The Practick part of the law shewing the office of a compleat attorney in the full prosecution of any action whether reall, personall, or mixt (1656)

Anon

The Practick part of the law shewing the office of a compleat attorney in the full prosecution of any action whether reall, personall, or mixt

Compleat attorney.

Anon.

[Edition statement:] The fourth impression corrected and amendedwith an exact table wherein are contained all the principall matters in the whole book.

Running title: The Compleat attorney.

Includes index.

Imperfect: numerous errors in paging.

[4], 409 [i.e. 421], [19] p.

London : Printed by Tho. Roycroft, for H. Twyford and are to be sold at his shop,

Wing / P3140A

English

Reproduction of the original in the Harvard Law School Library

Early English Books Online (EEBO) Editions

Imagine holding history in your hands.

Now you can. Digitally preserved and previously accessible only through libraries as Early English Books Online, this rare material is now available in single print editions. Thousands of books written between 1475 and 1700 and ranging from religion to astronomy, medicine to music, can be delivered to your doorstep in individual volumes of high-quality historical reproductions.

We have been compiling these historic treasures for more than 70 years. Long before such a thing as "digital" even existed, ProQuest founder Eugene Power began the noble task of preserving the British Museum's collection on microfilm. He then sought out other rare and endangered titles, providing unparalleled access to these works and collaborating with the world's top academic institutions to make them widely available for the first time. This project furthers that original vision.

These texts have now made the full journey -- from their original printing-press versions available only in rare-book rooms to online library access to new single volumes made possible by the partnership between artifact preservation and modern printing technology. A portion of the proceeds from every book sold supports the libraries and institutions that made this collection possible, and that still work to preserve these invaluable treasures passed down through time.

This is history, traveling through time since the dawn of printing to your own personal library.

Initial Proquest EEBO Print Editions collections include:

Early Literature

This comprehensive collection begins with the famous Elizabethan Era that saw such literary giants as Chaucer, Shakespeare and Marlowe, as well as the introduction of the sonnet. Traveling through Jacobean and Restoration literature, the highlight of this series is the Pollard and Redgrave 1475-1640 selection of the rarest works from the English Renaissance.

Early Documents of World History

This collection combines early English perspectives on world history with documentation of Parliament records, royal decrees and military documents that reveal the delicate balance of Church and State in early English government. For social historians, almanacs and calendars offer insight into daily life of common citizens. This exhaustively complete series presents a thorough picture of history through the English Civil War.

Historical Almanacs

Historically, almanacs served a variety of purposes from the more practical, such as planting and harvesting crops and plotting nautical routes, to predicting the future through the movements of the stars. This collection provides a wide range of consecutive years of "almanacks" and calendars that depict a vast array of everyday life as it was several hundred years ago.

Early History of Astronomy & Space

Humankind has studied the skies for centuries, seeking to find our place in the universe. Some of the most important discoveries in the field of astronomy were made in these texts recorded by ancient stargazers, but almost as impactful were the perspectives of those who considered their discoveries to be heresy. Any independent astronomer will find this an invaluable collection of titles arguing the truth of the cosmic system.

Early History of Industry & Science

Acting as a kind of historical Wall Street, this collection of industry manuals and records explores the thriving industries of construction; textile, especially wool and linen; salt; livestock; and many more.

Early English Wit, Poetry & Satire

The power of literary device was never more in its prime than during this period of history, where a wide array of political and religious satire mocked the status quo and poetry called humankind to transcend the rigors of daily life through love, God or principle. This series comments on historical patterns of the human condition that are still visible today.

Early English Drama & Theatre

This collection needs no introduction, combining the works of some of the greatest canonical writers of all time, including many plays composed for royalty such as Queen Elizabeth I and King Edward VI. In addition, this series includes history and criticism of drama, as well as examinations of technique.

Early History of Travel & Geography

Offering a fascinating view into the perception of the world during the sixteenth and seventeenth centuries, this collection includes accounts of Columbus's discovery of the Americas and encompasses most of the Age of Discovery, during which Europeans and their descendants intensively explored and mapped the world. This series is a wealth of information from some the most groundbreaking explorers.

Early Fables & Fairy Tales

This series includes many translations, some illustrated, of some of the most well-known mythologies of today, including Aesop's Fables and English fairy tales, as well as many Greek, Latin and even Oriental parables and criticism and interpretation on the subject.

Early Documents of Language & Linguistics

The evolution of English and foreign languages is documented in these original texts studying and recording early philology from the study of a variety of languages including Greek, Latin and Chinese, as well as multilingual volumes, to current slang and obscure words. Translations from Latin, Hebrew and Aramaic, grammar treatises and even dictionaries and guides to translation make this collection rich in cultures from around the world.

Early History of the Law

With extensive collections of land tenure and business law "forms" in Great Britain, this is a comprehensive resource for all kinds of early English legal precedents from feudal to constitutional law, Jewish and Jesuit law, laws about public finance to food supply and forestry, and even "immoral conditions." An abundance of law dictionaries, philosophy and history and criticism completes this series.

Early History of Kings, Queens and Royalty

This collection includes debates on the divine right of kings, royal statutes and proclamations, and political ballads and songs as related to a number of English kings and queens, with notable concentrations on foreign rulers King Louis IX and King Louis XIV of France, and King Philip II of Spain. Writings on ancient rulers and royal tradition focus on Scottish and Roman kings, Cleopatra and the Biblical kings Nebuchadnezzar and Solomon.

Early History of Love, Marriage & Sex

Human relationships intrigued and baffled thinkers and writers well before the postmodern age of psychology and self-help. Now readers can access the insights and intricacies of Anglo-Saxon interactions in sex and love, marriage and politics, and the truth that lies somewhere in between action and thought.

Early History of Medicine, Health & Disease

This series includes fascinating studies on the human brain from as early as the 16th century, as well as early studies on the physiological effects of tobacco use. Anatomy texts, medical treatises and wound treatment are also discussed, revealing the exponential development of medical theory and practice over more than two hundred years.

Early History of Logic, Science and Math

The "hard sciences" developed exponentially during the 16th and 17th centuries, both relying upon centuries of tradition and adding to the foundation of modern application, as is evidenced by this extensive collection. This is a rich collection of practical mathematics as applied to business, carpentry and geography as well as explorations of mathematical instruments and arithmetic; logic and logicians such as Aristotle and Socrates; and a number of scientific disciplines from natural history to physics.

Early History of Military, War and Weaponry

Any professional or amateur student of war will thrill at the untold riches in this collection of war theory and practice in the early Western World. The Age of Discovery and Enlightenment was also a time of great political and religious unrest, revealed in accounts of conflicts such as the Wars of the Roses.

Early History of Food

This collection combines the commercial aspects of food handling, preservation and supply to the more specific aspects of canning and preserving, meat carving, brewing beer and even candy-making with fruits and flowers, with a large resource of cookery and recipe books. Not to be forgotten is a "the great eater of Kent," a study in food habits.

Early History of Religion

From the beginning of recorded history we have looked to the heavens for inspiration and guidance. In these early religious documents, sermons, and pamphlets, we see the spiritual impact on the lives of both royalty and the commoner. We also get insights into a clergy that was growing ever more powerful as a political force. This is one of the world's largest collections of religious works of this type, revealing much about our interpretation of the modern church and spirituality.

Early Social Customs

Social customs, human interaction and leisure are the driving force of any culture. These unique and quirky works give us a glimpse of interesting aspects of day-to-day life as it existed in an earlier time. With books on games, sports, traditions, festivals, and hobbies it is one of the most fascinating collections in the series.

The BiblioLife Network

This project was made possible in part by the BiblioLife Network (BLN), a project aimed at addressing some of the huge challenges facing book preservationists around the world. The BLN includes libraries, library networks, archives, subject matter experts, online communities and library service providers. We believe every book ever published should be available as a high-quality print reproduction; printed on-demand anywhere in the world. This insures the ongoing accessibility of the content and helps generate sustainable revenue for the libraries and organizations that work to preserve these important materials.

The following book is in the "public domain" and represents an authentic reproduction of the text as printed by the original publisher. While we have attempted to accurately maintain the integrity of the original work, there are sometimes problems with the original work or the micro-film from which the books were digitized. This can result in minor errors in reproduction. Possible imperfections include missing and blurred pages, poor pictures, markings and other reproduction issues beyond our control. Because this work is culturally important, we have made it available as part of our commitment to protecting, preserving, and promoting the world's literature.

GUIDE TO FOLD-OUTS MAPS and OVERSIZED IMAGES

The book you are reading was digitized from microfilm captured over the past thirty to forty years. Years after the creation of the original microfilm, the book was converted to digital files and made available in an online database.

In an online database, page images do not need to conform to the size restrictions found in a printed book. When converting these images back into a printed bound book, the page sizes are standardized in ways that maintain the detail of the original. For large images, such as fold-out maps, the original page image is split into two or more pages

Guidelines used to determine how to split the page image follows:

• Some images are split vertically; large images require vertical and horizontal splits.
• For horizontal splits, the content is split left to right.
• For vertical splits, the content is split from top to bottom.
• For both vertical and horizontal splits, the image is processed from top left to bottom right.

E

common Pleas ... ...
642: ... this ... ...
... publishe... ...
1648 ... week a ... ...
... ... of the ...
... of this ... ...
... ... that ...
... ...

After ... ...
... 40 ... fo. 9
... fo. 10. 11
... ...
... ... forfeit ...
... fo. 12 ... ...
... for ... ... fo. 13
... ...
... to 38

... ... fo. 210.

... ... workes ...
... one ... ...
... these ... ...
... ...

THE
PRACTICK PART
OF THE
LAW:

Shewing the Office of a
COMPLEAT ATTORNEY

In the full profecution of any Action,
whether Reall, Perfonall or Mixt;
(from the very Originall to the Execution) in all Courts : With the exact Fees
of all Officers and Minifters of the Courts.

TOGETHER

With fpeciall Inftructions for the Solicitation of any Caufe in *Chancery*, or
elfe where, relating to the prefent Government; being ufefull for all men.

_____

*The fourth Impreffion corrected and amended.
With an exact Table, wherein are contained all the Principall Matters in the whole Book.*

_____

LONDON,
Printed by *Tho. Roycroft*, for *H. Twyford,*
and are to be fold at his Shop, in *Vine-
Court, Middle-Temple,* 1656.

...the Office of an Attorney, and a Guide for Solicitors in all the Courts at Westminster, with their Proceedings in any Action Real, Personal, or mixed. As also the Practice of the Courts in the City of London, Courts of Admiralty, Ecclesiastical Courts and other inferior Courts in the Country. 5th Edition enlarged. Octavo. 1724. — Practick Part of the Law 4th Edition 1711. — Practick Part of the Law, preceded... in English 1653. This is called the Compleat Attorney... and the Attorney...

TO THE

READER.

Reader,

Having obſerved the many Errours daily committed through the miſtake of the nature of the Action to be ſued, and conſequently, as well the miſgrounding of the Action, as the undue proſecution thereof, to the utter loſſe of many a Cauſe, hath put my intentions on work to give thee ſome light in ſuch waies, where either thou doſt voluntarily go to purſue thy right, or art Involuntarily driven to defend thy right : To that purpoſe was this Compoſure undertaken, wherein thou ſhalt find the whole progreſſe of the Law in the Practicall part : So that whether thou haſt buſineſſe of thine owne

The Epistle.

er on the behalf of another, hereupon all
occasions, thou mayest find Instructions for
a due and full prosecution thereof; there
being scarce any Action, Reall, Personall, or Mixt, in what Court soever, but
its Nature, Progresse, Judgment, and Execution is here explained, with the duty of
all Officers, Judiciary, and Ministeriall;
as also the justifiable Fees and Allowances
of the Prothonotaries, Masters of Officer, Secondaries, Clarks, Attorneys,
Sheriffs, Under-Sheriffs, Bayliffs of
Franchises, and prescribed Liberties; the
Practice of the high Court of Chancery,
the Fees of the Six Clarks, &c. All which
being methodically disposed, with an exact Table to every particular, will, I hope,
render thee a benefit worthy of thy kind
acceptance.

[handwritten annotation]

Farewell.

[handwritten annotation]

The Compleat Attorney.

Being full and exact directions for all man-
ner of Proceedings at Law, in all Courts
whatsoever: Together with all Fees incident
thereunto.

THE Office of an Attorney requires much knowledge both of the Theorique and Practick parts of the Law.

The one is to be gained out of the body of the Law, and cannot be expected to be ascertained in this small tract.

For the better enabling of him to the later is this ensuing Discourse intended, wherein we shall begin with the Court of Common-Pleas, as being of the largest Extent, in relation to the multiplicity of Actions, both real, personal, and mixt, properly incident to that Court, wherein all persons of the Nation, either as Plaintiffs or Defendants, are more or lesse concerned.

This Court consists of a chief Justice, and three other Judges.

The Subordinate Officers are;

The *Custos Brevium*, or Keeper of the Writs.

Three Prothonotaries (one of which was antiently incident to the *Custos Brevium* for the time being) who by themselves and their Clarks, draw all pleadings and enter them, and exemplifie and record all common Recoveries.

The clark of the Warrants, who entreth all VVarrants of Attorney, and inrolleth all deeds acknowledged before the Juſtices of the Court.

Philizers, who make all manner of mean proceſſe upon originall Writs before *appearance.*

The Clark of the Eſſoynes, who doth enter the Eſſoynes and exceptions in all actions wherein Eſſoines lye, and prepareth and marketh all the Rolls uſed for the court.

The clark of the Outlawries who maketh the *Capias utlegatum,* upon the return of the exigents brought in unto them? This Office is properly incident to the Attorney Generall for the time being.

The clark of the Superſedeas, who makes VVrits to ſuperſede the Outlawing of perſons, granted by Letters Patents under the great Seal of *England.*

The Exigenters, who are   in number, and make the VVrits of Exigents and Proclamations, in order to Outlawry upon the *plures capias*, brought in unto them.

The clark of the Juries, who makes the VVrits of *Habeas corpora* and *diſtringas Jur.* for the tryall of Iſſues.

The Chyrographer, who doth make the Indentures of Fines levyed, and hath many ſubordinate Clarks for the ſeverall Counties where the Lands lie.

The Clark of the Kings-ſilver, ſo antiently called, who doth enter on record the Money which the State is to have upon Fines, for the Poſt-Fines, according to the yearly value of the Land, as the ſame is rated on the Writs of Covenant.

The clark of the Errors, who makes all *Superſedeas* upon Writs of Errour, and doth tranſcribe the Records out of the Treaſury, belonging to the Common Bench, into the Upper Bench.

The Keeper of the Treaſury, who hath the keeping

of the Rolls entered of Record in the Court, and the making forth of Copies and Exemplifications thereof, and also of all records of *Nisi-prius*.

The Proclamator of the Court; the Keeper of the Court; The Office of the Inrollment of Fines and Recoveries erected by Statute.

Foure Cryers, or Tipstaves, Substitutes to the Proclamator.

The Warden of the Fleet, who by himselfe or his Deputy is to attend the Court, that Prison being proper for all Commitments out of that Court.

The Pleaders are all Sergeants of the Coife, none under that degree being allowed to plead in that Court.

The Attorneys are very many, being not limited to any set number; antiently they were such as either had studied the Law for some years in some Inne of *Chancery*, where was usually their residence, or had served for the space of 6. or 7. years, with some able Attorney of the Court, whereby they come to be very knowing in the Practise of the Court, the better to mannage their Clients causes with ability and integrity, to the honour of the Court, and their owne credit.

At the time of their being admitted Attorneys, there is an Oath administered unto them as followes.

YOu shall doe no falshood, nor consent to any to be done in the Court; and if you know of any to be done, you shall give knowledg thereof to my Lord Chief Justice, or other his Brethren, that it may be reformed. You shall delay no man for lucre or malice, nor shall encrease no fees, but be contented with the old accustomed fees. You shall plead no forreign plea, nor sue no forreign suites unlawfully to hurt any man, but such as shall stand with the order of the Law and your Conscience. You shall seale all such Processe as you shall sue out of this Court, with the Seale thereof, and see the Kings Majestie, and my Lord chiefe Justice discharged of the same. You shall not wittingly nor willingly sue, nor procure to be sued, any false suite, nor give aid or consent to the same, on paine of being expulsed from the Court for ever. And further, you shall use your selfe in the Office of an Attorney within the court according to your learning and discretion, so helpe you God.

Having taken his Oath, he is to pay the fees of Court incident thereunto, as followes,

Imprimis, to the Judges box, 20 *s*.

To the Secondary of the Chiefe Prothonotary, who giveth the Oath, 12 *d*.

To the Cryers, Court-Keeper, and other Officers 1 *s*.

Then must he have a note from the Prothonotary, in whose Office he intends to enter, directed to the Clark of the Warrants, which is usually made, as follows,

Of the Term of St. *Hillary* in the year, 1651.

T.D. Gent. sworn in Court the 10 day of *February*, in the selfe same Term, in the Office of Attorney of the Common-wealth of the Common Bench.

To which the Prothonotary subscribeth his name.

Which note being delivered to the Clark of the Warrants, he enters the name into the Roll of the Attorneys names.

The Clarks of the Warrants hath for the entring thereof 4 *s*. and 4 *d*. for the Roll of that Terme, 4 *d*.

And so he stands charged to pay 4 *d*. for the future, so long as he continueth an Attorney of the Court each Term.

The Attorney thus fitted for practise, he must

very carefull in taking right and due instruction from his Client, and informe himselfe of whatsoever is materially incident to his Cause; that so he may know what manner of Action is most proper to be brought on the behalfe of his Client; for a Cause once throughly weighed, and rightly grounded, goes on with a great deale of ease and satisfaction, both to the Attorney and Client.

The Attorney ought to be throughly versed in the nature of all sorts of VVrits, as in the Register, Terms of the Law, and other Books now extant.

To begin with Actions of Debt.

FIrst, you are to take notice of your Plaintiffe name, and of his cause of Action, whether it arise by Bond, or Bil, which are called Specialties, and otherwise for arrears of Rent, VVares, Cattell sold, or any other Chattels, or for worke or service done, &c. If by Bond or Bill, you must take an exact note of the Defendants name, together with his addition precisely, as he is written in the Obligation or Bill, that so you may make your Originall and your other processe to agree with the Obligation, otherwise it is Errour.

That done you must make a short note to the Cursitor, if in debt, as follows;

London. ss. Command *I. C.* late *London.* Gent. otherwise called *I. C.* of *L.* in the County of *H.* Gent. that justly, and so forth, he render T. B. 40 *l. &c.* Originall returnable 15. dayes after *Easter.*

VVhich being done, you must carry your note or notes to the Cursitors Office, and deliver it to that particular Cursitor, who is for the County you lay your Action in, who maketh your Originall, and delivereth it you under Seale.

This Originall is your first Processe, and is a Summons: and although it issue out of the *Chancery,* yet

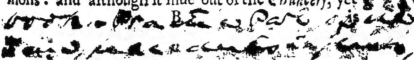

it is made returnable before the Justices of the *Common Pleas* at a certain return : And between the Teste and return of the same (as also in all other ordinary Writs to be sued forth, and procured upon the same) must be 15. daies at the least.

Note, that this Writ may bear Teste out of the Term, because it is to be understood that the Court of *Chancery* is alwaies open.

All other Process sued forth at the court of *Common Pleas*, must bear Teste sometime within the Term, and in the name of the chief Justice of the same court for the time being, and one writ is to bear Teste from the return of another, as namely the *Capias* (which is the next Writ to the Originall in an action of Debt) from the return of the Originall, the *Alias capias*, from the return of the *Capias*, and the *Plures* from the return of the *Alias*, and the Exigent and Proclamation from the return of the *Plures*; and these are the severall Writs in order to an Outlawry.

The return of your Originall in debt is thus;

Pledges of prosecuting { John Doe.
{ Richard Roe.

The within named *I. S.* hath nothing within our Bayliwick whereby he may besummoned.

The answer of *R. B.* and *I. S.* Sheriffs.

If there be two Defendants in the Originall, t return must be thus:

The within named *I. C.* and *D. L.* have nothin within our Bayliwick wherby they may be summoned If there be more then two Defendants, then thus *I. C.* and the rest of the Defendants within written have nothing within our Bayliwick whereby the may be summoned.

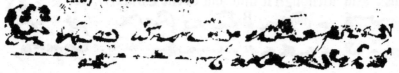

Note, it is said (within our Bayliwick) because the
ction lies in *London,* where there are two Sheriffs,
therwise where there is but one Sheriff, you say
with my Bayliwick) and the like for all other ci-
ies that have two Sheriffs, and likewise the words,
the answer of) are intended onely where there is two
heriffs, otherwise you barely recite the Sheriffs name
nd stile at the bottome of the back of the Writ.

Your Originall being thus made and returned, you
ust deliver the same to the Philizer of the county,
ty, or shire, where your action is laid, to have such
rther processe made thereon, either in suing to the
utlawry or otherwise, as the present Term wherein
u sue forth the same;shal by reason of the length or
ortnesse of the time allow,observing the former rule
fifteen daies betwixt the Teste and the returne of
ery Processe.

he Ordinary and usuall proces thereupon with the
ilizer, are those formerly mentioned which he ma-
th upon the Originall Writ brought to him, for
ich you deliver him **4** *d.* as payable to the *Custos*
evium for filing the Originall.

First, A *Capias,* for which you pay **10** *d.*
Secondly, An *Alias Capias* which costs *6 d.*
Thirdly, A *Plures capias,* for which you pay *6 d.*

The returns whereof as followes.

he within named *I. C.* is not found within our Bay-
vick.

And if more then two Defendants, then thus.

I C. and the rest of the Defendants within written
: not found within our Bayliwick.

The answer of R. B. and J. S. Sheriffs.

Ut if you intend not to sue the Defendant to an
outlawry,but that his body may be easily and rea-
y arrested,then you need not proceed further then

to the *Capias* onely, and deliver the same to the Under-Sheriff of the County, and procure a VVarrant thereupon, and get him arrested by the Sheriffs Bayliffs, which is a great furtherance to your Clients cause, in relation to Tryall, and procuring Judgement.

Note that you are to pay 4 *d.* as a *post-diem* for each of the aforesaid Processe, which you bring not into the Philizer by the day of the return.

The two cheife Termes wherein to commence Suits to the Outlawry, are *Easter* and *Michaelmas* Termes, they having in them the most returns, for if you begin in *Easter*, you shall Outlaw the party, if he appear not in *Michaelmas* Terme next following, and if you begin in *Michaelmas* Terme, you shall doe the like in *Easter* or *Trinity* Terme then next following.

Note that you may have an Originall VVrit made returnable of a precedent Terme, upon bringing a Note to the Curſitor within the firſt week of the following Terme, but if you slack that time, you lose your advantage.

Anciently the courſe hath been, that if an Originall VVrit be made againſt a Knight, Eſquire, Gentleman of worth, or other ſubſtantiall Free-holder, that hath ſufficient Lands and Tenements in the ſame County where the Action is laid. then ought a Summons to be returned by the Sheriff of the County, who is to execute it: And you cannot return that Originall of Courſe by the return of (having nothing, &c.) For otherwiſe the Defendant, if he have ſufficient in the ſame County, and he be returned, (to have nothing, &c.) may bring an Action of the Caſe, for diſabling of him in his Eſtate, againſt the Attorney for the Plaintiff, or againſt the Under-Sheriff of the County, who ſhall make ſuch return, to difable him upon a Summons ; if he appear not, you proceed by *Pone*, and fo to a diftrefs, and if he appear not upon the *Diftringas*, you have an *Alias diftringas*, and fo diftrefs upon diftrefs, untill he appeare ; but this manner of proceedings by way of Summons hath not been ufed of late.

Upon the making and fuing forth of the Originall Writ, if the debt or damages therein fpecified do exceed forty pounds : Then there is a certain Fine due for the fame, to be paid formerly to the King, now to the State as followes;

Imprimis, from forty pounds to a hundred marks, paies 6 *s.* 8 *d.*

From a hundred marks to a hundred pounds, paies 10 *s.* 0.

From a hundred pounds to two hundred marks, paies 13 *s.* 4 *d.*

From a hundred thirty three pounds fix fhillings and eight pence, to a hundred fixty fix pounds thirteen fhillings and four pence, paies 16 *s.* 8 *d.*

From a hundred fixty fix pounds thirteen fhillings and foure pence , to two hundred pounds, paies 20 *s.* 0.

And fo confequentiy for every hundred marks more, paies, 6 *s.* 8 *d.*

And for every hundred pounds more , paies 10 *s.* 0.

If you begin in *Eafter* Term, you may procure your *Capias* and *Alias capias* , returnable in *Trinity* Term, and in *Trinity* Term fue forth your *Plures capias,* Exigent, and Proclamation ; if in *Michaelmas* Term, you may fue forth the Originall *Capias,* and *Alias capias* returnable the fame Term ; and a *Plures capias* returnable in *Hillary* Term then next following, and in the fame Term procure your Exigent and Proclamation. Note

Note, that if you lay your action in *London*, the party will be the sooner outlawed, in respect of the Hustinge, being oftner there then elsewhere.

Now if the party have sued out his Originall in *London*, and the party live elsewhere, and that he would have him more speedily arrested then by way of Outlawry upon the return (of the parties not being found, *&c.*) by the Sheriff, he may have a *Testatum* into the county where he liveth, to arrest him there; the fee of which Writ is twelve-pence.

All the Writs before mentioned must be filed with the *Custos brevium*, either by your self or the Philizer, or else there will be Error in the proceedings.

The *Plures Capias* being orderly procured, sued forth and returned, must be delivered to the Exigenter of the county where the action is laid, and he will make an Exigent, and proclamation thereupon.

The Exigent and Proclamation must be delivered to the under Sheriff of the same county, where the Defendant dwelleth, to be executed according to the forme of a Statute, in that case made and provided, and according to the tenure and forme of the said Writ.

The charges of a Suit to the Outlawry are as followeth.

Doe
against }   *Easter Term*, 1651.
Roe.

	l.	s.	d.	
For the Fine to the State,	0	10	0	}
For the Original, *Post diem* and Entry,	0	1	5	}
For the *Capias*, Scale and *Post diem*,	0	1	9	} s. d.
For the *Alias capias*, Seal, & *Post diem*,	0	1	5	} 17-11
For the Attorneys fee,	0	3	4	}

Trinity

Trinity Term following. *l. s. d.*

For the *Plures capias*, Seale and *Post diem*.	0-1-5	
For the Warrant of Attorney,	0-0-4	
For the Exigent and Seale	0-1-7	*s. d.* 8—9
For the return thereof,	0-1-0	
For the Attorneys fee,	0-3-4	

The sum totall is 1-6-8

If the Exigent be against several Defendants living in severall Counties, severall Proclamations must go to the Sheriff of the severall Counties, which will increase the charge:And further take notice there must be of necessity five county-daies, between the Teste and the return of the Exigent, or else you must be necessitated to sue forth another Writ, called an *Allocatus,* from the said Exigenter, to be delivered to the said Under-sheriff, to the great hinderance and charge of the client; and your *Allocatus* must beare Teste with the return of your former Exigent, and be returnable the next return, after the fifth county-day and your Exigent and Proclamation must have one and the same Teste and return.

You must carefully examine all the aforesaid Processes, that there be no difference or variance either in the summes, names, or additions, from your Originall Writ, that so they may each warrant the other.

The same Term that you sue forth your Exigent and Proclamation, you must then file a Warrant of Attorney (for the Plaintiff who is your client) with the clark of the Warrants, in failer whereof you commit manifest Error in the prosecution of your cause, to the great hinderance and hurt of your Client, and danger of your selfe, by incurring the forfeiture of ten pounds, by a Statute made in that behalf.

The forme of a Warrant of Attorney is as followes, and must be ingrossed in Parchment.

London ſſ. *A. B.* puts in his place *C. D.* his Attorney, against *T. F.* lately of *London* Gentleman, otherwise called *T. F.* of *S.* in the Countie of *Gloceſter*, Gentleman, of a Plea of Debt: Thus upon ſpecialtie.

In Action of Treſpaſſe thus.

DOrſet ſ. *G. W.* puts in his place *T. F.* against *I.* late of *Blanford* in the County aforeſaid, of a plea of Treſpaſſe and the like in other Actions.

The Exigent and Proclamation being returned, you must then file the proclamation with the *Cuſtos Brevium,* and if you file the same or any other Writ there, before the return be paſt, or upon the return day, then you must pay nothing for filing the same; otherwise every writ payes 4 *d.*

Well-experienced Practiſers know how to ſave many of their *poſt-diems,* by having their writs made ready in an early manner.

In caſe of not filing your Writ or Writs, in or of the ſame Term they are returnable, they force you to pay when you file them with the *Cuſtos Brevium,* for the Poſt *Terminum* of them, which is 20 *d.* for every Writ, every Term the same is unfiled, except Exigents, for which you pay onely one Poſt *Terminum,* which as aforeſaid, is 20 *d.*

It is very unſafe in relation both to your ſelfe and Client, to keep your Writs unfiled (the filing of them

them being the substantiall warranty for the proceedings had upon them)least a Caveat be obtained from
some of the Judges in that behalfe, which is called a
Ne recipiatur.

The Exigent being returned by the Sheriff of
the County, and you being willing to procure process
of Outlawry against the Defendant to Arrest him,
upon the same he being outlawed, you must then
carry the Exigent so returned, to the Clark of the
outlawryes, for the time being, and he will make you
a Writ or writs, into any County you shall desire
him, where you can any wayes discover the Party to
be, or any Estate of his, either in Lands or Goods,
yea into severall Counties at one time; because those
writs are as well on the behalfe of the King, as for
the Plaintiff.

There be two severall writs of *Capias Vtlegat.* the
one called a Generall *Capias Vtlegatum*, being for
the apprehending of the body of the Defendant only:
The other especiall, being against his body, Lands,
and Goods.

You having now the Exigent in your hands, ready to file, I thought fit to let you know the accustomed Fees for suing the Outlawry out, and Processe
thereon.

The Fees of the *Capias Vtlegat.*

THe filing of the Exigent with the Clark of the
Outlawries in the same Terme it is returnable,

	payes 1 *d.*
If it be with a *post Terminum*	payes 20 *d.*
The Generall *Capias Vtlegat*	payes 10 *d.*
The Speciall	payes 2 *s.* 4 *d.*
The Seale of either	payes 1 *d.*
The fee of the Attorney suing it forth ;	3 *s.* 4 *d.*

Severall ways there are to discharge and avoid the
same as occasion serves, whether the party be taken or
otherwise.   The

The firſt and moſt uſuall way is, to reverſe it by
Error, found in the returne of the Exigent, which
may be committed many ways, and is not unfrequent,
either by miſtaking the County-dayes, in not allowing inſufficient time between any of them, or in miſ-
naming of the perſon, or omitting, or miſtaking of
the Sheriffs name to the ſame Writ or Returne, or by
words which will bear no ſignification, or otherwiſe,
as Experience and Practiſe will better inſtruct you:
And ſecondly by any Error to be found in the Return
of the Proclamation, which may be committed many
wayes, as aforeſaid.

Likewiſe for want of filing the Proclamation with
the *Cuſtos Brevium*, as alſo for want either of the Return or a due Return or Miſ-entry, or miſtakes, either in the Originall *Capias*, *Alias*, and *Plures*, afore
recited.

For all which there muſt be diligent ſearch with
the *Cuſtos Brevium*, or in the other Offices where the
proceedings have been.

Upon the finding of any ſufficient Error, either in
thoſe or any other the proceedings : Then the file of
Writs, in which ſaid matter of Error in Writ is filed,
muſt be brought by the *Cuſtos Brevium* into the open
Court, there to be ſeen and peruſed by one of the
Judges of the ſame Court, and the Errors to be al-
lowed, or diſ-allowed, according to his diſcretion and
Judgment.

Upon Reverſall of an Outlawry for want of Proclamation in all caſes, or for any other default, if
the debt or damage amount to 20 *l.* or above, there
muſt be ſpeciall Bayle entred by the Defendant with
Sureties to anſwer to the Plaintiffs ſuite, and pay the
debt and damage demanded, or yeeld his body to
Priſon, if the Defendant ſhall be condemned in the
Action, which Baile muſt be taken out into the Remembrance

membrance in the same Prothonotaries office, where the same is reversed. And then if the party outlawed be taken, and arrested, or fear to be so upon notice of an Exigent against him, he may have a Writ of *Supersedeas* directed to the Sheriffe of the County where he is, or feareth to be taken, for his discharge, which writ is to be made and signed in the same Prothonotaries Office where the Outlawry was reversed.

The Outlawry thus reversed, the Defendant is bound by his Attorney to appeare, and to accept of a Declaration at any time within two Terms then next following after the said reversall, and then to answer according to course of Law.

Upon the reversall of every Outlawry, the Attorney ought to have a note or Certificate thereof from the Prothonotary to the Clark of the Outlawry, that no further Processe may be made against the Defendant upon the same, and to see the Outlawry Book discharged, for which he must pay   2 *s.* 8 *d.*

The Fees of the reversalls according to the occasions are uncertaine, but the usuall and accustomed fees follow.

For search and Copie of the Outlawry,   8 *d.*

For search with the *Custos Brevium* for every particular Term you need to use,   5 *d.*

For carrying the bundle of Writs to the Hall,
     2 *s.* 9 *d.*

For putting in the Bayle.   6 *s.* 4 *d.*

To the Box.   1 *s.*

To the Prothonotary for entring the Reversal upon insufficiency of the Return,   8 *s.*

For the Judges Fee,   4 *s.*

To the Clark of the Outlawries for discharging the Book,   3 *s.* 6 *d.*

For the Supersedeas,   2 *s.* 7 *d*

For the allowing thereof with the Sheriff,   2 *s.* 4 *d.*

An Ourlawry alſo may be reverſed, although there be no Error in return or Entries of the Exigent or Proclamation: and although the Proclamation be filed with the *Cuſtos Brevium,* as namely, if that the ſame proclamation were not awarded according to the forme and effect of a Statute, in that caſe provided, into the County, and the Defendant named of the Pariſh where he had been reſident *infra annum & diem,* when next before the ſame Suite was begun, and commenced, or that the Defendant be miſnamed therein, in his Surname, Degree or Myſterie. And this Reverſall is to be done by way of a Plea, drawn by a Clerk to that purpoſe; for which you ſhall finde precedents in the Book of Entries, to which pleas the Attorney Generalls hand muſt be procured; but this way as being both very troubleſome and chargeable, is much out of uſe.

An Outlawry may be alſo reverſed by the Kings Generall pardon, which is uſually granted at every Parliament, if ſo be the Defendant were outlawed before the day thereby limited, or by a ſpeciall pardon, which muſt be done by way of plea, and *Scire Facias* directed to the Sheriff of the ſame County, wherein the action was firſt layd: And if the Sheriff doe returne a *Scire feci* upon the ſaid *Scire facias;* then you ſhall need but one Writ of *Scire Facias;* if not, then you muſt have two returned with *Nihil,* &c. in this manner.

The within named A. C. (the Plaintiffe) hath nothing within my Bayliwick, by which I am able to make known unto him, nor is found in the ſame.

D. L. *Knight,* Sheriffe.

Theſe *Scire facias's* are to be drawn by the prothonotaries Clark, and then entred into a rememberance in the ſame Office, and a *Superſedeas* made, and a Certificate alſo made as above from the Prothonotary to the

the Clark of the Outlawries, that from thenceforth no further Proceſſe may be made againſt the Defendant, and alſo entred upon Record.

And note in this caſe alſo, the Defendant muſt by his Attorney appear, and anſwer the Plaintiff in his Action, but no bail need be put in.

The Fees thereof.

For the Copie of the Exigent,	8 d.
The two *Scire facias's* and Seals,	5 s. 2 d.
The Returns thereof,	8 s.
The filing of them,	2 d.
The taking out in the Remembrance	1 s.
The Copies,	3 s. 4 d.
The Prothonotary,	5 s. 4 d.
The *Superſedeas*, and allowing thereof,	4 s. 11 d.
The Certificate,	1 s.
The Clark of the Outlawries.	2 s. 8 d.
The Attorneys Fee,	3 s. 4 d.

An Outlawry alſo may be reverſed by Writ of Error upon Error in the proceedings, as the want of the Warrant of Attorney, the not filing of the Originall; *Capias, Alias*, or *Pluyes*, and then your courſe therein followes:

In the firſt place you are to have a Copie of the Exigent, or *Capias Utlegat.* which is to be carried to the Curſiter of the County where the action lies, and where the Defendant is returned outlawed, to have a Writ of Error made thereupon, which Writ muſt be brought under Seale to the Lord chiefe Juſtice of the Common Bench, or his clark of the Errors of the time being, with the copie of the Outlawry, and thereupon the clark of the Errors of the Common Bench makes a *Superſedeas* to the Sheriff of the County, where the Defendant either is, or fears to be arreſted, for his diſcharge, and from him procure a Certificate to the Clark of the Outlawries, (as formerly) the charge of the *Superfedeas* is 33 s. 4 d. besides the search and copie of the Outlawry. And in this case the Defendant by his Attorney must appear upon a new Originall sued out by the Plaintiff within two Termes : And this is the most usuall and ready way (though most chargeable) for discharging of an Outlawry (especially in the Vacation) if the Defendant be either under arrest, or fear to be arrested ; but baile must be put in, if the debt or damages amount to 20 *l.* as in the like cases before recited.

It's requisite in this case the Attorney should take money of the Defendant for the Declaration, and his fee against the next Term, at the time of the delivery of the *Superfedeas* (especially if the Defendant be not well known unto him) and a Warrant under his hand to appeare, plead, or confesse the Action : for many times the Attorney is put to a great charge and trouble to find out his Client.

These are the generall and particular instructions and directions to sue to the Outlawry, and to arrest thereupon, and how to reverse the same, both in the behalf of the Plaintiff and Defendant ; besides which there are other waies of suing by mean processe, when they proceed no further then to the taking out of an Originall, and then make an arrest upon the *capias* ; or in case the partie cannot be taken before the return of the said *capias*, then you may take out a *capias* by continuance, which costs you 10 *d.* to the Philizer, and 7 *d.* for the Seale.

And having now dilated at large the severall proceeds in Actions of debt, in order to Outlawry, or otherwise, and likewise the reversal of such Outlawries, whereby the Defendant comes to appear, it now rest we should shew how they may declare, and in what manner those Declarations must be ; But before we proceed

ura6G.

proceed fo far, it will not be amiffe to infert fome few rules or obfervations as a guide for the Attorney, both in the taking of inftructions, and drawing his feverall Declarations in other perfonall Actions, as follow.

IN Actions of debt, either upon fpecialty, as Bond or Bill, or for Rent arrear upon a demife by Indenture or otherwife, or upon an action of Covenant, you muft have recourfe to the feverall writings, by which you warrant your faid Actions, and the circumftance of time, either for the date of the faid writings, the place, the quantity of what Rent arreare, for what time, when commencing and ending, and what particular Covenant; if but one in an action of Covenant, you intend to infift on for the laying of the breach aright, and likewife you muft informe your felfe how your Client came to be Entituled to the Debt, whether as Obligee, or by fome Affignment, by Letter of Attorney, or otherwife, as Executor or Adminiftrator of the Obligee: And if for arreare of rent, whether the party came to it by mean affignment or reverfion, in which cafes you are to informe your felfe of the Attornment of the Tenant, and for what time the rent is arrear, and look what right the immediate Leffor or Leffees have; the fame is in their Affignes.

If Rent grow due by Leafe-paroll from year to year, which is fo called, in refpect there is nothing under hand and feale, but barely by word of mouth, to fignifie the Demife, you muft know the time of the Demife, afcertaine the thing demifed, the Terme, the Rent, and time of payment of it: the time of the Leffees entry, and what Rent is arreare by the Defendant.

If in Debt upon an Award.

YOu are to informe your selves of the Arbitrators names, the time of the Award made, and what was awarded, and if you can get the Award it self, it is far better.

Note, that if any under the age of one and twenty years, either in this or any other Action, commence Suit, he muſt come in by his Guardian in proper perſon to be admitted, which coſts two ſhillings the admittance; otherwiſe if the Defendant take notice of his Nonage, and that he appear not by Guardian, but otherwiſe, the Defendant may plead it in Bar to his Action.

And now take ſome few inſtructions in other Actions, as Treſpaſſe, upon Aſſault and Battery, falſe Impriſonment, &c.

In the firſt place, take notice of the time, or any time after the treſpaſſe done, before the Teſte of your Originall of the Treſpaſſe, by Aſſault and Impriſonment, and the place where (although I think neither of them Locall) together with the time the Party remaineth deceaſed, or impriſoned, and what it coſt him by way of Fine or otherwiſe, to be releaſed.

And note for the Aſſault of the Wife, Children, or Servant, the Father and Maſter, as well as the Servant, may bring an Action, for the loſſe or hinderance he receives thereby.

For Treſpaſs either in Cloſes, or Houſes, or chaſing of Cattell, or fiſhing where another man hath right, as followes: and firſt,

For breaking your Cloſe, the certainer you lay it in naming the place, the time of the Treſpaſs done and with what Cattell, and how long the Treſpaſ continue continued, and what corn was confumed and eaten up, or trodden down with the Feet, and what Grafs, and of what value; and it were to be wifhed, in relation to the faving much charge, there were the fame courfe taken in the Court of common Bench, that is done in the Upper Bench, that is, To afcertain the place of the Trefpaffe done, by giving it his particular name and bounds, which if done in the Declaration, would prevent pleading the common Barre and new Affignment, and this with much eafe, by faying (The clofe of A. called C. in D. hee broke, &c.)

If any Trefpafs done for chafing of cattell, you muft lay the time and place of chafing, worrying, and beating your cattell, what cattell, and how many they were, and what you were damnified by it, either in Ewes cafting their Lambs, or being torne with doggs: Or Kine in loofing their Milke, cafting their Calves, or Mares in the Loffe of their colts, and the like.

An action of Trefpaffe alfo lyes againft one, for the refcuing of his owne cattell out of your hands, in cafe you are driving them to the pound, for Trefpaffe, or otherwife, or in cafe he break the Pound, where you had impounded them, and drive them away; in both which cafes, you muft fhew what right you had to take them, either as damage feafant, or that you did diftrain them for Rent, or Services arrear.

If your Trefpaffe be, for taking away of Goods, or chattells, out of your ground or houfe (albeit money) and fuch things are commonly taken out of your houfe, they are to be named particularly, and their value, if money in a bagg, the particular Sum.

In cafe a man take away a Ward, an action lyes, wherein you muft fhew how the Plaintif came to have

Right to the Ward, which the Defendant detaineth, as if it be Knights service by his Fathers holding of such a Mannor of the Plaintiffs, the Lands he dyed seized of, &c. shew the manner of the Tenure, and that the Childs Father dyed in the Homage of the Lord, whereby the right of the Childs Marriage belongeth unto him: You must likewise know the time and place of taking him away, the age of the Ward, together with the Damage the Plaintiff sustained.

If by Socage Tenure the Lands holden, then the next of kindred (to whom the Lands cannot descend) hath the like Action for his Ward, wherein hee must shew what he dyed of in Socage-Tenure, and of whose Mannor it was holden, together with the time the Plaintiff was seized of him, and the time, manner, and place of his taking away.

In an Action of Trespasse for spoyling or turning your Water-course, you first shew how hee held the Water-course, from, where, and whither the water-course came, and that it had used so to come time out of mind; then what benefit it did the Plaintiff, as in making his Gronnds fertile, and for watering his Cattell, then how the Defendant did stop that Course and with what, and the time, by reason whereof, the Plaintiff hath lost the benefit of it for such a time, or if the Ground be overflowed by the like course, then shew how the Defendant, having such a Water-course or Mills, lying neer the Plaintiffs ground, did open his Flood-gate and stopped the Water-course, and caused it to overflow the banks and drown the Lands.

In Actions of Account, take these ensuing.

IF an Action be brought for Arrearages of account as where diverse Reckonings are between two Per-sons ns, and they account together, and upon that account the one is found indebtred to the other; then now the time when the parties accounts were, and before whom, if they had any Auditors, and what the sum was, he was to account for, and the time when was appointed to be paid by the Auditors.

If you charge any as Receiver for monies delivered, name the time when, and the place where, and the person that delivered it, and the Sum that was delivered; if he received it for the Rent of any thing, it best to name the thing for what it was.

If you charge him as a Bayliff of Lands and Goods, shew from what time he hath been so of the things under his charge, and of all things he received, and how long since he was Bayliff.

If you charge him as Bayliff for any thing he hath had for you, recite the thing to be accounted for.

Detinue.

you would bring an Action of Detinue for any thing that you have bought cannot have shew time when you bought it, and what you paid, the time for the delivery of it.

If you have delivered any thing to any man, and not have it again, you may have the like Action, shewing the value of the thing delivered, and to what use you did deliver it, and what time was appointed for the delivery of it, in case it be for writs, either upon the delivery, or that it came to the defendants hands by chance, know the Date and the effect of the writing, the time when the Plaintiffe possessed of it, and the time when the Defendant it.

In Actions of the Case take these ensuing.

First for Trover, which is the Recovery of Goods that come to any mans hands by chance or not in a warrantable way, know the nature of the goods, the value of them, the time and place when and where the Plaintiff was possessed of them, and how they came to the Defendants hands.

In an Action of the Case for words, if the Plaintiffe have borne any Office of credit, it would do well to recite it in the Declaration, and know the time and place of speaking the words, either to the Plaintiff, or of the Plaintiff, together with what other Circumstances may make to aggravate the words spoken by the Defendant.

In an action of the case, where felony is laid to ones charge, and the Party carried before a Justice of Peace, and so bound over to the Assizes; be sure in this case to take notice of the time when, and the place where he laid the Felony to him, and for what, and the Constables name that detained him, and the Justices name before whom he was brought, and the bayling or committing of him till the Assizes, the day of the Assizes held, and before whom the Copy of his Inditement, and his Acquittall thereupon.

Upon an escape upon a meane Processe.

If the Bayliff have Arrested the Partie you are to sue upon meane Process, and either for favor or Bribes release him afterwards, so that you lose thereby the benefit of your Arrest. For Instructions,

First know what caufe your Client had againft the perfon fo Arrefted, and for how much money, and then fet forth that for the recovery therof, he took out fuch a Writ, returnable fuch a time, directed to fuch a Sherif, whereupon a Warrant was made and delivered to the Bayliff, by vertue whereof he Arrefted the Party, and fuch a day releafed him.

When you buy any thing upon Warranty, whether it be living Cattell, or any Chattels or goods that are warranted to be found, ufefull, and good, or that fhould contain fuch a number, either of loads, Pounds, weight or meafure, and it holdeth not out fo, an Action lyes in which cafe you muft take notice of the quantity and quality of the thing, when fold, and for how much the time and place, and that the Defendant did warrant it to be good, &c.

An Action likewife lyes againft a Farrier, who for a Sum of money undertakes a cure, and wholly neglects it, or ufes contrary or poyfonous Medicines, wherby your Horfe dyeth or it worfted.

And likewife againft a Smith that pricks your Horfe in fhooing of him, whereby he becomes lame and unufefull, and you lofe the benefit of his Service.

And where a Taylor taketh a quantity of cloath or Stuff to make a Suite, and cutteth it fo fcanty as that it will not be for the Parties ufe.

And likewife for many other frauds and deceits, both in Shop-keepers, Artificers and men almoft of all Myfteries and profeffions.

Having thus given fome breife directions what to take by way of Inftruction and Information for the Attorney in behalfe of his Client, in order to drawing a Declaration, I fhall now proceed to the faid declaration, Iffue, and judgement, after appearance made by Super-

sedeas to the Exigent, or upon any other appearance upon arrest had by vertue of mean Proceß.

THe Defendant appearing by putting in speciall Bail to the Action, or otherwise upon the *Capias*, *Alias*, or *Plures* in the Philizers Office, where the same was sued forth, or by *Supersedeas* to the *Exigent*, brought and allowed with the Sheriff, you must informe your selfe what Attorney doth appear for the Defendant; that done, you must declare either upon Bond, Bill, Indenture, Trespasse, or otherwise, as your Case requires, allwayes observing this rule, that there be no difference between the Additions in the Writs or Summes therein contained, and your Declarations, for they must literally agree, the one being a Warrant for the other; for if there be variance, and the Defendant take notice of it, he may plead that variance in abatement to the Writ.

And for the drawing of those Declarations, it rerequires the skill, studie, and experience of an able Clark of the *Prothonotaries* Office, and some helps there have been formerly by Books of *Entries*, which being at an Extraordinary rate, have not been so much in use amongst Attornies, but there is now a Book extant of select *Presidents* in *English*, for almost all Declarations, out of the Works of the learned *Prothonotary* Mr. *Brownlow*, and is of small price, sold by Mr. *Twysford* in *Vine-court* Middle Temple, to which I referre you.

Having your Declaration drawn, you must enter it upon some Roll of the Court, in one or other of the *Prothonotaries* Office, either by your selfe or some Clark of the Office, who must see it put in the Docquet of that Office, and thereto put the number-Roll, and so enter it in your owne Docquet Book, and keep your number-roll, that so you may have recourse to the Roll afterwards to enter up your Continuances, if the Caufe continue above one Term before Judgment or Tryall had.

By the courfe of the Court, the Defendants are to anfwer the fame Term they appear, if the Writs be returnable at the beginning of the Term, efpecially in Iffuable Terms, which are *Trinity* and *Hillary*, but in other Terms, if the action be not layd in *London*, the Defendants have for the moft part imparlance, or time to plead till the next Term.

And here take notice, there be two kinds of imparlance, the one Generall, the other Speciall; after a generall imparlance had, the Defendant cannot plead in abatement to the VVrit, Excommunication, or the like, nor any priviledge out of another Court as a priviledged man.

But after a fpeciall imparlance, many pleas may be pleaded, which after the generall imparlance cannot be allowed: If a fpeciall imparlance be prayed, you muft take for the entry thereof of the Defendants Attorney, the fumm of 2 s-

If the Attorney for the Defendant upon receiving a Declaration do not crave that the condition of the Bond may be entred with the imparlance, and do not pay for the fame, then he is debarred from pleading Conditions performed at any time after, without moving the Court, and paying 5 s. to the Judges Box.

Rules to anfwer muft be entred in fome of the Remembrances in one of the *Prothonotaries* Office, which is done breifly thus.

Hereford ff. An imparlance between A. B. plaintiffe, and L D. lately of S. in the county of H. Yeoman, otherwise called A.B. of L. in the county of H. Yeoman, Defendant of a plea of Debt.

WHich being thus written, you put either in the Margent, or over head, your rule, which is unless the Defendant plead (within some few days) let Judgement be entred.

And these are entred either by the Secondary of the Office, where the Plaintiffs Attorney enters his causes on the Bill of pleas ; or as before I have said, by the Attorney or Clark for him, upon the common remembrance, for which there is 4 *d.* and upon the Expiration of the same rule, no plea being brought in, you must signe Judgement with the Prothonotary for want of answer.

If the Attorney for the Plaintiff do not declare against the Defendant upon his appearance within reasonable time in the Term after the appearance made, then the Attorney for the Defendant, may also enter a rule in the Bill of pleas against the Plaintiff, to declare ; and thereupon cause a *Non profecutus* to be entred, which must be signed with the Prothonotary, and cost given for the unjust vexation; for which costs he shall have Execution against the Plaintiff. But if the Plaintiff sue as Executor, or Administrator, he shall pay no costs upon any Non-suit.

The imparlance is a time of leave, or licence given from one Terme to the Terme succeeding, by the Plaintiff to the Defendant, either to plead to his action brought, or to let it passe by default; and to that purpose the next Term after the imparlance had, as aforesaid, the Attorney for the Plaintiff may call to the Attorney of the Defendant, to answer to the Declaration

Declaration, and if he do not plead in due time, give him rule to anfwer, which done and the Rule expired, he may enter Judgement as before is declared, either by *Nihil dicit*, for the Debt and cofts, as is fit and very ufuall in eafes before expreffed, if Debt.

Where the Defendant pleads generall Iffues or pleas as is moft ufuall, aud now directed to be done by a Statute lately made, wherby the fpeciall matter if any be, may be given in Evidence, as in an action of debt, that he owes nothing by the Country, *&c.* Or to Debt upon Bond, or Bill penall, that he did feale and deliver through threats, *&c.* Or by reafon of hard Imprifonment, or that it is not his Deed, or that he hath performed conditions, or the like; or in action of the cafe, the generall iffue not guilty for words, if upon promife, that he did not affume, *&c.* and for not guilty likewife in action of Trefpaffe or Battery. In thefe or the like cafes of commonn Pleas or iffues, there is no more requifite, but that the Attorney for the Defendant, do put his hand to the Plaintiffs Attorneys *Docquet* book, and that done, the Plaintiffs Attorney doth draw up the Plea, and make a copy of the Iffue, and there delivereth it to the Defendants Attorney, who muft receive it, and pay for entring fuch his plea, and for the Book, and then ufually they give warning of a Tryall, unlefs they forbear Tryall the next Affizes.

But if the Defendant plead fpecially (which will not be fo ufuall as formerly) he is to bring it to the Plaintiffs Attorney under a Serjeants hand, and if the Plaintiff reply fpecially either by traverfe or otherwife, the Replication is alfo to be under a Serjeants hand, and he is to give it to the Defendants Attorney.

So if the Defendant demurre to a Declaration, it is alfo to be brought under a Serjeants hand.

note   It's most generall, that the Jury arise out of that County and Town, or Parish where the action is laid for tryal, unlesse it be removed by pleading, as where an Action is brought upon a Bond or Bill, and the Action laid in *Herefordshire*, and the Defendant pleads Conditions performed, for the money paid at *Stow* in *Glocestershire*, according to the Condition, here the *Venire* shall not arise in *Hereford*, but in *Stow* in the County of *Glocester*, and thither shall the Record be carried to be tried.

note   If an Action upon the Statute of *Hue and Cry* be brought against a Hundred for a robbery done within the Hundred, the *Venire* shall not arise in that Hundred, where the fact was done (for then they would be Judges in their owne caule, which is against common reason) but the *Venire* shall arise in the Hundred next adjoyning, and to this purpose the *Venire* must be awarded specially, which is worthy observation.

note   After the Issue joyned and entred, there may be severall causes of challenge, as where the Defendant is of kindred to the Sheriff, either by blood, or marriage, the Plaintiff may pray the *Venire facias* directed to the Coroners, and if the Defendant agree thereto, it shall be accordingly. This must be specially awarded upon the Issue roll, and in the awarding of it, it must be set down and derived how the Sheriff is of kindred, and then is the *Venire facias* directed to the Coroners, and this is called a challenge to the array.

note   You cannot make a challenge to the Jury, till after they are called, and before they are sworn, for afterwards it comes too late.

note   If your tryall be by *Nisi prius* at the Assises in the Country, and your Jury appeare not full upon the Panell, the Plaintiffs Attorney may crave a *Decem tales*

tales de circumstantibus, ten of the standers by to fill up the Jury, or a lesse number, according as is requisite, which *Tales* must be mentioned upon returne of the *Postea*, and the judgment thereupon on the Issue Roll.

And upon the Plaintiffs default, after the first Term the Defendants Attorney may bring the cause to tryall by *Venire facias* by *Proviso*.

If at the tryall of any *Nisi prius*, the witnesses of the Plaintiff or Defendant will not voluntarily appeare, without being served with the processe, to testifie the truth of their knowledge, in the matter or cause in question, then you may have a *Subpœna ad testificand.* for the said witnesses out of the Prothonotaries Office, and therewith serve them, and compell them to appear, the fee whereof is,   2 s. 7 d.

When you proceed unto your tryall, you must, having entred as before your Declaration with the Issue joyned in the Prothonotaries Office, you must make out a *Venire facias* upon your Issue, and get it signed with the Prothonotary, and having sealed it, you must get it returned by the Sheriff of the County or City, where you lay your Action, and upon return thereof, you must also sue forth a *Habeas corpora*, which is made by a particular Officer of the Court, called the Clark of the Iuries, and deliver the same to the Sheriff in due time, that so he may warne the Jury, and get the same returned before the Assises.

Note, that if a Cause be brought to triall, and a *Habeas corpora Juratorum* be delivered to the Sheriff who summons the Jurie, and if you for reasons best knowne unto your self, defer the triall untill some longer time, and afterwards you think fit to bring it again to triall, you need not be at charge of a second *Venire facias*, but may take a Copy from the *custos brevium* of your first Writ, if you keep it not in your hands, paying him for it 8 *d*. and for the search of it 5 *d*.

Upon which Copie or old Writ, the Clark of the Juries will make you an *Alias habeas corpera*, or *Plures*, paying for it, in Debt or Trespass,   10 *d*.

And in other actions   1 *s*. 6 *d*.

And for the continuance of it every Term,   4 *d*.

Then you must in suing forth your *Nisi prius*, ingrosse your Record in Parchment, *verbatim*, according to the copie of the Issue made up, and the entry of it upon the Roll, in the Prothonotaries Office, and then examine the same with the Prothonotary, if it be upon an issue joyned the same Term, whose hand must be to it, and then carry the same to the clark of the Treasury for the time being, giving him such Fees for signing and making up the Record, as are hereafter specified.

But if the issue were entred of a former Term, then must you deliver the paper-book of the issue to the clark of the Treasury, who will examine the same by the Roll, and make up the Record thereupon; which done, and the same signed by him or his Deputy, you must seale the same with the Lord chief Justice of the Court, for the time being, who hath a Seale for that purpose, and then deliver the Record so sealed, together with the *Habeas corpus Jur.* returned by the Sheriff to the clark of the Assise for the same county where the matter is to be tried.

The generall fees in an action of debt, trepass, &c. follow, as to making up the Record.   *s*.   *d*.

For the *Venire facias*,   2 *s*. 7 *d*.

For the return thereof,   2 *s*. 4 *d*.

For the *Post diem* thereof,   4 *d*.

For the *Habeas corpora Jurator*, and *Expedition*, 2 *s*.

For summoning the Jury,   12 *s*.

If in *London,* or a Corporation, but   4 *s.* 4 *d.*
For signing the Record with the Clark of the Trea-
    sury, if the same exceed not three sheets   2 *s.*
For every sheet exceeding   4 *d.*
For Examining the *Jurators.*   4 *d.*
For writing the Record, for every sheet   4 *d.*
For examining the same by the *Prothonotary*   1 *s.*
For the Seal   2 *s.* 2 *d.*

Having thus procured your Record of *Nisi prius,* you
are to carry it at the time of the Assize and deliver it
in to the Clark of the Assize, and there pay the Judges
fee, having retained your councell, and your witnesses
being in readinesse for the tryall of the Truth of your
Cause, according to the Issue.

The Fees you are to pay at the Assizes are as follow,

For the Judges Fee in putting in the Record of *Nisi*
   prius   11 *s.* 8 *d.*
To each Counselour you retaine, at the least   10 *s.*
For reading the Record   10 *s.*
For the Marshalls Fees   2 *s.*
For the Jury, eight pence a piece   8 *s.*
To the Bailiff that keeps the Jury   2 *s.*
For the Crier   1 *s.*
For the Oath of every witness   4 *d.*
For a *Non-suit*
For a *Tales de Circumstantibus*
For a Privy Verdict
For a Warrant of Attorney if the Attorney be ab-
sent   4 *s.*

The Fees doe somewhat differ, by custome in seve-
all Counties; But if the tryall be had before the
Lord chief Justice of the common Bench in *London,*

thofe are common fees to be added unto the former.

For the Green cloath	1 s. 6 d.
To the Bar-Keeper and Hall-keeper	2 s.
To the Judges Groom or Foot-cloath man	1 s.
To procure the Record to be read	
For Lights, if the cafe be tryed by candle light	

The Affizes ended, your tryall being had, and Verdict paffed for your Client, at the next Term following, you are to call for the return of the *Poftea* from the Clark of the Affize, and thereupon bring the fame to the Prothonotaries Office to get cofts affeffed, for which end (if your charges have been extraordinary) you muft bring a Bill of disburfements under your hand, otherwife not, and thereupon caufe Judgement to be entred : For the Entry whereof, the gener Fees are as follow,

For the returne of the *Poftea*.	2 l.
For figning the Cofts.	1
For entring the Judgement, if the Jury did fully appeare.	2 s. 4 d.
If there were a *Tales*, then more.	3
For the Copy of the Judgement.	1 s. 4

Having thus far proceeded, you may now procu Proceffe and Writs of Execution, by *Capias ad Satisfaciendum, Fieri Facias, Elegit,* or otherwife, accord' to your defire, and as the nature of your Actio brought, doth allow to require ; wherein,

Note that the *Capias ad fatisfaciendum,* is the taki of the Body only of the Party in Execution, till h fatisfie for the Debt and Damages, the *Fieri fac* againft the Goods onely, and the *Elegit* againft t Moietie or any one half of his Lands and Tenemen and all his Goods, and Chattells (his Oxen and Plow-Cattel only excepted) to have and to hold the Goods as his owne Goods, and the said Moietie of the Lands untill his Debt and costs shall be fully satisfied and paid. But note this, that after an *Elegit* executed and filed you can never have any other Execution, it being your owne Election.

Note also, that if you first sue forth a VVrit of *Fieri facias* against the Goods of the Defendant, and by vertue therof levy part of the Debt and not the whole then you may have afterwards a *Capias ad Satisfaciendum* against his Body, or an *Elegit* for the rest, but if you first Imprison his body by vertue of a *Capias ad Satisfaciend.* then you cannot have a *fieri facias* against the Goods, or an *Elegit*: if you have severall judgements against severall men for one and the same Debt, they being joyntly and severally bound for the same; you may have two or three severall Executions against them all, untill the Debt and Costs be satisfied by one of them, but cannot have the whole of every of them; and if the Defendant be in another County, and not to be found in the same County where the Action was laid, then you must sue forth a *Capias ad Satisfaciend.* into the same County where the Action was laid, and get the Sheriff to returne upon it (that he is not to be found) and then sue forth a *Testatum* into the County where he is to be found: And those Executions made immediately after Verdicts, &c. Judgments had upon them are made by the Clark of the Judgements in the respective Prothonotaries Office, who keep the Judgment papers where they are transcribed.

We have now shewed you the course how to proceed to tryall, after Outlawry reversed or an appearance, in case the Defendant plead an issuable Plea, or indeed upon any other appearance made upon

mean Proceſſe : Onely take notice of this, that if the
Plaintiffs Action be juſt, and right, and for good Debts
or juſt cauſes of Action ; the Attorney for the Defendant ſhall doe well to counſell his Client to yeeld to
judgment, either by way of not being informed, Con-
feſſion, or otherwiſe, ſo that he procure ſtay of Execution againſt his Client for ſuch time as ſhall be agreed
on by both Attorneys, which muſt be carefully looked
unto by the Attorney of the Defendant in time, before
the rule be on and they take judgement by default:
And this he ſhall do by putting his hand to the Plaintiffs Attorneys Docquet-Book, in this manner.

　　I am not informed, ſo that Execution be ſtaid till the
Mortow after the holy Trinity.

　　Hereford. ſ. Bridges for *Lacie*　　　　*Dowdeſwell.*
　　　　Dowdeſwell for *Hunt. Rot.*

　　After which you draw up the judgment ſhort in paper and carry it to the *Prothonotary*, who is to tax
Coſts and for that you pay him 3 *s.* 4 *d.* if in debt upon one ſingle contract, and then you are to take it out
(the Plaintifs name, and the Defendants and the Attorney for the Plaintiff, in the Judgment Book) after
which you enter it upon ſome Roll of the Court in the
Prothonotaries Office, and keep the number-Roll by
you to your Docquet Book, that ſo upon all occaſions
you may have ready recourſe to it ; and the Plaintifs
Attorney muſt be carefull of keeping together the Copies of all his judgments, that ſo when he hath occaſion to renew them by *Scire facias*, he need not be driven to take out new Copies, which are chargeable
out of the Treaſury.

　　And note, that in caſe the judgment have continued above a year and a day, and no Execution taken out, he muſt be put to renew it by *Scire faci-*

so must he likewise due, in case the Plaintiff or Defendant die.

And in case, or any Judgment had in Debt against an Executor or Administrator, you can have but a *Fieri facias* of the Goods of the party deceased, in the hands of the Executor or Administrator, but if the Sheriff return upon your *scire facias* a *devastavit*, then shall you have a *Fieri facias* of the proper Goods of the Executor, or Administrator; and if the Sheriff return that he hath no Goods, you shall have a *Capias* against his Body and after an Exigent, and so to the Outlawry after Judgment, if you please, in case you find him not easily to be arrested.

The course whereof is thus.

FIrst then he must have a *Capias ad satisfaciendum* to be made for the Debt and Costs, if it be in Debt or after a judgement had for Trespasse for the Damages and costs, as in the Judgment with which must be made into the same County where the Action was laid, and get the same returned to the Sheriff, with (*that he is not found, &c.*) Then he must carry the same to the *Exigenter* of the same County, who will make an Exigent thereupon which must be delivered unto the Under Sheriff to be executed and returned accordingly, as other *Exigents*.

NOte that in this case there shall need no Declaration at all against the Defendant, to give him notice thereof.

The Exigent being returned, you may sue forth the Processe of Outlawry from the Clark of the Outlawries, either generall or speciall, as in other Actions afore specified; whereupon the Defendant, if he

be arrested, cannot be discharged without satisfaction
to the Plaintiffe, and reversing, or pardon of the Outlawry; this is the utmost and last proceeding the
Common Law doth or can afford in any Case whatsoever.

The Fees to the Outlawry after Judgement are
   as follow;

	s. d.
FOR the *Capias ad Satisfaciendum*	I-I
For the return thereof	0-4
For the Post-*diem*	0-4
For the *Exigent*	I-7
For the returne thereof	0-4
For the generall *Capias Utlegatum*	0 II
For the speciall *Capias utlegatum*	2-2

Note that in this Case you may have either generall or speciall *Capias Utlegat.* into as many severall
Counties as you will, either in *England* or *Wales*;
but observe further, that no Processe whatsoever issuing or to be made in or out of the Common-Pleas, can
be directed or executed to or by any Under-Seriff in
Wales, but onely *Elegits*, *Extents*, Proclamations upon
the meane Processe, as before: *Capias Utlegatum*,
generall or speciall, or upon Outlawries after Judgement. If the Defendant be Outlawed after Judgement, if he cannot be arrested within a year and day,
yet the Plaintiff shall not need to renue judgement by
way of *Scire facias*, but otherwise in case he be not
Outlawed, he must, as I before recited.

The manner of renewing the Judgement by Scire Facias.

FIRST, the Plaintiff muſt ſue forth a *Scire Facias* againſt the Defendant in the County where the Action was laid, directed to the Sheriff to give notice to the Defendant to appear and ſhew cauſe why the Plaintiff ſhould not have Execution againſt him, for the Debt and coſts formerly recovered : To which Writ if the Defendant can ſhew any good cauſe as a releaſe, ſatisfaction, or any other juſt cauſe or ſufficient diſcharge, then he may appeare and plead in bar his diſcharge.

If the Defendant upon returne of the ſame *Scire facias*, do not forthwith appear and plead, the Plaintiff ſhall have preſent Execution againſt him.

But if the Defendant, after the ſaid Judgement obtained, and before ſatisfaction of the ſaid Debt had, unleſſe the Plaintiff procure a *Scire facias, &c.* to be returned upon the firſt *ſcire facias* againſt the Executor or Adminiſtrator, then the Plaintiff muſt ſue forth a ſecond *ſcire facias* againſt the Executor or Adminiſtrator of the Defendant, and upon their ſecond default, the Plaintiff ſhall have preſent Execution againſt them, having after the return of the ſaid *ſcire facias*, taken it out, and given a Rule in the remembrance in the Prothonotaris Office to this purpoſe, that unleſſe the Defendant plead ſomething to his Writ (by ſuch a day) Execution is to be made by default.

NOte that theſe ſeverall Writs are to be made and ſued forth together with the Execution, in and out of the ſame *Prothonotaries* Office, and where

D 4   the

the first Judgment was entered : And the said Writs of *Scire facias*, together with the new Judgment had thereupon, to be entered upon Record, in the same Office, and the Writs carefully filed with the *Custos brevium*.

The severall Fees are these.

For search in the Docquet for the Number-Roll,
　　　　　　　　　　　　　　　　　　　　4 d.
For searching in the Treasury　　　　　　4 d.
For the Copy of the Judgment usually　　2 s.
For the Clark for making the Writ　　　8 d.
To the Prothonotary for signing of it　1 s. 4 d.
For the Seale of it,　　　　　　　　　　7 d.
For the Return with a *Nihil*　　　　　1 s.
For the Return with a *Scire feci*　　2 s.
For entring the Judgment upon default, upon one
Scire facias.　　　　　　　　　　　　　2 s.
If upon two *Scire facias's*　　　　　　4 s.
For the Copy　　　　　　　　　　　　　2 s.
For taking the Writs into a Remembrance　1 s.
For the Rule　　　　　　　　　　　　　4 d.
For a Warrant of Attorney　　　　　　　8 d.

Upon these proceedings duely and truely performed the Plaintiff may have Execution against the Defendant, by *Capias ad satisfaciendum*, by *Elegit*, or otherwise at his pleasure (as is before told you in Writs of Execution :) And if the Defendant be dead, then there shall issue against the Executor, a *scire facias de bonis testatoris*.

Thus

THus far having proceeded in debt againſt the Defendant himſelfe, his Executor, or Adminiſtrator either by way of *ſcire facias*, or otherwiſe, we now proceed to proſecution to Judgement and Execution upon ſpeciall Baile; wherein obſerve theſe Rules following.

IF the Defendant be arreſted by meane Proceſſe, as *Capias*, *Alias*, or *Plures*, and the Plaintiff holdeth him not ſufficient to anſwer the debt or damages contained in the Writ, the ſame amounting to 20 *l*. or upwards: In this Caſe the Plaintiff upon the return of the Writ, may crave ſpeciall Baile to be put in to his Action, which the Defendant muſt put in before ſome Judge of the Court where the Cauſe depends, who wil accept of ſuch Baile as the validity or weight of the Cauſe doth require, or in his diſcretion ſhall be thought fit.

If the appearance be upon arreſt, by the *Capias*, *Alias*, or *Plures*, then the Bail muſt be taken, and entred by the Philizer of the ſame County where the Action was laid, and who made the ſaid Proceſſe.

BUt if the Defendant be arreſted in the Mayor, Bayliffs, or Sheriffs Court, of any City or Corporation, and the Defendant by any Writ of priviledge, or *Habeas Corpus*, doe remove the ſame out of the ſame Corporation to be tried at Common Law above;

Then the Baile being taken by any Judge of the ſame Court, muſt be entred in the ſame *Prothonotaries* Office, where the ſaid Writ of priviledge or *Habeas Corpus* iſſued and was ſued out.

THe Defendant being as aforeſaid bayled, the Plaintiff may proceed and declare againſt him

as

as the nature of his Cause or Action shall require, observing the same form and manner in every respect or point to procure Judgement and Execution by way of *Nihil dicit, non sum informatus,* Confession of the Action, tryall by *Nisi prius,* or otherwise, as is formerly set down and expressed by Supersedeas.

And the Plaintiff having obtained judgment against the Defendant, and perceiving that he is not easily to be arrested and taken in Execution, or not sufficient to satisfie the same, but knoweth the Bail to be better able, then the Plaintiff, may at his choice leave the Defendant, and prosecute the Baile in this manner following.

First, the Judgement being entred, he must sue forth an Execution by *Capias ad satisfaciendum* against the Defendant, directed to the Sheriff of the same Countie where the Action was first laid, and upon the return thereof, get the same returned by *Non est inventus,* that is, (he is not to be found) then he must procure a Writ of *scire facias* against the Baile, to shew cause how the Plaintiff should not have Execution against them according to the Recovery or Judgement so had against the Defendant, upon which Writ if the Sheriff doth returne a *scire feci,* then there needs no second Writ to be made; but if he return a *Nihil* then there must be a second Writ of *scire facias,* which being returned likewise with a *Nihil* then the two Writs of *scire facias* must be taken out upon Remembrance in the *Prothonotaries* Office with the returnes of them, and Rules thereupon given, and filed accordingly with the *Custos Brevium,* and thereupon if the Baile shew not cause to the contrary, Judgment by default shall be entred against them in the said *Prothonotaries* Office, for the sum in which they became Baile as aforesaid, whereupon the Plaintiff may take Execution out againſt them, either by *Fieri Facias*, or *Elegit*, but not by *Capias ad ſatisfaciendum*.

ANd in this caſe obſerve, that the Plaintiff may likewiſe ſue and arreſt the Baile going by way of Originall at the common Law, for the ſum for which they became bail, and arreſt their bodies, either upon the *Capias alias*, or *Plures*, or ſue them to the Exigent thereupon, and declare upon the ſaid Recognizance, uſing all proceedings therein as in an Action of Debt, but in this the Action muſt be laid in the County of *Middleſex* onely, where the Records do lie, and whence the *Venue* out of that reſpect muſt riſe.

And if the bail cannot be arreſted in the County of *Middleſex* upon a *Capias*, &c. you may return (he can not be found, &c.) and ſue forth thereupon a Writ of *Teſtatum*, and by that means arreſt them in any other County where they may be found, obſerving all the Proceedings, as in an Action of Debt,

WEe have now ſhewed you how to proceed againſt the Bail, as well as againſt the Defendant himſelf, we come next to ſhew you how to proſecute a Writ of Errour and reverſe Judgement thereupon (which is not ſo abſolutely taken away as moſt men conceive by the late ſtatute) but that ſtill if there be ſubſtantiall matter of Error to be allowed of the Court, it holds good after Verdict, and is not at all taken away in Judgement upon *Nihil dicit &c.*

And there are various cauſes of reverſing an Outlawry; as we formerly ſhewed, ſo ſome of them may ſerve to reverſe a Judgement, which I ſhall here particularly relate.

After

After a Judgment had and recovered by (*Non sum informatus*,) Confession or otherwise (if it be not by triall of *Nisi prius*) these causes of Errour or any of them being duely found, may serve to reverse and make void the same.

First if there be any materiall difference or variance between the additions in the Originall, or the Procefs of *Capias*, *Alias*, *Plures*, and Exigent, and the Judgment which is warranted by them ; this is good caufe of Errour.

Secondly, if the Debt demanded in the Procefse or either of them, and the debt in the judgment recovered doe not agree, but are different, this is good cause of Errour.

Thirdly, if the Writ be not ordinarily and duely returned and filed with the *Cuftos brevium*, there is a juft cause of Errour.

Fourthly, if there be not warrants of Attorney duly filed, and put in the Office accordingly, as the caufe requireth, as one for the Plaintiff upon fuing forth of the Exigent, or upon the entry of the Judgment, there is good cause of Errour, for which you are to make fearch with the Clark of the warrants for the time being.

And for thefe and all other Errors, you are to fearch and get Copies of the Writs from the *Cuftos Brevium*, and obferve diligently both them and their returnes and confer them with the Judgement as it is entred upon Record in the Prothonotaries Office, where you are to take your Number-Roll out of the Docquets to that purpofe, that fo you may goe readily to it in the Treafury.

Fifthly, if the Defendant be arrefted by a Writ of *Teftatum* in a forraine County, and no Writ of *Capias ad fatisfaciendum* returned againft the Defendant with a *Non eft inventus*, in the fame Countie, where
the

the Action was laid and filed with the *Cuſtos Brevium* that is good cauſe of Errour in the Execution, but not in the Judgment.

NOw being informed of the cauſes of Errour, and that the Defendant be not arreſted and taken in Execution, but would avoid the ſame, then muſt he proceed as follows.

IN the firſt place, having the Number-roll, he ſhall do well to get a copie of the judgement, with the Additions of the party Defendant, and of the Debt and Coſts of Suit literally as it is entered upon the Record.

The Prothonotaries Office as I formerly told you, is the place where you are firſt to reſort, and there to the Docquet-Houſe to find out your Number-Roll in the Docquets of that Terme, when the judgment was entred; and having found the Cauſe, take the number-Roll, and then repair to the Records in the Treaſury at *Weſtminſter*, and ſo the Roll, and take a true Copie of the Judgement in all things, as above.

Then carry the ſame or a copie of the Præcipe, debt and Coſts, to the Curſitor of the ſame Countie where the Action is laid, who thereupon will make you a Writ of Errour.

THen you muſt goe with the Writ of Errour to the Clark of the Errours, for the time being, who will take out the Judgment with the Debt and Coſts of Suit, in his Book of Remembrance for Baile, and be ſure you carry with you good Sureties, ſuch as the Validity of the cauſe doth require.

Thereupon your Sureties, together with the Writ, muſt be brought to the Lord Chiefe Juſtice of the
common

common Bench for the time being, and there enter
Bail in a Recognizance, together with the Defend-
in double of the Debt, that the Defendant hath good
cause of Error, and shall follow the same Writ with
effect : And if the Defendant shall happen to be condemned therein, and not able to prove a sufficient Error therein, then that Defendant shall pay the
condemnation therein with further costs of Suite, such
as shall be allowed, or they the Sureties for to doe the
same ; To this the Judge subscribeth his hand and
thereupon giveth Warrant to the said Clark of the
Errors to make *Supersedeas*, 1. 2. or more as the Defendant for his Indempnity, or safegard from Arrest
shall require; which Writ or writs the Defendant is to
allow with the Sheriff of the same County or Counties where he standeth in danger or fear of Execution
before he be Arrested, or the said Execution Executed, either upon Body or Goods, or else the said *supersedeas* is of no force, nor can be allowed, whereof the
Defendant is to have speciall care, that he have it in
an early manner.

And this may be done as well in the Vacation, as
in Term time, if the Defendant be not arrested, or
have his Goods taken in Execution, by vertue of the
said judgement.

But if the Defendant be taken in Execution before
the *Supersedeas* be procured, then the Supersedeas
comes too late, for the Defendant shall not thereupon
be released, but must continue in durance, untill such
time as the judgement shall be reversed by the said
writ of Errour, in the Upper Bench.

FOR Reversall whereof he must not onely sue
forth his writ of Errour, as above, but also cause
the whole Record of all the Proceedings, from the
Originall and the beginning of the same cause (if Er-

rour be not found in entry of the Judgement it selfe)
to be certified by the said Clark of the Errours, out
of the Common Pleas into the Upper-Bench, and
Assign cause of Errour there.

The Record being thus certified, and Errour assigned upon the return of the said Writ of Error, he is
to take Copies thereof, and thereupon sue forth a
VVrit of *scire facias* to the Plaintiff, in the Action to
heare Errors.

To this the Plaintiff if he see cause may appear and
plead, and the most usuall and common Plea there, is,
that the Record is in nothing Erroneous.

The Plaintiff having so pleaded, and willing to have
the said Errour argued, and the Judgement confirmed
as cause shall require;

The Defendant according to his Recognizance;
must so follow the same with effect, or else he will be
condemned therein.

The Defendant, is then to labour for a day given,
for the arguing or the same Errour, if the Cause shall
so require.

But if the Defendant doe delay the Plaintiff, the
Plaintiff is to sue forth two *scire facias*'s against the
Defendant, to shew cause why he should not have exe-
cution: And if at return of the second *scire facias*,
Errors be not assigned, Judgement is confirmed for the
Plaintiff.

NOte that in this case upon a Writ of Error
brought upon a Judgement had in the Court of
Common Bench, and returned into the Upper Bench,
the proceeding thereupon must be only in the Upper
Bench, to which Court and no other it doth properly
belong after tis thither returned.

Bus

Ut a Writ of Errour upon a Judgment had in the Upper Bench muſt be returnable in the Excheꞇquer Chamber; and the cauſe of Error is onely heard and determined before the Lord chiefe Iuſtice of the Common Bench, the Lord chief Baron of the publique Exchequer, and the reſt of the Iudges and Barons, who are of the Coiſe of thoſe two Courts, and not before the Iuſtices of the Court of Upper Bench, where the Cauſe formerly depended; and received its Iudgeꞇment.

If the Errour be found and allowed by them, to be ſufficient and good, then the ſaid Iudgment is by their full conſent and Iudgment to be reverſed and made void.

But take notice, that notwithſtanding the reverſall thereof, it takes not away the Plaintiffs cauſe of Action, for the Plaintiff may commence a new Action againſt the Defendant for the ſame Cauſe, if he ſo think fit.

If the Errour be not found good and allowed, then is the former Iudgment affirmed, and further Coſts for delay of Execution allowed to the Plaintiff, who may preſently ſue forth Execution out of the Court of Upper Bench, either againſt the Defendant or his Suꞇreties as he thinks beſt, and proſecute againſt them either by *ſcire facias*, &c, as in the caſe of ſpeciall baile, as above, or by an action of Debt: But if any writ of Errour be ſued in any other Action then an Action of Debt, no Baile is required.

The Fees in this caſe are very uncertain, and canꞇnot be expreſſly ſet down, but the Heads of them, acꞇcording to their proceedings, are as follow.

For ſearch of the Record to find the Errour.

For

For the Copies of the Record.
For the Writ of Errour.
For the Lord chief Iustices Fee.
For putting in Baile.
For certifying the Record.
For assigning causes for Errour.
For an *Habeas Corpus.*
For the allowing.
For the return.
For the *Supersedeas,*
For the Copy of the Writ of Errour.
For drawing *Diminution,* if need require.
For the Copy thereof.
For entring the Errours and Plea,
For a *Certiorari,* if need require.
For a Certificate from the *custos brevium.*
For entring the same, and *Diminution.*
For the warrant of Attorney,
For the Copies of the Books for the Iudges.
For Counsellours Fees.
For affirming the Iudgment.
For the Copy thereof
For the *Scire facias* and entring.
For filing and returning.
For Attornyes Fees.

     Cum multis aliis quæ nunc, &c.

NOte that if upon any Iudgment recovered and had against the Defendant, he be taken in xecution, or have his Goods taken, or his Land exended for the same, and upon full payment or satisfaction of the Debt and costs, the Plaintiff, ether person, or by his Attorney, doe acknowledge satisaaction upon Record, in the said Court wherein the dgment was entred; and if the Defendant at no e, from thenceforth or after, made a Release of Errours to the Plaintif, and that there be good cause of errour found in the said judgment, the Defendant may bring a Writ of Errour upon the said judgment, and upon arguing thereof, (as before, the Errours being allowed by the Judges, and the Judgment thereupon reversed) the Defendant may sue forth a Writ of Restitution against the Plaintiffe, and recover back again the full Debt and costs of Suit specified in the said Judgment; but if he have made a release, he is void of remedy.

And take notice further, that if there be a judgement had and recovered against the Defendant by way of *nisi prius*, and Verdict of twelve men, Then unlesse he can find some cause in the Originall or the entring or giving of the said Judgment after the Verdict so given and had, he cannot be admitted to sue forth a Writ of Error, for by many Statutes, and particularly the Statute of *Jeofailes*, many great faults, misprisions, or causes of Errour had or committed in prosecution of the said Cause before the said Verdict, are taken away.

Observe further, that if the Defendant be outlawed after judgment, and there be good cause of Errour to be found, as well for or in the said judgment as Outlawry, the Defendant may bring a Writ of Errour, and be bayled for both, and have a *Supersedeas*, as well for the safeguard of his bodie as good before they be arrested or taken upon the same.

NOw because we have omitted to speake of acknowledging of satisfaction where the debt satisfied and judgement had, whereby the Defendant in Case the satisfaction be not acknowledged may be in danger in paying twice one and the same debt, therefore observe the ensuing rules.

When you are to acknowledge satisfaction, be

De 6C.

to have a sufficient warrant for it from your Client, and likewise let the Defendant seal a release of Errours for the reason before alledged.

If it be in Terme time, get the Cryer to bring the Roll into Court, and lay it before the Secondary, with the cause ready before him, and pray him to enter satisfaction, which the Secondary of that *Prothonotary* in whose Office the cause was entred, will do you, paying the Fees as follow.

To the cryer for bringing in the Roll.	6 d
To the box, if the debt be not above forty pound	6 d
If above forty pounds, for every hundred pounds	1 s
To the Prothonary	2 s. 4 d
To the Secondary	4 d.
For the Attorneys fee	3 s. 4 d

HAving gone thus far in actions of Debt it rests now wee should speak something of a wager at Law, which is a plea usuall by the Defendant where an action of Debt is brought against him; either for money lent, or upon a Book-debt, or upon detinue, or any other action of Debt which is not grounded upon specialty (unlesse it be where an account hath formerly been before Auditors) in all which cases the Defendant may wage his law, and there are two wayes of waging Law.

The first is called *Lex justanetr*, which is when your client will presently upon pleading come into court & swear that he oweth or detaineth nothing, in which case it behoves you to have your client ready, at the time when you plead, and the next day, or second bring him into court, and let him do his law, in which case the Plaintiffe cannot become

sion-non-ſuit ; but upon a wager at Law at a day aſſigned he may be non-ſuited.

Note *Lex inſtanter*, cannot be after a generall imparlance, nor doth an Eſſoyn lie in that caſe.

FOr the other kind of wager of Law, which is *Lex ad diem*, where a day is aſſigned, there is to be given fifteen dayes at the leaſt, after the Law pleaded for doing thereof, that is, fifteen dayes after the comming in of your Imparlance, at which time, if your Client be not ready to do his Law, he may be Eſſoyned (that is to be excuſed for that time) and have a longer day to do it, which you muſt doe upon the Eſſoyn day of that returne, wherein your Law ſhould have been done in Court.

Note that the Plaintiffs Attorney muſt ever look on the dayes of Exceptions, in caſe there be no Eſſoyne caſt, to enter a *Ne recipiatur*, but if there be an Eſſoyn caſt, then to adjourn it ; and to look to the continuances, as this, and the nature of the Actions, the Eſſoyns are caſt in, require.

Note further, that upon an Eſſoyn caſt, if it be not adjourned by the Plaintif, he may be non-ſuited, is before ſhewed.

If an Eſſoyn be caſt where it will not properly lie you may have it diſſolved, which is called qua ing, which ſhall return the Defendant or Tenant d fault.

NOte, the Tenant or Defendant may (for the moſt part,) be Eſſoyned upon every Original before appearance, with cauſe or without cauſe, wh by doth enſue great delay to the Plaintiff, and ſome time the Defendant may be Eſſoyned after an Eſſo in Action reall (of which we ſhall hereafter tre more at large by it ſelfe.) The Tenant for life at eturne of the originall Writ may be Eſſoined, and then the Defendant muſt adjourne the ſame, wherein muſt be given common daies of returne , and at the day given by the Eſſoyn, the tenant may demand the view, wherin muſt be given other daies of returne and at the day of view, the Tenant may be Eſſoyned again, and then he may pray in aid of him in the Reverſion, and at the returne of the ſummons *Ad Auxiand:* he that is prayed in aid, may alſo be Eſſoyned or nine returnes , at which time the firſt Tenant may be Eſſoyned again : And all theſe delayes the Tenant may inforce the Demandant to ſuffer.

Note that in all reall Actions upon the Summons, the Tenant may be adjourned by the Demandant unto the ninth returne following , Incluſive , but of this more in its proper place.

The Fees incident to the wager of Law and Eſſoyns, Exceptions and Adjournments follow in a Table amongſt other Fees.

NOte, that many of theſe Actions of Debt are brought in inferiour Courts, as in in the Sheriffs or Majors Court in *London,* and in other corporaions, where they hold plea by their Charters for very great ſums, where the Defendant for delay or otherwiſe doth uſually bring a *Habeas Corpus* or Writ f priviledge , which doth remove both the body if in Priſon) together with the cauſe.

This *Habeas Corpus* or Writ of Priveldge , muſt be made by one of the *Prothonoaries* Clarks , and muſt be ſigned by one of the Judges of the court , and ter by the *Prothonotary,* and after ſealed and carred under ſeale, and delivered to the Judge or Steward, or other Officer in chiefe , of ſuch inferiour urt where the cauſe is depending , where upon alwance of it , they returne it , and certifie the cauſes

E 3   which

which done, he that brings the *Habeas Corpus*, must put in baile above, before the Judge, most usually that signes the Writ, such as the Judge shall approve of, when he sees what the causes are.

BUT if the party do not appear at the return of the said Writ, and put in good baile, in some short time (for they cannot put in common baile, though the Action be never so small) you may have a *Procedend*, to carry back the Cause or Causes to the Court below, from whence they were removed, there to be proceeded into Judgment.

The Fees of a *Habeas Corpus* are as follow.

	s-d.
To the Clark for the Writ	0-8.
To the Prothonotarie for signing it	1-4.
For the Seale	0-7.
To the Iudge for his hand thereunto	4-0.
For the Attorneys Fee	3-4.
For allowing the Writ	2-8.
For the returne of the first Cause	2-6.
For every other cause	1-0.
For a bill of *Multas causas*, if in *London* for search	0-4.
To the Serjeant, if in *London*, for his Fee at least	10-0.
For putting in baile before the Iudge for the first Cause	10-8.
For every other Cause	3-0.
To the Prothonotary for filing the baile, for the first Cause	6-4.
For every other cause	2-0.
For the Attorneys Fee	3-4.

Now becaufe there are many mifcariages in thefe *abeas Corpus*, whereby the Writs themfelves become nufefull, in being not allowed, all which proceeds oft ufually from the miftake of title of the Corpora-on or Court to which it is directed, I have thought to infert the titles of the moft corporations rougout *England*, as follows Alphabetically.

A

St. *Albons.*

O the Major, principall Burgeffes and Recorder of our Burrough of Saint *Albons* in the County of *rtf.* greeting.

Abenden.

To the Major and Bayliffs of our Burrough of *A-den* in the County of *Hertford*, greeting.

B.

Briftoll.

O the Major, Aldermen, and Sheriffs of the city or Town of *Briftoll*, and to the Major and con-bles of the fame City or Towne, and alfo to the ilifs and commonalty of the fame City or Towne *Briftoll*, and to the Bayliffs of the faid Major and nmonalty of the fame City or Towne in Court, l to either of them, greeting: (Note this City h divers Courts within it, which caufes the divers ellations.)

Burgavenie.

To the Steward and Bayliffs of *L. Nevill*, Lord *A-gavenie* of his Town of *Burgaveney*, greeting.

Bridgewater.

To the Major and Bailiffs of the Town of *Bridge-ter*, greeting.

Bedford.

To the Major and Bailiffs of the Towne of *Bedford* greeting.

Bridgenorth.

To the Bayliffs & Burgesses of our Town of *Bridgenorth,* greeting.

Boston

To the Major & Burgesses of our Burrough of *Boston* in the county of *Lincoln,* greeting.

Barnstable.

To the Major, Aldermen, and Burgesses of our Burrough and town of *Barnstable,* greeting.

Banbury.

To the Bayliffs of our court of *Banbury,* greeting.

Barwick.

To the Major of the town of *Barwick* upon *Tweed,* greeting.

Battell.

To the Steward and Bayliffs of *A. Brown* Knight Lord *Mountague,* of his Liberty of *Battel* in the county of *Suffex,* greeting.

Bath.

To Major, Recorder, Aldermen, and Justices of the city of *Bath,* greeting.

Bodmyn.

To the Major commonalty, and Clarks, of our Burrough of *Bodmyn* in the county of *Cornwall,* greeting.

Buckingham.

To the Major, Burgesses, and Steward of the Burrough and Parish of *Buckingham,* greeting.

St. Edmonds Bury.

To our head-Bayliff of our town of *Bury, St. Edmonds* and

and to our head-Steward of our Liberty of the Burrough of S. *Edmonds*, & to every one of them, greting.

Bewdley.

To the Bayliff, Recorder, and Burgesses of the Burrough of *Bewdley*.

Bridewell.

To the Major, commonalty, and Citizens of the city of *London*, and to the Governours of the Hospitall of *Edward* the sixth, late King of *England*, to wit, Christs *Bridewell* St. *Thomas* the Apostle, greeting.

Beverley.

To the Major, and Governors of the Town of *Beverley*, greeting.

Biddiford.

To the Major, Aldermen, head Burgesses, and to the Recorder, or his sufficient Deputy of the Town of the Burrough of *Biddiford*, and to either of them, greeting.

Newcastle upon Tyne.

To the Major, Aldermen, and Sheriff of the Town of *Newcastle upon Tyne*, greeting,

C.

Cirencester.

TO the Maior, Aldermen, and Citizens of the city of *Cicester* greeting.

Colchester.

To the Bayliffs of the Town of *Colchester*, greeting.

Canterbury.

To the Major and Bailiffs of the towne of *Canterbury*

bury, and to either of them, greeting.

Coventry.

To the Major and Baylifs of the city of *Coventry*, greeting.

Chipping-Wiccomb.

To the Major, Steward and Bayliffs of the Burrough of *Chipping-Wiccomb*, greeting.

Carlisle.

To the Major and Bayliffs of the City of *Carlisle*, greeting.

Cheftenham.

To the head Steward, Bayliff of the Mannor of the Borrough or Town of *Cheftenham*, and to either of them greeting.

Chepftow.

To the Steward and Bailiffs of the town of *Chepftow* in the county of *Monmouth*, greeting.

Caftle-rifing.

To the Major and Burgeffes of the town of *Caftle-rifing*, greeting.

Chipping-Norton.

To the Baylifs of the Burrough of *Chipping-Norton*, or otherwife, to the common Clark, or Deputy there, greeting.

D.

Downehewot.

To the Major, Aldermen, and Recorder of the Burrough of *Downehewot*, otherwife called *Launtefton* in the county of *Cornwall*, greeting.

Doncafter.

To the Major and Recorder of the Town of Don-
cafter

caster, and to both of them, greeting.

Derby.

To the Major, Recorder, and Burgesses of the town or Borrough of *Derby*, or to either of them.

Downwick.

To the Baliffs of the Burrough or Town of *Downwick* in the County of *Suffolk*, greeting.

Clifton, Dartmouth-hardness.

To the Major, Bayliffs, and Burgesses of the Burrough of *Clifton, Dartmouth hardneße*, greeting.

Dover.

To our Constable of the Castle of *Dover*, and one of the Keepers of our five Ports, or to him that holds the place there.

E.

Ely.

TO the Justice of Pleas within our Isle of *Ely*, held and assigned, greeting.

Exeter.

To the Major and Bailiffs of our City of *Exeter*, and to the Bayliff in Court of the said City, and to either of them.

F.

Ferriet neere Shrewsbury.

TO the Steward and Bailiffs of the Liberty of *Ferriet* behind the Town of *Shrewsbury*, greeting.

Fleet.

To the Warden of the Prison of the *Fleet*, or to him
holding

holding the place, heret.

G.

Gilford.

TO the Major of our Town of *Gilford*, greeting.
   City of Gloucester.

To the Major, and Sheriffs of our City of *Gloucester*, greeting.
   Gravesend and Milton.

To the Major, Jurors, and Inhabitants of the town and Parish of *Gravesend* and *Milton* in the county of *Kent*, greeting.

H.

City of Hereford.

TO the Major of our City of *Hereford*, greeting.
   Hebson.

To the Major and Burgesses of our borrough of *Hebson* in the county of *Cornwall*, greeting.
   Haveringe.

To the Steward of our Mannor of *Haveringe A-thowry*, greeting.
   Higham-Ferries.

To the Major and Aldermen of our Town of *Higham-Ferries*, and to either of them, greeting.
   Hertford.

To the Major and head Burgesses of our Burrough of *Hertford*, and also to the Steward in Court of Record there, greeting.

Huntingdon.

Huntingdon.

To the Major and Bailifs of the Towne of *Hunting-don.*

I.

Ipſwich.

TO the Bayliff of our Town of *Ipſwich* in the County of *Suffolk*, greeting.

Great Irnemouth.

To the Bailifs of the Town of Burrough, and Liberty of great *Irnemouth*, greeting.

K.

Kingſton upon Hull.

TO the Major and Sheriff of our Town of *Kingſton upon Hull*, greeting.

Kingſton upon Thames.

To the Bayliffs of our own Town of *Kingſton upon Thames*, and Steward of the Town-Court there, and in the abſence of the ſaid Steward, to the Bayliffs and Recorder of the ſaid Town, or to two of them, greeting.

St. Katharines next the Tower.

To the Steward of the Maſters, Brethren, and Siſters of St. *Katharines* behind our Tower of *London*, in Court there, greeting.

L.

Lincoln.

TO the Major and Sheriffs of the City of *Lincoln*, and to either of them, greeting.

Ludlow.

To the Bayliffs of the Town of *Ludlow*, greeting.

Lichfield

Litchefild.

To the Bayliffs, Burgeffes, and citizens of the city of *Litchfield.*

Kings Lenne.

To the Major and Recorder of the Town or Burrough of *Kings Lenne* in the county of *Norfolk*, and to either of them.

Kings Lyn.

To the Major of our Town of *Kings Lyn*, in the county of *Dorfet.*

Leicefter.

To the Major, Bayliffs, and Burgeffes of the Town of *Leicefter*, greeting.

Lidford,

To the Major and Burgeffes of the Burrough of *Lidford*

M.

Maidftone.

TO the Major of the Kings Town and Parifh of *Maidftone.*

Monmouth.

To the Major and Bayliffs of the towne of *Monmouth.*

Kings Milcomb.

To the Major and Bayliffs of the Town or Burrough of *Kings Milcomb.*

Mincholts.

To the Burgeffes of the Burrough of *Minchilots*, in the county of *Somerfet*, greeting.

Marleborough.

To the Major and head-Burgeffes of the Burrough

rough of *Marleborough*, greeting

Middleton.

To the Steward of our court of *Middleton* behind *Sittingborne*.

N.

Norwick.

TO the Major and Sheriffs of the city of *Norwick*, and to either of them, greeting.

Newport.

To the Major, and Baylifs of the Burrough or town of *Newport*.

Northampton.

To the Major and Bayliffs of the town of *Northhampton*, greeting.

Nottingham.

To the Major and Sheriffs of the town of *Nottingham*, greeting.

Newark.

To the Major and Aldermen of the town of *Newark* upon *Trent*, in the county of *Nottingham*.

O

Oxford.

TO the Major and Bailiffs of the city of *Oxford*, greeting.

P.

Plymmouth.

TO the Major of the Burrough of *Plymmouth*, greeting.

Plympton

Plymton.

To the Major, Bailiffs and Burgesses of the Burrough of *Plymton.*

R.

Reading.

TO the Major and Burgesses of our Burrough of *Reading,* greeting.

Rochester.

To the Major, Aldermen, and citizens of our City of *Roffen,* and to either of them, greeting.

S.

Sudbury.

TO the Major, Aldermen, Burgesses, and Steward, of our town of *Sudbury,* greeting.

Stafford.

To the Major and Burgesses of our town of *Stafford,* greeting.

Southhampton.

To the Major and Bailiffs of our towne of *Southhampton* in Court there, and also the Keeper of our Goale within the same towne, or to his Deputy, or to either of them, greeting.

Saltash.

To the Maior, Aldermen, and burgesses, of the borrough of *Saltash,* greeting.

Southwark.

To the Steward in Court and Maior of the comminalty, and Citizens of the city of *London,* and burrough of *Southwarke* in the county of *Surrey,* or to his Deputy, greeting.

Shrewsbury

Shrewsbury

To the Baylifs of our Town of *Shrewsbury,*

Startford upon Avon.

To the Baylife of our Burrough or Town of *Strat*ord upon *Avon*, and also to the head Alderman of he same Burrough, or Town, and Common Clark here.

Southmolton.

To the Major and head Burgesses of the Burrough of *Southmolton*, greeting.

T.

Talboth.

TO the Baylifs in Court of *Talboth* or Town of Bishops *Lenne*, greeting.

Tavestock.

To the Steward or baylifs in Court of the Earle of dford, his liberty of *Tavestoke*, greeting.

Totnes.

To the Major of the Burrough of *Totnes*, greeting.

Towre of London.

To the Constable holding the place of the Tower London, and also the Steward of our *Court* there, eeting.

Truroe.

To the Major and Burgesses of the Burrough of roe in the County of *Cornwall.*

Trematon.

To the Steward of *Trematon* in the County of De n, or to his Deputy, holding the place there, greeg.

F   *Toreing=*

Torrington.

To the Major, Aldermen, Burgesses and Steward of the Burrough or Town of great *Torrington.*

Tewkesbury.

To the bayliff and principall Burgesses and Steward of *Tewkesbury* in the County of *Gloucester.*

Uske.

TO the Major and Bayliffs of the Town or Burrough of *Uske*, greeting.

W.

Wallingford.

TO the Major and Burgesses of the Burrough or Town of *wallingford*, greeting.

New Windsor.

To the Major, Aldermen, Bayliffs, and Steward of the Burrough of *New windsor*, in the County of *Berk* or to either of them, greeting.

Woodstock.

To the Major of the Town of *New woodstock.*

Wye.

To the Steward in Court of the Mannor of *Wye* in the County of *Kent*, greeting.

Witteroll,

To the Bayliff in Court of *witteroll*, greeting.

Winchester.

To the Major, Baylifs and Commonalty of our City of *winton*, greeting.

Worcester.

To the Major, Recorder, and Aldermen

our city of *Worcefter.*, greeting.

Wenlock.

To the Bayliff and Steward of the town and liber-ty of great *Wenlock*, greeting.

Wigmore.

To the Steward and bayliff of the towne and Bur-rough of *Wigmore*, in the County of *Hereford*, gree-ting.

Warwick.

To the Bayliffs and Recorder of our Burrough of *Warwick*, greeting.

Weftbich.

To the Keeper of our Prifon and Caftle of *weftbich* or to his Deputy there being, greeting.

Thefe are the feverall titles of feverall Corporati-ons which happily may fome of them alter in fome particular, by reafon of renuing their Charters and having larger Grants, by which they are incor-porated a new, and which may alter the title, of which the Attorney muft the beft he may, informe him-felf.

Some few rules have been omitted, which concern what hath been premifed concerning actions of debt, and may be of much ufe in other actions; which take as followes, and firft of Amerciaments and of the E-ftreating of them.

NOte, that if the party be arrefted, and at the returne of the Writ the Sheriff return (that he hath taken the body of the Defendant which he hath ready, &c.) and yet the Defendant appears not, you may if the Sheriff will be fo content, take the bond of appearance given to the high Sheriff, and have it affigned to you, & fo you fhall be inabled to fue

the

the Defendant and his Sureties in the high Sheriffs name, or if you will not so do, or the Sheriff will not let you have the bond, then you must give the Sheriff a day by rule to bring in the body, &c. in the Prothonotaries remembrance, which if he doe not, he shall be amerced, and then you may sue out an *Habeas Corpus*, with the Prothonotaries Clark, and if hee bring him not in upon that, you shall continue amercing of him, and in case the Sheriff returne that he is (*Languidus in persona*) That is to say, that he is so sick he cannot bring him, then if it be found a delay, issue forth a *Duces tecum*, &c. and still upon the amerciament you shall increase issues untill you force an appearance: But you may have your *Habeas Corpus*, and also give your rules for amercing the Defendant as well in the Philizers, as in the Prothonotaries office.

When you come to the estreating of your amerciaments you must see them entred with the Philizer or Prothonotary where the rule was given, and then the clark of the warrants through whose office this prothonotaries Rolls pass, whereby he may take notice of the Defendant his (*Misericordia*) or being in mercy upon judgments, will certifie the amerciaments as he doth all other of that nature of course into the Exchequer. But if it be in the Philizers office, you must get a certificate from the Philizer to the Clark of the warrants who will return it into the Exchequer where the Sheriff shall, when he passeth his account, be inforced to pay it.

NOw if the Sheriff who made the arrest bee out of his office before you make your proceed or have appearance, you shall have a Writ called a *Distringas nuper vicecomitem*, that is to say, a distraining of the late Sheriff, which Writ must be made

out

out of that office whence the laſt proceedings were had.

NOte, that every Attorney, Clark, or Officer of the Court, may have an attachment of Priviledge, which is to be made in one of the Prothonotaries office, and muſt be made returnable at a day certaine, and is as effectuall on their behalfe as an originall, for if the debt be fineable you ſave the fine, and although the Debt be ſmall, or that it be any other action, yet ſhall you hold him to ſpeciall bayle, and upon a *Cepi* returned, you may proceed to amerce the Sheriff as is in other Proceſſes.

NOte, that if you cannot arreſt the party upon your firſt proceſſe taken from the Philizers, you muſt be ſure to ſee them ſo carefully continued, which coſts you four pence for each terme from the time of taking them forth, for if upon a ſecond writ the Defendant find your Writ diſcontinued, he may enter a diſcontinuance, and the want of any one continuance is Errour at the time of Judgment.

NOte that when you deliver unto the Defendant his Attorney, the copy of your Declaration, you are to ſhew your Bond, Bill, Will, Letters of Adminiſtration, Indenture, or other writings under ſeal, whereby you intitle your ſelfe, and this, for that you have (*A Perfect. hic in curia*) of theſe Writings in your declaration, which is in ſubſtance an acknowledgment of them to be brought into Court, but if the Defendants Attorney receive the declaration and then call not for ſight or hearing of the Bond, &c. and after pleads or takes an imparlance, you are

not

not bound afterwards to shew it him.

OBserve further, that if you bring your action against two or more for one debt due upon one specialty, when you draw your (*Precipe*) for the Curfiter, take heed whether your specialty be joyntly or severally; Joyntly thus, (we binde us our Heires Executors, *&c.*) or (*Obligamus nos, heredes,* &c.) not having therein the word, either of us, then your originall must be, and so your Declaration (that they render to the Plaintife so much money, *&c.*) but if the specialty be, as is most usuall, joyntly and severally, then must your *Precipe* be severall, and then must you make delivery, and enter so many severall Declarations as there are Defendants in your Writ.

NOte, that in Actions of Debt upon *Emisset*, for wares or Merchandizes, or other things upon *Mutuatus*, for money or other thing lent upon an *In simul computasset*, Actions of Trespasse, Battery or upon the case, *&c.* you are not tyed to lay the certaine day; but you may lay it any time after the cause of Action accrued, and before the *Test* of your Originall, but in an *Ejectione firmæ* the date of the Demise must be your guide, from which you must not vary.

NOte, that as I said before, there are some Actions reall, some personall, some mixt, whereof some are locall, as tyed to be layed in the County where the cause of action accrued; every personall Action, as an Action of debt, trespasse, Covenant, Battery, *&c.* may be commenced and layd in any County whatsoever, according as the Plaintif pleaseth, although both the Plaintif and Defendant

fendant do dwell out of the fame ; but every reall and mixt action is to be laid in the fame County where the caufe of the faid Action arifes as before, or where the Lands and Tenements do lye, &c.

The like courfe muft be taken to continue an iffue joyned and entred upon the roll from terme to term as before was fhewed in the cafe of imparlances.

NOte, that when you declare upon feverall fpecialties, in the clofe of your Declaration upon the (profect. hic in cur.) you muft mention their feverall dayes.

NOte alfo, that if feverall Defendants appeare by one Attorney, who are bound in a Bond joyntly and feverally, if they declare feverally againft them, yet the condition muft be recited but in one of the Declarations ; but if they appeare by feverall Attornsys you muft infert the condition to all the Declarations.

ANd note, that in many of the foregoing actions of Debt, you fhall do very well, it is the fafeft way for your Clyent to make actions of the cafe of them by indebitat affumpfit, where if you have the money lent, or wares delivered, &c. the Law implyes the promife, and in that cafe the Defendant is barred from waging his Law.

ANd note further, that if you bring an action of debt againft one within age, he may plead in Bar that he is within age, but in cafe it be for neceffaries, as Meat, Drinke, Apparrell, &c. there is no Bar to the Plaintiff.

And in cafe any one is fued who is within age, he muft defend himfelf by his Guardian ; and if he will sue, it must be his *Prochein amie*, or next of kindred.

NOte, that you may sue an Heire as well as the Executor or Administrator for the debt due by the Obligor; but in case you cannot find any Lands to descend unto him, he pleading *Riens* per discent (that is, hath nothing discended unto him) he shall not be charged.

If money be payable upon demand, there in that case it must be demanded before you can sue, and the Plaintiff must lay a demand in his Declaration, and the action accrues by vertue of that Demand.

NOte, that if a man shall bring an action either upon Bond, Bill, or otherwise, upon which he formerly had judgment, the Defendant may plead the former judgment in Bar, and it may be held good.

NOte, how and to what cases you may plead the Statute of Limitations, which will guide you to bring your actions within the time limited, or to cause you to forbear bringing them at all; all actions of Debt, Account, Detinue, Trespass, Replevin, and all other actions of the case, unless for words, must be put in suit within six years after the cause of Action; all Actions of Assault, and Battery, and Imprisonment, are to be put in suit within foure years and after cause of action and all actions of the case for scandalous words within two years after the words spoken, if in any of these cases they be brought after the time limited as above, the Statute of 21 Jacobi pleaded, is a good plea in Bar to any of them, no time limited for specialties.

If

If a man Arrest another or cause him to bee Arrested in another mans name, without the consent of the party in whose name he is Arrested, the Statute gives an action of Debt to the party so Arrested.

An action of Debt lies by the Statute of 2. *Edw.* the sixth, *Cap.* 13. For a Parson against his Parishoners for not setting out of Tythes, upon which action the Parson shall recover the treble value of the tythes so carryed away untythed.

An Action of Debt by the Statute of 32. *Henry* the 8. Chapter the thirtieth, lyes against an Attorney for not filing of Warrants of Attorney, in the Causes he is towards.

Where no place of payment is set down in a Bond, there the Obligor must be enforced to find out the Obligee, to pay him the money.

We now proceed to actions of Detinue; wherein we shall neede to say the less, for that the same Rules that have been given in actions of Debt, either in relation to the Process or the manner of declaring do hold in this, the one being in the *Debet* and *Detinet*, and the other the *Detinet* onely: And this action properly lyes where a man delivers Goods or Chattells to another to keep, and the Party to whom they were so delivered, refuses to redeliver them.

And observe that in this action of Detinue, you ought to ascertaine the thing, as a Horse, Cow, or other Cattell, or Cattells, naming them and making them certaine, for that the Plaintiff, is to recover the thing detained, and therefore it must be so certaine, as it may be known; for money delivered, an action of Detinue lyes not, but an action of account, and your Originall in this action runs thus;

THE

THE Keepers, &c. To the Sheriff of H. greeting, command J. G. lately of I. in the county of H. Yeoman, that justly and without delay, he render T. B. one Cow, which he unjustly detaines, &c.

If for a mans Evidences of his Land, in a Box or Bagg sealed up, in which case also an Action of Detinue lyes; then the Writ runs thus,

THat justly and without delay he render him one box, with Deeds, Writings, and other Minuments in the same box contained, which he unjustly detaines, &c.

The Defendant hath not in this action that variety of Plea as before in Debt, the most usuall Plea being (that he detaines not the thing sued for) and upon this he puts himselfe upon the country to be tryed, and the Plaintiff in like manner, &c.

Note that in this case, if the Plaintiff have a Verdict, his Judgement is a recovery of the thing detained, or the value thereof; in which case, as also where the Judgment is had by default for want of pleading, there is after the judgment had, a Writ of enquiry awarded, to enquire of the value of the thing detained: Upon the returne of which Writ of enquiry, what value the Jury finde the thing of, and what damages they give him for the detainder of it, is together with increase of Costs entred up for Judgment.

Note, that a man may wage his Law in an Action of Detinue, as formerly in debt was shewn, wherein the same course for the manner of the wager of Law, is to be observed as before.

But it is otherwise in case you declare for one Evidence in speciall, delivered by the Plaintiff to the De-

Defendant; in this cafe the Defendant fhall not wage his Law.

Note, that in cafe of Evidents detained; it is not proper for the Executor, nor hath he any Right to this Action, but the Heire who is to have the Lands.

Note, that if it be of any thing delivered to be kept, whether by the immediate party that brings the Action, or his Father, Anceftor, &c. Properly this Action lyes, if detained, but otherwife an Action of Trover and Converfion.

In the next place we come to Actions of Account.

THis Action lyes upon feverall occafions, as againft one that is Guardian in Socage, againft one as Receiver of monies, either by way of Rents or otherwife, or as Bayliff of an Office or as Bayliff in general: In all which cafes, you muft be fure to frame your Action rightly, by informing your felfe for what time he continued bailiff, receiver, &c. Of what his charge was, and what it amounts unto, and when he entred upon fuch his charge.

To begin with Guardian in Socage, your Proceffe are by Summons, *Capias ad computand. &c.* And you declare upon the Statute of *Marlebridge,* the eighteenth Chapter, of a Plea, that whereas by the common Counfell of the Kingdome of our Lord King of *England*; it is provided for, that the Guardians of the Lands and Tenements which are held in Socage, fhould render their reafonable account of the Iffues and Profits of the faid Lands, to the Heires of the fame Lands and Tenements, when they come to full age, &c.

They

The intendment of Baylif is one that hath the Administration and charge of Lands, Goods or chattels, to make the best benefit for the Owner; against this Person properly lyes an action of account, for the profits which have been made or raised, during the time he hath had the care of them.

And observe this, that a Baylif may be charged to account, and accordingly doth account, and upon account, nothing doth appear to be arreare in his hands but rather the Plaintif indebted to him, in which case the Baylif shall bring his Action of debt, for the surplusage of what he hath expended and laid out over and above his Receits.

If I appoint a man to receive money to my use, to render me an account, I shall have my action of account against him for the said moneys, he also having his reasonable Expences and Disbursements.

Where a man declares against one as receiver of moneys; and he must ascertain by whose hands the money was received; which lyes not against a Baylif, and if the receit be from any hands, other then the party Plaintif, the Defendant shall not wage his Law, but if it be alledged to be received by his own hands, and not by another mans hands, in this Case the Defendant may wage his Law.

Where there be two Copartners in Merchandize, that occupy and Merchandize in common, by the Statute, one shall have his action of account against the other, they being both named Merchants.

Where there be two Joynt-Tenants, and the one makes the other Baylif of his Moyety, in this case he that makes the Baylife may bring his action of account.

The Executors of a Baylif or receiver, are not chargeable with an Account.

An account may be brought against the Collectors

lectors, for money given to the use of the poore.

Note that if a man brings his Action of Account against one as Bayliff, and the Defendant to his action pleades, that he was never his bayliff to render an account &c. And upon that Issue joyned, and upon the tryall a Verdict for the Plantiff, in such case the Judgement is, that the Defendant shall account with the Plaintiff of the time and profits aforesaid, &c. And that hee be in mercy, because he did not sooner account.

Upon his Verdict and Judgement, the Court assignes Auditors, before whom the Defendant is to account upon such a day or time, as the Auditors shall appoint to heare the account ; and in the *Interim* the party either puts in Baile to account, or otherwise stands committed to the Fleet.

NOte that if the defendant acknowledg the action and that there be Auditors assigned by the court,
  in this case hee shall not bee inforced to put in Bayle.

There are two Pleas most usuall in these actions of account, the one is (that he was never his receiver, &c.) And the other (that he hath fully accounted, &c.)

Note that the Auditors assigned by Court, have power upon his accounting, to make him allowance of what reasonable Disbursments and charges hee brings in, as laid out, and if after the Defendant be over and above in arreare found by the Auditors the Plaintiff may bring his action of Debt, to which as is before said, the Defendant shall not wage his Law.

In an action of account a man may plead doubly, as where he stands charged to have received severall moneys, severall times from divers Persons, there

there he may plead as to part (that he stood not bailiff, *&c.*) and as to the other part (that hee hath
fully accounted, *&c.*) Upon the joyning of which
Issue, it being double, you say ; Therefore as to the
trying as well of this Issue as the aforesaid other issue
formerly joyned, command is given to the Sheriff
&c.

Note that an Action of Account lyes against a
Church-Warden after he is out of Office, by the succeeding Church-Warden to be brought.

Where an Infant within the age of fourteene
yeares, being seized of Lands in Socage tenure, a
Stranger enters into the Lands of the Infant, and
takes the Profits of the same, though he be not the
next of Kindred nor Guardian in Socage, yet the
Infant shall charge him as Guardian in Socage; and
it is no Plea for him to deeme that he is the next of
Kindred, but he must answer to the taking of the profits, the Writ being that he should render his reasonable account of the Issues and profits, comming of the
Lands and Tenements in S. which are held in Socage, *&c.*

Note that if it be for the profits of the Land, for
the time after the Infant is come to fourteen yeares
of Age, he must be sued as Bayliff, and not as Guardian.

Note also, that if any man have cause of Action of
Account against any as Receiver and bayliff, and dye,
his Executors shall have this action.

This Action may likewise be brought in the County where the cause of Action arises, and if so brought,
it may be removed into the common Bench, at the
suit of the Plaintiff, by a *Pone*, without shewing the
cause in the Writ, but it shall not be removed at the
suit of the Defendant, without shewing the cause
in the Writ of *Pone*, as if the Defendant have release,
and

and then it shall bee named in the *Poxe*, &c.

An Apprentice shall not be charged with an action of account, but if a man have a Servant whom hee commands to receive Money, the Master shall have a Writ of account against him, if hee were his Receiver.

The Fees incident to this Action, and the proceedings thereupon, follow in a table amongst others.

Actions upon the Case.

THese Actions are very numerous, and grounded upon severall occasions, as for scandalous words, for promises not performed, for speciall Nusances, &c. The Processe upon them are; first an Originall, and then by way of *Capias*, if you can arrest upon the first Processe, if not, then you may proceed to the Outlawry, as before in Debt, only the charge will be more in respect of the length of your Processe, and for returne of those Writs, you must returne (that the Defendant hath nothing within my Bayliwick whereby he may be attached) this for the Originall: And for the *Capias* and other Procefs (that the Defendant is not found within my Bailiwick).

In Actions of the Case for words, you must carefully observe what the nature of the words are, what they import, the manner of speaking of them, and what the party Plaintiff may be any wayes damnified by the speaking of them, what his credit was, and how impaired, and take the whole words as neere as you can; and before you bring your Action let the witnesses set downe the words as they were spoken, and as they will be able to prove them, and the time and place when and where they were spoken, and before whom. This Action oftentimes miscarries, by sca-

reason the Attorneys weigh not well whether the words be actionable or not, and many times, though some part of the words taken by themselves may be actionable, yet the subsequent words may quallifie the sense or the precedent; as where a man saies of another, that he is a thiefe, and hath stolne something of small or no value: For generally where one stands charged by words for any theft, which is onely criminall and not capitall, there the party plaintiff shall never enter Judgment, although he brings his action.

An action of the Case lyes against the Husband and Wife for words spoken by the wife, but in case the Wife be arrested and not the Husband, you cannot declare.

This Action lies in these severall cases following.

WHere one becomes Surety for another at his instance and request upon Bond, and he saveth him not harmelesse, but the surety is inforced to pay the money, in this case he may bring his action upon the case, wherein he must recite how such a time, at such a place, at the instance and request of the Defendant, he became bound to such a one in such a sum conditioned for the payment of such a sum at a day then to come, and that the Defendant in consideration thereof, did assume and promise to save him harmeless; that notwithstanding the promise aforesaid, he hath beene sued by the Obligee, and shew how and where and what he is damnified.

It lies where a contract is made betweene two by word of mouth, either for the delivery of Corn, Cattell, or any Merchandize whatsoever, and the party that promises so to deliver it, makes breach.

It lies for money borrowed, when you would make

sure the Defendant should not wage his law.

NOte, that in all Actions of the Case upon speciall promises you must be sure to lay a good consideration to ground your promise on, otherwise it is said to be *Nudum pactum*, as where it is for money owing by a stranger, and his Friend promises payment upon forbearance, there you must lay, that whereas such a one was indebted to the plaintiff in forty pounds, and that for the more speedy obtaining of the said Debt; the Plaintiff intended to implead him, and that in consideration the Plaintiff would forbeare to sue or implead the party owing the Money for such a time, the Defendant himselfe would pay it, in case the other did not.

It lies for money promised in consideration of marriage, wherein the Plaintiff must aver, that he married her such a time.

To call a man a Bastard if he be the Eldest Son, and in a capacity at the time of the words spoken, to inherit an Estate after his Father, and be disinherited, an action lies.

To call a maid Whore, or to say she hath a Bastard, whereby she loseth her preferment in marriage, is likewise actionable.

To call a married wife whore would not formerly hold action at Common Law, but in *London*, by custome it hath, but *Quære* whether it will not now be actionable in respect of the Statute, that makes the crime capitall.

If a man speaks scandalous words of any, for which is action brought against him; if the Defendant be able to make proof of the words spoken, he may plead a speciall justification; but if he plead such plea, and make it not good, the damages wil be much aggravated thereby.

If the Defendant fpake other words then what are, layed in the Declaration, he muſt plead eſpecially, and traverfe the word layd in the declaration; but quære, whether in both cafes by this late act he may not plead the generall iſſue, and give the fpeciall matter in evidence.

Where the Defendant pleads the generall iſſue which is, not guilty, for words ſcandalous, &c. there it refts on the Plaintiffs part, to prove the words as he hath laid them.

It hath been uſuall, and yet is the courſe to arreft upon a *clauſum fregit*, & then upon filing a new Originall, to declare fpecially in an Action of the cafe.

It lies for the hire of a horfe, which is returned back, and the hire unpaid.

It lies likewife, where a man abuſeth a horfe by immoderate riding, or otherwife by miſuſing of him.

The party likewife that hires a horfe, if he have given earneft for the Horfe, and that it bee promiſed him, it ſhall be delivered unto him by ſuch a time, and then he refuſes to deliver him, whereby he is diſappointed.

It lies for the Maſter againſt his Servant, for leaving of his fervice, before the time contracted for be expired.

Likewife for a fervant in cafe the Mr. without juft cauſe ſhall turne him out of fervice, before his time be expired.

It lies for a mutuall contract made between two, by word of mouth, and to bind the fame, a piece of money is given by the one to the other in earneft; now if either will not perform what is agreed upon, the other may bring his action of the cafe.

It lies, where a man upon fale of ſheep, warrants them ſound, and they prove rotten, or otherwife unſound.

An

An action of the case lies where one sells a Horse and warrants him to be sound, and the horse proves to be unsound at the time of the sale.

It lies against a Farrier, who shooes a horse and pricks him, whereby he grows lame.

It lies where a man, who is a Goaler, lets a Prisoner at large, and this as well as escape.

Where a man hath made a Distress of Cattell, &c. and is driving of them to the Pound, and another comes and rescues them, an Action of the Case lyes.

It lies against any that shall entice his Covenant-Servant from him.

If a man lose goods brought into a common Inne, or Hostrie house, an Action of the Case lies.

If a man deliver goods to a Carryer, and agree upon the rate for carrying, and they are lost, and miscarried, an Action of the Case lies.

It lies for stopping of a Water-course through his Ground, whereby the Plaintiff watered his Beasts and did other necessaryes, and if this be stopped either by Stones, Turfes, or otherwise diverted, an Action of the Case lies.

If a man stop up a way, whether Cart-way or Foot-way, and another hath right to that way, and can prescribe to it, an Action of the Case lies.

Where a man is to pay money, and gives a Bill of Exchange which is not accepted, but afterwards comes to bee protested, an Action of the Case lies.

Where a man sells another mans Cattell or goods, or Merchandizes, and warrants them to be his owne, an Action of the Case lies.

An Action of the Case lies against a Taylor, who doth undertake to make cloathes, and spoyles them, so that they are not usefull for the Party they are made for.

It lies againſt an Executor upon the promiſe of the Teſtatour, provided there be a conſideration to ground the promiſe on.

It lies in the behalfe of a Commoner againſt any that hinder him from uſe of his common.

Where a man hath an Office granted unto him, & another either diſturbes him in the Execution of his place, or otherwiſe receives the profits due to the office, an action of the caſe lies.

It lies againſt a cheat, for playing with falſe Dice.

Where a man diſturbs the keeping of a Court Leer, an Action of the caſe lyes.

It lies againſt an under-Sheriff for an ill or falſe return.

It lies againſt an under-Sheriff, who makes returne of Writs within any Liberty granted to another.

It lies on the behalfe of a Phyſitian or a Chyrugeon for Phyſick or performing a cure.

Where a man builds a houſe ſo neer his neighbours, or raiſes any ſhed or other out-houſe, or laies piles of wood, or Stacks of hay or corne ſo neer his neighbours windows, as that they ſtop up his light, an action of the caſe lyes.

And for any other nuſance, whereby a man is any wayes damnified, as where a man builds a ſtable or privy houſe ſo neere his neighbours houſe, that the ſmell thereof annoyes him.

It lies againſt an under Sheriff, for taking greater Fees then is allowed by the ſtatute.

It lies againſt one who ſhall break downe a mans Wall or Sluce, whereby his land comes to be drowned.

It lies for ſelling corrupt Wine, without warranting it to be good, for that it is prohibited by law.

It lies where a man hath pawned goods and tenders,

ders the money due, and Demands his Goods, and it will not be accepted.

It lies for not carefully keeping fire, whereby a mans house who is a neigbour comes to be burned either in part or whole.

It lies for digging of Lime pits.

It lies against one for keeping a dog that worries sheep.

It lies for a Soliciter, for his Disbursements and Fees.

It lies so many severall wayes for promises, as that they are not to be named in particular, but are to be drawn as the case falls out, onely observe some particulars following.

It lies where a man for money lent, upon forbearance promises to become security.

It lies upon a promise to pay money for Land contracted for.

It lies against any one that makes an arrest in a liberty not being Bayliff.

It lies for the Lord of a Mannor in ancient demesne against a Tenant that levies a fine above in the Common Pleas.

It lies in the nature of an action of conspiracy for one indicted of Felony, and afterwards acquitted.

It lies against a Steward of a Court for not taking security in Replevin.

It lies against the Husband and Wife, for meat, drink, &c. had by the wife before the intermarriage.

It lies for a Keeper of a prison for Meat and Drink had by a prisoner.

It lies against an Attorney or Clark of the Kings Bench for appearing or filing a bayle without Warrant.

It

It lies likewise against an Attorney that shall do any act in any mans name, whereby the party is prejudiced in relation to the Law, without Warrant had.

It lyes for erroneous prosecuting a Writ of Execution.

It lyes also against an Officer who takes money by extortion.

It lyes for a rescue made upon a *Capias*, or other processe whatsoever.

It lyes against the Sheriff for not returning a *Venditioni exponas.*

It lyes likewise on the behalfe of an Executor against an under Sheriff, for returning falsly a *Devastavit.*

If a man sells cloathes, and warrants them to be of such a length, if they hold not out accordingly, he which buyes them, may bring his action upon the case.

It one takes a mans cattell, and another take them from him, an action of the case lyes by way of Trover and conversion for the cattell.

An action of the case lyes against Tenant at will, who commits wast by burning houses, or pulling them down, but not an action of wast.

An action of the case lyes against the Bayliff for killing or spoiling any of his Masters cattell.

If a man deliver to another his Sheep to dung his Land, or his Oxen to Plow his Land, and he killeth them, an action of the case lies.

An action of the case lyes against a Sheriff, where the Plaintiff hath a Charter of exception, that he shall not be impannelled upon any Jury, and shewed that to the Sheriff, and yet he impannells him.

If the Sheriff upon a writ of second deliverance to the Plaintif of the distresse, and will not return the

Writ

Writ, so that the Defendant may constrain the Plaintiff to come and declare, so that he may avow, the Defendant shall have his remedy by action of the case against the Sheriff.

Actions of the case lye against the Sheriff, where he makes a *Precipe* to one who is no Bayliff of the Franchise, who returns a Jury which is quashed, to the damage of the Plaintiff.

Where a Guardian pleads falsely for an Infant, or vouches one who is not sufficient to render in value to the Infant, the Infant shall have an action of the Case.

An action of the Case lyes against a Chirurgeon, who undertakes to cure a man of a wound, and neglects it, whereby a man grows worse, and makes it through his negligence incurable.

Where a man promises in consideration of an hundred pounds, or any other summ in hand paid, to enfeoff another in such and such Land, by such a day, and doth it not, he shall have an action upon the Case.

There are many other cases wherein action of the Case lyes, which cannot be certainly recited, in respect of the various occasions of them; but in these before recited, and all others, the proceed is one and the same, onely the Declarations must vary as your Case requires; after your Declaration drawn, upon appearance made, you deliver it to the Attorney for the Defendant, and most usually with an Imparlance, which done you enter it accordingly of that Terme you deliver your Declaration, upon one of the *Prothonotaries* Rolls, and then Docquet it, and keep the Number-Roll by you, whereby you may be able to continue your Imparlance if need be.

The Terme following you give a Rule within some short time of the beginning of the Terme, with the

Second

Secondary of the Office for the Defendant to plead by such a day, or otherwise the Plaintiff have Judgement.

There is not much diversity of pleading to this Action, especially since the late Statute, the most usuall Pleas are, either, not guilty, or in case of promises, *Non assumpsit.*

Either of these being pleaded, you make up a Copy of the Issue, and deliver it to the Defendants Attorny, who is to pay for the Copy of the Issue, as before for the Declaration, four pence for every sheet, and also to pay for entring his Plea two shillings, that done, if you intend to try it, you must give warning to the Attorney of the Defendant when you intend to try it, and in order thereunto make out your *Venire Facias,* and get it returned by the Sheriff, and then sue out your *Habeas Corpus,* and so proceed to the making of your Record; and in all other things, both before, at the tryall, and after, as you are directed before in the case of Debt.

But in case they plead not, but let it goe by default, then upon the entring up of your Judgment you are to award a Writ of Inquiry of Damages, returnable, some returne the Terme following, which done, you make out your writ and procure it to be signed with the *Prothonotary,* and then Seale it, and be carefull to keep your Number-Roll likewise of your judgment when you have Docquetted it.

Note, that you are to give notice to the Attorney of the Defendant of the time when you intend to execute your Writ of Inquiry, if you practice fairely,

And having so done, and brought your Writ under Seale, and delivered it to the Sheriff, you may proceed upon it according to the time agreed on.

The Sheriff to summon an Inquest, who are

in

inquire what Damages the Party Plaintiff hath su-
ftained, as alfo for his Cofts and Expenfes of Suit.

The Inqueft having paffed, the Sheriff draws
a fhort fchedule, and annexes it to the Writ of Inquiry, and returns the Writ of Inquiry, which is called
an Inquifition, which he delivers you upon payment
of his and the Juries Fees.

Having your VVrit of Inquiry thus returned, and
the Inquifition annexed, you muft bring it to the
Prothonotaries Office and there take it out in the
Bill of Pleas, together with the Return and Inquifition, and give a Rule upon it, which done and the
Rule out, you carry to the Prothonotary, and he tax-
eth your Cofts, and then you pay him for it, and carry it to the Clark of the Judgments, and be fure you
give him likewife your Number-roll, and Term when
the Judgement was entred, and he will make you out,
either a *Capias ad fatisfaciendum* or a *Fieri facias* for
your Damages and Cofts. The Fees incident to this
action, you will follow.

Actions of Trover and Conversion.

THis Action is called alfo an Action of the
cafe and differs not at all in the Proceedings
from what hath been faid before, in Actions of the
Cafe.

It properly lies where the Defendant hath found
any of the Plaintiffs Goods, and refufeth to deliver
them upon demand, or where the Defendant comes
by the Goods, by the delivery of any other then the
Plaintif, wherein he fhall recover as much damages as
the Goods are worth.

It is not as in an Action of Detinue, that the thing
it felfe, whether Goods or Cattell fhall be recovered,

ed, but Damages to the value of them.

Note that a demand is absolutely necessary to this action before it be brought.

In this action if the Defendant plead that he is not guilty, which is the most generall Plea in this action, the property of the Goods must be proved to have been in the Plaintiff, before such time as they came to the Defendant his hands.

This action is now very usuall, and takes place instead of actions of Detinue, for in them the Defendant was at liberty to wage his Law, whereas this debars him.

In many Cases a speciall justification may be pleaded to an action of Trover, as where a man justified the taking of it as a stray, and refuseth not to deliver it, being a Horse, Sheep, or the like, upon payment for their Meat and keeping.

Many times in this action, the arrest is made upon a *Clausum fregit*, and then file a new Originall, and so declare in Trover; or in case you cannot arrest, you may sue to an Outlawry.

Where a man brings his action of Trover and conversion against another, with whom he findes any of his Goods lost or purloyned, here if the Defendant brought them in open Market or Faire, and that they be tolled in the Book, this alters the property of the Goods, and I can never recover them, but this must be specially pleaded.

Otherwise it is where they are brought privatly and not in open Market, or Faire, by this there is no property altered.

It is generally held, a mans shop is said to be open Market; but if Plate be stollen and sold to any other Tradesman, or in any other shop, then the Goldsmiths to whom it is proved to buy it, it hath been held the property is not altered, but that the Party

losing

loſing of it, may recover the value of it in Damages by action of Trover.

All the proceedings in this action are generally the ſame immediatly before going in all particulars, whether it be by triall at the Aſſizes, or by Writ of Inquiry; which Writ of Inquiry, Inquiſition thereupon, as that alſo in caſe are to be filed by the Clark of the judgments, with the *Cuſtos brevium*, after judgment entred up.

In this action you muſt be carefull of the dayes when you lay the Plaintiff to be poſſeſſed, and what time after you lay it to be loſt, and what time after the Converſion.

Action of Treſpaſſe and Battery.

THis action lyes where a man aſſaults another, and ſtrikes, kick, or beat, or do him any manner of violence, either with hand, foot, or with any weapon, or throw any thing at him, or upon him, whereby he is hurt.

The Writs in Battery are by way of originall *Capias, alias*, &c. If not arreſted upon the firſt Proceſſe, you may take out a *Capias* by continuance, or otherwiſe ſue to the Outlawry.

Your originall writ runs thus: wherefore by force and armes on him the ſaid Plaintif at *L.* he made an aſſault, and him beat, wounded, evill entreated, ſo that of his life he did deſpair, and other harms to him he did, to the great Damage of the Plaintiff, and againſt the Peace, &c.

In ſome caſes you add (after wounded and Impriſoned) in caſe the Party were kept in Priſon and then in the Court, you name for what time.

In caſe you have the Party arreſted, you muſt inform

form your selfe of the time when the Battery was done, and what the manner of the Battery was, and with what Weapons, and whether the Party were Imprisoned, and what Damage your Clyent sustained.

This done, and having an appearance (which is usually made on the Philizers Roll, if the Attorneys take not one anothers word in the Countrey, or put their hands to the Sheriffs Warrant for to appear according to the returne of the Writ) you draw your Declaration, which is no more but a recital of the writ above, only in the second place, when you count upon the Writ, you are to insert the time, and when you say, by force and armes, you then add (that is to say, with Swords, Staves, and Knives) and if the Party were Imprisoned, you then shew, how long, and whether he were forced to pay a fine for his redemption: your Declaration drawn must be delivered to the Defendants Attorney, as before in case, &c. And you must enter it with an Imparlance, if you give one.

And you are to give Rules, the Imparlance out, and call for answer; and make up your Issue, or for want of pleading, enter up Iudgement by default, and take your writ of Inquiry; in all things observing the Rules before given, either for tryal or proceeding with your Writ of Inquiry.

The generall Plea to this action is, not guilty, but there are severall other Pleas, in justification of a mans selfe, as where it is done in defence of a mans person or Goods; also a man may justifie, in the defence of the person of his wife, Father, Mother, or Master : But note, that if it be not in these Cases, or in the Maintenance of Justice, if he be not constrained by a necessary cause, he is punishable if he beat another.

If

If a man come into anothers House againſt his will, and there offer violence either to his Wife, Children, Servants, or to any of his goods, he may lawfully thruſt him away, to hinder him, and if hee bring an action in ſuch like caſe, he may plead ſpecially as the Caſe was, and conclude that to hinder him, or put him out of doors, he did (*Molliter manus imponere*, &c.) that is, ſoftly lay his hands upon him.

To all ſuch ſpeciall Pleas it is uſuall they ſhould be pleaded under Councels hand.

Where a man for preſervation of the peace, goeth about to part a Fray, by holding either of the parties from ſtriking, in Caſe the Party that was ſo holden, doe bring an action of Battery, the Defendant may plead ſpecially, that to preſerve the perſon of one from killing, and preſervation of the Publike Peace, he did come in to ayd him, and did ſoftly lay his hands upon him.

To this the Plaintiff may reply, that he did it of his own proper injury, without any ſuch cauſe, and then the Defendant muſt maintain his Plea, with an (*ut prius dicit*,) And of this he puts himſelfe upon the Country, &c.

There is a Plea called (*Son aſſalt demeſne*) which is, where a man juſtifies in his owne defence, as being firſt ſtruck, which falls out to be very frequently pleaded. Thus much for Battery.

Of Traſpaſſe in generall.

Theſe are the moſt generall Actions next Actions of Debt, that are brought, and vary in the orilinall Proceſſe and Declaration, according as the

Treſpaſs

Trespass is ; and the cause of Action thereby accrued.

It may be brought for breaking the Close, without adding any manner of other Trespass.

Sometime for breaking both Close and House, in which case the Originall is ; Wherefore by Force and Armes, the Close of the Plaintiff at L. he brake and other harmes to him he did, to the great damage of the Plaintiff, and against the pulique Peace, &c.

You may lay it for severall Trespsses at severall dayes, or one Trespass with (a *Continuando*) that is, continuing of it for some certain daies or weeks, from the time laid in the Declaration.

It lies for chasing of Cattell, whereby they either dyed, or were bitten or worryed with Doggs.

It lies for taking away of Pales, Posts, Rails, breaking of Hedges or Fences.

It lies for digging in a Leaden Mine, and taking away the Oare, or for breaking the Ground, and digging there.

Where a man breaks another mans Dove-cote, and takes away Pigeons, an action lies.

For drawing a Cart and Horses over any mans Ground; where there can be no way prescribed for, an Action of Trespass lyes.

It lies for fishing in an other mans Ponds, and for breaking the Pond, and letting out the water.

For chasing in a free Warren, an Action lyes.

For breaking of a Close, mowing of Grass, and eating of Corne with a mans Cattell, this Action lyes.

For Trespass done in a Garden, by plucking up
by

by the Roots, *Rosemary, Lavender*, and other Herbes.

It lies in the behalfe of a Minister against any that hinder or oppose him, in carrying away of his tithes.

It lies for impounding a Horse or other cattell, and not giving them sustenance in the pound.

It lies for taking away Hay in cocks, and Corne in sheafes.

It lies for taking away of Horses or any other like Cattell, wherein you say (of the price of such, &c.) or if goods and Chattels, then you say, to the value of so much.

It lies for breaking of the Doores, Windowes, Walls or other forces of a house.

An action of trespass lies, where one having right to a Toll in a Market, and imployes his servant to gather it, and he is disturbed in it.

It lies likewise where a man hath right to keepe a Fayr, and is hindred.

It lies on the behalfe of one that hath returne of Writs within his Hundred, and hath a Disturbance by any.

And where a man hath right to keepe a Court Baron, and is any wayes disturbed, this Action lies.

For digging in a mans Cole mines, and carrying away Coles, and for digging in a mans quarries, he shall have his Action.

WEE have now given you some particular hints in what case an action of trespass lies, I shall now proceed to the processes thereupon, which as I told you, are by Originall, in the first place *Capias*, in case you can arrest them, or otherwise to the Outlawry

If you arrest the party, and have an appearance, you must draw your Declaration, wherein you must be sure to take perfect notice from your Client of the day when the Trespasse was done, that so you may lay it to be done before the *Teste* of your Originall, and likewise how long the trespas continued, that so if there be Occasion, you may lay it with a *Continuando*, and whether there were not severall Trespasses at severall dayes, and the place where the Trespasse was done, in that Town or Parish, for from thence your *Venue* must arise.

To this action the most generall Plea is, not guilty, yet is there much speciall pleading by way of Justification or otherwise, but most usually that is after the common Barre hath beene pleaded in an Action of Trespasse, and that there be a new assignment of the place, then they plead as to the Trespasse in the place of new assignment, either in justification for a Foot-way, or a Cart-way or some other speciall Plea, &c. Or not guilty to the new assignment: this new assignement is used very oft, to cleere a Title, which upon it comes in question; here in case the Title appeare to be the Plaintiffs, hee shall recover Damages.

This action brings to the party Plaintiff if he recover, Damages, but not recovery of any possession, as in the case of an *Ejectione Firma*.

All manner of Proceedings after the Declaration any waies had, relating to this action, whether by tryall of *Nisi prius*, or Writ of inquiry, upon default or confession, are altogether the same with what hath been delivered, as to actions of the case.

Actions of Covenant.

THis Action lies where an Agreement or Compact is by Deed, Articles, or other Writing,
sealed betweene two persons, where every of them is
bound to the other, to performe certaine Covenants
for his part, and if the one of them holdeth not his
Covenant but breaketh it, then hee which findeth
himselfe agrieved, may have thereupon a Writ of
Covenant : And Covenants are either in Law or
Fact, *or*

A Covenant in Law is that which the Law intendeth to be done, although it be not expressed in words,
as if a man demise any thing to another for a certaine Terme, the Law intendeth a Covenant of the
part of the Lessor, that the Lessee shall hold all his
Term against all lawfull Incumbrances.

Covenant in fact, is that which is expresly agreed
between the parties.

Also there is a Covenant meerly personall, and
a Covenant that is reall, as sayes *Fitzherbert* in his
Natura brevium, Fol. I. 5.

Covenant reall, is where a man tyeth himselfe to
passe a thing reall, as Lands or Tenements, where a
man covenants to levy a fine of Lands; *&c.*

Covenant meerly personall is where a man covenants with another by Deed, to build a house or to
serve him.

Note well, that no Writ of Covenant shall bee
maintainable without a specialty, but in the City of
London or in some other place priviledged by custome
or use.

Note, that a man may bring an action of Covenant
upon a Letter of Attorney.

H   Where

Where a Covenant perfonall is made to any and the Covenantee dyes, the Covenant being unperformed, here his Executor fhall maintain an action of Covenant.

The Heire fhall likewife maintaine an action of Covenantry, where one had covenanted by writing with his Father, to Enfeoff him in certaine Lands, and doth it not.

The Proceffes incident to this Action is an Originall which is a fummons, for in this Action as in Debt, you fay (was fummoned, and not attached.)

Your Originall runs thus (Of a Plea that he hold the Plaintiffs Covenant between them made, according to the force, form, and effect, of certain Indentures between them made, &c.)

After your Originall taken out, you may have a Capias, and if you arreft him not upon the Capias, you may proceed to the Outlawry, as in other cafes.

Upon appearance had, you muft declare as in the example following, wherein you muft obferve, that in this Action as in Debt, you have an (*Alias dictus*) which muft be made literally to agree with the Indenture.

Effex. ff.

I Glover; late of &c. otherwife called *John Glover*, Gentleman, was Summoned to anfwer *E. M.* of a Plea, that he hold to him Covenant between them made, according to the force, forme, and effect, of certain Indentures between them made, &c. And whereupon the faid *E.* by *T. G.* his Attorney faith, that whereas by a certaine Indenture made (fuch a day, yeare, and place,) between him the faid Plaintiff, on the one part, and the faid *I.* of the other part, which other part figned with the Seale of the

faine

fame I. the aforefaid *E.* brings here into Court, the Date whereof is the fame day and year: it is teftified (reciting the whole Indenture, till you come to in Witnefle whereof) as by the fame indenture more fully appeareth: And the faid Plaintiff faith, that although hee hath fulfilled and performed, all and fingular the Covenants and Grants in the indenture aforefaid above fpecified on his part to bee fulfilled and kept in Fact, the fame *E.* faith, that within the aforefaid feven years after the making of the indenture aforefaid, *&c.* (that is to fay) fuch a day and year, one *T. D. Efq.* then being of the learned Councell of him the faid *E.* at *B.* aforefaid, in the County aforefaid, did devife and caufe to be written for further affurance of the aforefaid Clofe with the Appurtenances, to be made to the faid *E.* a certain Writing of releafe of the aforefaid Clofe of the Appurtenances, to be made to the faid *E.* by the faid *J.* in which faid Writing it was contained, that the aforefaid *J.* fhould remife, releafe, and alwayes for himfelfe and his Heires, quit claime to the faid *E.* and his Heires, the whole Right, Title, and Claime which he had, or at any time from thence following might have, of an in the aforefaid Clofe with the Appurtenances: And the fame *E.* afterwards the fame day and yeare at *C.* aforefaid, did requeft the aforefaid *J.* to feale, and as his Deed to deliver to the faid *E.* the aforefaid Writings of releafe in forme aforefaid devifed; and the aforefaid I. that to doe, then and there altogether refufed, againft the forme of the indenture aforefaid; yet the faid *J.* although often required, hath not held the Covenant aforefaid; for that hee the faid *J.* and his Heires, and all perfons and their Heires, claiming in or by the aforefaid *J.* at any time, during the fpace of the aforefaid feven yeares, upon reafonable demand thereof, to them or any of them to be made, shall make, permit, & acknowledge, or cause to be made, permitted, & acknowldeged, all & singular act & acts, thing or things for the better and further assurance and sure making of the Premises with the appurtenances to the said *E.* and his assignes, as by learned Councell of him the said *B.* his Heires or assignes, should be reasonably devised, but hath broken it, and to hold that covenant to him the said *E.* hitherto hath denied , and yet doth deny, whereupon he saith that he is damnified , and hath damage to the value of two hundred pounds, and thereupon he brings his Suit, *&c.*

Here you have an action of Covenant brought for making further assurance; wherein you see the laying of the breach, and what the further assurance is , and indeed the whole difficulty of an action of Covenant, lies in the laying well the breach.

To this the Defendant pleads as followes.

And the aforesaid *I.* by *F. N.* his Attorney comes and defends the force and injury when *&c.* and saith, that the aforesaid *E.* did not require him the said *I* to seale, and as his Deed to deliver to the aforesaid *E.* the aforesaid writing of release , for further assurance of the aforesaid close with the appurtenances, to the aforesaid *E.* to be made , as the aforesaid *E.* by his Declaration aforesaid above hath supposed, and of this he puts himselfe upon the country, and the aforesaid *E* in like manner, therefore command is given to the Sheriff , that he cause to come here on the morrow after the holy Trinity, twelve, *&c.* by whom *&c.* and who neither, *&c.* to recognize, *&c.* Because as well *&c.*

Observe by this issue you see joyned, that where the Defendant takes issue, you say, (and of this hee puts himselfe upon the country) and where the Plaintiff

tiff takes the issue, you say (and this he prayes may be inquired of by the Country)

In this action you recover Damages assessed by the Jury for what you are damnified, by the breach of Covenant and costs of suit.

Note, that an Administrator may have an Action of Covenant, as well as an Executor, and the Writ of Covenant ought to be brought in the County where the Deed is made; but if it be brought in another County, then where the Deed was made, the party Defendant shall not have a Plea in bar to the Writ, unlesse that the Deed bare date in another County.

A Writ of Covenant also lyes against pledges, who become sureties that another man shall perform a covenant.

The assignee of the Lessee shall maintain an action of covenant against the Lessor, although he be not specified in the said Deed of Covenant to be an assignee.

Having given you before, an issue joyned in an action of covenant, you are (in case you proceed to tryall) to make out your *Venire facias* as in others, with this difference, onely that you say, (of a Plea of covenant broken) and then your *Habeas Corpus*, and the rest of your proceedings in order to tryall, as before in other actions.

But if after your Imparlance and rule being out, the Defendant plead not, you must take your Judgment by default, which is to be signed by the *Prothonotary*, and then you are to have your Writs of Inquiry, which be awarded upon your Iudgment Roll, and signed by the *Prothonotary*.

There may be one or more breaches assigned, as the case may require.

But

But in an action of debt upon Bond for performance of Covenants, he can assigne but one.

NOw because within the Title of that Covenant reall, fall Writs of Covenant, it will not be a-misse to insert here the form of suing out a fine.

And first how to acknowledge a fine at the Barre in the Court.

IN the first place you are to take notice, that it is in the parties Election, whether they will acknowledge a Fine in open Court or before the Lord cheif Justice of the common Pleas, at his Chamber, or elsewhere out of the Court, as before some Judge of the same Court, or before the Iustices of Assize in the Country, when they go *Circuit*, or before Commissioners in the Country by vertue of a speciall *Dedimus potestatem*, to give them authority to take the knowledge thereof, none of all those saving the Lord cheife Iustice, having power to take without *Dedimus &c.*

If the acknowledgment be to be made in open court, you must have your Writ of Covenant made by the Cursiter, and there compound it at the Office of Alienation, where it must be likewise indorsed and entred, and so fitted for the Seal, to which must be annexed your *Precipe*, and concord in Parchment which you must deliver to some one of the Serjeants at Bar to draw it for you, and then you pay him three shillings four pence, the other Fees payable in Court are certain and are not great; for by the acknowledgment in Court, the Client saves divers Fees and charges, which otherwise the Caption would cost.

Th

The Caption being paſt, you proceed with your *Precipe,* and Concord, and Writ of Covenant, through the Alienation Office, Kings Silver, *Cuſtos Brevium,* and Chirographer, as hereafter is ſhewed in other acknowledgments.

How to acknowledge a Fine before the Lord chiefe Juſtice.

IF you would acknowledge your Fine before the Lord cheife Juſtice of the common Pleas, out of Court, firſt draw your *Precipe* and concord in a ſheet of paper, and then bring the parties that muſt acnowledge the fine to my Lords chamber, and deli-er your *Precipe* to my Lords Clark of the Fines, who ill read it to them in preſence of my Lord, and heir hands being firſt ſet to it, he acknowledgeth it efore my Lord and he putteth his hand to it.

The Fee of my Lord cheife Juſtice is   9*s*——8*d,* hich being paid by you or your Client to my Lords lark, after the acknowledgment, the Clarke will terwards ingroſſe the *Precipe* and concord in Parchent, and get my Lords hand to that which you uſt fetch from him, and give him his fee for the in-oſſing thereof, which is, that done, you muſt carry to the Curſitor of the ſhire where the Land lies and ave it with him to make a VVrit of Covenant by, en the VVrit is made, before you paſſe it under l, you carry it to the alienation office, where you are pay a fine for licence or leave to alien, and there is you muſt make your Compoſition, which is ſet by e Commiſſioners ſitting for that purpoſe, and that u may doe it with the leſſe charge to your Client, u muſt informe your ſelfe of the value of the

H 4   land

land by year, and in cafe there have been a former fine, if you have it not to know the terme when it was and in cafe you informe the value, there is one fits purpofely with the Commiffioners to take it, who was formerly a Doctor, you muft by Entreaty, per-fwafion, or otherwife draw the fine to be fet at as low a rate as poffibly you may.

The value being fet down by one of the Commiffioners, if it exceed forty fhillings, (for elfe there is nothing to be paid) you muft goe to the Receiver in the fame office, and pay the fine fo affeffed which is the Kings filver, for the Kings licenfe, which li-cenfe the Clark of the Kings filver entereth, as is hereafter fhewed, when the mony is paid, the Recei-ver will fet his hand to the back of the VVrit, then give it to the Doctor to fign, who hath four pence, as I take it, for his hand, then get the hands of the two Commiffioners to the back of the VVrit, which done, you muft carry it to the three Clarks fitting to be indorfed and entred.

This being done you bring back your VVrit to the Curfitor and he will get it fealed, and then you pay him the Fee of two fhillings and fix pence, then having broke it open you are to return it as follows.

Towards the upper end of the VVrit thus,	}	*John Doo* Pledges of profe- cuting *Richard Roe.*
Towards the middle of the VVrit thus,	}	*John Dem.* *Richard Fen.*

And at the lower end of the VVrit the Sheriffs Name.

This

This is now by a late erected Office done by an Officer who takes for the doing of it, and making an entry of it, 1s. 6d.

Note, you are to file a Warrant of Attorney with the Clark of the Warrants where your Writ of Covenant must be signed, which warrant is as follows (the Shire in the Margin) *G. W. puts in his place T. L. to prosecute a Writ of Covenant against T. H. of Lands and Tenements in A. and C.*

That done file your Writ of Covenant and your Concord which you had from the Lords Clark together, and carry them to the *Custos brevium* his Office in *Lincolns Inne*, to the Clarke who dealeth for that Shire, and leave them with him to enter in his Book and to indorse the Writ, when he hath done, fetch them from him, and pay him for the same, 3s.8d.

Then take them and carry them to the Kings-silver Office to enter the Kings-silver, which is the Fine for the value which you paid to the Receiver in the Alienation Office.

The forme of his entry you may see in the Rolls the Kings-silver Office, amongst the Plea-Rolls of any Term in the Treasury at *Westminster*, his Fee is for entring of it, 6d. which when he hath done, you must fetch it away and deliver it to the Secundary in the Chirographers Office, who takes it forth in his Book, and hath for his Fee 5s. 8d. if it be in the Term, but if it be not in the Terme, then you must give him twelve pence more, which he will have for allowing the Proclamation in the same Terme : That done, you must in the same Office deliver it to the Clark of the Office, who is appointed to write for that Shire wherein the Land lyes to ingrosse, he hath for the ingrossing of it, 2 s. 6 d. if small, but if great 3 s. 6 d. or more in case it be exemplified.

When

When your Fines are Ingroffed, which are by way of Indentures, get one part from him, and deliver it your Client to keep.

In making up your Clients Bill, you alwayes take for your owne Fee, as allowed for your paines, fix fhillings eight pence.

How to acknowledg a Fine before a Judg out of Court, by Dedimus potestatem.

YOU fhall proceed in taking the acknowledgement; and in pafing the Writ of Covenant thorow the Alienation Office, in like manner as is before fhewed, which being done, and delivering your Writ back to the Curfitor, you mufl befpeake a *Dedimus poteflatem,* which the Curfitor mufl make, and when you have your Writ of Covenant and *Dedimus potestatem* under feale, you mufl deliver the *Dedimus* to the Iudges Clark of the Fines, and he will Ingrofs the *precipe* and *Concord* as before is fhewed, and return the *Dedimus,* and get the Iudges hand to it; which *Dedimus* fo returned, *Concord* and Writ of Covenant you mufl annex together, and paffe them through the *Custos Brevium,* Clark of the Warranty, Clark of the Kings filver, Mr. *Jones* his office of Inrolments, as its termed, and the Chirographers Office in like manner, as is before fhewed: The courfe of Proceeding and Fees being all one more then this, that you pay to the Curfitor for your *Dedimus poteflatem,* 9s 2 d.

How

How to sue forth a Fine to be acknowledged before Commissioners in the Countrey, by especiall Dedimus Potestatem.

WHere in regard of the Cognizors debility of Body, or remoteness from *London* or *Westminster*, or other occasion, you are to sue out a Fine, and passe it by speciall *Dedimus*, inabling Commissioners in the Country to take the acknowledgment; you are to proceed as followes.

Irst draw your *Precipe* in a Sheet of Paper, as a Note for the Cursitor to draw the *Dedimus* by, then ingrosse your *Precipe* and *Concord* in a faire peice of Parchment, and goe therewith to the Cursitor of the Shire, where your Land lies, and upon your *Precipe* in paper insert your Commissioners names, which must be four in number, whereof one at least must be a Knight, and get him to make your *Dedimus potestatem*, for which you must pay him   and in paying of him (for he takes for them all) you pay a Fine, and for a Iudges hand, and for the Master of the Rolls his hand, which hands must be had before it be sealed, and then having it under Seale, deliver it so, and the Concord before any two of the Commissioners named in the *Dedimus*, and your Cognizors being present, let them take the *Caption* as is before shewed: Which being done, they must return the Writ of *Of Dedimus*, and their Execution thereof in manner and form following on the back of the Writ.

The Execution of this Writ appears in a certain
Schedule

Schedule to the Writ annexed.

And they must write the day of the *Caption* of the Cognizance, underneath the Concord as followes: (taken and acknowledged at C. in the County of D, the twelfth day of *August* 1650.)

Underneath the which the Commissioners are to Subscribe their names.

Having your *Dedimus potestatem* thus returned, you must file your *Dedimus* and *Concord* together, and carry them to the Cursitor for the making of your Writ of Covenant, which having had and compounded, your proceed is as in all other Fines through the severall Offices.

NOte, that upon every Fine past, where a Fine is paid, there is within foure or five Termes a post-Fine, that comes in charge to the Sheriff to levy in the County where the Land lyeth; and that Fine is as much and halfe as much, as was payd before in the Alienation Office.

How to sue forth a license of Alienation of Lands holden in Capite.

IF you levy a Fine of Lands holden in *Capite* of the Kings, you must be driven to sue forth your license of Alienation, for if you should enter into the Land without a license, the King would have a Writ of intrusion against you and receive all the main profits, untill you have sued out a pardon, which is both troublesome and chargeable: The fine whereof besides the main Profits between the Intrusion and the Pardon, and the other charges, is above a years value cleerly, according to such composition

or

or *Affidavit* of the under value, as is said, before the other Compositions of the Alienation Office, unlesse the Commissioners inquire, and will more favourably compound for the meane Profits, as in some cases upon reasonable cause shewed, they use to doe.

And your licence of Alienation is to be sued in this manner, first, you must get the Clark of the Alienations, to make you a *Docquet* in paper, which you must carry to the Alienation Office, and there compound for the value of the Land, which must be also by composition or *affidavit*, as is shewed before.

The value being set down underneath your *Docquet*, you must pay a third part of the value so assessed by way of Fine for your licence, which you must likewise pay there in the same Office, and you must give the Receiver over and above what you pay, six pence.

Then you must there get the Doctors hand to your *Docquet*, for which you must give him, 2 s. and you must then get the Commissioners in the same Office, to set their hands to the *Docquet*, then deliver it to the Register, there to enter, for which you must give him 6 d. And after it is entred, then carry it to the Clark of the Alienation again, and hee will get the Lord Chancellor or Lord Keepers hand to it, and will afterwards ingrosse your licence of Alienation, and passe it under the great Seale for you. The Charges are as followeth;

The Charge of acknowledging a Fine before the Lord chief Justice, and a Licence of Alienation upon the same.

	l	s	d
For drawing the Concord,	0	3	4
For my Lord chiefe Justices fee for acknowledgement.	0	9	8
To his Clark for ingrossing the Concord,	0	1	6

For

For the Writ of Covenant.	0-2-6
For the return	0-2-0
For the *post diem* thereof.	0 0-4
For the Fine,	0-0-0
To the Receiver for marking the Writ of Covenant	0-0-6
For the entry and endorsment	0-1-6
For the Doctors hand	0-0-4
For the Warrant of Attorney and filing it	0-0-8
To the *Custos brevium.*	0-3-8
To the Clark of the Kings Silver	0-1-4
To the Chirographer	0-6-8
For ingrossing the Fine	0-3-0
For the Attorneys Fee,	0-6-8

Charges of the fine acknow-
ledged at Bar.

FOR drawing the *precipe* and Concord	3-4
For the Writ of covenant	2-6
For return of the same	2-0
For the filing thereof	10
To the Sarjeant at Bar	3-4
To the Prothonotary	6
To the Secondary	6
To the Crier, Tipstaves, and court-keeper	1-6
For the Fine	
To the Receiver	6
For entry and endorsment	1-6
For the Doctors hand	4
For the Warrant of Attorney and filing of it	8
To the *Custos brevium.*	3-8
To the Clark of the Kings silver	1-4

To

To the Chircgrapher   6-8.
For ingroffing the indentures of the fine   3-0.
For the Fee.   6-8.

Charges of a Fine acknowledged by Dedimus poteftatem, before a Judge, and exemplified.

FOR drawing the *precipe* and concord   3-4.
  To the Judge for his fee   9-8.
To the Clark for the return of the *Dedimus*, and ingroffing the Concord,   2-6.
For the Writ of *Dedimus poteftatem*,   9-2.
For all other Fees, as in the next proceeding, for the feverall Offices.
For the Exemplification,   2-8.
For the Exemplifying,   5-6.
For the Seale thereof.   2-2.

Charges of a Fine by fpeciall Dedimus poteftatem taken before Commiffioners.

FOR drawing the *Precipe* and Concord.   0-3-4
For the fpeciall *Dedimus poteftatem*,   1-0-0
For the Returne,   0-3-0
For the reft of the Fees, they differ very little from what are paid upon Fines otherwise acknowledged

HAving fpoken fo largely of Fines, it now refts we fhould fpeak fomewhat of Recoveries, that
relate

relate thereunto, for in many cases where a Fine is had, if there be Remainders over, it is very necessary for the Purchasers security to have a recovery, to bar those in remainder.

We shall therefore begin to shew you how to sue forth a Recovery, the Tenant and Voucher comming in person into court.

When you would sue forth a Recovery to be suffered by the parties in open Court, you must doe thus:

Draw your *Precipe* for your Writ of entry, naming the Demandants and the Tenants, the quantity of Lands, and of what nature, how many Acres, what Mannors, Messuages, and in what place or places they lye or extend.

Then take your *Precipe* and enter it upon the Bill of Pleas or Remembrance of the *Prothonotary*, in whose Office you enter and put the Voucher or Vouchers names in the Margin of the Remembrance, if it be a single Voucher, then thus: the proper tenant calls *Howse* to warranty.

If a double Voucher, the proper Tenant calls *J. L.* Esq; who calls *J. Howse* (who is the common Voucher and the last Voucher in all Recoveries) if a treble Voucher, then you must name another person to be Vouched over.

Upon this remembrance you must enter after your *Precipe*, the Returne and *Teste* of your Writ of entry, and how it is returned, and the Sheriffs name, but this you make perfect before you examine your Recovery with the Prothonotary.

Those remembrances are alwayes brought to the Hall in the Term time at the first sitting of the court, so that when you would draw your Recovery at Bar, your fittest time will be in a morning when the Judges first sit down, before they enter upon businesse.

Having

Having your client in readinesse at the Bar, the Tenants and Vouchers, and the Remembrance in your hand, call them up between the Serjeants, and then deliver the Remembrance, and shew him your *Precipe* into one of the Serjeants hands, who will aske which is the Tenant, and cause him to stand up, as also the Vouchers, to the intent that they may be shewed to the court, then the Iudges will aske, who knowes the parties, which you or some other must answer, you know them to be such parties, or else might others come either in men or womens names and suffer a Recovery of their Lands, to the Losse of their Lands, as hath been heretofore seen; where the husband brought in another woman a stranger, saying, she was his wife, and suffered a Recovery of his wives lands to cut off her estate without her consent.

After the Tenant or Tenants with the Vouchers, have their appearance recorded, then must you give for every Serjeant that speakes, (and one there is for each person personated, whether Demandant, Tenant, or Voucher or Vouchers) two shilling and six pence, which done, and the rest of the fees paid in Court, which follow after amongst others.

Then get the Cursitor to make your VVrit of Entry by the *Precipe*, and having your writ of Entry unsealed, you must proceed therewith in the Alienation Office and other Offices, in all things as was shewed in a VVrit of covenant, for the Fees and the Fine are all one, only you must have the Attorney Generalls hand to the Back of your VVrit of Entry, which you have not to the VVrit of covenant, for you which pay ten shillings, formerly but eight shillings, and is for that you should enter into that, the land is not holden in *Capite*, but when they did enter bond, they did pay but six pence; and also where

I   she

the Land is holden, and you sue forth license of Alienation, you should pay nothing.

Then take your Writ and get it sealed, and then open it and returne it, as you do your Writ of Covenant.

Then deliver your Writ to one of the Clarks of the Prothonotaries Office, who entreth for you, and he will enter and exemplifie your Recovery for you rnd make your writ of Seizin, and returne that, and examine the Recovery with the Remembrance, writs of Entry and Seizin, and the Roll your Recovery is entred on with the Prothonotary, who must sign your Exemplification, which being carefully examined and signed, you must get sealed, and then deliver it to your Clyent: And you must be very carefull to see both your writ of Entry and seizin filed with the *Custos brevium*, for that is the warranty for your Proceedings had.

Note, your writ of Seizin may be made returnable *Indilate*, or at a day certaine, or of the Term following, all which your owne further experience and practice will shew.

How to sue forth a Recovery by Dedimus Potestatem, *and Warrant of Attorney.*

IF either the Tenant or Vouchers cannot come into the Court in person, you must passe it by warrant of Attorney, which warrant of Attorney may be taken by any of the Judges of either Bench, Barons of the Exchequer, or Serjeants at law in their circuits without *Dedimus potestatem*, or by Commissioners in the Country,

Country, where you muft proceed as in the Fine by *Dedimus poteftatem.*

When you acknowledge your warrant before a Judge you muft draw up your warrant as before in Parchment; and go with the Partyes before a Judge and acknowledge them, and he will under-write the Day of the Caption, and fubfcribe his name, then get your Writ of Entry made and paffed through the Alienation Office, which done, feal it, and deliver it to your Prothonotaries Clark, and he will enter it, and will award the Writ of Summons; which will come in nine Returns after the *Tefle* of the Writ of Entry inclufive, and he will make a Copy of the Declaration he entereth in Parchment, which together with the Writ of Summons, and the warrant of Attorney, he will examine with the Prothonotary by the Writ of Entry and the Roll.

Then will he returne a Writ of Entry, and give it you fixt together with the Writ of Summons, warrant of Attorney, and Copy of the Declaration.

The Writ of Entry you muft file, the Writ of Summons you muft Seale and keep them fo fixt together fafely till the Writ of Summons be returnable; at which time you muft bring the fame into Court, and deliver it to one of the Serjeants, who will call it at the Barr, as the manner is, and you muft pay the Fees in Court, which done you muft take it from the Serjeant and give it to the Prothonotary, who will marke it thus (*A Barram*) and give it you againe, which you muft deliver to your Clark in the Prothonotaries Office, who will Exemplifie and make your Recovery perfect and fitted for the Seale.

NOte, that although the Tenant be by warrant of Attorney, if either the Recovery be a fingle

Voucher,

Voucher, or the Vouchers come in perſon, it needeth no Summons, and ſo may be a perfect Recovery of one term.

Note alſo, where you will take your Warrant by *Dedimus poteſtatem* before ſpeciall Commiſſioners, you muſt carry a Note of your *precipe*, and of your Commiſſioners names to the Curſitor, and get him to make your *Dedimus*, and proceed in that as is ſhewed you in caſe of a Fine, as to the Caption: And when your Warrants are acknowledged, get them certified, and then by the helpe of your Prothonotaries Clark, you may ſoon proceed to perfect your Recovery, either to Summons or *Alias* Summons, or ſo as your cauſe ſhall require.

It behoveth the Attorney to be very carefull of the true returning and filing of his Writs, and the examining and filing of his VVarrants, and other proceedings, for fear of committing errour: And to that purpoſe by the Statute of 23. *Eliz.* it hath been uſed, eſpecially in weighty matters, to exemplifie the VVrits, Returns, and VVarrants of Attorney, for fear of being imbezeled, whereby the Recoveries might be overthrown.

If you are to ſearch for any Recovery of an old terme, you muſt ſearch in the Office of the Clark of the VVarrants of Attorney, where you ſhall ſooneſt find it of any place, by reaſon all the Prothonotaries bring in their Plea-Rolls, on which the recoveries are entred, to the Clark of the Warrants to take them out into a Book.

It hath been the conſtant practice formerly, in caſe the Land were holden in *Capite*, to ſue forth a licenſe of Alienation, as you doe in the caſe of a Fine, and that before your VVrit of entry, for elſe you may be inforced to ſue forth a pardon afterward, which was a very great miſchiefe.

Charge

Charges of a Recovery with two Vouchers in Person at the Barr.

	s - d
FOR drawing *Precipe*,	2 - 6
For taking it into the Remembrance,	1 - 0
For your VVrit of Entrie,	2 - 6
For the Fine of it.	
To the Receiver,	0 - 6
For the Doctors hand, entring, and endorsing,	1 - 6
For drawing it at Bar, and four Serjeants,	13 - 4
To the Criers,	1 - 0
To the Box,	1 - 0
To the VVarden of the Fleet,	0 - 6
For the common Vouchee,	0 - 4
For the Attorney Generals hand to the VVrit,	10 - 6
For making the Remembrance, when the Recovery is drawn at the Barr,	2 - 0
For the returne of the VVrit of Entry,	2 - 0
For the *Post diem* of the VVrit of Entry,	0 - 4
For return of the VVrit of Seisin,	2 - 0
To the Prothonotary for the Entry of the Recovery,	14 - 6
To the Clark for exemplifying of it, and making the VVrit of Seisin,	7 - 6
For sealing the Exemplification, and VVrit of Seisin,	2 - 9
For filing the writs of Entry and Seisin,	2 - 0
For the Fee of Demandant, Tenant, and Vouchee in the Recovery,	10 - 0

I 3   *Charges*

Charges of a Recovery by Summons upon a Warrant of Attorney

s. d

FOr drawing your Recovery, *Precipe,* and the Warrant of Attorney. } 3-4

For entry of the Summons,   6-6

For making the Writ of Summons, and the Seale,
2-7

To the Clark from drawing the Summons, and the entry in Parckment,   2-6

For filing every Warrant of Attorney,   0-8

For return of the Writ of Summons,   2-0

For the filing of it.   1-0

Note, that every single Voucher hath three Serjeants, a double Voucher foure Serjeants, and a trebble Voucher hath five Serjeants, and so further.

The Prothonotarie hath, as you see before, for his entry for every Summons,   6-6

For every single Voucher,   10-6

For every double Voucher,   14-6

For a trebble Voucher,   18-6

For every *Dedimus* and *Mittimus,*   4-0

The Charges of a Recovery under the Great Seale of England.

l. s.

FOR the *Certiorare,*   0-13

For the allowance thereof.   1-0

I

To the Clarke for his paines,	0-06-8
For the Exemplification for every Skyn,	1-06-8
For the Scale,	1-00-6

Come we now to the Action called Ejectione Firmæ.

THis Action is the moſt generall Action now in uſe, for triall of a Title, and comes in place of many reall Actions, which were both very tedious, difficult and chargeable. This lies, where a man makes a Leaſe to another of Lands, Houſes, *&c.* And ſeales and delivers it upon the Premiſſes, and leaves the Leſſee in poſſeſſion, and afterwards the Leſſee is outed by the Entry of a Stranger; here in this caſe the Leſſee ſhall bring his *Ejectione Firmæ.*

And in bringing this Action, hee muſt have recourſe to his Leaſe, both for the thing demiſed, and the Term, and the Date of the Demiſe, and the place preciſely where the Land lyes, but thoſe onely are to be mentioned in the Court, but not in the Writ.

You muſt be ſure your Originall beare Teſte, after the entry of the Ejector. And after.

In this Action is recovered the Poſſeſſion of the Land or Houſe demiſed, and that by an Execution of *habere facias Poſſeſſionem*, which is awarded upon the Judgement Roll, and alſo Damages.

The Proceſſe in it are Originall, *capias, alias &c.*

The Originall runs thus.

THE Keepers of the Liberty, *&c.* Greeting, *&c.* Wherefore by Force and Armes two Meſſuages,

one

one Garden, eight Acres of Land, two Acres of Meadow, and three Acres of Pasture, with the Appurtenances in *H.* which *R. C.* to the aforesaid *T. P.* did demise for a Terme which is not yet past, did enter and him the said *T. P.* from his Farm aforesaid he did eject, and other harmes to him he did, to the great Damage of him the said *T. P.* and against the publick peace, *&c.*

This is the form of your Originall, and must be made thus by the Cursitor of the Shire, where the Land lyeth.

Note, that although in your Lease you many times name severall Closes, either of Land, Meadow or Pasture, by their particular names, yet in your Writ you must name the quantity of Acres of each, and how many Houses, Cottages, Mills, *&c.*

After your Originall is sued out, and a *Nihil* returned thereupon, you proceed to take out a *Capias,* and so arrest the Ejector, but if you cannot arrest upon the *Capias,* you may, as in other Actions, proceed to the Outlawry.

But the party against whom you bring your Action, either appearing after Arrest, or voluntarily, you must prepare your Declaration.

The Declaration goeth thus.

Bedford. ſſ.

R. G. lately of *H.* in the County aforesaid Yeoman, was attached to answer *T. P.* of Plea, wherefore by force and Armes, two Messuages, one Garden, eight Acres of Land, Two Acres of Meadow, and three Acres of Pasture, with the Appurtenances in *H.* which *R. G.* to the aforesaid *T. P.* did demise for a Terme which is not yet past, did enter, and him the said *T. P.* from his Farm aforesaid he did eject, and other harmes to him he did, to the great Damage of him the said *T. P.* and against the publick peace,

&c.

&c. And whereupon the said T.P. by *F. N.* his Attorney complaines, that whereas the aforesaid R. G. (such a day, and yeare, and place, naming the date of the Demise) did demise to him the said T. P. the Tenements aforesaid with the Appurtenances, to have and to occupy to him and his Assignes, from (such a day then last past) unto the end and Terme of three yeares then next following, and fully to be compleat and ended : by vertue of which Demise, the aforesaid T. P. into the Tenements aforesaid with the Appurtenances did enter, and was thereof possessed, and the said T. P. so being thereof possessed, the aforesaid R. G. afterwards, to wit (such a day and yeare aforesaid) by Force and Armes, *&c.* Into the Tenements aforesaid with the Appurtenances, which the aforesaid R. G. to him the said T. P. in form aforesaid did demise, for the Terme aforesaid, which is not yet past, did enter, and him from his Farme aforesaid did eject, and other harmes, *&c.* to the great Damage, *&c.* and against the publick Peace, *&c.* Whereupon he saith, that he is damnified and hath Damage to the value of forty Pounds, and thereupon he brings his Suit, *&c,*

To this the most generall plea is, Not guilty, nor is there indeed any other Plea in use, sometimes the Defendant confesseth the action, and here you see following a Plea if not guilty and a confession both to one action.

And the aforesaid R. by T. L. his Attorney, comes and defends the force and injury when, *&c.* And as to the whole Trespasse and Ejectment aforesaid, above supposed to be done, besides the Trespasse and Ejectment in three Acres of Land of the Tenements aforesaid with the Appurtenances, he the said R. sayes, that he is no wise thereof guilty as the aforesaid T. P. above against him declareth, and of this he puts himselfe

selfe upon the Country, and the aforesaid *T. P.* in like manner, and as to the trespass and Ejectment aforsaid in the aforesaid 3 acres of Land of the tenements aforesaid with the appurtenances, above supposed to be made, he the said attorney of the aforsaid R. says that he is not informed by the aforesaid *R. G* his Client, of any answer for him the said *R. G.* to the aforesaid T. P. in the complaint aforesaid to be given, and nothing other he thereupon sayes by which the said said T. P. should remaine against him the said G. for which the said T. P. his aforesaid Terme of and in the aforesaid three acres of Land with the appurtenances, and his damages by reason of the Trespasse and Ejectment aforesaid, in the same three acres of Land ought not to recover, but because it is convenient and necessary, that there be one onely tax of the Damages for the whole trespass and Ejectment aforesaid, if it shall happen that upon the determining of the issue aforesaid, Judgement shall bee rendred for the aforesaid T. P. Therefore the Writ for giving of possession in that behalfe is to cease, and also of inquiring of damages by reason of the trespasse and Ejectment aforesaid, in the same three acres of Land with the appurtenances, untill the issue above-joyned bee determined, and as to the trying of that Issue, command is given to the Sherif, that he cause to come here twelve *&c.* By whom *&c.* and who neither *&c.* to recognize, *&c.* Because as well *&c.*

Here you have an issue ioyned which if you intend to try, you must proceed as is directed you in other actions, and so consequently for your judgement after verdict.

In this Action as I told you, there is a possession, recovered as well as Damages, and for Execution in both which is for possession, your *Habere facias possessionem*, which is made; you must usually by the Clark

of

of the Judgements after your Cofts are taxed and the Judgement figned, and likewife a *Capias ad fatisfaciendum* againft the Body for the Damage, or a *Fieri facias* againft the goods or Lands, which are alfo made by the Clark of the Judgments, and may likewife be made by any of the Prothonotaries Clarks.

Having your Writ of *Habere facias poffeffionem*, in cafe you cannot voluntary have quiet and peaceable poffeffion, you muft deliver your Writ to the under-Sheriff, who will put you into poffeffion, and remove whomfoever are in.

The fees incident to this action follow in a Table amongft others.

REplevin and Avowry comes in the next place to bee handled as that which brings a title many times in queftion by reafon of the Avowry, wherein we fhall fhew you the nature of the action, and in what cafes it lies, and for what things, what is incident to it by way of proceeding.

And to give you the fuller knowledge of this Action, we will begin to treat briefly of Diftreffes in generall.

Diftreffe is a thing which is diftrained in a houfe or upon any Land for Rent behind, or other duty or fervices, or for hurt done, although the property of the thing belongeth unto a ftranger : But if they be Cattell that belong to a Stranger, it is requifite that they were leavant and couchant upon the fame Ground; that is to fay, that the Beafts have beene upon the Ground a certain fpace, and have well refted themfelves there, or elfe they are not diftrainable for rent or Service.

And if a man diftrain for Rent, Services, or other thing, without a lawfull caufe; then the party grieved fhall have a Replevin, and upon fecurity found,

to

to pursue his Action, shall have the Distresse delivered to him again : But there be divers things that be not distrainable, *Viz.* another mans Garment in the House of a Taylor, a Strangers Cloath in the house of a Fuller, Shearman, or VVeaver, for that they be common Artificers, and that the common presumption is, that such things belong not to the Artificers in their own right, but to other persons which put them there to be wrought: The lessor cannot distrain fats fixt by his Lessee for a dying Pan, although the Lessee may remove them during his Terme.

The Lessor cannot distrain Glasse fixt by the Lessee, for his Rent.

The Lord cannot distrain Shocks of Corn for his Rent, but doing Damage he may, Sheaves of Corn in a Cart may be distrained, Victuall is not distrainable.

A Distresse ought allwayes to be made of such things, whereof the Sheriff may make Replevin, and deliver again in as good case, as they were at the time of the taking.

A man may distrain for Homage of his Tenant, for Fealty and Escuage and other Services.

He may distrain also for Fines and Amerciaments, which be assessed in a Court-Leet, but not in a Court Baron.

He may likewise distrain for Damage Fesant; that is to say, when he findeth the Beasts or Goods of any other, doing him wrong, by eating his Grasse or Corn, or trampling them down, or for incombring his Ground.

Note, a man may not distrain for any Rent or thing due for any Land, but upon the same Land that is charged therewith.

But in case when a man comes to distrain, the other
seeing

feeing his purpofe, chafeth his Beafts or Cattel away, or beareth his Goods out, to the intent they fhall not be taken for a Diftreffe upon the Ground; in fuch cafe I may well purfue, and if I take it prefently in the High-way or in another mans Ground, the taking is lawfull as well there as upon the Land charged, to whomfoever the property of the Goods be.

And for Fines and Amerciaments, which be affeffed in a Leet, one may allwayes take the Goods of him that is fo amerced, within whofe Ground foever they be within the Iurisdiction of the Court.

VVhere one is amerced in a Leet, and another takes Leather from him, and makes thereof Bootes and fhooes, whereby there feemes to be an altering of the property, in this cafe, thofe Bootes or fhooes being within the Precinct of the Leet may be diftrained for the amerciament.

Note, when one hath taken a Diftreffe, it behooveth to bring it to the common Pound, or elfe he may keep it in an open place, provided that he give notice to the party, who was owner of it, of his fo taking of it, and the place where it is, that he, if the Diftreffe be a quick Beaft, may give it food, and then if the beaft or beafts, dye for default of food, he that was diftrained, will receive the loffe, for the party diftraining, may take another Diftreffe for the fame rent or duty.

But if he carry the Diftreffe to a Hold, or out of the County, fo that the Sheriff may not make deliverance upon the Replevin, then the party upon the Sheriffs return of the Replevin may have a VVrit of *withernam* directed to the Sheriff, that he take as many of his beafts, or as much goods of the other in his keeping till he hath made deliverance of the firft Diftreffe: And alfo if the Beafts or Goods be conveyed to a Fort or Caftle, the Sheriff may take

with

with him the *Posse Comitatus*,   that is the power of the County, and beat downe the Castle , as appeares by the Statute of *Westminster* the first,   Chapter the seventeenth.

There is Distresse finite and infinite.

Distresse finite, is limited by Law, how often it shall be made to bring the party to a tryall of the Action, as once or twice.

Distresse infinite, is within limitation untill the party come, as against a Jury that refuseth to appeare upon Certificate of Assize,   the processe are a *Venire facias*, *Habeas Corpora*, and distresse infinite.

It is divided also into Grand Distresse , and an ordinary Distresse.

A Grand Distresse is that which is made of all the Goods and Chattels which the party hath within the County, and seemeth sometimes to be all one with Distresse infinite.

If a man proffer sufficient amends before the distresse made, for the wrong done by a mans Cattell, or otherwise, he cannot Distrain and Avow.

Note, that it is not lawfull for any common person to make Distresses out of their Fee, not in the Kings high way, nor in the common Street ; but the King might, and so might any who are substituted as his Ministers, and have especiall Authority derived from him.

Thus much for Distresses in generall, we come now to the Replevying of the Distresse taken.

THis Replevin (as we touched before in Distress) is a Writ that lieth where any man distraineth another for Rent or other thing, then the party distrained ftrained fhall have this writ to the Sheriff to deliver to him the Diftreffe, and fhall find Surety (as we faid before) to purfue his Action, and if he purfue it not, or if it be found or adjudged againft him, then he that took the Diftreffe fhall have again the diftreffe, and, that is called the returne of the Beafts, or other things, and he fhall have in fuch Cafes, a writ that is called a *Returno Habendo*.

Alfo if it be in any Franchife or Bailiwick, the party fhall have a Replevin of the Sheriff, directed to the Baylifof the fame franchife, for to deliver them againe, and he fhall find furety to purfue his action at the next County-Court, and this Replevin may be removed out of the country unto the common Pleas, by a Writ of *Reordare*.

Note, that a man may have a writ of *Homine replegeando*, which lies, where a man is in prifon, and not by the efpeciall commandement of the King, nor of his Juftices, nor for the death of a man, nor for the Kings Forreft, nor for fuch caufe that is not repleviable; then he fhall have this writ directed to the Sheriff, that he caufe him to be replevied.

This writ is a Juftices and not returneable, and if the Sherif do it not, then there fhall go forth another Writ (*Sicut alias*) and afterwards another Writ, (*Sicut plures vel caufam nobis fignifices*) which fhall be returneable, and if the Sheriff yet make no replevin, then there fhall go forth an Attachment againft the Sheriff, directed to the Corners to attach the Sheriff, and to bring him before the Juftices at a certain day, and furthermore that they make execution of the firft writ.

If a man take living Cattell, and more then one Beaft, then the Writ of Replevin runs thus.

The

The Writ of Replevin.

THe Keepers, *&c.* We command thee that juſtly and without delay, thou cauſeſt to be replevied, unto B. his Cattell, which C. took and unjuſtly detaines, as its ſaid, and afterwards to him then thereupon, juſtly cauſe to be brought back, leaſt that we any more thereupon, heare a complaint for want of Juſtice, *&c.*

If it be but one ſingle Beaſt that is taken, then the VVrit ſhall be.

The Keepers, *&c.* VVe command thee, *&c.* that thou cauſeſt to be replevied unto B. his Horſe, Heyfer, or Bull, *&c.*

If it be of any dead Chattell, the VVrit ſhall go thus,

The Keepers, *&c.* We command thee, *&c.* that thou cauſeſt to be replevied unto B. his Goods and Chattells.

In his Declaration it behoveth him, to declare of divers things, naming them.

But if he take but one thing that is a dead Chattell, then the VVrit ſhall be thus,

The Keepers, *&c.* VVe command thee, *&c.* that thou cauſeſt to be replevied unto B. a certain Net or a certain Iron of his Mill, *&c.*

NOte, that if the Sheriff return upon the Replevin, the *Alias* or *Plures* (where the Replevy is to be made within a Liberty or Franchiſe) that he hath commanded the Bailiff of the Franchiſe, who hath given him no anſwer, or that the Bayliff will not make deliverance, that then the Plaintiff ſhall have a *Non omittas* directed to the Sheriff, commanding him to enter into the Franchiſe, and make the Return, and if the Sheriff do it not, the Plaintiff
ſhall

shall have an *Alias non omittas* directed unto the Sheriff, and afterwards a *Plures non omittas*, &c.

But this return, that he hath commanded the Bailiff of the liberty, &c. who gave me no answer, &c. or the other return, that that the Bayliff will make no deliverance, are no good returns, for by the statute of *Westminster* 1 *Chapter th* 27. in the end of the same statute appears that the Sheriff upon such a return made to him by the Bayliff ought presently to enter into the franchise or liberty, and make deliverance of the thing taken.

And if the Sheriff upon the *Plures*, return, that the aforesaid B. the cattell of the aforesaid A. hath taken and them hath driven out of the County into the County of F. by which he cannot replevy them unto him, or if the Sherif returne that he hath commanded the Bayliff of the Franchise of D. who hath returne of Writs, &c who hath answered him, that the Cattell are Esloyned into divers liberties, that he cannot have the view of them, whereby to make deliverance.

And if the Sheriff himselfe make return, that he cannot have view of the cattel wherby to make deliverance or if the Sherif returne, that after the taking of them, &c. the Defend. hath esloyned his beasts out of his Bailiwick, by which he cannot make deliverance, or if the Sheriff return, that the Defendant hath esloyned his beasts into places unknown, by which he cannot come to have a view of the Beasts, whereby to make deliverance, or if the Sheriff return that he hath commanded the Bayliff of the Franchise, &c. Who hath answered him, that the Defendant hath impounded the beasts within the Rectory of the Church of C. by which he cannot make deliverance; upon those returns made by the Sheriff, the Plaintiff may have a Writ of *Withernam* to take as many of the

K   beasts

beasts of the Defendant, and it shall be directed to the Sheriff, and the Writ shall be thus;

The *Writ* of Withernam.

THE Keepers, *&c.* Whereas we have many times commanded thee justly, *&c.* To *A.* his Cattell which *B.* took, *&c.* and detaineth, as its said, thou shouldest replevy or signifie the cause to us, wherefore our commandement to thee many times therupon directed, thou couldest not, nor wouldest not execute: And thou hast signified unto us, that after the aforesaid *B.* took the Cattell of the aforesaid *A.* he drove them in your Country, and from that County into the County of *C.* by which you could not replevy them to him the said *A.* we willing to stop the malice of him the said *B.* in that behalfe, command thee, that the Cattell of the aforesaid *B.* within thy Bayliwick, thou take without delay in *Withernam*, and them thou detain untill, according to the custome of our Realm of *England*, thou canst replevy the aforesaid A. his Cattell, according to the Tenor of our aforesaid Command to thee formerly directed, *&c.*

Note, in this Writ of *withernam*, that whatsoever the Sheriff return upon the *Plures*, it ought to be inserted and rehearsed in the Writ of *Withernam*, as is before specified, and if the Sheriff returne upon the *Plures*, that he hath commanded the Bayliff of the Franchise, *&c.* who answereth him, that the Cattell are essoyned, *&c.* then the Plaintiff shall have a Writ of *withernam*, directed to the Sheriff, and the Sheriff shall command the Bayliff of the Franchise to serve the *withernam*, and if the Bayliff do not Execution, or give not any answer to the Sheriff of the precept directed to him, then the Plaintiff shall have a *Withernam* directed to the Sheriff, with a (*non omittas propter aliquam libertatem*, &c. *Quin eam ingrediaris*, &c.

Replevin.

&c.) and shall take in *Withernam* &c.

Note, that the Sheriff upon complaint made unto him of the taking of Cattell, may command his Bailif by word of mouth to make Replevin, and this as well as if the Sheriff had made a precept to his Bayliff to make a Replevin, for it may so fall out the Sheriff nor his Bayliff may not be able to write, or may want Pen, Inke, or paper.

If a man take Cattell Damage Feasant, that is doing hurt, and offer sufficient amends before the Cattell be impounded, and the party refuseth it, *&c.* Now if he sue Replevin for the Cattell, he shall recover damages onely for the detaining of them; but not for the taking of them, for that was warrantable.

And if the Lord take the Beasts of his Tenant wrongfully, and after the beasts return unto the Tenant, yet the Tenant shall have a Replevin against the Lord for those beasts, and shall recover his damages for the wrongfull taking of them.

And if a man distrain in one County, and drive the cattell into another County, the party whose Cattell they were may sue a Replevin in either of the Counties, which he please, or in both.

And if the Cattell of a feme sole, that is, a woman unmarried, be taken, and afterwards she take a Husband, the Husband soley may sue a Replevin.

Note, in Replevin, if the Plaintiff declare that the Defendant now hath and detaineth the Cattell, *&c.* and the Defendant appeares, and after makes default, the Plaintiff shall have judgment to recover all in damages, as well the value of the Cattell, as damage for the taking of them, and his costs.

IN this action of Replevin the processe are Summons, Attachment, and Distresse, upon a *Ni-*

bil, proceſſe of Outlawry, and then the Originall muſt come forth of the Chancery, except the Sheriff who may make a replevin, *Ex Officio*, (which ſhall be tried in the Sherifs court, called the County-court) do make it, which is moſt uſuall, and then it may be removed forth of the Sheriffs Court, by a (*Recordare*) or forth of any Lords Court or Hundred Court, by an (*Accedas ad curiam*) upon either of which writs returnable, either into the upper Bench or common Bench, if the Plaintiff declare not againſt the avowant for taking his Goods or Chattells which were taken before, the Avowant is to ſue out a Writ of *Returno Habendo* to be made by the Phillizer of the County, upon the return of which Writ, if the Plaintiff, that is, he whoſe Cattell were taken declare not, there ſhall be a Writ to inquire of Damages, &c.

And if the Sheriff upon the *Returno Habendo*, do return that the Cattell were Eſloyned, &c. then a *Capias* in *Withernam* as was beforeſaid, ſhall be awarded to take other Cattell ; and if the Sheriff returne that he hath no Cattell, then a *Capias* againſt the Body, and thoſe Proceſſe are likewiſe made by the Phillizer of the County, &c. And the like Proceſſe may be had in a Court Baron, in Replevin there.

Having ſhewed you the nature of this action, and how and in what caſes it lyes, and the Proceſſes that are incident to it : We come now to the Declaration upon it.

Devon. ſſ.

IN. was ſummoned to anſwer W. D. of a Plea wherefore he tooke the Cattell of him the ſaid W and them unjuſtly detained againſt ſureties an Pledges, &c. and whereupon the ſame W. by I. D his Attorney complaines, that the aforeſaid I. N
(ſuc

(such a day and yeare) at R. in a certaine place there called E. he took the Cattell, that is to say, five Heyfers and two Bullocks of him the said W. and them unjustly detained, against Sureties and Pledges, untill, &c. Whereupon he saith, that he is damnified and hath Damage to the value of twenty Pounds, and thereupon he brings his suit, &c.

The Avoury or damage seasant.

ANd the aforesaid I. by R. F. his Attorney, comes and defends the Force and injury when &c. And as the Bailifl of I. E. well acknowledgeth the taking of the said Cattell, in the aforesaid place in which, &c. and justly, &c. because he saith, that the same place in which the taking of the Cattell aforesaid was supposed to be done, containeth, and, the aforesaid time of the taking aforesaid above suposed to be done, did containe in it sixteene Acres of Land with the Appurtenances, in R. aforesaid, which said sixteen Acres of Land with the Appurtenances are, and the aforesaid time of taking aforesaid above supposed to be done, were the sole and free Tenement of the said I. E. And because the Cattell aforesaid, the aforesaid time wherein, &c. were in the aforesaid place in which &c. feeding upon the Grasse growing therein, and doing Damage there, the same I. as the Bayliff of the aforesaid I. E, well acknowledgeth the taking of the aforesaid Cattell, in the aforesaid place in which, &c. and justly &c. doing there Damage, &c.

K 3 *A Plea*

A Plea in Barre to the Avoury, by a Guardian in Socage.

AND the aforesaid W. saith that the aforesaid I for the reason before alledged, ought not to acknowledge the taking of the aforesaid Cattell, in the aforesaid place in which, &c. as the Bayliff of the aforesaid I. E. to be just, because he saith, that before the aforesaid time of the taking aforesaid, and long before the aforesaid I. E. had any thing in the aforesaid sixteen acres of Land with the appurtenances, one R. E. was seized of the Mannor of H. with the Appurtenances, in the County aforesaid whereof the aforesaid Place in which, &c. is, and the aforesaid time of taking aforesaid, was parcell in his Demesne as of Fee, and being so thereof seized, the Mannor with the Appurtenances whereof, &c. hee held of one R. W. Knight, as of his Mannor of L. in the County aforesaid, in Socage, that is to say, by Fealty and the Rent of twenty pound by yeare, every yeare, at the Feast of Saint *Michael* the Arch-Angell yearely to be paid, as also by the service of doing suite to the Court of the said R. of his aforesaid Mannor of L. from three weekes to three weekes, at the aforesaid Mannor yearly to be held; and the same R. E. of the Mannor of H. aforesaid, with the Appurtenances whereof, &c. being so seized, dyed thereof seized, after whose Death the said Mannor with the Appurtenances whereof, &c. descended to the aforesaid I. E. as to the Daughter and Heire of him the said R. E. the same I. E. being then within the age of fourteen yeares, that is to say, at the age of twelve yeares, and the said W. is the next of Kindred to the said I. E. that is to say, the Brother of *Eliaror*, the wife of the aforesaid R. E. and Mother

of

of the aforesaid *J. E.* to whom the aforesaid Mannor of *H.* with the Appurtenances whereof, *&c.* cannot from the aforesaid *I. E.* by hereditary Right descend, by which the custody of the aforesaid Mannor of *H.* with the Appurtenances whereof, *&c.* and of the a-foresaid *I. E.* untill the lawfull age of fourteen years, of her the said *I.E.* pertaines, by which the said *W.* the aforesaid time of taking aforesaid, was of the Custody of the said Mannor of *H.* with the Appurtenances whereof, *&c.* and of the aforesaid *I. E.* possessed, for that at the same time in which, *&c.* the said *I. E.* was within the age of fourteen years. And being so thereof possessed, afterwards, and before the aforesaid time of taking aforesaid, he put his aforesaid Cattell, on the aforesaid place in which, *&c.* to feed on the grass them thereupon growing: Which said Cattell were in the aforesaid place in which, *&c.* feeding up-on the grass then growing, untill the aforesaid *I.* the day and yeare in the Declaration above specified, at *K.* aforesaid, took the aforesaid Cattell of him the said *W.* and them unjustly detained, against Sureties and Pledges, untill, *&c.* as the said *W.* against him complaines; and this is he is ready to aver, whereupon for that the aforesaid *I.* above acknowledgeth the taking of the aforesaid Cattell, in the aforesaid place in which *&c.* the said *W.* prayes Judgement and his Damages, by reason of the taking and unjust detainiug of the aforesaid Cattell, to bee adjudged unto him, *&c.*

The defendant maintaines his Plea, and traverses the Tenure in Socage.

AND the aforesaid I. N. as formerly saith, that the aforesaid sixteen acres of Land with the Appurtenances, are, and at the aforesaid time of taking

aforesaid,

aforesaid, above suppofed to be done , where the sole and free Tenement of the aforesaid I. E. as he before hath alledged, without that , that the aforesaid R.E. held the aforesaid Mannor of H. with the Appurtenances whereof, &c. of the aforesaid R W. Knight, as of his Mannor of L. in Socage ; that is to say , by fealty and the Rent of twenty pence by the yeare, every yeare , at the Feaft of S. *Michael* the Arch-Angell yearly to be paid , and by the service of doing suite at the Court of the aforesaid R. W. of his aforesaid Mannor of L. from three weeks to three weeks , at the Mannor aforesaid yearly to be held , as the aforesaid W. hath above alledged , and this he is ready to aver, whereupon he praies Judgement, and the return of his Cattell, together with his Damages to him the said I. N. to be adjudged, &c.

Issue upon the Traverse.

AN E the aforesaid W. as formerly saith , that the aforesaid R. E. held the aforesaid Mannor of H. with the appurtenances, whereof , &c. of the aforesaid R. W. as of his Mannor of L. in socage , that is to say, by fealty, and the rent of twenty pence by yeare, each yeare at the Feaft of S. *Michael* the Arch-Angell, yearly to be paid, as also by the service of doing suit at the Court of the aforesaid R. W. of his aforesaid Mannor of L. from three weeks to three weeks; at the said manner yearly to be held , as he hath before alledged, and this he prayes may bee inquired of by the Country , and the aforesaid I. N. in like manner, therefore command is given to the Sheriff that he cause to come here twelve, &c. By whom &c. And who neither, &c To recognize , &c. Because as well, &c.

Here you have both a declaration , an Avowry, a
bar

barto the avowry, a Rejoynder, and a Sur-rejoynder, whereby you have a full and a compleat Iffue made up.

And here note, that this avowry is for damage fea-fant, but there are feverall other avowries, as,

Firft, A man may avow for fervices due to his Mannor, as Suit to his Court, or Suit at the Mill, *&c.*

Or for a Rent Charge, upon Prefcription to di-ftrain.

Or for a Rent Charge generally, hee may a-vow.

A Man may avow for an amerciament in a Court Baron.

After iffue joyned, in cafe you would proceed to a Triall, your proceeds are for the making your *Venire*, and fuing out your Record, and *Habeas Corpus*, as in other actions.

Partition.

THis Action lyes in feverall cafes, as where Lands defcend by the courfe of the Common-Law, or by Cuftome, as *Gavelkinde* Land amongft Coheires or Copartners, where there muft be two at the leaft, whe-ther they be Sons, Daughters, Sifters, Aunts, or otherwife of Kin to the Anceftor from whom the Land defcended to them.

And this Partition is made four wayes for the moft part, whereof three are at pleafure, and by agreement amongft themfelves, the other is by compulfion, when any refufe.

One partition is, where they themfelves divide the Land equally by agreement into fo many parts as there be of them Copartners, and each cheofeth

one

one share or part, the eldest first, and so the one after the other, as they be of age, except the eldest by consent made the partition, then the choice belongeth to the next, and so to the eldest last, according to the old Rule, he that divides, must not choose.

Another partition is, when they choose certaine of their friends to make division for them.

The third partition by agreement, is by drawing of Lots thus, 1. to divide the land into so many parts as there be Copartners, then to write every part severally, in a little Scrowle or piece of Paper, or Parchment, and put the same Scrowles up close into a Hat or Cap, or other such like thing, and then, each Partner, one after the other as they be of age to draw out thereof one peice or Scroule, whereon is written a part of the Land which by this drawing, is now severally allotted unto them in Fee simple.

The fourth partition, which as we said, is by compulsion, comes now to be treated of, which is, where one or some of the Copartners would have partition, and other some will not agree therto, then they that so would have Partion, may bring a Writ, *De partitione facienda*, against the others that would not make partition, by vertue whereof they shall be compelled to part, &c.

In Kent where the Lands are of the nature of Gavelkind, they call at this day their partition, Shifting, which is the same with that the Saxons used, namely, *Shaftan*, which signifies to make betweene Coheires partition, and to assigne to each of them their portion, in Latine it is called *Herciscere*.

Partition may also be made by joynt Tenants, or Tenants in common by their assent by deed between them, or by writ, by the Statute of 32 *Henry the eight*, *chapter* 32. and by the Statute of 33. *Henry the eighth*.

The

The processe in this action is Summons, Attachment, and Distresse infinite.

Your Summons is as follows;

The Summons in partition.

THe Keepers , &c. If *A.* &c. then summon *B.* to
shew wherefore when they the said *A.* and *B.* together and undivided , hold three acres of Land with
the appurtenances of the inheritance which was *M.*
Mother of the aforesaid *A.* and *B.* whose heires they
are in I. the same B. to make partition therof between
them , according to the Law and Custome of the
Common-wealth of *England*, denieth , and the same
permitteth not to be done , most unjustly as she faith,
and have you there this Writ , &c.

NOte that the Summons varies in the case where
there are three or four Copartners , and likewise
where it is between Joynt-Tenants , or Tenants in
Comomn, the Summons according to the severall cases were too large here to insert.

Having your Summons thus made returnable of
any Terme , the Defendant may Essoyne if hee
will.

If the Defendant doe Essoine, it rests on the Plaintiffs part to adjourn it, as if the Summons, *Tres Mi-*
chaelis, he may adjourn to *Crastino Martini,* and then
issues out from the Phillizor , a Writ called a *Pone,*
returnable , *Octabilis Hillarii* and then upon that returned by the Sheriff, you must file your *Pone* with
the Phillizor , which Warrants the making out of a
Distringas, returnable, *Octabis Purificationis,* and upon that get an Amerciament of five pounds, if the Defendant appeare not , then you may have an *Alias*
Distringas returnable in *Easter* Terme , doubling your
Issues,

Iſſues, and ſo Diſtreſſe infinite till he do appeare.

Where the Defendant as before doth caſt an Eſſoyn, and there is no adjournment made thereof, the Defendant may enter a *Non-ſuite* againſt the Plaintiff, it he be carefull firſt to enter a *Ne recipiatur* with the Clark of the Eſſoynes, upon the day of the Exceptions, upon which non-ſuire, the Plaintiff muſt begin againe.

Where there are ſeverall Defendants, they may ſeveally Eſſoyn, if they would protract time before appearance, and where they Eſſoyn not upon the Summons, they may upon the *Pone.*

If they do not Eſſoyn but appear, you may declare, and your declaration ;

Buck. ſſ.

ANtony *Cooke* Knight, in mercy for many defaults: And the ſame *Anthony* and *Thomas Wootton Eſq.* were ſummoned to anſwer *Peter Temple* Gentleman, of a Plea , that whereas they the ſaid *Peter* and the aforeſaid *Anthony,* and *Thomas* together and undivided , do hold to them and their Heires, the Mannor of *Doſſet alias Dorſſet,* with the appurtenances, they the ſaid *Anthony* and *Thomas* to make partition, thereof between them , according to the forme of the ſtatute in that caſe publiſhed and provided , doe deny, and the ſame moſt unjuſtly permit not to be done, againſt the forme of the ſtatute aforeſaid , &c. And whereupon the ſaid *Peter* by T. L. his Attorney ſaies , that whereas he and the aforeſaid A. and T. together and undivided , do hold to them and their Heires , the Mannor aforeſaid with the Appurtenances, whereofunto him the ſaid *Peter* and his Heires it belongs, to have one part of the Maunor aforeſaid with the Appurtenances , in three parts equally to be divided, and to the aforeſaid *Anthony* and his Heires,

it

it pertaines to have another part of the same Mannor with the Appurtenances, in three equall parts, as is aforesaid to be divided, and unto the aforesaid *Thomas* and his Heires it pertaines to have a third part, the residue thereof to hold to them in severalty, so that the same *Peter* of his part of the Mannor aforesaid with the Apurtenances to him belonging, and the aforesaid *Anthony* of his part of the Mannor aforesaid, with the Appurtenances to him thereof belonging, and the aforesaid *Thomas* of his part of the Mannor aforesaid with the Appurtenances, to him thereof belonging; may be able severally to appart, they the said *Anthony* and *Thomas* to make partition thereof between them; according to the forme of the Statute in that case made and provided, do deny, and the same most unjustly permit not to be done, against the form of the Statute aforesaid; whereupon he saith that he is damnified, and hath Damage to the value of a hundred pounds, and thereupon he brings his Suite, &c.

In these Actions the Pleas are various, as the Title may be.

The Defendant may plead the freehold solely in himselfe at the time of the Plaintiffs issuing forth his originall Writ, and traverse that they hold it together and undivided, &c. whereupon he praies Judgement, whether Partition ought to be made between them, &c.

To this Plea the Plaintiff may take issue upon the Traverse, and if so, they may joyne issue, and so proceed to tryall.

Upon a verdict and judgement had for the Plaintif, he may have his Writ of partition directed to the Sheriff, commanding him to take twelve men of the County, and of the *Venue*, in the presence of the Copartners to make partition, by vertue of which Writ

he

he Summons a Jury of the said twelve men, and in the presence of the parties concerned, he makes partition, and then his return is as follows;

By vertue of this Writ of the Keepers of the liberty of *England* to me directed, and to this partition indented annexed J.T.D. Knight Sheriff of the county aforesaid (such a day, year, and place) having taken with me *L. N. R. R.* and twelve free and legall men of my County, and of the *Venue* within written, in presence of *H. L. R. M.* in the Writ aforesaid named, in my proper person, I came to the Tenements in the said VVrit named, and there by their oath (having respect to the true value of the same Tenements with the appurtenances,) the same Tenements into partition into three parts equally to be parted, I have caused, and one part of the same three parts (*Videlicet,* such and such Land so butted and bounded) I the Sheriff aforesaid, the aforesaid day and yeare, &c. Those to be delivered and assigned, have caused to *H. L.* in the said Writ named to be had to her, in severalty, according to the forme and effect of the Writ aforesaid, and as to two parts of the residue of the aforesaid Tenements in the aforesaid writ specified, I the Sheriff aforesaid, certifie the Justices within written, that none of the part of the other 2 came to receive of me, the aforesaid Sheriff, the same 2 parts, so that the same 2 parts to the other two assign, and, deliver I could not, as the writ aforesaid exacteth and requireth, in Testimony whereof, as well the Seal of me the aforesaid Sheriff, as the seals of the aforesaid twelve Jurors to this Partition indented, or set, given the day and yeare abovesaid : Upon this Return of the Sheriff, the Judgment is entred, that the Partition aforesaid made, in form aforesaid shall be held firme and stable for ever, &c.

A partition thus made by the Sheriff, and by the
Oath

Oath of twelve men, and Judgement thereupon given, shall bind an Infant, though his part be unequall.

Note, a partition between Joynt-Tenants, is not good without deed, albeit it be of Lands, and that they be compellable to make partition, by the Statute of 32. *Henry* the eighth, Chapter the tenth, and 32. *Hen.* the eighth, Chapter 32. because they must pursue that Act by Writ, *De partitione faciend.*

And note, that you are to take out this Writ *De partitione faciend.* Executed by the Sheriff, together with the Sheriffs return *Verbatim*, into the remembrance in the Prothonotaries Office, and then the Prothonotary signes Judgment thereupon.

The Fees incident to this Action you will find in the generall Table of Fees.

We preceed now to treat of Dower.

Dower in the Common Law is taken for that portion, &c. which the Widow hath for Terme of her life, of the Lands or Tenements of her Husbands, it is called *Dower or dowery*, as a gift, because the Law it selfe doth (without any gift of the Husband himselfe) give it to her, its commonly taken for the third part, which she hath of her Husbands Lands after his decease.

To the consummation of this *Dower*, three things are necessary, Marriage, Seizin, and the death of the Husband.

This provision the Law hath made for a Widow, where the Husband hath not assigned in his life-time part of his Lands to his wife.

Dower by the custome of some places, as (*Gavel-kind,*

kinde Land, &c. is to have halfe the Husbands
Lands.

This Writ of Dower, lyes where a man is sole seized of Lands or Tenements in Fee-simple or Fee-taile, during the Coverture between him and his Wife, where by possibility the Issue between them may Inherit, if such a man dye, his Wife shall recover the third part of all the Lands, whereof the Husband was sole seized, any time during the Coverture, by a VVrit of Dower, though he dyed not seized, and although that he made Alienation thereof in his life time.

VVhere the Husband dyed seized, and the VVife brings a VVrit of Dower, and recovers, she shall recover Damages, for the Profits of the Land incurred, from the time of the Death of her Husband, but if there were any Estate or Alienation made of the Lands, &c. during coverture, so that the Husband dyed not seized, in that case she shall recover no Damages for mean profits, although she recover the Land.

It is not necessary that seizin should continue during Coverture, for being once seized it sufficeth, although he alien Lands or Extinguish Rents; yet the woman shall be Endowed.

But it is absolutely necessary that the Marriage continue, for if that be dissolved, the Dower ceaseth.

In case of *Elopement*, which is where a VVoman leaves her Husband, and goes away with an Adulterer, and dwelleth with the Adulterer, without voluntary reconcilement to her Husband, by this she shall lose her Dower.

A woman

A VVoman shall not be endowed of a Common without number in grosse, nor of an annuity, &c. nor of Rents, &c. if the Freehold of the Rents were suspended before the Coverture; but she shall be endowed of Tithes; of the third part of the profits of Courts, Fines, Heriots, &c.

Shee shall be endowed according to the value of the Land at the time of the assignment, and not according to the value as it was in the time of her Husband, whether the value of the Land by building or otherwise be improved, or whether it be impaired by the Heir.

If the VVife be past the age of nine years at the time of the death of her Husband (albeit shee were but four years old when she was married) yet shee shall be endowed.

If a VVoman marry before shee be of years to consent, which is twelve in a VVoman, and fourteen in a Man, yet that imperfect or incheat Marriage (from which either of the parties at the age of consent may disagree,) after the Death of the Husband, shall give Dower to the VVife.

If the Heire, &c. put her out within forty dayes she shall have a Writ *De quærentina habenda,* which is a Writ that the Law gives, where a man dies seized of a Mannor, Place, and other Lands, whereof the Wife ought to be indowed, there the Woman may abide in the Mannor, Place, and there live of the store and profits thereof for the space of forty dayes, within which time, her dower is to be assigned, as by *Magna Charta,* Chapter 6.

There needeth neither liberty of seisin nor writing to any assignment of Dower, because it is due of Common right, and the assignment must be of some part of the Land or of a Rent, &c. issuing out of the same.

L.   The

The affignment muft be certain and abfolute, and by fuch as have freehold, or againft whom a Writ of dower lies.

Affignment of Dower muft be either by the Sheriff by the Kings Writ, or elfe by the Heir or other Tenant of the Land by confent and agreement betweene them.

A Joynture was formerly no bar of Dower at the Common Law, but now it is by the Statute of 27. *Henry the eighth*, if the Joynture be made to the Wife, according to the Purview of that Statute.

Six things are required to a perfect joynture.

Firft, it is to take effect for her life in poffeffion, or profit, prefently after the Deceafe of her Hufband.

Secondly, that it be for terme of her owne life, or greater Eftate.

Thirdly, it muft be made to her felfe, and no other for her.

Fourthly, it muft be made in fatisfaction of her whole dower, and not of part, &c.

Fiftly, it muft be either expreffed or averred to be in fatisfaction, &c.

Sixthly, it may be made either before or after marriage.

If the Joynture be made, for Marriage, the Wife cannot wave it and claim her Dower at the common Law; but if it be made after Marriage, fhe may wave the fame.

A Joynture made to the Wife above or under the age of nine years is good.

The Wife fhall not be endowed of Lands which the Husband holdeth joyntly with another at the time

of his Death, &c. for that the Joynt-Tenant which
surviveth, claimeth the Land by the Feoffments, and
by the Survivorship, which is above the title of Dower; but the Tenants in common hath severall Freeholds and inheritances, and their moities shall descend to their severall Heires, and therefore their
wives shall thereof be indowed.

THe processe incident to this Action of Dower
are,

First. A Summons between the *Teste*, and return,
whereof there is five returnes.

And if the Tenant neither appeare, nor cast an
Essoyne, entring a *Nerecipiatur*, a grand *Cape* lies to
seize the Lands, &c. for that for such his default, the
Tenant shall lose his Land.

But if he wage his Law of *Non Summons*, he shall
save his default, and then he may plead with the Demandant.

NOte, that in the Grand *Cape*, the Tenant shall
be summoned to answer to the Default, and further to the demandant; but in *Petite Cape*, he shall be
summoned to answer to the default onely, and not to
the Demandant, and it is called a *Petite Cape*, because
it includes lesse then the other.

And if the Tenant by the returne of the Summons,
essoyne, the Demandant adjournes fifteen dayes longer, in such case, the Attorney for the Tenant, may
enter with the Philizer, that the Tenant appeares
and prayes view, &c.

Then a writ of view goes out, whereby the Sheriff
is to shew the Tenant the lands in question, which supposeth the tenant knows not well what lands it is that
the Demandant asketh, by the returne of which writ

of

of View, the Tenants Attorney takes a Declaration.

NOte, that where a default is made after appearance, there a *Petite Cape* is to issue forth at the Demandant his suit, which is made, as likewise the Grand *Cape* by the Philizer of the County where the Land lieth.

The forme of the Summons is thus;

THe Keepers of the liberty, *&c.* to the Sheriff of *L.* greeting, command *J. D.* that Justly, *&c.* he render *E. D.* the third part of ten Messuages, five Cottages, two hundred Acres of Land, three hundred acres of Meadow, and two hundred acres of pasture, in *C.* and *B.* as her Dowry, by the Endowment of *G.D.* in time past her Husband, *&c.* whereof she hath nothing, *&c.*

In case the Tenant appear upon the Summons, *&c.* Then you delare as follows;

Lincolne ß.

E. D. Widow, which was the Wife of *G. D.* by *A.B.* their Attorney, demand against I. D. the third part of ten Messuages, five Cottages, and two hundred acres of Land, three hundred acres of Meadow, and two hundred acres of Pasture with the Appurtenances in *C.* and *B. &c.* as the Dowry of her the said E. D. by the Endowment of *G. D.* in time past her Husband, *&c.*

To this action there may be severall Pleas, as the case may require.

The most generall Plea is, (*Ne unque seizi que dower*) That is to say, that the Husband was never seized of any Estate, whereof the Wife can be endowed, the form whereof is as follows,

L *Ne unque feizi que Dower, pleaded in Dower.*

AND the aforefaid Defendant by *A. B.* his Attorney comes and fayes, that the aforefaid *A.* ought not to have her Dowry of the Meffuage and Tenements aforefaid, with the Appurtenances whereof, *&c.* Of the Indowment of the aforefaid *D.* once her Husband, *&c.* Becaufe he faith that the aforefaid *D.* once her Husband, *&c.* neither at the day wherein he married the aforefaid *A.* nor at any time after, was feized of the fame Meffuage and Tenements, with the Appurtenances whereof, *&c.* of fuch an Eftate, fo that the aforefaid A. thereof might be indowed.

And of this he puts himfelfe upon the Country, and the Plaintiff in like manner, therefore command is given to the Sheriff, that he caufe to come here twelve, *&c.*

There is a Plea likewife of *Non-tenure,* which is as followes;

Non-tenure pleaded in bar of Dowry.

AND the Defendant by I. D. his Attorney, comes and fayes, that he cannot render the aforefaid A. her Dowry, of the Mannor aforefaid with the Appurtenances, becaufe that he is not thereof Tenant, as of the free-hold, nor was, the day of the iffuing forth of the originall Writ of her the faid A. nor at any time after: And this he is ready to aver, whereupon he prayes Judgement of the VVrit aforefaid, *&c.*

Iffue

Issue upon the Non-tenure.

AND the aforesaid *A.* saith, that the Writ aforesaid, for the reasons before alledged, ought not to be quashed, because shee saith, that the day of the issuing forth of the originall Writ of her the said *A.* (to wit, such a day and yeare) the aforesaid Defendant was Tenant of the Mannor aforesaid with the Appurtenances, as of his Free-hold, as by the same Writ is supposed; and this he prayes may be inquired by the Country, and the aforesaid Defendant in like manner, therefore Command is given to the Sheriff, that he cause to come here twelve, &c.

Also *Nonage* may be pleaded in bar of Dower, and then it is thus;

Nonage in Bar of Dower.

AND the aforesaid *R. M.* by T G. his Attorney, comes and sayes, that the aforesaid *N.* ought not in this behalfe to have Dowry, because he saith, that the aforesaid *N.* at the time of the Death of the aforesaid R. in time past her Husband, of whose Endowment, &c. she was not of that full age, that she should deserve Dowry, that is to say of nine yeares and a halfe: and this he is ready to aver, whereupon he prayes Judgment, whether the aforesaid *N.* ought to have her Dowry of the Tenements aforesaid with the Appurtenances, &c.

Issue of full age.

AND the aforesaid *N.* saith, that shee the aforesaid *N.* was at the time of the Death of him the

the said R. in time past her Husband, &c. of such age as that she might deserve Dowry; that is to say, of nine yeares and a halfe and above, and this she prayes may be inquired of the Country, and the said R.M. in like manner, &c. Therefore command is given to the Sheriff, that hee cause to come here twelve, &c.

Elopement may also be pleaded in bar of Dower and then it is thus;

Elopement in Bar.

AND the aforesaid I. and L. by T. L. his Attorney, comes and sayes, that the aforesaid R. and A. ought not to have against them the Dowry aforesaid, of the Mannor and Tenements aforesaid with the Appurtenances, of the Endowment of the aforesaid E. in times past her Husband, &c. Because they say, that the aforesaid A. in the life time of the aforesaid E. in time past her Husband, &c Of her own voluntary will and accord at B. in the County of M. left him the said E. in time past her husband, and went from him with one M. R. in the Parish of S. in the County of M. and after there with the same M. did lead her continued life in Adultery, during the life of him the said E. in time past her Husband, &c. Without that, that the aforesaid A. to the said E. her Husband, in the life time of the said E. in time past her Husband &c. was reconciled unto him; and this they are ready to aver, whereupon they pray Judgement, whether the aforesaid R. and A. in this behalfe, ought to have her Dowry, of the Mannor and Tenements aforesaid with the Appurtenances, of the Endowment of the aforesaid E. in time past her Husband, &c.

L 4 Recon-

Reconcilement pleaded to the Elopement.

AND the aforesaid R. and A. say, that they by any thing before alledged, ought not to be debarred from haviug the Dowry of the aforesaid, A. of the Mannor and Tenements aforesaid with the appurtenances, against them the aforesaid I. L. because they say, that after the departure aforesaid, by the said I. and L. supposed to be made, the aforesaid E. in his life time, her the said A. of his owne accord, and without Ecclesiasticall compelling, at L, did reconcile, and suffered her to live with him; and this they are ready to aver, whereupon they pray Judgement, and the Dowry of her the said A. of the Mannor and Tenements aforesaid with the appurtenances, together with their Damages, by reason of the Detainer of the Dowry aforesaid, to be adjudged unto them, &c.

Issue upon the Reconcilement.

AND the aforesaid I. and L. say, that the aforesaid E. in his life-time, did not reconcile in manner and forme, as the aforesaid R and A have above alledged, and of this they put themselves upon the Country, and the aforesaid R. and A. in like manner; therefore Command is given to the Sheriff, that hee cause to come here on three weeks after the holy *Trinity,* twelve, &c.

A man may call to warranty in Dower, and then is the Fart so called to warranty, summoned in the County where he lies, and that by the ayde of the Court, and this is called a Counter-plea of the Voucher in Dower, and is thus.

Counter-

Counter-plea of the Voucher in Dower.

AND the aforesaid I. by C. B. his Attorney, comes and calls thereupon to warranty R. C. Gentleman, summoned in the County aforesaid, by the ayd of the Court. &c.

To this the Defendant may reply, that the party calls to warranty: hath nothing in the Lands, &c.

And the aforesaid I. sayes, that neither the aforesaid R. whom &c. nor any of his Ancestors, had any thing in the Tenements aforesaid with the appurtenances, in his Demeine as of Fee, in Reversion, or, &c. from the time of the Death of the aforesaid W. C. in time past her Husband, &c. unto the day of the issuing forth of the original Writ of her the said I. (to wit, such a day and yeare) so that he could thereof Enfeoff the aforesaid *John*, or any of his Ancestors: And this he prayes may be enquired of by the Country, and the aforesaid *John* in like manner, herefore Command is given to the Sheriff, that he cause to come twelve, &c.

An Annuity may also be pleaded in bar of Dowry, but is too long here to recite.

To this Action, in case the Tenant have no speciall matter to plead in bar, then he may confesse the action by *Non sum Informatus,* or let it passe by default, as in the ensuing.

Non Informatus in Dower.

AND the aforesaid E. by T. S. his Attorney, comes, and the same Attorney sayes, that he is not informed by the sayd E. his Clyent, of any answer for the aforesaid E. to the aforesaid P. S. in the

the Plaint aforesaid to be given , and nothing other he thereupon saith, by which the same P. S. should remaine against the aforesaid E. thereupon undefended : Therefore it is considered, that the aforesaid P. S. shall recover her seizin against the aforesaid E. of the third part of the Mannor , Park, Free-warren, Tenements, and Advowson aforesaid with the appurtenances, and the aforesaid E. in mercy, *&c.*

And upon this the aforesaid P.S. prayes the Writ of the Keepers of the Liberty of *England* to the sheriff of the County aforesaid to be directed , to cause him to give her full possession of the third part aforesaid with the appurtenances , and it is granted unto her, returnable here in eight daies after S. *Michael*; and also the same P. S. sayes, that the aforesaid T. in time past her Husband , *&c.* died seized of the Mannor, *&c.* in his Demesne as of a Fee, and of the Advowson aforesaid , as of his Fee and right, and prayes the Writ of the said Keepers of the Liberty , *&c.* to the Sheriff of the County aforesaid to be directed , to inquire of Damages, and it is granted unto her , returnable at the aforesaid Term, *&c.*

Note, that in this as other reall actions , when you plead for the Defendant you say onely (*Comes and saies*) and not as in other Actions , Defends the force and injury , *&c.*

When upon issue joyned you would go to tryall, you must proceed with your *Venire facias* , and *Habeas Corpora* , and Record, as in other actions , and upon tryal the Jury do give in damages for the main profits, from the death of the Husband, and for that you shall have Execution made by the Clark of the Judgments who entreh up your Judgement.

And then you have a writ to the Sheriff , to give possession of a full third part, *&.* which writ being executed by the Sheriff, is thus turned.

BY vertue, *&c.* and to the Shedule annexed (such a day and yeare) I have caused to be delivered to *J. B.* Widow in the aforesaid VVrit named, plenary seizin of the third part of the Mannor of *L.* with the Appurtenances in the same Writ specified (*Viz.* and rehearse the particulars in the Writ) to be held to the aforesaid *I. B.* in the severalty by meets and bounds, in the name of the whole Dower of her the said *I. B.* to her the said *I. B.* contingent of her whole Mannor in the Writ specified, as by the Writ aforesaid to me is commanded *&c.*

Formedon.

In the next place we come to treat of an Action called Formedon; *which is a reall action, and that is in three wayes.*

THE first is *Formedon* in the Discender, which lieth where Tenant in taile enfeoffed a stranger, or is disseized and dyeth, the Heir shall have a Writ of *Formedon* to recover the estate.

The second is *Formedon* in the Remainder, and that lieth where one gives lands in the tayl, and for default of issue, the remainder to another in tail, and that for fault of such issue the land shall revert to the Donor, if the first Tenant in tail dye without issue, he in the Remainder shall have this VVrit.

The third is a *Formedon* in Reverter, and that lieth, where the Tenant in Tayle dies without issue, and he in the Remainder dies also wrthout issue, then the Donor or his Heirs, shall have a *Formedon* in Reverter.

VVhere

VVhere Tenant in taile aliens or is diffeized, or if a Recovery be had againft him by default, and that he die, his Heir fhall have a *Formedon*, for the Heir fhall not have other Recovery for the poffeffion of his Anceftor then by *Formedon*; but if he be outed, of his own poffeffion, as if he be feized and put out, he fhall have his VVrit of Affize.

Formedon lies by the Heire of a gift made before the Statute of *weftminfter* 2. where the Donee after the Statute aliens and dies.

VVhere there is a Tenant in Dower or by the Curtefie.

The reverfion to another in tayl, if one intrude after the Death of the Tenant in Dower, or by the Heire of courtefie, he in the Reverfion fhall not have intrufion, but a *Formedon.*

VVoman in tayle takes a Husband, which aliens, and after they are divorced, and after the ~~VVife~~ dyes, the VVife fhall in this cafe have a *Formedon*, and not a *Cui in vita.*

If Tenant in tayle lets for life, and the Tenant for life aliens in Fee, the Tenant in tayle fhall have a *Formedon* at his pleafure.

VVhere Land is given to one for life, the Remainder to the Father in Tayl (if it were executed in the Father) and he aliens, the Iffue may have a *Formedon in Defcender* generally, or may have a fpeciall VVrit, making mention how it was given for life, the Remainder to his Father in Tayle, and one or other is good.

In conveyance of degrees, you need not name him Heire, but Son of him which was not feized, but it is a furer way to name him Son and Heire to every one, if he were feized or not; but he cannot omit any in his VVrits which were feized.

If the Demandant omit in *Formedon*, one who held
the

the Estate, that is to say, who was seized the Writ shal abate.

The Demandant in this VVrit ought to make his difcent by all which hold the Estate, otherwife the VVrit fhall abate.

Though the Demandant be made Heire to him which dyed in the life time of his Father, which was not feized, yet the VVrit fhall not abate, but is good.

Note, by the Regifter it is held, that he ought to make him Sonne to every one, and Sonne and Heire to him which laft holdes the Estate; but if he makes him Sonne and Heire to every one, that is more, and good, notwithftanding that every one did not hold the Estate.

The VVrit is not the worfe, although in the fame it be mentioned that he is Heire of one, or that he fhould have fcarce been Heir to him if he had lived, if he be Heire to him, that laft was feized.

The Demandant in *Formedon*, ought to name him Sonne and Heire to him that was feized, but if one furvive his Father, and were not feized, he need not name himfelfe Heir, but Son onely.

Formedon did abate, for that the Demandant made himfelfe Cofin and Heire to the Donee, where his Father was feized after the Death of the Donee, and no mention was made of him.

Efplees fhall be alledged in *Formedon in Reverter*, in the Donor and in the Donee, and in *Formedon in Defcender*, and Remainder, in the Donee onely.

Thofe Efplees is as it were the feizen or poffeffion of a thing, Profit, or Commodity, that is to be taken, as of a common, the Efplees is the taking of the graffe or Common by the mouthes of the Beafts that Common there, of an Advowfon by taking the graffe, Tithes by the Parfon prefented thereto, of VVood,

the

the felling of Wood, of an Orchard, the felling of Apples and other fruit growing there: Of a Mill, the taking of Toll is Efplees, and of fuch like.

NOte, that in a Writ of Right of Land or Advowfon, &c. The Demandant ought to alledge in his Declaration, that he or his Anceftors took the Efplees of a thing in demand, or otherwife the Pleading is not good.

Formedon in Remainder, he alleadgeth Efplees in the Tenant for life, and not in the Donor.

Formedon in the Remainder, he counts upon the matter without laying Efplees in the Donor, and it is good.

Of what things a Formedon lyeth, and of what not.

FOrmedon lyeth of Gorfe, but not of an Avowfon.

It lies of Pafture for ten beafts, or a certain number, but not of common, for there a Writ called (*Quod permittas,*) &c.

Formedon lies of common in groffe.

Formedon lies of a Corody, that is to fay, of Rent and certain breads, &c.

It lies for the Moiety, profit of a Mill, which is granted to one and the Heires of his body, and the Donee dyeth, and his Heire is deforced of this profit; now the Heire fhall have a Writ of *Formedon in the defcender* for this profit.

The forme of the Writ when it is in the *defcender* runs thus.

Is

In the discender.

THe Keepers , &c. to the Sheriff of L. greeting, command T B. that &c. he render I. C. the Moiety of the profits comming of two Mills of him the said T. B. in M. which R. B. &c. gave to T. C. and to the heires of his Body issuing, and which after the Death of him the said T. C. &c. Ought to descend &c.

If the *Formedon* be in the Remainder , then the Writ runs thus ;

In the remainder.

THe Keepers of the Liberty , &c. to the Sheriff of G. Greeting, command A. that he render B. one Messuage and twenty acres of land, &c. which C. gave to D. and the heires of his body issuing , so that if the same D. dyed without heir issuing of his Body, the aforesaid Messuage and twenty acres of Land with the appurtenances, should remaine to the aforesaid B. and his Heires , and which after the death of the aforesaid D. to the aforesaid B. ought to remain by the form of the Donation aforesaid; because the aforesaid D. dyed without Heire of his Body issuing , as its said, &c. unlesse, &c.

If the *Formedon* be in the Reverter , then thus ;

In the Reverter.

THe Keepers of the Liberty , &c. to the Sheriff of G. greeting , command A. that hee render B. one Messuage and twenty acres of Land with the appurtenances. in G. which C. father of the aforesaid B. whose

B. whose Heire he is, gave to J. and E. his wife, and to the Heires of their body issuing, and which after the Death of the aforesaid J. and E. ought to revert to the aforesaid B. by form of the gift aforesaid, for that the aforesaid J. and E. died without Heires issuing of their bodies, as he saies, &c.

This writ is called a Summons and hath nine returnes, betwixt the Teste and the returne, and the Processe are the same which are in Dower after the Summons, that is a Grand *Cape*, Writ of *View*, and *Petite Cape*.

In this Action, as also in that of Dower, and other reall Actions, the Plaintiff is called Demandant, and the Defendant Tenant, and in mixt Actions, Plaintiff and Defendant.

Note, that there is great care to be taken by the Atturneys on both sides, in the course of casting Essoines, adjourning and entring *Ne recipiatur* with the Clark of the Essoyes, and getting *Non suites*, for that thereby much prejudice or advantage may come to their Clyents causes.

If we should now in this action, as in that of Dower, descend to the severall declarations, in order to the severall *Formedons*, *in Descender*, *Remainder*, and *Reverter*, together with the various Pleas thereto, it would take up more roome, then can be spared in this little Tract.

Let it suffice that we told you that the Proceedes were much alike to that in Dower.

Let's *Proceed to* Quare impedit.

Quare impedit is a Writ, and it lyeth where a man hath an advowson, and the Parson dyeth, and
another

another prefenteth his Clark, or difturbeth me to prefent, then he may have the faid Writ.

Affize of *Darreyn prefentment* lies, where I, or my Anceftors have prefented before, and where a man may have an affize of *Darreyn prefentment*, he may have alfo a *Quare impedit*, but not contrariwife.

Alfo if the Plea be depending between two Parties, and be not difcuffed within fix Months, then the Bifhop may prefent by *Lapfe*, and he that hath right to prefent, fhall recover his damages, as it appears by the Statute of *weftminfter* 2. Chapter the fifth.

Alfo if one have right to prefent after the death of a Parfon, and bringeth no *Quare impedit*, or *Darreyn prefentment*, but fuffereth a Stranger to ufurpe upon him, yet he fhall have a Writ of right Advowfon, but this Writ lieth not, unleffe he claim to have the Advowfon to him and his Heires in Fee-fimple.

A *Quare impedit* may be brought by him who hath a Grant of the next avoydance.

It lies for the Moiety, or third parr of the Advowfon, and of the Advowfon, or Moiety of the third part.

It lies for a Chantry, which is a Donative, and he hath it by Letters Patents, and that it be void, and he prefent to it his Clark, who is difturbed by another, or another prefented to the faid Chantry, he which hath the Right, fhall have his *Quare impedit*.

Formerly a *Quare impedit* might be brought for an *Abby* or *Priory*.

A *Quare impedit* lay likewife for an Hermitary, it's brought formerly againft the Bishop, together with others that claim or difturb : The form of the Writ generally is thus.

M   *Quare*

Quare impedit.

THE Keepers of the Liberty of *England*, &c. to the Sheriff of *L.* Greeting, &c. conumand *A. B.* that juftly, &c. he permit *T. L.* to prefent a fit Parfon to the Church of *L.* which is void, and belongs unto his Donation, &c.

This Writ is a Summons at the Plaintiffs fuite, and if there be two or three Defendants, they may all Effoyn one after the other, and after they have effoyned, your proceeds are the fame, as in the Action of Partition by a *Pone* and *Diftringas*, which makes the Proceedings of this Action very tedious, the Defendant ufing all the poffible delayes he can, for that moft ufually he hath gotten into poffeffion, and fo holds them Plea with their owne Weapons, and gaines many times a yeare or two the profits of the Tithes.

But in cafe the Church be voide, and that the Plaintiff do feare that the Defendant will get in, or formerly that the Bifhop would Collate his Clarke, then he might have a Writ directed to the Bifhop, which is called *Ne admittas*, and this Writ muft be brought, while the Action is depending in the Common Bench; whether by *Quare impedit*, or *Darreyn prefentment*, and this Writ ought to be fued within the fix Months after the voydance, for after the fix Months he fhall not have this Writ, for then the Living may be prefented unto by *Lapfe*, and therefore it is in vain then to fue this Writ, for that the Title of prefenting is devolved to the Bifhop, but the King might fue this Writ after the fix months, having a Writ of *Quare impedit* or *Darreyn prefentment* depending, according to that *Maxim, Nullum tempus occurrit regi*, and the Writ of *Ne admittas*, is as followes,

lows; in case it were for the King in his time.

A Ne admittas.

CHARLES by the grace of God, &c. To the Venerable Father in Christ *W*. by the same grace Bishop of *Winchester*, greeting. We prohibit you, that you admit not any Parson to the Church of S. which is void, as it is said, and for the Advowson whereof there is contention moved in our Court between us and *A*. (If between private persons) then (between *A*. and *B*.) untill it be discussed in the same Court; whether unto us or unto the aforesaid *A*. it pertaineth to present unto the Advowson of the same Church, &c.

Note, that the Defendant as well as the Plaintiff may sue out his Writ, if the Defendant do suppose that the Bishop will admit the Clark of the Plaintiff the suite depending, but as we said before, this Writ of *Ne admittas* lies not, unlesse the Plea be depending in Court, by *Quare impedit* or *Darreyn presentment*, and for that purpose there is a Writ in the Register, directed unto the chief Justice of the Common Bench, to certifie the King in the Chancery, whether there be any Plea depending before him and his companions by Writ between (such and such) and by this it seemed, that the *Ne admittas* should not be granted, before the King were certified in Chancery, that such a Plea of *Quare impedit*, or *Darreyn presentment*, were depending in the Common Bench. But at this time the course is otherwise, that the *Ne admittas* may be granted out of the Chancery directed unto the Bishop, that he shall not admit, &c. before that the King be certified in Chancery, that such Plea of *Quare impedit* or *Darreyn presentment* is depending in the Common Bench.

And if the Truth be that there be no such Plea depending in the common Bench, then the party greived may require the chiefe Justice to certifie the King in his Chancery, that no such plea is there depending, upon which the party greived shall have a Writ to avoid the *Ne admittas.*

If the Defendant or Defendants in this Action do appear, you must prepare your Declaration, wherein you must lay down your Title, which many times causeth the Declarations and pleadings to be very long in this Action, and therefore cannot be expected to be inserted here, as in other small ones.

In case after speciall pleadings, you come to an Issue, and having your Issue joyned, and your paper book made up, and that you would go to tryall, you must make your *Venire Facias,* which differs not from other *Venire Facias's,* but onely in these words, (of a Plea *Quare impedit*) and that made, signed, sealed, and returned, you must sue out your *Habeas Corpus,* and proceed with your Record, as in other.

When you have a verdict for the Plaintiff, and the *Postea* returned, and Judgment entred, you may then have a Writ to the Bishop, to admit your Clark, or to the Metropolitan, which is as thus, when the Recovery is had against the Bishop himselfe.

The King, *&c.* To the venerable Father in Christ *W. Bishop* of *Winchester,* greeting, Whereas *T. L* Knight in our Court, *&c.* hath recovered against you his presentation to the Vicaridge of *W.* Wee command you, that at the presentation of him the said *T.* to the aforesaid Vicaridge, you admit a fit person *&c.*

And if a man have his recovery against any othe then the Bishop, then the Writ that shall be mad unto the Bishop shall be in this wise;

Where

WHereas T. L. Knight, hath recovered againſt I. P. his preſentation, &c. We command you, that notwihſtanding the claime of the aforeſaid I. P. at the preſentation of the aforeſaid T. L. you admit a fit perſon, &c.

Note, that upon this VVrit, he ſhall have an *Alias* and a *Plures*, if the Biſhop do not execute the VVrit, and an Attachment againſt the Biſhop, if need be.

Come we now to Actions of waſte.

THIS Action lies, where Tenant for Terme of years, Tenant for Terme of life, Tenant for Terme of anothers life, Tenant in Dower, Tenant by the Courteſie of *England*, or Guardian in Chivalry, doth make waſte or Deſtruction upon the Land or Houſes, that is to ſay, pulleth down the Houſe, cutting down Timber, or ſuffereth the Houſe willingly to fall, or diggeth the ground, then he in the Reverſion ſhall have a VVrit for the waſte, and ſhall recover the place where the waſte was done, and trebble damages againſt him that ſo committed waſte.

But if a man cut downe Timber without licence, and therewith repaire old Houſes, that is held no waſte, but if hee therewith build new Houſes, then the cutting down of ſuch Timber is VVaſte alſo.

The cutting downe of under-wood, or VVillowes, which are no Timber, ſhall not be ſaid to be waſte; but where they grow in the ſight and ſhaddow of the Houſe.

M 3   There

There are both negligent and voluntary wastes, and these alike punishable, as where the Tenant or lessee, is bound by Law to keepe the Houses in good repaire, as they were, when hee came to them.

In this case, if he do not so, but suffer any part of it, by his negligence to grow ruinous, this is VVaste, for which the Lessor may sue the Lessee.

VVhere there is no Timber upon the Lands to make repaire, yet is it waste to suffer it to decay, for this, that the Tenant must procure Timber at his own charge.

Its waste where a man prostrates, abates, or breaks down any of the housing, either the whole or part, (that is) any of the principall VValls, or VValls of partition in Chambers, whether they be of stone or Mud.

VVhere by a violent tempest, &c. the House comes to be uncovered, it ought to be repaired by the Tenant in convenient time, otherwise it is waste, to suffer the House to be burnt by negligence, &c. is waste.

If the House be ruinous, when the Tenant first comes into it, and he pull it down and do not build it up againe, this is waste.

VVhere a man either takes away, pulls, or breaks down the VVainescots, Doores, VVindowes, Benches, or any other things that are inseparable incidents of the House, being set up and fastned by the Lessor or Lessee, or other, is waste.

What is said to be Waste in Trees or Woods.

WHere there is Oake or Ash which are held Timber in most Countrys, (and Elme in some Countries where Timber is scarce) whether young or old, above or under twenty years of age, to sell this, or to imploy it to build a new House, or a new Room, or any other purpose then to the repaire of the old House, or Housing which are on the Land, or were at the time of the Lease, &c. in decay by age or Tempest, is waste.

If a man fell Timber, although with an intent for Reparations, and if he after sell it, or imploy it to any other use, this is waste, and if after sale he buy it again, and then imploy it for Reparations, yet this hath been held to be waste.

VVhere a man fells Timber for Reparations and so imploys it, yet if it be done at such an unseasonable time, as that the Timber die in the root; this is waste.

To cut down a VVood, and after to suffer cattell to crop it when its newly felled, whereby it is killed, or to root and stub it up, this is waste.

To cut down Timber Trees for fire-boote, hedge-boote, &c. where there is enough of other boote, this is waste.

To cut down such Trees for fireing, as are fit for better use, being Timber, and onely hollow, and dry at the top, is said to be waste.

But if they be hollow, dry, and dead throughout, that they beare neither fruits nor leaves in Summer, if the Tenant cut down such Trees for fire-boote, it is no waste.

To cut down more for fire-boote, hedge-boot, and

M 4   House

house-boote, (to keep it as he found it) then is necessary, or to cut down green wood, when there is sufficient dry, and dead wood, is waste.

To cut down Fruit-Trees, Apple-Trees, or Pear-Trees, is waste, if they be growing in a Garden, although for Reparation, is waste.

Such Fruit-Trees although halfe broken by the winde or otherwise, if they do yet beare Fruite, or the young springs of them, that may beare fruite, if the Tenant cut them downe, or pull them up, it is waste.

Where a man ares up deepe Meadow, not plowed in mans memory, or grubs up wood by the roots, and turns it into arable, or on the contrary, turns arable into wood, its waste.

To open or digg new Quarries, for Coale, Stones Mettall, Gravell, Lyme, Clay, or the like, this, unless there be speciall words in the Lease to warrant it, is waste, although it be not waste for a man to dig forward in a Mine that was opened before.

Its no waste to dig the Land, for Gravell, Clay, &c. For necessary reparations, &c.

HAving gone thus far in shewing what is waste, let the Attorney be well advised he bring not an Action of waste, where the Lease or other writing, by which the Tenant holdeth or claimeth, have that clause in it (without impeachment of waste) in which case the Lessee can do no waste, &c.

For the unfolding of this clause (without impeachment of waste) observe that,

An impeachment of waste doth signifie a restraint from committing of waste, in Lands or Tenements, &c.

And this word (without) added to impeachment of waste, intimates a liberty to commit waste, and an

Estate

Eftate without any fuch reftraint.

Thofe and the like words inferted in the Deed, &c. are faid to be annexed to the Eftate, and they doe change the quality of the Eftate, and make the Tenant herein, in the nature of a Tenant in Taile, and it adds that priviledge thereunto, that they give the Leffee a Power and Intereft to make wafte, and to difpofe the things to his owne ufe, and here if the Leffor bring an Action of wafte, the Tenant may bar him with this claufe.

If it be not thofe very words, or of the like fenfe, they are not good, for if the words be, without impeachment of wafte by any Writ of Wafte, the words in this cafe are more tyed up, and are not fo large, they give not fuch a power to the Tenant, nor alter the property; they onely difcharge the Action, fo that the Land-Lords can bring no action againft the Tenant for the Wafte done.

The words (without impeachment of Wafte) muft be inferted in the fame Deed, whereby the Eftate is made, or another Deed made at the fame time, for if he make his Leafe without this claufe, and after willeth that the Leffee fhall hold without impeachment of wafte; its held, thofe words work nothing, either to difcharge the Action, or give an intereft.

If a man make a Leafe for life, and by his Deed grant that if any wafte be done, it fhall be redreffed by Neighbours, and not by Suite or Plea, yet an Action of Wafte will lye.

This priviledge gained by thofe words, where it is, may be loft, for it is annexed onely to privity of Eftate: And therefore if one that hath this priviledge annexed to his Eftate, agree to change his Eftate, the priviledge is gone; as where he that hath a Leafe for yeares, with this claufe in his Deed, accept

cept of a Deed of confirmation of his Estate without this clause.

The Processes incident to this Action are,

1. A Summons which is made by the Cursitor of the County, where the House or Land lies.

This Summons, if against a Tenant in Dower, is as followes,

THE Keepers of the Liberty of *England* ; *&c.* To the Sheriff of *L. &c.* If *A.D.* shall secure thee, *&c.* Then Summon by good Summoners *T. B.* which was the VVife of *C.* that she be before our Justices at *Westminster*, on the morrow after the holy *Trinity*, to shew wherefore she hath made waste, sale, and Destruction, in the Lands, Houses, Woods, and Gardens which shee holds in Dowry of the Inheritance of the aforesaid *A.* in *N.* to the disinheriting of him the said *A. &c.*

Neither in this Writ nor in a Writ of Waste against a Guardian, a man shall not be tyed to rehearse the Statute which gives a Writ of Waste, for that very reason, that they were actionable before the Statute.

If the Writ be against Tenant for Terme of life, or of yeers, then it goes in this form,

THE Keepers, *&c.* if *A. &c.* Wherefore by the Common Councell of the Common-wealth of *England*, It is provided that it shall not be lawfull, for any to make Waste, sale, or destruction, in Lands, Houses, Woods, or Gardens; the said *B.* of Lands, Houses, and Gardens in *L.* which the aforesaid *A.* demised unto her, *&c.* hath made waste, *&c.*

This Writ being returnable on the day of three weekes after Saint *Michael*, the Defendant may if he please, Essoyn upon that return, which if he do, then

the

the Plaintiff may adjourne it unto the morrow after St. *Martin*, which if so, then the next Proceſs is a *Pone*, which is to be made by the Philizer of the County, and may be made returnable in eight dayes of Saint *Hillary*.

Vpon the returne of this *Pone*, and filing it with the Philizer, he maketh out a *Diſtringas* which you may have returnable in eight dayes of the Purification of the bleſſed Virgin *Mary*, as we ſhewed before in the caſe of Partition, *&c.* And upon that *Diſtringas* you may have an Amerciament, in caſe the Defendant appeare not; and then an *Alias* and *Plures* *Diſtringas*, and further Amerciaments. And as I told you before in other Actions, in caſe the Defendant Eſſoyn not upon the Summons, he may upon the *Pone*. In caſe the Defendant appear, and that you declare, your form is as follows; in caſe it be againſt Tenant for years,

Wilt. ß.

A. *A.* Knight and Baronet, was ſummoned to anſwer *W. Earle* of *S.* of a Plea wherefore, whereas by the Common Councell of the Common-wealth of *England*, it is provided, that it ſhall not be lawfull for any to make waſte, ſale, or deſtruction of Lands, Houſes, Woods, or Gardens, to him demiſed for Terme of life or yeares, he the ſaid *A.* of Houſes in *D.* which he held for terme of yeares, by the demiſe of the aforeſaid Earle, hath made Waſte, Sale, and deſtruction, to the diſinheritance of him the ſaid *Earle*, and againſt the forme of the proviſion aforeſaid, *&c.* and whereupon the ſame *Earle* by *E. H.* his Attorney ſayes, that whereas he himſelfe was ſeized of one Meſſuage with the Appurtenances called *B.* Farme Houſe in D. aforeſaid in his Demeſne as of Fee, and being ſo thereof ſeized, (ſuch a day and year)

yeare) at D. aforesaid, did demise the messuage a-
foresaid, with the appurtenances, (amongst other
things) to the aforesaid *Anthony*, to have and to hold
to him the said A. and to his Assignes, from the
Feast of St. *Michael* the Arch-Angell then last past,
unto the end and Terme of twelve yeares from
thence next following, fully to be compleat and ended; by virtue of which demise, the Aforesaid A. into
that Messuage with the Appurtenances did enter, and
was thereof possessed, and he being thereof possessed,
the same A. made waste, sale, and destruction in
the messuage aforesaid with the Appurtenances, of
Houses, that is to say, by throwing down two Barnes,
the price of either of them twenty pounds, parcell
of the messuage aforesaid above demised, and two
Houses called out-Houses, the price of each of them
eight pounds, in like manner parcell of the Messuage aforesaid, above, as aforesaid demised, and the
Timber of the same Barnes and Houses so thrown
down, taking, burning, and selling to the disinheri-
tance of him the said *Earle*, and against the form of
the provision aforesaid, whereupon he saith that he is
damnified, and hath damage to the value of one hundred and fifty pounds, and thereupon he brings his
suite, *&c.*

And the aforesaid A. by I. D. his Attorney, comes
and defends the force and injury when, *&c.* and
whatsoever, *&c.* And by protestation that the aforesaid two Barnes, and two out-Houses, were not parcell of the messuage aforesaid, in him the said A. by
the aforesaid *Earle*, in forme aforesaid demised; by
protestation also, that the same Barnes or out-Houses
were not of so much value as the said Earle by his
Declaration aforesaid, hath above supposed, for Plea
he saith, that he hath made no waste, sale, or destruction in the Messuage aforesaid, as the aforesaid *Earle*
hath

bath above against him declared, and of this he puts himselfe upon the Country, and the aforesaid *Earle* in like manner. Therefore command is given to the Sherif that he cause to come there in eight dayes after the purification of the blessed *Virgin Mary*, twelve, *&c.* By whom, *&c.* And who neither, *&c.* To recognize, *&c.* Because as well, *&c.*

Thus you have a Declaration in waste, and a Plea pleaded to it, and issue joyned, and this is against Tenant for Terme of yeares; now the Declarations in this action vary, as to the several persons that bring the Action, and the severall persons against whom it is brought.

As where it is brought by the Heire in tail, against Tenant for life.

Where it is against Tenant in Dower, as before you saw in the Summons.

Also where the Purchaser of the Reversion brings it against Tenant for years.

Also it may be brought after a Fine levied; in all which cases the Declaration must vary according to the cause, in all which cases, as also in divers other proceedings of other natures, I refer you to a Book printed in *Easter* Term last, intituled, Declarations and Pleadings in English, Collected by *Richard Brownlow* Esq. which would swell this small Tract beyond its intended bignesse.

Now, as the Declarations are various, so are the Pleas incident to them, for they may be either Generall or Special.

The generall Plea is, No waste made, *&c.*

The speciall Pleas are many, either in way of Justification, or excuse, as the case is.

It is a good Plea, if the waste be laid, to be in not repairing, *&c.* That it was repaired before the Action brought, and this must be pleaded specially.

But

But to plead it was repaired after the action brought, it is no good Plea.

It is a good Plea to any waste, that the Leſſor gave Authority to do it.

It is no good Plea to ſay, that the Plaintiff did covenant to deliver Timber from off the Land, to do it, and refuſeth, for the Defendant in this caſe may take it.

It is a good Plea to ſay, the Houſe or Trees were burnt or ſpoyled, by fire, water, or winde, or that the ruine of them was cauſed by ſome extraordinary Act of God.

It is a good Plea to ſay, that the Houſe fell before the Leaſe, or that it was ſo extraordinary ruinous, and the Timber ſo rotten, as that it would not bear repairing.

It is a good Plea to ſay, that the leaſe is ſurrendred to the Leſſor, and he hath accepted it.

It is a good Plea that the Plaintiff hath entred upon the Land, and before ſuch his entry, there was no waſte committed.

It is a good Plea to plead that the Plaintiff hath granted away his Eſtate, and before the grant there was no waſte committed.

If the Plaintiff by good words do effectually releaſe the waſte, this is a good Plea.

VVhere the Leaſe was made without impeachment of waſte, it is a good Plea on the part of the Defendant.

It is no good Plea in this action for cutting down Timber, or pulling down the houſe, that the Leſſor took away the Timber or materialls, &c.

It is no good Plea, that the Leſſor hath a covenant from the Leſſee not to do waſte.

It is no good Plea for the tenant in an action of waſt for cutting of timber, to ſay, that he cut it and keeps it it till there shall be need, nor to say he cut it generally for necessary reparations, unlesse he say withall that he imployed it to that purpose.

And yet it were but reason it should be justified to cut it a little before it be used, for the drying of it and making of it otherwise usefull, when an occasion of use is apparantly at hand.

It is a good Plea for the Defendant to say, that he cut it to make posts for inclosures, if he can withall prescribe that there have been alwayes such inclosures there.

But these and many other, may now ?at the Election of the Defendant be omitted, and by the late Act of 22. *Octob.* 1650. he may plead not guilty, or some such other generall issue may be pleaded, and the speciall matter may be given in Evidence.

Upon these or any other issue joyned, and that you intend to go to tryall, the directions that were given before in Partition, Dower, &c. will guide you, both for the making your *Venire Facias, Habeas Corpora*, and *Record*, and likewise for your tryall and return of your *Postea*, and entring of Judgement.

In this Action, as before you have heard, your judgment is, that the Plaintiff shall recover the place wasted and his trebble damages.

In case the Defendant pleads not, but let it go by default or confesseth the Action, then a Writ of inquiry is awarded, and upon that the Sheriff is to inquire by the Oath of twelve Jurors, what damage the Plaintiff hath sustained, which he returns in an Inquisition, and then the party hath Judgment to recover the trebble of it, and then hath he as in a Verdict after judgment entred, a Writ of seizin awarded, which is directed to the Sheriff of the County, where the House or lands lye, to give possession to the Plaintiff of the place or places wasted, &c.

War-

Warrantia Carta *comes next to be treated of.*

WArrentia Carta is a Writ that lies for him that is enfeoffed with Warranty, and is afterwards impleaded in an Affize, or other Action, in which he cannot Vouch, then he may have this Writ againft the Feoffor, or his Heire, to compell them to warrant the faid unto them.

The Proceffe in this Action are Summons in the firft place, which is as follows,

The Summons *in* Warrantia Carta.

THE Keepers of the Liberty of *England*, *&c.* Command A. that juftly, *&c.* he warrant to B. one Meffuage with the appurtenances in D. which holdeth and claimeth to hold of him, and whereof he hath his Deed as he faith ; and unleffe, *&c.* Or otherwife that juftly, *&c.* he warrant to B. the Mannor of N. with the appurtenances, and the Advowfon of the Church of N. which he holdeth, *&c.* And whereof he hath his Deed; or the Deeds of D. his Father or Mother, or any other of his Anceftors, whofe Heire he is as he faith, *&c.*

And although this Writ fuppofeth that he holdeth of the Defendant ; yet is it not materiall whether he holdeth of him or no.

And alfo if the Plaintiff hold by Homage *Avaftrell* of the Defendant any Land, and is impleaded, and hath not any Deed of it, yet he fhall have this Writ of *warrantia Carta* againft the Defendant, and the Writ will fay, (whereof he hath his Deed) and yet he hath not the Deed to fhew, but onely holdeth by

Homage

Homage Anceſtrel, which imployes a Warranty, and for this in this caſe, theſe words (whereof he hath his Deed) is not materiall.

If a man leaſe Land for Terme of life, rendring a certaine Rent, or make a Gift in taile, rendring Rent without Deed, and after the Leſſee, or Donee is impleaded, in ſuch Action where he cannot vouch then he ſhall have this Writ of *warrantia Carta*, againſt the Leſſor or Donor, or his Heire, who hath the Reverſion; for this Reverſion and Rent reſerved makes a Warranty in Law, by the Statute of Bigamis the laſt Chapter, although he had not any Deed of it.

If a man give Land to another in Fee, by Deed, by theſe words, (I have given and granted, &c.) In this caſe, he ſhall be held to warranty of this Land to the Feoffee, by theſe words, and if the Feoffee be impleaded, he ſhall have a Writ of *warrantia Carta* againſt the Feoffor by theſe words, (I have given and granted, &c.) but not againſt his Heir, for the Heir ſhall not be bound unto Warranty by the Deed of the Father, unleſſe he oblige himſelfe and his Heirs to warranty, &c. by expreſſe words in the Deed, as to ſay (I and my Heirs all the aforeſaid Lands, &c. will warrant, &c.)

Note, that he ſhall not have this Action of *warrantia Carta* againſt the Feoffee, or againſt him againſt whom he hath Warranty, if he be impleaded in any action wherein he may vouch him, for then he ought to vouch him to Warranty, and if he will not vouch him in the Action, he ſhall not afterwards have a Writ of *warrantia Carta*.

Note, that the Vouchee is either to defend the Right againſt the Demandant, or to yeeld him other Lands. &c. in value, and extendeth to Lands, &c. of an Eſtate of Free-hold or inheritance, and not to

N   any

any Chattell, reall, personall, or mixt, saving onely in case of a Wardship granted with Warranty; for in the other cases concerning Chattells, &c. the Voucher shall have an Action of Covenant, if he hath a Deed: And an Action of the case, or an Action of deceipt, if it be by word of mouth, &c.

The Processe whereby the Voucher is called, is a Summons *Ad Warrantizandum*, and whereupon if the Sheriff returne that the Vouchee is summoned, and he maketh default, then there is awarded a *Magnum Cape ad Valentiam*, &c. When if he make default again, then Judgment is given against the Tenant, and he to have over in value against the Vouchee; but if the Sheriff return that he hath nothing, then after a Writ of *Alias* and *Plures*, a Writ of *Sequuntur sub periculo suo* is awarded, &c. And the Demandant shall not have Judgement to recover in value, &c. because the Vouchee was never awarded.

In the case of Homage *Ancestrell*, which is a special Warranty in Law, and Lands that the Lord hath generally at the time of the Voucher, shall be liable to Execution in value, where he hath them by discent or purchase: But in the case of an expresse Warranty, the Heire shall be charged but onely for such Lands as he had by discent from the Ancestor, which creates the Warranty.

Note, the Lands of the Vouchee shall be liable to warranty, that the Vouchee hath at the time of the Voucher, for that the Voucher is in liew of an Action, and in a *Warrantia Carta*, the Land which the Defendant hath at the time of the Writ brought, shall be liable to the warranty.

If a man give Lands in Fee with warranty, and bindes certaine Lands especially to warranty, the person of the Feoffer is hereby bound, and not the Land, unlesse

unlesse he had it at the time of the Voucher.

A man may bring his Writ of warranty of Charters, &c. in what County he will, if the Deed beare not Date at a certaine place or County, for then he ought to bring the VVrit where the Deed beares Date.

But if a man bring a VVrit of *Warrantia Carta*, by reason of Homage *Anceſtrell*, &c. Then he ought to bring the writ in the County where the Land lies.

The Summons in this VVrit we have shewed you before, upon which VVrit as in the caſe of waſte, the Defendant may eſſoyn, and the Plaintiff adjourn; and for want of an Adjournment of the Plaintiff, the Defendant may enter a Non-ſuit againſt the Plaintiff, provided there were a *Ne recipiatur* firſt entred with the Clarke of the Eſſoynes, upon the day of Exception; and then in that caſe the Plaintiff is put to begin again.

After the Summons comes a *Pone*, and then a *Diſtringas*, and if the Defendant appeare not, an *Alias Diſtringas* ſetting Iſſues, &c. And ſo Diſtreſſes in *Infinitum*, till there be appearance given.

In caſe the Defendant do appear, then you may declare as in the form following;

The Declaration in Warrantia Carta.

Licolne, ſſ.

E. A. was ſummoned to anſwer H. B. Clark, of a Plea; that he warrant to him three Meſſuages, &c. with the appurtenances in C. which he holdeth, and claimeth to hold of him, and whereupon he hath his Deed, &c. and whereupon the ſaid H. by *J. W.* his Attorney, ſaith, that whereas a certaine Fine was

levied

levied in the Court of the Keepers, &c. here, that is
to say, at *Westminster*, from the day of Saint Hillary
in fifteen dayes (such a yeare before O. S. *John* and
others, naming them) then Justices of the Common
Bench here, that is to say, at *Westminster* aforesaid,
and other faithfull persons then being present between him the said H. B. Plaintiff and the aforesaid
E. and one *Joane* then his Wife, and R. H. Deforci-
ents of the said three Messuages, &c. with the appurtenances, whereof the Plea of Covenant was summoned between them in the same Court, that is to say,
that the aforesaid E. I. and R. did acknowledge the
aforesaid Tenements, with the Appurtenances to be
right of him the said H. B. as those which the said
H. B. had of the gift of the aforesaid E. I. and R.
and the same remised and quite claimed, from
them the said E. I. and R. and their Heires, to the
aforesaid H. B. and his Heires for ever, and moreover the said E. granted for himselfe and his Heirs,
that they would warrant the aforesaid H. and his
Heirs, the aforesaid Tenements, with the appurtenances against all men for ever. By virtue of which fine
the said H. B. was seized of the Tenements aforesaid
with the appurtenances in his Demesne as of Fee,
and he the said H. B. so being thereof seized, one I. D.
arrayed against him the said H. a certaine assize of
novell disseisin of the Tenements aforesaid with the
appurtenances, before P. W. one of the Justices of the
Common Bench, and R. C. one other, &c. Justices
assigned to take the assises in the County of I. aforesaid, which said Assise depending, he the said H.
often required the aforesaid E. that he would warrant to him the Tenements aforesaid with the appurtenances, yet the said E. hitherto hath denied to warrant to the said H. the Tenements, aforesaid with
the

the Appurtenances, and yet doth deny. Whereupon he faith he is damnified, and hath damage to the value of five hundred pounds, and thereupon he brings his suite, &c.

The Defendant acknowledgeth the Action.

ANd the aforesaid E. by J.E. his Attorney comes &c and saith, that he cannot deny the aforesaid action of the said H. neither but that the writing aforesaid is the deed of him the said E. nor but that he did give and grant by that writing to the said H. and his Heires, the tenements aforesaid with the appurtenances, neither, but that he by that writing is held to warrant to the said H. the Tenements aforesaid with the appurtenances in the forme in the which the said H. hath above declared against him : therefore it is considered of, that the said E. shall warrant to the said H. the tenements aforesaid with the appurtenances for the place and time, and nothing of being in mercy of him the said H. because he came the first day by summons, &c.

Here you have a Declaration and judgment by confession.

NOte, if a man recover his Warranty in *Warrantia Carta*, and after he is impleaded in an action in which he cannot vouch as by assise, or by *Scire facias* upon a fine, now it seemes that he ought to have notice to him against whom he had received his warranty of his action; and to pray him to shew what plea he will plead to defend the Land.

NOte, that a man may bring a Writ of *Warrantia Carta* at the Common Law, for warranty made of Lands holden in ancient Demesne.

H 2.

Having gone through Warrantia Carta, *we come now to* Audita Querela.

What the Writ is.

Audita *Querela* is a VVrit, and lyeth where one is bound in a Statute Merchant, Statute Staple, or Recognizance, or where Judgement is given against him for Debt, and his body in Execution thereupon, then if he have a release, or other matter sufficient to be discharged of Execution, and hath no day in Court there to plead it, then he shall have this VVrit against him that hath so recovered, or against his Executors.

Against whom, and for whom this VVrit is brought.

THis VVrit lieth for the Party himselfe against whom the Judgement is had, by whom the Statute is made, or his Heire, Executor, or Administrator, upon whom the charge is come, or comming. Sometimes it is to be had against the Prosecutor himselfe, and sometimes against him and others that ought to bear a part of the burthen with him.

It lies against Ter-Tenant, without naming him Party, or Privy.

VVherefore this remedy is given, there must be these three things in the case;

1. There must be a charge or burthen come, or comming upon him that is to have it.

2. It must be such a charge, &c. as by Law, hee ought to be discharged of, in part or in whole.

3. It is such a case as where he hath no other remedy for his reliefe.

These

These following Cases will cleare these particulars.

If a Judgement, or Judgement and Execution be had against one, and the Plaintiff release him of the Debt in fact, or that he be released of it all, or part of it in law, and yet he sueth out Execution.

If a Judgement be had against me and another, and one of us be taken in Execution, and after are released of the Debt, or discharged of the Execution by the party himselfe, the other may take advantage of this.

If Judgement be against two trespassors, and one taken, and the damage satisfied by him.

The like case if a Judgement be against two or more, upon one bond, and Execution is done upon, and satisfaction made by one of them.

If Executors sue for, and recover a Debt, and after the Testament is revoked, in this case, the Party that hath paid the money, may get the same certified by the Bishop and then he shall have his remedy against the Executors.

If the Conusor after Execution tender the money due upon the Statute to the conusee, and he refuse it, or if part of it were paid at the day, and he tender the rest in court, and yet the conusee go on to extend it, in these cases the Party grieved may have this remedy.

If the Statute were delivered to a stranger to keep till certaine conditions were performed, and he doth deliver it to the conusee, or he doth get it by fraud from him, before the condition be performed, in this case he shall be relieved by this Writ.

If an Infant enter into a Statute, he may avoide it whilst hee is in his *Minority*, by this Writ, and the course is this: In case he be in prison, this Writ may be sued out by some of his Friends to the Justices,

who

who thereupon command the Sheriff to bring the Infant into Court to be seen; and if the Judges judg him to be within age, after processe sent to the Conusee, they wil discharge him. But if one that hath been an Infant, be sued upon it, after he is of full age, this Writ doth not lie for him.

If divers be bound by one specialty [Conjunctim and divisim] and the Obligee get Judgment and Execution against one of them, and after sue the Especialty against the other, he shall have this Writ for his reliefe.

If in the *Interim* betwixt Verdict and Judgement, the parties have put themselves into Arbitrement for the Suit, or the Defendant get a Release from the Plaintiff, and yet the Plaintiff doth proceed, the Defendant may have this Action; but where these cases are put, its to be conceived before the Writ brought the judgement is given.

Where a man sues for a thing, for which he had formerly judgement and Execution, there this Writ lies.

Where a man and his Heires are bound by any Bond, or bill, &c. and the Obligee sue it, and recover against the Heirs, and after sue the Executors for the same cause; or on the other side after recovery had against the Executors, he sue the Heirs, here the Heir or Executor so sued may have this remedy, for that he cannot plead it in Bar.

Where a Lessee covenants for him and his Assignes, to repair Houses, or to do any other thing chargeable upon him, after assignment of his Estate, and he assign his Estate, and after the Lessor, who may sue either of them, sue and recover against one of them; in this case, if after he sue the other for the same cause, he may have this remedy.

The Proceedings in this Action are as follow,

Where

Where before Execution this Writ is brought by the Party grieved himselfe, or by his Heirs, or Executors, he surmising good cause for this Writ, must give good baile to prosecute, and stand to the Judgement of the Court, upon which he may have a *Superfedeas*, to stay Execution; but when the Party is in prison, then it seems there is no Baile put in, till the Conusee or Obligee answer in the *Audita querela*.

Note, that after Execution executed, no *Superfedeas* doth lie.

The Processe before Execution are a *Venire facias*, and an *Alias*, &c. And then if he come not in, the use hath been that upon motion, the party in prison may be discharged.

After those Processe a *Distringas* and upon default after appearance, and a plea pleaded, a *Distringas ad audiendum judicium*, for by such default Judgement shall be given against him, and after Execution the Processe is a *Scire facias*, when the Party is in Prison upon a *Capias ad satisfaciend.*

Where a man puts in Baile in this Action, he shall not be discharged of this Baile, but must continue till the Suit by the *Audita Querela* be determined, for albeit the Party do not prosecute after the appearance of the Defendant, yet he must continue in prison, or stand upon his Baile.

If a man be Non-suited in one *Audita querela*, yet he may have another, but he shall have no *Superfedeas* in the second as he had in the first.

Audita Querela upon the Statute of Usury.

IT was commanded to the Sheriff &c. whereas out of the grievous complaint of T.B. of, &c. R.B. of, &c. And A. B. of, &c. it was shewed to the Keepers, &c. Complaining, that whereas in the Statute in the Parliament held, &c. (reciting the Statute of Usury) as by the said Statute more fully appeareth And whereas one N. W. such a day and year at C. did lend unto one R.B. ninety pounds, for one year then next following, and that in consideration thereof, it was then and there agreed, between him the said N.W. and the aforesaid R. B. that the said N. W. should have by way of gaine and profit for deferring and giving day of payment of the aforesaid ninety pounds for the time aforesaid, ten pounds, to be paid to the said N. W. together with the aforesaid ninety pounds, and also eighteen yards of black Frizes, of the price of every yard sixteen pence, which said R. B. afterwards, that is to say, such a day and yeare at C. aforesaid, made his Testament, and appointed and ordained *Agnes*, the wife of the aforesaid A. A. and one T. *Bartram*, L. B. and I. B. his Children, Executors of his Testament aforesaid, and the same A. A. and one W. L. Gentlemen, Guardians of the aforesaid T. B. Sonne and Heire apparant of the said R. B. during the minority of the aforesaid T. B. and afterwards there dyed, after whose death, that is to say, (such a day and yeare, at C. aforesaid) it was agreed between him the said N. W. and the same A. A. and W. L. that the aforesaid N. W. should defer and give day of payment of the aforesaid ninety pounds, of the principall Debt, and of the aforesaid ten pounds for the Use aforesaid, from the end of the aforesaid yeare, for

the

the payment thereof as aforesaid, before agreed, untill Wednesday next after the Feast of *Easter* then next following, and that the said A. A. and *W. L.* or one of them would pay to the said *N. W.* six pounds thirteen shillings and four pence for gaine and use, for deferring and giving day of payment of the same ninety pounds of principall Debt aforesaid, and ten pounds for the first use aforesaid, and also that A. A. and *W. L.* and the aforesaid *T. B.* and *R. B.* should by Recognizance acknowledge before *R. M.* then one of the Justices, &c. themselves to owe to the aforesaid *N. W.* foure hundred pounds, for the secure payment of the aforesaid ninety pounds of principall Debt aforesaid, and ten pounds for the first use aforesaid, and also of the aforesaid six pounds thirteene shillings and foure pence for the said second usury aforesaid, on the aforesaid Wednesday next, after the Feast of *Easter*, betweene the hours of one and foure in the afternoone of the same day, which said severall sums in the whole, doe amount unto one hundred six pounds thirteene shillings and foure pence, whereupon the said *T. B. W. L. R. B.* and *A. A.* (such a day and yeare aforesaid) at *C.* aforesaid, before the aforesaid *R. M.* did acknowledge themselves to owe to the aforesaid *N. W.* the aforesaid foure hundred pounds for the secure payment of the aforesaid one hundred six pounds, thirteene shillings and fourepence, on the aforesaid Wednesday next after the aforesaid Feast of *Easter*, according to the forme, and effect of the agreement aforesaid, and so that recognizance and forme aforesaid acknowledged for the payment of the said ninety pounds of principall debt aforesaid, and the aforesaid sixteene pounds, thirteen shillings and four pence for the use aforesaid, exceeding the rates of ten pounds for a hundred pounds

pounds by the yeare, by virtue of the Statute aforesaid, published in the Parliament holden, &c. is void
in the Law; as the said T. B. R. B. and A. A.
by wayes and meanes convenient, are ready to make
appear. Notwithstanding which the aforesaid N. W.
now lately hath unjustly prosecuted Execution of
the aforesaid foure hundred pounds, by reason of the
Recognizance aforesaid in forme aforesaid acknowledged against them the said T. B. R. B. and A. A. to
the great damage and grievance of them the said T. B.
R. B. and A. A. whereupon the said T. B. R. B. and
A. A. to the Keepers, &c. have supplicated to provide
for them a fit remedy in this behalfe; the said Keepers, being willing to do herein that which is just,
and to exhibit full and speedy Justice therein to the
said T. B. R. B. and A. A. have commanded the
Justices here, that hearing the complaint of them the
said T. B. R. B. and A. A. and calling before them
the parties aforesaid in this behalfe to be called, and
hearing their reasons thereof, they cause due and
speedy accomplishment of Justice to be done to them
the said T. B. R. B. and A. A. as of right, and according to the Law and Custome of the Common
Wealth of *England*, ought to be done, and to that
purpose, that they should cause to come here at this
day, that is to say (such a returne) the aforesaid N.
W. to answer in and upon the premisses, and further
to do that which the Justices here shall think convenient, and consider of, and now here at this day (naming the return) came as well the aforesaid T. B.
R. B. and A. A. by W. B. their Attorney, as the aforesaid N W. by L. C. his Attorney, and hereupon the
said T. B. R. B. and A. A. say that the aforesaid N. W.
(such a day and yeare) lent unto one R. B. ninety
pounds for one yeare then next following, and that
in consideration thereof, it was then and there a-
greed

agreed between him the said N. W. and the aforesaid T. that the said N. W. should have in gaine and
profit, &c. and so go on as before in the Writ, untill
you come to void in the Law. And this he is ready to
aver, whereupon he prayes judgment, and that the
aforesaid N. W. may be barred from having his Execution aforesaid, by virtue of the Recognizance and
judgement thereupon in Court here had, and that the
said T. B. and A. B. may be discharged thereof,
&c.

And hereupon the said N. W. prayeth liberty to
plead, &c.

NOte, that if a man enter into a Statute or Recognizance, which either is defective in it selfe, or
is avoydable by some Law, or because the Contract
is usurious, as in the Declaration before specified;
or that there be a defeazance upon it, which is kept
from the Conusor, or that the Statute is delivered
up by the Conusee (which is a release in Law) and
the Conusee get it againe, and the Conusee doth go
on in the Execution of it. In all these cases, the Party grieved may have this remedy and Writ for his reliefe.

If the Statute were made through hard imprisonment of the Conusor, he may have this Writ, &c.

NOte, I. W. brought an *Audita querela*, upon the
Statute of Usury, to be relieved in making void
a judgement given upon a Bond, where he hath pleaded that it was not his Deed, and it was disallowed,
and judgement thereupon as followeth;

AND hereupon the Premises being seen, and by
the Justices here more fully understood; it seemed to the same Justices here that the aforesaid Writ
of

of hearing the complaint, and the matter in the same contained, was insufficient in Law to bar the said R. from having his Execution aforesaid, by reason of the Recognizance aforesaid: Therefore it is considered of, that the aforesaid *J. W.* take nothing by his Writ of hearing the complaint, that the aforesaid R. may prosecute for the Execution, if, &c.

If a man sue an *Audita Querela* upon a Release, and afterwards he is Non-suit, he shall not have an *Audita Querela* upon new matter, and yet the Law seems contrary to this, where it says, he shall not delay Execution upon a new *Audita Querela.*

If the Conusor after Execution tender the money due upon the Statute to the Conusee, and he refuse it, or if part of it were paid at the day, and he tender the rest in Court, and yet the Conusee go on to extend it, in these cases the Party grieved may have this remedy.

The Process, as we told you in *Audita Querela*, were *Venire facias, Distringas, Alias* and *Plures Distringas*; only take this further, that if the Sheriff return, that he hath nothing &c. Or that he cannot be found, &c. Then he shall have a *Capias* against the Defendant.

Curia Claudenda. *This is a Writ which lies at Common Law, and is for reparation of Fences and Hedges, Mounds, &c.*

THis Writ lyes, where a man ought to inclose his Soyl or Land from his Neighbours, and will not doe this, then he may have this Writ, and it may be sued before the Sheriff in his County Court,

or

or in the Court of Common Bench. If the Writ be before the Sheriff, then it runs thus,

THe Keepers, &c. To the Sheriff, &c. That justly &c. he close his field in N. which is open to the nocument of the Free-hold of B. in the same Towne, or in another Village, which he ought, and was wont to inclose, as the said B. sayes, and as he is reasonably to shew that he ought to inclose it, &c.

If in the Common Bench, then the Writ is thus,

THe Keepers, &c. Command A. that justly. &c. he close his field in N. which is open to the Nocument of the Free-hold of B. in N. aforesaid, which he ought, and was wont to inclose, and unlesse, &c.

This Writ may be removed out of the County, at the Suit of the Plaintiff, without cause.

But if the Defendant will remove it, he ought to shew cause in the Writ.

And in the Writ to remove it by the Defendant, shall be this clause, (let Execution of this Writ be made, &c. if the cause be true, otherwise not.)

This Writ lies not, unlesse against him who hath the Close next adjoyning unto the Land of the Plaintiff, and lies not, unlesse for him who hath an Estate of free-hold in the Land, for Tenant for Term of years shall not have this Writ.

If a man have a Common in a great waste, to him and his Heirs, or for Terme of life, and he who hath the Land adjoyning to this waste, who ought to inclose betwixt the waste and his Land, will not make his Inclosure, yet the Commoner shall not have this Action for the Damage which he hath sustained, &c. Although the Common may distraine the Beasts;

Damage

Damage feafant to the Land which is his Common. For the Writ fuppofes to the Nocument of the Free-hold of the Plaintiff, which proveth that the Plaintiff ought to have the Land adjoyning, if he will have this action.

The Proceffes in this action is Summons, Attachment, and Diftreffe, *&c.*

The view lies in this Writ.

If the Defendant appeare, and afterwards make default, he fhall have a *Diftringas* in lieu of the Petite *Cape*, &c. and if he make default at the day of the Returne of this Writ, he fhall have a Writ to inquire of damages, and alfo a Writ to diftrain to the Reparations.

It the Party appear, and that you come to declare, take thefe obfervations.

IN your Declaration you ought to fhew the certainty of the Land which the Plaintiff hath there adjoyning unto the Defendants Land, and the certainty of the Land which the Defendant hath there adjoyning, who ought to inclofe, and then you ought to alledge prefcription to inclofe.

Parco Fracto, or breaking the pound comes next to be handled.

THIS Writ lies, where a man diftrained the Beafts of another man doing hurt in his Land, or for Rent or Service behind, and fends them into the Common Pound, or into any other Pound or place, which may be called a lawfull pound, and he which hath the property of the beafts, or another

ther perfon take the Beafts out of the pound, and dri-
veth them to a place where he pleafeth; In this cafe,
he that diftrains for Damage done unto him, or for
Rent or Services behind, may have this Writ; wherein he fhall have Judgement to recover Damages for
it, and to diftrain the Catteli again wherefoever he
fhall find them.

For this caufe alfo is the party offending punifh-
able in a Court Leet.

If a man command his fervant to diftrain for Rent
or fervices arrear, and the fervant diftrain the Beafts
and put them in pound, &c. and a ftranger take
them out of the Pound; in this cafe the Mafter, and
not the fervant fhall have an Action of *Parco Fracto,*
for it is the Pound of the Mafter.

If a man diftrain for Rent or Services, or for Damage feafant, and put the Beafts in the Soile, or in
the Clofe of his find by his Licenfe, and he which
owes the Beafts takes them out of the Clofe; here
he which diftraines fhall have this Action, and not
he who owed the Clofe, for he which owed the clofe
may have his Action, wherefore he brake his Clofe,
&c. For it is not his Pound, but the Pound of him
that diftraineth, &c. The forme of the Writ is thus,

THe Keepers. &c. to the Sheriff of *Lincon.* greeting, if A. &c. Then put, &c. B. to fhew, wherefore whereas he the faid A. in his damage at N. certaine Cattell, or fo, the Cattell of the aforefaid B. had
took, and them according to the Law and Cuftome
of the Common-wealth of *England,* had there impounded : The fame B. the aforefaid pound by Force
and Armes brake, and the Cattell aforefaid he tooke
and led away, and other harms to him he did to the
great Damage, &c.

Note here, this Writ is by Force and Armes, and it
is not put in the Writ what manner of Beafts they

O   were

were, nor what number, nor to whom the property of the Beasts are, unlesse at the pleasure of the Plaintiff.

Where a man commands his servant to distraine for Rent or Services, or for damage-feasant, then the Writ is thus,

TO shew wherefore whereas he the said A. in this damage of N. by B. his servant, hath caused a certaine Bull, or Certaine Cattell, to be taken and the same B. the said Bull or Cattell according to the Law and Custome of the Common-wealth of *England* had there impounded : the aforesaid C. that pound by force and Armes did break, &c.

Where a man distrains for an Amerciament in a hundred; and impounds the Beasts, and the other Party takes them out, the VVrit shall be thus,

WHereas the said A. by B. and C. his Bayliff of the hundred of N. certaine young Cattell of him the said F. at S. within the precinct of the Hundred aforesaid, for a certaine Amerciament, to which he the said F. was amerced in the same Hundred, to the use of the aforesaid A. to be levied, had caused to be taken, and the same B. and C. the same young Cattell, &c.

Here in this VVrit it ought to be shewed, that the property of the Beasts were in him who was amercied for that, that he cannot distrain a Strangers Cattell for this Amerciament.

But for Rent or Services arreare. it is otherwise, for there the party to whom those Rents or Services were arrear, may distrain what Cattell he finds upon the Ground, levant and couchant.

This VVrit lies. albeit the impounding be unlawfull, as where the Party that is distrained for Damage

feasant

feasant do offer sufficient amends after taking, and before the impounding, and the Party so distraining doth refuse it.

The like case of one that hath a Replevin, or other coloured Authority (not good in Law) by virtue whereof he gets out the Cattell.

VVhere a man hath a good Authority, and breaks the Pound before he demand the Cattell of the Keepers of the Pound, and he do interrupt him in the taking of them, in all these Cases the Party grieved may have this VVrit for his remedy.

The Processes in this Action after the Summons, are Attachment and distresse infinite.

Rescues *we come now to treat of, and the rather for that it hath some relation to what we spake formerly of.*

THE word *Rescues* is two wayes applyable, either to persons or things.

To Persons, and that is, when a man is arrested, and he himselfe, or another in his behalfe, doth rescue him.

The other relates to things, and of that we now treat, as having affinity to that of [*Parco Fratto*] immediately before spoken of.

This is a VVrit lying, where one or his servant doth distrain for Rent services, or Damage-feasant, or for any other cause, and being about to impound the Distresse, another taketh it away from him, and will not suffer him to impound it; in this case the Party hurt or grieved may have this VVrit for his reliefe against him that made the rescue, and shall recover Damages for it.

VVhere a man distrains Cattell, and in driving

them

them to the Pound, they get into the Owners House, and he doth withold them from the distraining, and he will not suffer him to drive them to the Pound, this is a Rescous, for which the Action lies.

It a man be comming to distrain, and the Owner drive away the Cattel, and he that is about to distran doth follow them upon a fresh pursuit, and the Party will not let him have them, but drive them away, in this cale he may have this Writ as his remedy.

But if before one he come in sight, the Owner drive out the Cattell, or they go out themselves, so that he misseth of that distresse he intended, this Writ will lie for this.

If the Lord distrain his very Tenant without cause, and unjustly, and it be rescued, it seemes this Action doth lie.

Note, that if any other but the Lord do distrain upon his Tenant without cause, or out of time or place, in any of the Cases before recited this Action will not lie,

The Processes in this Action are as follows.

The first is a Summons, and then Attachment, and Distringas, and then Alias and Plures Distringas.

The Writ of Summons is thus,

THe Keepers &c. To the Sheriff of L. &c. If A. shall cause thee &c. Then put, &c. To shew wherefore; whereas he the said A. in his Damage at S. certaine cattell (or thus) The cattell of the aforesaid B. he took, and them according to the Law and Custome of the common Wealth of *England*, would have there impounded, the aforesaid B. the aforesaid cattell by Force and Armes he did rescue, &c. And other harmes, &c.

If for services due, as follows.   The

THe Keepers, &c. to the Sheriff, &c. if A. shall cause thee, then put &c. to shew wherefore whereas he the said A. in his Fee at S. for Customes and Services to him due by C. his Servant, certaine Cattell, he caused to be taken and them according to the Law, and Custome of the Common-wealth of *England*, &c.

Note, where a man distrains Beasts, and dead Chattels, there the Writ is thus,

To shew wherefore, whereas he the said A. in his Fee at S. for Customes and Services to him due, the Cattell and Chattels of him the said B. he took, and those Cattell he would have impounded, and the aforesaid Chattels in the name of distresse, according to the Law and Custome of the Common-wealth of *England*, he would have detained, he the said B. the same Cattell did Rescue, and the Chattels aforesaid from him the said A. he tooke, and other Harmes, &c.

If the Party appeare not upon the Summons, then as before you are to proceed to Attachment and Distresse infinite.

In case he appeare, you may declare as follows,

Yorke ss.

W.C. lately of B. in the County of E. Yeoman, and W.B. lately of B in the County aforesaid, were attached to answer I. C. Knight, of a lea, that whereas he the said I. in his Fee at B. for Customes and Services to him due, by N. T. his Servant had caused to be taken certain cattel, & the same cattell, according to the Law and Custome of the Common wealth of *England* , would have impounded, there the said *W.* and *W.* the same Cattell by force and Armes did rescue, and other Enormities to him they offered, to the great damage of him the said I. and against the publick peace, &c. And whereupon the said I. by *I. W.* his Attorney, complaines that whereas he (such a day and yeare) in his Fee at B. that is to say, in one hundred of acres of Land, called *W.* parcell of the Mannor of B. with the appurtenances in the County aforesaid, which T. B. then held of him the said I. as of his Mannor of B. in the County aforesaid, by Homage, Fealty, and unto Escuage of our Lord the King, of forty shillings, when it shall happen 2 s. and unto more, &c. And unto lesse, &c. And by the Rent of five and twenty shillings, each yeare, at the Feast of Saint *Michael* the Arch-Angell to be paid, as also by the service of doing Suit to his Court of Wapentage of H. in the County aforesaid, from three weekes to three weekes, at the Wapentage aforesaid to be held, & by the Sheriff-gild of five shillings every yeare at the same Feast of St. *Michael* the Arch-Angell, yearely to be payd, of which said services the said I. was seized by the hands of the aforesaid T. as by the hands of the true Tenant, That is to say, of the Homage, Fealty, and Suit of Court aforesaid, as of his Fee and right, and of the Escuage and Rent aforesaid in his demesne as of Fee; and being so seized by the aforesaid N. T. his Servant, did cause to be taken certaine Cattell, that is to say, two Cowes feeding upon the aforesaid hundred acres of Land for the Rent, Customes and Services, unto him due and unperformed, that is to say, for the Homage, and Fealty, and for the Rent of five and twenty shillings, for one whole yeare, ended at the Feast of Saint *Michael* the Arch-Angell (such a yeare) being in arreare, as also

fo for the Suit of the aforefaid Court of *wepentage*
held at H. aforefaid (fuch a day and yeare) undone
and the fame N. the fame Cattell according to the
Law and Cuftome of the Common wealth of *Eng-*
land there would have impounded, th :y the faid W.
and *w.* the aforefaid Cattell the day and yeare aforefaid, at E. aforefaid by force of Armes, that is to
fay, with Swords, Staves and Knives, they did refcue, and other harmes, *&c.* And againft the Peace,
&c. Whereupon he fayes that he is worfted, and hath
damage to the value of foity pounds, and thereupon
he brings his Suit, *&c.*

ANd the aforefaid *w.* and *w.* by H. D. their Attorney comes and defends the force and injury,
when, *&c.* and the aforefaid *w.* fayes that he is in
no wife guilty of the trefpafs and refcue aforefaid, as
aforefaid *I.C.* hath above declared againft him, and of
this he puts himfelfe upon the country, & the aforefaid
I.C. in like manner, and the faid *w. B.* as to the coming by force and armes, fayes, that he is in no wife
thereof guilty, and upon this he puts himfelfe upon
the Country, and the aforefaid *I. C.* in like manner.
And as to the refidue of the trefpafs, and refcue aforefaid above fuppofed to be done, the faid *w. B.* fayes
that the aforefaid *I. C.* ought not to have againft him
his aforefaid Action, becaufe he fayes, that the aforefaid T. B. held not of the aforefaid I.C. the aforefaid
hundred acres of Land, as of his Mannor of B. aforefaid by the fervices aforefaid, as the aforefaid I. C. by
his Declaration aforefaid hath above fuppofed, and
of this he puts himfelfe upon the Country, and the
aforefaid I. C. in like manner, therefore as well to the
trying this iffue, as iffues above joyned, command is
given to the Sheriff that he caufe to come here 1ʃ
dayes after Eafter 12 *&c.* by whom, *&c.* And who nei-

ther

ther, &c. to recognize &c. Because as well, &c.

HEre you have a Declaration against two and he one pleadeth generally, not guilty, the other, not guilty as to force and arms, and as to the residue he pleads *Non tenure*, upon which you have an Issue joyned in the cause, where if you were to descend to triall in any of the like nature, your course of proceedings must be as is formerly directed in other Actions.

In this Action you recover damages and costs only.

Assize comes now to be treated of, an Action which formerly was much in use, and although for the present not so much in practice, yet to preserve the knowledge of it, we shall here discover somewhat of the nature of the action, together with the proceedings thereupon.

ASSIZE is a Writ, and it lyeth, where a man is put out of his Lands, Tenements, or of any profits to be taken in a certaine place, as of an Office, &c. and so disseised of his Free-hold (which Free-hold to any man is where he is seised of Lands or Tenements, or profits to be taken in Fee-simple, Fee-taile, for terme of his owne life, or for terme of another mans life) but Tenant by *Elegit*, Tenant by Statute Merchant, Tenant by Statute-Staple, may have Assize, although they have not Free-hold, and this directed by divers Statutes.

IN an assize it is allwayes needfull that there be a Disseisor and a Tenant, or otherwise the Writ shall abate.

Also where a man is disseised, and recovereth by an assize of Novell disseisin, and afterwards is againe disseised by the same Disseisor, he shal have against him a Writ of Re-disseisin directed to the Sheriff to

make

make inquifition, and if the Re-diffeifin be found, he shall be sent to prison. Also if one Recover by an Affife of Mordanceffer, or by other Jury, or default or by reddition, and it he be another time diffeised, then he shall have a Writ, *De poft diffeifin*, and he which is taken and imprifoned for Re-aiffeifin, shall not be delivered without speciall commandment of the King. See the Statutes thereof, *Merton*, Chapter the 3. *Marlebridge*, Chapter the 8. and *Weftminfter*, 2 Chapter the 26.

There is also another Affife called an Affife of fresh Force, and lyeth where a man is diffeised of Tenements, which are devifable, as in the City of *London*, or other Burroughs or Townes that be Fanchifes, then the Plaintiff shall come into the Court of the faid Town, and enter his plaint, and shall have a writ directed to the Major or Baylists, and thereupon shall pass a Jury in the manner of Affife of Novell Diffeifin; but it behoveth that he doth enter Plaint within forty dayes, as it is faid, or otherwife he shall be fent to the common Law, and if the Officers delay the Execution, then the Plaintiff shall have another Writ to have Execution, and a *Sicut alias*, and a *Plures*.

This Affife branches it felf further into an

1. Affize of *Darreyn Prefentment*, of which we have before fpoken.

2 Affife *de Mordanceffer*.

An Affife of *Mordanceffer* shall be brought in like manner, as an Affize of Novell Diffeifin shall be, and in Affife of Novell Diffeifin before the Juftices of the Common Bench, or of the Upper Bench, a certaine day shall be put in there, as unto Thurfday after fifteen dayes after *Eafter*, &c. But in an Affife of *Mordanceffer*, a common day shall be given, and fifteen dayes, &c or in eight dayes, &c.

IN an *Aſſize* of *novel diſſeiſin* in the *Common-Bench,* or in the *Upper-Bench,* the *Juſtices* may give a day out of *Terme,* ſo unto *Thurſday* next after ſuch a *Feaſt* &c. for that an *Aſſize* hath not any day of a day of retu. in in the *Term,* but a certaine day which the *Juſtices* will give him, and this may be as well out of the *Terme*.s in the *Terme,* and that by the *Statute* of *Articuli* ſuper *chartas* which directs that in every *Writ* of *Summons* and *At-tachment,* there ought to be fifteen dayes betwin the date and the returne of it: But in an *Aſſize* of *Novel Diſ-ſeiſin* in the *Common Bench,* or in the *Upper Bench* there needs not to be had fifteen dayes between the date, and the returne of it, as it ſeems by the *Statute.*

In an *Aſſize* of Novel diſſeiſin ſued before *Juſtices* in *Eyre,* or before *Juſtices* of the *Upper Bench* or of the *Common Bench,* the *Plaintiff* need not to have any *Pat-tent* to the *Juſtices,* for they have authority without *Pa-tent,* and ſo have the *Juſtices* of *Aſſize* authority to take *Aſſize* of Novell diſſeiſin without any patent made unto them, and that by the *Statute* of Weſtminſter, *Chap. the* 13.

If the *Aſſize* be brought in the *Upper Bench,* or in the *Common-Bench,* then the *Writ* runs thus,

THe Keepers, &c. To the Sheriff, &c. Com-plaint is made to us by A. that B. unjuſtly and without Judgement, hath diſſeiſed him of his Free-hold in C. after, &c. And therefore we com-mand thee, that if the ſaid A. ſhall ſecure thee of proſecuting his complaint, then thou cauſeſt that Te-nement to be reſeized of the Cattel, which in it were taken, That the Tenement with the Cattell to be in
                                                                    peace

peace untill Saturday, in eight dayes after Saint
Michaell, or unto Saturday next after the Morrow
of *All Soules* next comming, &c. And in the meane
time then cause twelve free and lawfull men of that
Visenage to see that Tenement, and imbreviate their
names, and so summon them by good Summoners,
that they be before us at *Westminster* (if in the upper
Bench) or before our Justices at *Westminster* (if in the
Common Bench) at the aforesaid time ready to make
Recognition, and put by Sureties and sure pledges,
the aforesaid B. or his Baile, if he cannot be found,
that he be there to hear that Recognition; and that
thou have there the Summoner, the names of the
Pledges and this Writ.

If the Writ be brought before the Justices of assize,
then the alteration is thus,

The Writ is all one with the former, till after the
word (Peace) and then you say, untill the next Af-
sizes, when our Justices shall come into those
parts.

If the Writ of Assize be brought before other Justices then the Justices of Assize in the same County,
then the Writ is as above, untill you come to the word
(Peace) and then you say, untill a certaine day, which
our beloved and faithfull R. and F. shall make known
unto you, &c. and in the meane time, &c. That thou
summon them before the aforesaid R. F. and those
whom we have associated unto them, at a certaine
place which the said R. and F. shall make known unto thee, ready thereupon to make recognition, &c.
And put &c.

Upon this Writ here ought to be a speciall Patent
directed to the same Justices, for that they are not Justices of Assize for that County.

If a man have Rent-service, Rent-charge, or a
Rent-seek, issuing out of Land for terme of life, or

in

in Fee-taile, or Fee-simple, if he be disseised of this
Rent, he shall have a Writ of Assise of this Rent, and
the Writ shall be generall, That unjustly, &c. he did
disseise him of his Free-hold in N. and he shall make
his Title to the Rent, &c. When hee declares,
&c.

A man may have an Assise of divers Rents, or of
Land and Rent and Offices, and Profits, to be taken
in a mans Soile, and all in one Writ.

If a man have any profit granted unto him out of
any Land for Term of life, or in Fee, as to have the
Fruites, whether Aples, Pears, Nuts or Achorns, or
other profit whatsoever, he may have an Assie of
them, if he be deforced of them.

So likewise of a Toll of a Market, of a passage or
Ferry, of *Pontage* or *Pannage*, and other like things, he
may have this Writ of Assise.

What Seizin is sufficient to have an Assize.

Seisin of parcell of the Rent is sufficient to have
Assise of all the Rent.

The Provost or Warden of a Colledge shall have an
Assise for Rent, where his Predecessor was seised, and
not he himselfe ; for the Seisin of the Predecessor is
the Seisin of the House. The same case of the Warden of an Hospitall.

If a man which hath a Title to enter, set his foot
upon the Land, and is outed, that is a sufficient Seisin
to have an Assie.

If one put in his beasts to use my Common by my
Commandment, that is a sufficient Seisin for me to
have an Assise.

Using

Using of Common by Tenant at will is sufficient Seisin for him in the Reversion to have an Assise of Common, if he or his Tenant at will be disturbed.

Reversion was granted to *J. S.* and the Tenant for life attorns and dies, and *J. S.* enters by the Windowes (for that he cannot enter by the Door) when one half of his body was in, he was pulled out, and yet that is a sufficient Seisin to have an Assise.

The Processes in this Action are Summons, Attachment, and distresse.

Where you are to declare, you may, in case it be for Common of Pasture, make the insuing your president.

Westmerland.

THe Assise comes to recognise, whether T. W. Knight, unjustly and without Judgement, have disseised *Henry* Earle of *Cumberland* of his Common of Pasture in R. which pertaines to his Free-hold in R. within thirty years now last past, *&c.* And whereupon the said Earle by H. D. his Attorney complains, that the aforesaid T. W. hath disseised him of his Common of Pasture, to wit, for comming every year all times of the year, in five hundred acres of Pasture with the Appurtenances in R. aforesaid with all Horses, Oxen, Cows, Sheep, Swine, and other Cattell in his mannor of R. in the County of W. Levant or couchant, which pertaine to his Free-hold in R. that is to say, to his Mannor aforesaid.

And for the title of the common Pasture aforesaid, and the Assise aforesaid thereupon to be had, the said Earle saith, that one H. lately Earle of *Cumberland,* and Father of him the said now Earle, whose Heir he is, was seised of the Mannor aforesaid with the Appurtenances in his Demesne as of Fee, and
that

that he the said late Earle, and all they whose Estate the said late Earle in that Mannor with the appurtenances had for the time, whereof the contrary is not extant to the memory of man, have had and have been accustomed to use, and have for themselves, and their Tenants for Terme of life, yeares, or at will, of their Mannor aforesaid, and of every parcell thereof common of Pasture, with all manner of Cattell aforesaid in the Mannor aforesaid, Levant and Couchant every yeare, all times of the yeare, on the aforesaid five hundred Acres of Pasture, as unto the Mannor aforesaid pertaining.

And he the said late Earle of the Mannor aforesaid with the appurtenances, being so seised of such his Estate, he died thereof seized, after whose death the Mannor aforesaid with the appurtenances, did descend to him the said now Earle, as to the Son and Heir of the said late Earle, by which he the said now Earle into the Mannor aforesaid with the appurtenances did enter, and was, and yet is thereof seised in his Demesne as of Fee. And being so thereof seised, he the said now Earle before the day of the issuing forth of the originall Writ of Assize aforesaid put his Cattell, that is to say two Oxen and two Horses, into the aforesaid Mannor, Levant and Couchant, on the aforesaid five hundred acres of Pasture to feed upon the Grasse there then growing, using thereby his common aforesaid, and the said Cattell were eating the Grasse there then growing, untill the aforesaid *T. W.* before the day of the issuing forth of the aforesaid VVrit; him the said now Earle of his common of Pasture aforesaid, unjustly, and without judgement he did disseize, as he above against him with complained : And this he is able to aver, and thereupon he demands the Assize,

And

And the aforesaid *T. W.* by *J. P.* his Attorney, comes and saith, that he hath done no injury or disseisin to the aforesaid now Earle, of the common of Pasture aforesaid, in the aforesaid five hundred acres of Pasture in view, &c. put, and in the plaint aforesaid specified; and upon this he puts himselfe upon the Assize, and the said now Earle in like manner: Therefore the Assize is to be taken thereupon between them.

There are severall Pleas specially to be pleaded in this Action, both in Bar and Abatement, which arise according to the Title on the Defendants part.

A Lease for yeares, or for life, the Reversion to the Plaintiff or a Feofment of the Plaintiffs, with warranty, and rely upon the warranty, is a good Bar.

The Tenant may plead, that partition was made between the Plaintiff and J. S. whose Estate he hath, and it is a good Bar.

If the Plaintiff choose one to be his Tenant of all where he is not, the Writ shall abate.

An assize is brought of Tenements in D. and S. The Tenant sayes, that all is in S. that being so, the Writ shall abate, for he cannot abridge the whole Town, but see now by the Statute of 23. *Henry* the eighth, Chapter the third, where he may abridge.

The Plaintiff may plead *Non-tenure*, or Misnaming of the Plaintiff, but not of his Master, and conclude it, &c.

The Bayliff may plead that the Tenements are in another Town, for that is an Abatement.

The Bayliff may plead Misnaming, and Joyntenancy without Deed.

A Bayliff may plead not attached by fifteene dayes.

After adjournment upon the Plea of the Bayliff, the Tenant may plead matter which comes of later time.

The

The Tenant himſelfe, after the Aſſize awarded, may leave his Bar, and plead the generall Iſſue, but he cannot plead a new bar after Iſſue.

If a Plea be pleaded, and the Juſtices die, all ſhall be pleaded anew; but if they be at Iſſue, that ſhall ſtand.

Where they are adjourned upon a Plea in abatement, and after the Writ is awarded good, he may afterwards plead in Bar.

Thus much may ſuffice to have ſpoken of Aſſize.

We ſhould now come to treat of divers other actions, as *Contributione facienda, Quid iuris clamat, Per quæ ſe vitia, Et er quem reddit*; and divers others of thoſe natures, and finding them to be very obſolete, and out of uſe, and that the Law hath provided remedies, by the foregoing actions in moſt of thoſe caſes, and that the proceedings thereupon (chiefly for the trying of title) are far more expeditious, and more certaine, and with leſſe trouble and danger to the Client; I think it will not be time ill ſpent to inſert ſome briefe Rules, both in *Ejectione firmæ*, and ſome other actions before ſpoken of, which were then omitted, and hope though they come not in the direct places of thoſe Titles, will be very uſefull for the Attorney.

Theſe proceedings are referred to the Title foregoing, of this Subject, Fol. 199.

OF the proceſſe in this Action we have before ſpoken, and of the pleadings and proceedings upon it: but becauſe many of them miſcarry, by reaſon that the proceedings before proceſſe, relating to the Leſſors Entry, the making of the Leaſe, the entrie of the Leſſee, by virtue of the Leaſe, the Ejectors

tors Entry upon him, and his Outer and Ejectments where care is not taken, and they be not circumspect to prevent a defect in any of these, it causes much danger and prejudice to the Client, and causes no little disgrace to the Attorney. In this Action so very usefull we shall speak to these things in order,

1. The Entry of the Lessor that hath the right.
2. The Lease made by him for trial of the Title.
3. The Entry of the Lessee, by virtue of the Lease so made.
4. The Entry upon him, and his Ouster and Ejectment.

First, it is to be considered what right or title the Lessor hath to enter, whether he hath any right or title to the Land or no ; for if the right and title appear on the Defendants part, the Plaintiffs Action will fail.

Now a man may have a right or title to that Land whereof he hath no possession or property; as where Land is taken from a man wrongfully by Disseisin, in this case the challenge and claim of him from whom it is taken, is called a right. There is a right of Action, which is, where there is no remedy left, but an Action to recover the Land; and there is a right of Entry, when the party claiming, may for his relief either enter into the Land, or have an Action to recover it.

There is a title of Entry, which is where no wrong is done, and yet one who hath a lawfull course to enter upon the Land which another hath, but hath no Action to recover it; as where Entry is given to a man, for a Condition broken upon an Escheat, the Tenant dying without Heir.

In all which cases he must make his entry before he can bring his Action.

1. The Property and Title of Land is made, and may be gained several ways.

Either by Entry, as in case of occupation, where Land is granted to *I. S.* for another mans life, and *I. S.* dy; in this case he that first gets into possession shall have the Estate.

2. By Discent, where one hath Land of Inheritance, and dieth. not disposing of it.

3. By Escheat, where the Owner dieth seised without any Heir, which may be in case he have onely a Bastard, or because he is attained of Treason or Felony.

4. By Conveyance, and so the Property of Land is transferred, and so it is passed ten manner of ways, as follow,

Fine, Recovery, Feoffment, Grant, Lease, Bargain and Sale, Exchange, Surrender, Release, Confirmation.

A man may have Property in Land also by an Execution, as by *Elegit* or Extent.

If he ever had a right of Entry into the Land, it must be considered whether it doth continue and be not taken away, for one may have a right of Action, and no right of Entry to recover his Land; and he that will maintain this Action, must make himself Title under the Lessor, that had a right of Entry into the Land when he made the Lease; for he that makes the Lease must have power and right of Entry at the time of the Lease made, otherwise neither the Entry nor the Lease will be good.

Now that the Entry may be good and warrantable by the Lessor; for otherwise the Action is not maintainable, take these Rules following.

1. This Entry is to be made by the party that hath right.

2.

2. It is a purpofed going into, or fetting his foot upon the Land, as upon his own Land.

3. This may be done by the party himfelf that hath right to enter, or by his Attorney, by a Warrant from him, or by another to his ufe ; and if it be done by Attorney, he muft have a good Authority, and fee he do duly purfue it.

Note that one Joint-tenant, Tenant in Common, or Coparcener, having right to enter, may if he will, enter for all the reft.

If fuch a perfon enter generally, or for, or in the name of himfelf and the reft; and the reft do not afterwards difagree to it, this is a good Entry for himfelf and the reft; and therefore if one have Iffue, a Son and a Daughter by one Venter, and a Son by another, and being feifed of Copy-hold-land, devife all to the younger Son, and dy, and he enter into all, this Entry fhall avail the eldeft Son, to put him in poffeffion of the third part.

The Entry into one part may be fufficient to gain the poffeffion of the reft of the Land.

The Entry into parts muft be in the name of all, &c.

If one reftrain his own Entry, and make it fpecial, and fay, that it fhall be to fuch an acre onely whereon he puts his foot ; in this cafe it reduceth the Poffeffion of no more but that part, &c.

If a Leafe be made to *A.* and delivered to *B.* to the ufe of *A.* and *B.* enter to the ufe of *A.* and after is outed, *A.* may have this Action upon the Entry.

Having done with Entry, we come now to fpeak of Leafes ; for it is abfolutely requifite for the maintaining of this Action, that a good and warrantable Leafe be fhewed forth.

For the better enabling of you to make fuch Leafe, take thefe Rules following.

1. The

212

1. The Leafe to try the Title muft be well made, fealed, and delivered, as other Leafes and Deeds are done; and for that fee the Book of common Affurance, chapter the fourth and fourteenth: A Book very ufefull for many conveyances, both in this and other kindes.

2. The Leafe and Entry may be made by the party Leffor himfelf, if he be of full age, and not a Feme covert, or by his Attorney, by a Letter of Attorney, wherein the Leffor may feal and fign the Leafe, and feal and deliver the Letter of Attorney at one and the fame time, to fome friend of his; and in this Letter of Attorney he muft recite the Leafe, and give the Attorney power to enter into the Land, and there to deliver the Leafe of the Leffee as his Deed, and then the Attorney muft do it in fuch fort, as the Leffor himfelf ought to do it; and he muft not deliver it till he come to the Land.

3. The Leafe muft be delivered upon the Land, for if the Leffor feal and deliver the Leafe, before he hath made his Entry upon the Land, it is void.

The Husband and Wife may make a Leafe and Letter of Attorney, to enter and deliver it upon the Land, and this is good.

A Woman covert, or an Infant, cannot make a Letter of Attorney to feal a Leafe, to try a Title as a man of full age may do.

The Husband alone may make a Leafe of his Wifes Lands.

A copy-holder may make a Leafe to try the Title for a year without Licence.

A Tenant in common may make a Leafe to try the Title for his part, &c. for a year, &c.

The ufual Traft that is ufed in fealing this Leafe of Ejeftment, is as follows.

Where a man hath a Title to a Houfe, Land, or

both,

both, and defires to gain the poffeffion; it is ufefull to make a Leafe (to fome friend who he is affured will not deceive his truft, but will furrender up the Leafe, &c.) for two or three years or more, for fo long as he may be fure the time is not expired, before he get his Trial and Judgment.

This Leafe being made, he goes with fuch his friend the Leffee, to the Mannour or chief houfe, or ftands within the door, or to the Land where no houfe is, where he feals and delivers it to his friend, and taking the Ring or any part of the Door in his hand, delivers the Leafe, mentioning the houfe and lands with the appurtenances, which are contained in the Leafe, to his faid friend the Leffee.

This being done, and that you go away, whofoever after that ftays in the houfe, or whofoever next enters into the houfe, whether mafter, fervant, or ftranger, is an Ejector, and is proper to be made Defendant.

In cafe you finde no Ejector, you may, if you fo think fit, appoint one to that purpofe.

The Leafe being fealed and delivered to your friend as before, the party appointed to be the Ejector may go into the houfe, and thereby, you going away, he is become Ejector.

Where you thus appoint an Ejector, you muft be fure to give notice to the Tenant of the Land, to defend the Title upon the Ejectors appearance.

Where the Tenant of the Land hath but a Leafe he muft give notice to the Lord in whom the Fee-fimple is, that he may be ready with his Evidences,&c. to defend the Title.

Note, that if you cannot come into the houfe, you may deliver the Leafe upon the Lands, in the name of the Houfe and Lands contained in the Leafe; and he that comes next after your going away upon the Land, is an Ejector.

Where

Where it cannot be proved that the Lessee after the Lease made, did enter and was possessed, this Action will not be maintainable, and therefore we must now say something of the Entry of the Lessee.

1. He must make such an Entry as to gain the Possession, for he cannot be ejected out of the Possession of that wherein by Law he was never in.

2. His Possession must continue, for if upon Sealing of the Lease, and the Delivery of it to the Lessee upon the Premisses, the Lessor leave him upon the House or Land, and that he be outed, or come away, &c. and another enter; whether it be a continuance of the same Tenant in Possession, or the Entry of a Stranger; here his Possession is discontinued, and any of those parties are Ejectors. For the Ejectors take this

The Entry of a man upon the Land after the Lease sealed, or the putting in the beast upon the Land, in the like case is an Ejectmement.

The continuance of the same Tenant in Possession, that was in at the time of the sealing of the Lease, is an Ejection, and the Tenant an Ejector.

Where a Lease is made to try the Title, and the Servants of the former Possessour enter with their Masters Carts to do their utmost, and the Action is brought against the Master; it is maintainable without proof of the Masters commandment for this Entry.

In some cases this Writ lies, and not in others.

It lies of a Mannour House, Land, Meadow, Pasture, Tith, or such like things.

It lies of an Orchard, It lieth of a Kitchin, It lieth of a Chamber, It lieth also of a Coal-mine, It lieth also of a Bailery.

It lieth not upon a Lease of a Stock of Cattle,

nor

nor upon a Lease of a Sum of Money, nor of a water-course.

The Writ must set forth the certainty of the thing both for quantity and quality, as so many Messuages, so many Cottages, so many Acres of Land, so many Acres of Meadow, so many Acres of Pasture, &c.

Thus much for *Ejectione firme*, before omitted.

In Actions of Account take these Observations following.

NOw where a Bailiff doth make a Deputy, yet the Writ must be against the Bailiff himself.

If a Stranger take the Profit of my Wives Land during Marriage, and I dy; my Executor, and not my Wife shall have this Action.

This Action lies against the Husband for the receit of his Wife; and against the Wife and Husband for the receit of the Wife, whilest she was sole.

It lies against a Body politick, as against a single man.

It lies against the Keeper of a Park, that hath the charge of Deer, as Bailiff of his Park, &c.

An Action of Account lies not in these cases following.

1. Where the party to be sued claimeth the thing to his own use.

2. Where there is no privity between the parties, neither *Ex provisione Legis*, called privity in Law, as in the case of a Guardian, nor in Deed by the consent of the party; as when Goods are delivered to a Stranger, and not to my use, nor to be delivered over to more, there is no agreement between the parties.

3. When he that hath delivered the things hath taken an Obligation for security of the things delivered.

P 4　　　　4. Where

216 4. Where the party that hath the things, hath a bare overfight of them, as a Bailiff of a Plough, a Shepherd of Sheep, &c

A Bailiff shall have allowance upon his Accounts, but a Receiver shall have none.

If the Bailiff disburse any thing for his Master belonging to his Office, as to pay his Quit-rent, or the like; or if he be robbed, or suffer loss by other means without any default in him, it shall be allowed him upon his account. But if he pay his Masters Debts, or lay out any thing else, not appertaining to his Office, this will not be allowed him.

There are two Judgments upon this Writ, the first is, (*Quod computet*) which is interlocutory : the last is, *Quod querens recuperet versus Defendentem,* so much as he is found in Arrearages, and *Damna occasione inter-placitationis.*

The first is to account onely, and upon this the Defendant may be outlawed, and then before Outlary if he appear and enter into account, and be found in Arrearages, the Plaintiff shall have a definitive Judgment for the Arrearages, and after the first Judgment no abatement can be for any cause, but a discontinuance, or Non-suit may be.

The first Judgment is but an Award of the Court, like to a Writ of Inquiry of Damages, and not like to a final Judgment, for there the Action is clearly determined, and these two Judgments depend one upon another, for if Judgment be to account, and the Plaintiff dy before he hath accounted, the Executour cannot go on in that Suit, but he must begin again, and no Writ of Errour will be upon the first, till after the second Judgment.

We have now gone through the most general and usefull practice of the Common Bench, relating to the several Actions before going; as also of all Offi-

ces,

ees, and Officers incident to that Court, and now as before we promifed, hereto is added a Table of the Fees of that Court, of all Offices whatfoever relating to the Court, or the practice of it, belonging to every Office or Officer, which follow in order.

The Fees hereunder mention'd are the Fees due, and paid to the Lord Chief Juftice, and the other Juftices of the Court of Common Pleas at Weftminfter, as they were due, and ufually paid to the Juftices of the fame Court.

The Lord Chief Juftice his Fees.

FOr allowance of a Writ of Errour upon an Outlawry before Judgment, 20 s.

Writ of Errour.

For a Bail taken upon an Outlawry upon mean Procefs in Debt, if the Debt be 20 l. or above, 2 s. 4 d.

For the allowance of a Writ of Errour upon a Judgment, 20 s.

For Bail taken in cafe of Debt, after Judgment, 12 s.

For the allowance of a Writ of Errour upon a Judgment upon a *Scire fac.* and Outlawry after Judgment 35 s.

For making the Roll that a Writ of Errour is allowed on, 2 s.

Making the Roll.

For a *Superfedeas.* 3 s.

Superfedeas.

For the tranfcript of a Record, being a prefs, 6 s. 8 d.

Tranfcript.

For

For every press more, 6 s. 8 d,

Certiorari. For the Return of every *Certiorari*, 14 s. 9 d.

Seal Nisi prius. For the Seal of every Record of *Nisi prius*, 2 s. 1 d.

Sealing of Writs and Exemplif. Fines. For the Seal of every Writ sealed in Court, 1 d.

For the Seal of every Expemplification, 2 d.

The Fees following are due to such of the Judges who do perform the business.

Sign FOr acknowledgment of a Fine or Warrant of Attorney for a common Recovery out of Court, 6 s. 8 d.

For signing every Writ of Privilege to remove any cause, *Habeas corpus, Procedendo,* or *Supersedeas,* upon a *Procedendo,* 4 s.

Bails. For every Bail taken out of Court upon any such Writ of Privilege, wherein one cause onely is returned, 9 s. 8 d.

For every cause more, 2 s.

Confessions. For the confession of a Judgment out of court 9 s. 8 d.

Bails. For every Phillizers Bail, and other Bail taken out of court, 9 s. 8 d.

Satisfaction. For acknowledging satisfaction out of court, 9 s. 8 d.

Deeds acknow. For acknowledging out of court a Deed to be inrolled 9 s. 8 d.

Guardians: For admission of a Guardian out of court, 9 s. 8 d.

Suggestion. For the proof of a suggestion out of court

Court, for every witnefs, 9 s. 8 d.

For a Warrant for paffing of a Fine, *Warrant for* where there are more than three Co- *Fines.* gnizors or three Cognizees, parties to the Fine, 4 s.

For every *Affidavit* taken out of *Affidavit.* Court upon a forreign Plea, or Re-fcous, 2 s.

For any other *Affidavit* taken out of Court, 8 d.

For exhibiting of any Information *Informations.* out of Court, 8 d.

For figning a Bill of cofts to award an Attachment for not appearing upon a *Sub pœna,* 8 d.

For granting a Licence to compound upon a penal Law, 2 s.

For affeffing of the Kings part of a Forfeiture upon a penal Statute after compofition with the Informer, 2 s.

For the Commitment out of Court *Commitments.* of a Prifoner to the *Fleet,* charged with one caufe onely, 9 s. 8 d.

For every Bail taken out of Conrt *Bails on Outla-* upon an Outlary in Debt upon mean *ries.* Procefs reverfed, if the fame be twenty pounds, 2 s. 4 d.

Divident

Divident Fees.

Fees in Court to the Box.

These Fees following are due to the Lord Chief Justice, and the other Judges of the Court of Common Pleas, by way of Divident.

Judgment.

FOr confessing of a Judgment in Court,   6 d.

Satisfaction.
For acknowledging satisfaction in Court, if the Debt or Damage do not amount unto 100 l.   6 d.

If the Debt or Damage do amount to 100 l. 12 d. and for every 100 l. after the same rate,   12 d.

Guardian.
For admitting an Infant in Court to his Guardian,   12 d.

Vtl.
For reversing an Outlary in Court for Errour in the Exigent, or Retourn,   12 d.

For the like for the insufficiency of the Proclamation or Retourn, or for want of a Proclamation,   2 s.

Recovery.
For every common Recovery acknowledged in Court,   6 d.

Fines.
For a Fine acknowledged in Court,   6 d.

Bails.
Recognizance.
For a Bail taken in Court, or a Bail or Recognizance acknowledged in Court,   12 d.

Deeds.
For a Deed acknowledged in Court to be inrolled,   12 d.

Discontinuance
For a Discontinuance,   12 d.

Prohibition.
For a Prohibition granted,   9 s. 8 d.

For

For every wager of Law, or Non-suit *Wagers of Law* upon a wager of Law, 6 d.

For admission of an Attorney to be *Atturn sworn.* an Attorney of this court, 20 s.

The Puisne Judges Fees.

FOr every Fine drawn at Bar, 12 d. *Fines.*
For a Recovery drawn at the Bar *Recoveries.* with a single Voucher, 18 d.

For every Voucher more, 6 d.

For Reversal of an Outlary in court, *Reversals.* 4 s.

For taking a privy Verdict, 6 s. 8 d. *Privy Verdict.*

For taking of costs upon every Ver- *Costs Rec.* dict, 12 d.

From the Clerk of the Warrants *Feod. anuale.* every Term, to every of the Puisne *Clericus Warr.* Judges, 33 s.

For every Attorney whose name is *Rec. Att.* recorded in the Roll of Attorneys, every Term, 4 d.

For inrolling and examining the *Inrolling Fines* parts of a Fine, and Writs upon com- *and Recove-* mon Recoveries by the Statute, 23 *ries.* Eliz. 6 s.

For the exemplification and exami- *Exempliscati-* nation of the parts of a Fine, and *on thereof.* Writs upon common Recoveries by that Statute, 5 s.

For drawing and entring a Rule for *Rules for a-* an amendment upon that Stat. 12 d. *mendments.*

For a search made upon the Inrol- *Searches.* ment upon that Statute, 4 d.

For a copy of a Fine, or Writs in- *Copies.*
rolled

rolled upon common Recoveries inrolled by that Statute for every sheet, 4 d.

Return of Writs of Covenant and Entries.

For the Return of every Writ of Covenant brought to levy a Fine upon, 10 d.

For the Return of every Writ of Entry to suffer a common Recovery, every Writ of Summons and Seisin thereupon, 10 d.

Signing Dedimus potestatem.

An ancient Fee of 6 s. 8 d. for signing of a *Dedimus potestatem,* due to the Judges of any Court who do assign the same which is now, and of late hath been divided amongst all the Judges that ride the Circuits.

These Fees following are due to the Clerks of the Lord Chief Justice, and other the Justices of the said Court.

Fines.

TO the Judges Clerk of the Fines, For taking of a Fine, or Warrant of Attorney, 3 s. 4 d.

Warrants of Attornies.

For certifying of a Fine, or Return of a *Dedimus potestatem,* 16 d.

Bails.

To the Judges Clerk of Bails, for taking every Bail, 12 d.

Caveat.

For entring every Caveat to give notice that good Bail may be taken, 12 d.

Satisfaction.

For satisfaction acknowledged out of Court, 12 d.

Deeds acknowledged.

For a Deed acknowledged out of Court to be inrolled, 12 d.

Suggestion.

For the proof of a suggestion out of Court for every witness, 12 d.

Affidavits.

For an *Affidavit* taken out of Court, 4 d. For

For entring into his Book an Infor-mation exhibited out of Court, 4 d. *Information.*

For entring into his Book of Costs a Warrant signed to award an Attachment for not appearing upon a *Subpœna*,   4 d.

For Admission to a Guardian, 12 d. *Guardian.*

For entring into his Book a Licence to compound upon a penal Law, 4 d. *Licences.*

For entring into his Book the Kings part of the Forfeiture upon a penal Law assessed by the Judges, after composition with the Informer,   6 d.

For entring into his Book a Commitment out of Court of a Prisoner to the *Fleet*, charged with one cause onely,   12 d. *Commitment.*

To the puisne Judges Clerk of the Inrolments, for Copying, Enrolling, and Examining the parts of a Fine and Writs upon a Recovery, by the Statute, 23 *Eliz.*   8 s. 4 d. *Inrolment. Fines and Recoveries, &c.*

For a Search made for an Inrolment upon that Statute,   8 d.

For writing a Fine, or Writs inrolled upon a common Recovery inrolled by that Statute.   8 d.

The

2-2-9

The *Custos Brevium*, who is the prime and first Officer of the Court, his Fees.

These Fees following are the Fees which are taken by the Custos Brevium, *of his Majesties Court of* Common Pleas, *and his Clerks in right of his said Office, and as they were taken* 11 Eliz. *by the then Master of the said Office, and his Clerks.*

Pt. diem.

INprimis, for filing any Writ, or other Record, coming after the day of the return thereof, except Writ of Privilege *de veniendo, & redeundo,* and also Writs of Privilege, called *Prop.* or *post diem.* 4 d.

Pt. Term.

Item, For filing any Writ, or other Record (except before excepted) coming after the Term wherein it was returnable, called a *Post Term.* 20 d.

Item, For filing any Writ, or other Record coming after two Terms, called *Post Term.* for every Term after 20 d. a piece; except *Exigents* and Outlawries, which pay but onely 20 d.

Item, To the Clerk of the same Office (*ab antiquo*) who enters the same, 2 d.

Item, Upon the making of the Stat. 4 H.7. cap. 24. the *Custos Brevium* was allowed

allowed by the Court, for carrying and re-carrying of every fine levied according to that Statute, to *westminster*, to the Chirographer to proclame, four Terms, 8 d.

Item, for keeping three parts of the Record of every fine, consisting of five parts, 4 d. a piece, 12 d.

In tot. for every fine 3 s. 6 d. whereof the Master hath 2 s. 6 d. and 14 d. is allowed to the clerks 3 s. 8 d.

Item, for the amendment of every *Amendments.* Writ or other Record *per warrant. cur.* 20 d.

Item, for every *Non est factum* plead-*Non est fact.* ed in court, 2 s.

Item, for every Sheriffs bundle of *Sheriffs bundle.* Writs returnable of the precedent Term, and coming before Essoyn-day of the second Return of the new Term, 8 d.

The usual Fees allowed by the Custos Brevium *to the Clerks of his Office.*

INprimis, for every Temple-search, *Searches.* 4 d.

Item, out of every *westminster* search, 2 s. 1 d.

Item, To the clerks out of the allow-*Certiorari.* ance of every *Certiorari* 2 s. 8 d. and for certifying the same, *secundum longitudinem*, and according to reason, 2 s. 8 d.

Item, to the clerk for writing and *Exemplificat.* examining of every exemplification,

Q   *secundum*

secundum longitudinem.

Porta. Bre. in Cur. — Item, To the Clerk for any Writ, or other Record carried into the Court, 4 d.

Bre de Ingrum. & seia — Item, For entring a common Recovery-writ *super disseisinem in le post,* 8 d.

Fines. — Item, For every Fine passing in the Office, 14 d.

Ne recipiatur. — Item, For entring into a Book every *Recipiatur* coming under a Judges hand or by Order of Court, 12 d.

Nota Jur. — Item, For every note of Jurors names for the Clerk of the Juries to make further Process by, 4 d.

Caoia ex fa. — Item, For every Note of an *Exigent* for the Clerk of the Outlawris to make further Process by, 8 d.

Searches. — Item, For the search of any Book of Entries of any Writs for every Term, 8 d.

Copies. — Item, For the Copy of any Writ or other Record, for every sheet, 8 d.

The usual Fees allowed by the Custos Brevium, *to the Bag bearer of the Office, being always the common Voucher of the Court.*

Searches. — Inprimis, For every search under five years, 1 d

Item, For every Temple search, 5 d
For every *Westm.* search, 12 d

Porta. Bre. in Cur. — For any Writ or other Record carried into the Court, 5

Recupat. — For every common Recovery suffer in Court (being the common Vo ch chee) 4 d. a piece,   4 d.

For every Attorney sworn in Court, *Attorn. Jur.*
         6 d.

The Fees of the Clerk of the Inrolments of Warrants, and Estreats, in the Common Pleas, as are now and have been taken these two and thirty years, and as I conceive were taken ever since 31 Eliz. saving the Fees hereafter mentioned, allowed per ordin. Cur.

EVery Inrolment containing a side *Inrolments.*
of a Roll,   5 s.

For a full Roll,   10 s.

    And so according to the rate.

Every Warrant of Attorney *in debt War. Attorn.*
trans &c *detinue,*   4 d.

The Sheriffs Warrants,   12 d.

Every other Warrant, called Double Warrants.   8 d.

For a *Post Term.*   4 d.

The Lord Mayor of *London* his Warrant,   5 s. 8 d.

The Secondaries of the Compters in *Easter* Term yearly,   13 s. 4 d.

For entring of an Attornies name *Attorn. Jur.*
in the Roll of Attorneys, upon his first admittance,   3 s. 4 d.

For a Warrant upon a Writ of Co- *War. sur. fine.*
venant, *per ordin. Cur.*   4 d.

Paid to the Clerk by every Attorney *Rot. Attorn.*
four pence a Term, called the Roll groat, which is paid to the Judges Box, and I conceive it to be due ever since,

11 *Eliz.*   4 d.

Recuperat.   Paid also to the Clerk by the Prothonotaries 12 d. upon every Recovery
which is also paid to the Judges, 12 d.

Attorn. Jur.   To the Clerk when an Attorney is
first sworn.   12 d.

The Chirographers Fees.

Fines.   INprimis, the ancient Fee limited by
Statute 11 *Eliz.* for every Fine, 4 s.
Item, From 4 *H.*7. for the service in
proclaiming Fines,   8 d.
Item, By Stat. 23 *Eliz.* for writing the
Roll,   4 d.
So the Chirographers fee for every
fine is,   5 s.

Other Fees also due, and anciently paid to the Chirogyaphers, viz.

Exemplificat.   FOr exemplifying a fine the Term in
which it was ingrossed,   2 s. 8 d.

Copy.   For every sheet of every fine, of
twelve lines copied out of the Record,
12 d.
For the sight of every Record being
ancient, from *H.*8. upwards, 3 s. 4 d.

Searches.   For the search of every fine from
*H.*8. to this present, for every year,
8 d.
For the search of every fine durin
t

the Reign of *H. 8.* for every year, 12 d.

For certifying of every Record by a   *Certiorari.*
Writ of Errour,   12 s.

For a *Quid juris clamat quem reddi-*   *Quid jur. clam.*
tum, reddit & per que servie.   6 s. *&c.*

For entring a claim upon a Record,   *Claims.*
                                     5 s.

For allowing of Proclamations upon   *Pt. Fines.*
Fines brought into the Office after the
Term ended,   6 d.

For the *Post Termin.* of a Fine, 12 d.   *Pt. Term.*

The Chirographers Clerks Fees for in-
grossing of Fines by the Attorney which
sues them out.

THe Chirographers Clerks have re-   *Fines ingr.*
ceived an allowance of the Attor-
neys for their pains for them, which
heretofore have been more advantage-
ous unto them than now it is, being re-
puced to 2 s. 6 d. in certain, had, and
made at the request of 100. or 80. of
the most ancient Attorneys, with *John*
newer, Esq: Clerk of the said Office,
in 2. or 3. of King *James:* To which
agreement had and made in writing,
the said Attorneys set to their hands,
and the same was delivered to Sir *Ed-*
ward Cook Knight, then Chief Justice
of the Common Pleas, and hath so continued ever since,   2 s. 6 d.

For this allowance the Clerks do
write more than all the Officers through
which Fines do pass, *viz.* They write
every Fine long, or short, four times o-

ver in a great set hand.

Fees belonging to the Clerk of the Treasury.

Copy.   FOr the copy of every Issue and Imparlance, for every sheet,   4 d.

For every Judgment, Deed enrolled, and real Action, for every sheet,   8 d.

Searches.   For the search of every Term above ten years,   4 s.

Exemplification.   For every exemplication not exceeding three sheets,   7 s.

For every sheet more,   12 d.

Records of Nisi prius.   For every Record of *Nisi prius,* not exceeding three sheets,   2 s.

For every sheet more,   4 d.

Fees for the Keeper of the Treasury from 12 Eliz.

Searches.   INprimis, for search of a Term above ten years,   8 d.

For seven years under ten years, 4 d.

For three years,   0

Portam Rot.   For search of a Plea-roll,   4 d.

Ligam Rot.   For a Roll carried into the Court, 6 d.

For making up a Term & Record, 3 s.

Attorn. jur.   For every Attorney sworn in Court,   12 s.

Jur. at Bar.   For a Jury at Bar,   5 s.

Nisi prius Mid.   For a *Nisi prius,* in Mid.   2 s.

Wager deleg.   For a Wager in Law,   5 d.

For

For a Copy of a *Precipe*, after the Term, 18 d.

For a Fine acknowledged in the Treafury, 4 d. *Copy per fines.*

For a Warrant of Attorney left un-entred, and comes to be entred in the Roll after the Term, 4 d.

For an Entry left out of the Kings Silver, and comes to be entred in the Office, 4 d. *Intra. pl. Term.*

From the Clerk of the Treafury for my attendance every Term, 5 s. *Feod. annuale.*

For my Key after the Term, 18 d. *Claves Thef.*

The Fees of the Clerk of the Kings Sil-ver, as they were taken in the eleventh year of Queen Elizabeth, *in the fix-teenth year of King* James, *and in the late Kings time, and fince.*

INprimis, for the Fees of every ordi-nary Fine taken by the Lord Chief Juftice of the Common Pleas, or any Judg of Affize in the Weftern circuit, together with the Copy, or *Poft fine,* eighteen pence, for every Fine taken in the fame Circuit by fpecial Com-miffion, and for the Copy of the *Poft fine,* 22 d. *Fines in the Weftern Circuit.*

Fines by fpecial Deed.

For every ordinary Fine elfewhere in *England,* and *Monmouthfhire,* taken as aforefaid without Commiffion, and for the Copy, 10 d. *Ordinary fines.*

Q 4 For

Weſtern.   For every Fine taken by ſpecial Commiſſion out of the Weſtern circuit, and for the copy,   14 d.

Several capti.   For every ſeveral caption in any Fine where it is taken at ſeveral times by ſpecial Commiſſion, over and above the former rates,   4 d.

Certiorari.   For every Fine certified by *Certiorari* after the death of any Judg, or other Commiſſioners, over and above the former rates,   6 d.

Pt. Term.   For the *Poſt Termin.* of every Fine brought in the next vacation after return of the Writ of Covenant,   6 d.

Searches.   For every ſearch of any Fine every Term,   4 d.

Copia.   For every copy of the Entry of the Kings Silver,   8 d.

Ne recipiatur.   For every Fee of a *Ne recipiatur,* of any Fine either by Order, or Warrant, of the Court, or any Judg,   3 s. 4 d.

For the continuing of any ſuch Order or Warrant from Term to Term till it be diſſolved,   3 s. 4 d.

The Philizers Fees.

Cap. al. & plur.   INprimis, For every *Cap. Al. & Plur. Cap. in Debt, Detinue,* and *Treſpaſſ,* not having more than four names in a Writ, and Entry thereof,   6 d.

Delivery of Record of the Cap.   Item, for delivery of every firſt *Cap.* upon Record and Entry thereof,   4 d.

Teſtat.
Pone ſum.   For every *Teſtat.* upon any of the ſaid Writs, *Pon. in Replevin & Summons,*   12 d.

Item,

Item, For every *Cap. Al. & Plur. Bria. in comp.*
In Accompt, Covenant, Annuity *Ejectione firme,* and upon penal Statute,
12 d.

Item, For every Writ in an Action *Actions super* upon the cafe or more, according to the *cafum.* length, 12 d.

For every return *Habend.* and fe- *Return Habend.* cond deliverance, and Entry thereof,
2 s. 6 d.

For every *Non omit. & cap.* in *Wi- Non omit.* thernam, 2 s. *Withernam.*

For every Writ of Partition, *War- Partition, waft.* rant Charte, *Quare impedit,* and wafte, *Quare impedit.*
12 d. *War. Cart.*

For every Writ of inquiry of dama- *Inqui. de dam.* ges in real Actions, *Scire fac. & Super- Scire fat. fuper-* fedeas, 2 s. *fea. Gr. & pet.*

For every *grand cap. Al. Sum. pet. cap.* cap. *Copia in* and Entry thereof, <div align="center">2 s. 6 d.</div> *de.*

For the copy of the Entry thereof,
8 d.

For the demand in every Writ of *View.* View and Entry thereof, 2 s. 6 d.

For every Writ of Seifin and Entry *Seizin.* thereof, 4 s. 6 d.

For the view prayer, 2 s.
For a copy of the Entry thereof, 8 d.

For every Writ of *Habeas corpus, duc. Habeas corp.* coram, *diftring. nuper vicec. & diftring. & diftring.* ballivum, 2 s.

For every Writ of Refcous and En- *Adjornment.* try thereof, 2 s. *cont. refort.*

For the Entry of every Adjournment, *Refcous.* Difcontinuance, and Refort, 4 d.

For every fpecial Bail, and the Entry *Special Bail.*
there-

thereof,   2 s. 10 d.

For every Appearance in real and mixt Actions,   4 d.

Appearance.

For every Appearance upon Writs to arrest, and Entry thereof,   12 d.

Searches, rules, copies, number-rolls.

For searches, copies, number-rolls, and giving of rules, each of them, 4 d.

Exigenters Fees.

Prod. Exigenters.

EVer since the Statute of *Henry* the eighth, which gave the Proclamation upon the *Exigent*, the whole Estate of the Exigenters Office did consist in the making of three Writs, *Videlicet*, an *Exigent*, a *Supersedeas*, and a Proclamation, all which Writs are warranted by one and the same Record.

For all the time of our remembrance and experience in the said Court, which hath been (by the most ancient of us) for about thirty years or thereabout, the Fees of the said Writs were as followeth, *videlicet*,

The *Supersedeas*,   2 s.
The *Exigent*,   11 d.
The Proclamation,   6 d.

Which Fee of 6 d. was given by the Statute of 6 *Henry* the eighth, being now about an hundred and ten years since.

About eight or nine years since the *Supersedeas* (*quia improvid.*) being the

least

leaſt Writ in labour, and more in proſit than both the other, was granted by Letters Patents under the great Seal of *England*, by the late King of famous memory, to Mr *John Murray*, then of his Majeſties Bed-chamber, and partly to avoid conteſtation with his ſaid Majeſties grant, and upon hopes and promiſes of ſome recompence other way, the Exigenters did give way to the ſaid Patent, and have ever ſince loſt the benefit of the ſaid *Superſedeas*, whereupon the Judges did give increaſe onely of one penny to be taken upon the *Exigent*, for relief of the Exigenters, and their Clerks, and ſo the *Exigent* was made twelve pence, which increaſe of a penny is all the recompence which hitherto they have received for that great loſs of the *Superſedeas*.

We have likewiſe heard, that above fourty years ſince, and before our times by occaſion of an Act of Parliament, made 21 *Eliz.* whereby the Proclamation of the *Exigent* was much enlarged without any addition or increaſe of Fee, there was one penny added to the *Exigent*, to be given to the poor Clerks for writing the ſaid Writs, over and above the ancient allowance, which penny hath ever ſince been paid to the ſaid poor Clerks accordingly, without any benefit to the Maſters themſelves.

Other increaſe, addition, or alteration of Fees in our Offices we know not

2 4 6

of, nor ever heard of, although the length of the said *Exigent*, or Proclamation with their Entries considering the loss of the *Supersedeas*, (all which we humbly submit to his Majesties Commissioners) might perhaps have justly deserved some further improvement. And it is certainly true, that no other increase of Fees hath been in our Officers since 11 *Eliz.* nor for ought we ever heard, or can by any means conjecture for these hundred years at the least.

HILAR. TERTIO
CAROLI
Regis.

The Clerks of the Jurors.

A note of all such Fees as are now usually taken by the Clerks of the Jurors of his Majsties Court of Common Pleas at Westminster, *being the same, and no other than such as have been taken time out of minde.*

Habeas corpus. INprimis, For a Writ of *Habeas corpus Jurator.* in Debt and Trespass, 10 d.
For the like Writ in all other Actions, 16 d.

Distring. For a *Distringas cum decem Tales,* 2 s. 4 d.

Search copy. For a Terms search, the copy of a Jury

Jury, a number-roll, and a discontinu- *Court adjourn.*
ance and adjournment for every of
them,   4 d.

The Clerk of the Essoyns.

INprimis, for every Essoyn and Ex- *Essoyn except.*
ception,   4 d.
For the Copy,   4 d.
For every Adjournment,   4 d.
For the Copy,   2 d. *Copia.*
For every *Idem dies*,   4 d.
For every Non-suit for want of Ad- *Adjournment.*
journment in Actions personal, 2 s. 4 d.
For the copy,   12 d. *Copies.*
For every Non-suit in Actions real, *Idem dies.*
                                       4 s. 4 d. *Non pros.*
For the Copy,   12 d.
For the exemplification of every Es- *Exemplificat.*
soyn and Non-suit thereupon when it
shall happen, being very seldom,
                                       7 s. 6 d.
For the copy thereof,   3 s. 4 d.
For the Clerk,   12 d.
For several fees from several Offi- *Feod. anuale.*
cers of the Court towards the num-
bering and marking of the Rolls,
                                       4 l. 9 s.

Outlawry

Outlawry Office.

In the *Kings Attorney General his Office of the Outlawries executed by his Deputy* Mr: Johnson, *the Fees are as followeth,* viz.

Cap. utl. special. FOr a special *Cap. utlegat:* against Body, Lands, and Goods, 2 s. 4 d.
For a *Proprium,* 14 d.

Habeas Corpus duces tecum. For every Writ of Hab. Corp. & duces tecum, when they are sued forth, 2 s. 4 d.
If a Proper. 14 d.

Cap. utlegat. general. Certif. utl. in lect. For a general *Cap. utlegat.* 10 d.
If a Proper. 6 d.
For ingrossing and certifying a special Writ, with the inquisition returned by the Sheriff, of Lands, or Goods found thereupon, and for the *Exigent,* with the Return thereof at large certified into the Exchequer, when it is required, the Office-fee is eight shillings, unless it be commanded by the Lord Treasurer, Chancellour, or Barons of the Exchequer, or by the Kings Attorney General, or Solicitor for his Majesties service onely, then no Fees are due, 8 s. *aut nil.*

Certific. Reversal in secium. For ingrossing and certifying a Reversal into the Exchequer to discharge seizure upon Outlawries, when any is, 5 s.

Exon libri de utl. And to the Clerk, 4 d.
For entring the Reversal in the Outlawry

lawry Office to discharge all Process thereupon, or upon any Writ of Errour, 2 s. 8 d.

For certifying of an Outlawry, or *Certific. nisi.* Reversal when it is pleaded, 2 s. *vel Reversal.*
And to the Clerk, 4 d.

For the search of an Outlawry one *Search.* Term (as in all other Offices) 4 d. if above a year, then 3 d. a Term, which is the utmost, 3 d.

For entring and filing an *Exigent, Filace exfa.* with one Process thereupon, 4 d.

These several Fees aforesaid were paid and received in Easter Term 34 Eliz. *and ever since to mine own knowledg, for so long I have been and continued Clerk, and to all Attornies General that have been since that time.*

These (as I understand) are the true Fees.

The Fees of the Seal for Writs.

ALL Writs for the Kings Bench, *Seals of Writs.* and Common-pleas, 7 d.
The exemplification of the Kings *Exemplific.* Bench, 2 s. 6 d.
The exemplification of the Common-pleas, 2 s. 2 d.
Outlawries, 1 d.
Propr. 1 d.

Fees

Fees due to the Marshal, and Proclamator of the Court of Common Pleas, given by Order made by all the Judges of the Court, Term. Trin. 31. *H.* 1. *post conquestum, and received accordingly by the said Marshal and Proclamator, for any thing appeareth to the contrary, untill* 11 *Eliz. and ever since.*

Judgments.

INprimis, for every Judgment and Nonfuit, 4 d.

Fines.

Item, for every fine, 8 d.

Item, for every final Judgment, 12 d.

Chief Usher of the Exchequer, and Marshal and Proclamator of the said Court of Common Pleas by Lease from *Clement Walker* Esq: who hath the same Office in inheritance by grand Serjeanty.

The four Criers.

HEreafter do ensue the good Ordinances and Rules made as well by the Kings Justices of the Common Pleas in times past, as by the Justices now being, for the good Rule and Order of the said Court, which same now Justices do charge and command every of the said Officers and Attornies well and truly to observe and keep upon the pains therein limited.

Which

Which said Orders were inrolled *Termin. Trin.* 35 *H. I. post conquestum Rot.* 494. *Jo: Priest* chief Justice of the Common Pleas, *Ni Austen, Pet: Arder, Ro: Davers, Ro: Dawby, Wa: Moil,* and *John Needham* Justices of the same court.

The Criers Fees from 11 *Eliz.*

FOr every Judgment,	4 d.	*Judgments.*
For every final Judgment,	12 d.	
For every Non-suit,	4 d.	
For every Fine,	8 d.	*Fines.*
For every Recovery,	8 d.	*Recoveries.*
For calling a Jury, if they fill not,		*Juries.*
	2 s.	

For every Jury, if they fill, and serve, and give up their Verdict the same day, at the Bar the same day, and for keeping them till then,   6 s.

If the Jury ly all night, that we be forced to watch and wait on them all night,   30 s.

For carrying every bundle of Re- *Carrying Rolls.* cords out of the Treasury into the court, and back again into the Treasu- ry,   6 d.

For every Attorney that is sworn, *Attorn. jur.*   6 s.

For every Bail,	12 d.	*Bails.*
For every Oath in Court,	12 d.	*Oaths.*
For every Wager of Law, old Fees,		*Wager of Law.*
	4 s. 4 d.	

For every *Scire facias* called in court,   4 d.

R

The Compleat Attorney.

Nisi prius.	For every *Nisi prius* before my Lord Chief Justice,	4 s.
Guardians.	For every admittance to a Guardian,	12 d.

The Fees of the Keeper of the Court, from 11 Eliz.

Feod. annuale.	From the Clerk of the Treasury for hanging the Cloath of the Court,	6 s. 8 d.
Wagers of Law. Attorn. jur.	For a Wager of Law and Wager-men,	9 s. 6 d.
	For a Jury at Bar	5 s.
	For every Attorney sworn in Court,	12 d.
Nisi prius.	For a *Nisi prius* in *Midd.*	2 s.
Bails.	For a Bail,	4 d.
Fines.	For a fine,	4 d.
Deeds acknow.	For a Deed acknowledged,	4 d.
Satisfaction.	For satisfaction acknowledged,	2 s.

The Fees of the Clerk of the Inrolment of Fines and Recoveries.

Of fines and recoveries in grosſ.	Inprimis, the fee due to the Judges by the Statute of 23 *Eliz.* for inrolling of every Fine and Recovery,	6 s, 8 d.
Exemplific.	Item, due to the Judges by the same Statute for exemplifying every Inrolment,	5 s.
Searches.	For search of every Fine inrolled for every year,	16 d.

For

For copying every Fine inrolled, for *Copies.*
every sheet, 12 d

For the Clerks Fee for inrolling by *Inrolments.*
the Roll, 8 s. 8 d.

For exemplifying after the same *Exemplificat.*
rate, 8 s. 4 d.

For every Rule upon Amendments, *Rules for a-*
3 s. 4 d. *mendments.*

For returning Writs of Covenants *Return of*
upon Fines and Writs of Entry, Sum- *Writ of Entry.*
mons, and Seisins upon common *Covenant. Sei-*
Recoveries, as Deputy of Record for *zins, &c.*
Sheriffs appointed by the Court, the
ancient Fee is, 2 s.

The Porter of the Court his Fees from
11 *Eliz.*

FOr every Writ of Entry with Mr: *Writs of Entry.*
Attorney General, 4 d.

For a Jury at Bar, 5 s. *Juries at Bar.*

For a *Nisi prius.* 2 s. *Nisi prius.*

For a Wager of Law, 6 d. *Wagers of Law.*

For a Fine acknowledged, 4 d. *Fines.*

For a Bail, 4 d. *Bails.*

For satisfaction acknowledged, 2 d. *Satisfaction.*

For the Attorneys Oath, 12 d. *Atturn sworn.*

For a Guardian, 4 d. *Guardian.*

Alienation Office.

THomas Ravenscroft, Francis Poulton,
George Coultrop, Esq: Commissioners.

R 2 *Tho:*

Tho: Bond Esq: Receiver,
Take no Fees, but receive a certain
stipend from the King.

*Fees taken by the Master of the Chancery,
for that Office appointed.*

Docquet. FOr signing every Docquet upon Licence and pardon of Alienation,
2 s.

Pt. Writs. For every Writ of Entry, for Lands holden in chief,   2 s.
For Writs of Entry of Lands not holden in chief,   4 d.

Affidavits. For Affidavits upon discharge of Tenures,   2 s.

*The usual Fees taken in the Office of
Compositions for Alienations, by the
Clerks there.*

Certificate. FOR a Certificate upon a Writ of Entry,   3 s. 4 d.

Pardon. For the Warrant to the Great Seal for pardon of Alienation,   10 s.

Discharges of Process. For viewing the Subjects Evidences, search of the Tenures, and drawing of the Affidavit with Process, to be discharged,   6 s. 8.

Release. For a Release in nature of a pardon of alienation upon a common Recovery, and for the like Release upon a special Livery, and also for a Release upon
a genera

a general pardon at the Coronation, or other times for each of them, 1 l. 3 s. 4 d.

For the note of a Sheriffs Discharge *Discharge of* upon a Seizure,   3 s. 4 d. *Seizure.*

For every Exo. and for certifying thereof into the Exchequer,   1 2 d.

For the Sheriffs acquittance, 6 s. 8 d. *Acquittance.*

FOr entring in a large Book every *Entry of Writs.* Writ of Covenant finable, *videli-cet,* in the Term-time,   6 d.

And in the Vacation,   1 2 d.

For entring in another Book remaining in the said Office every Doc- *Licence of Alie-* quet upon a Licence of Alienation in *nation.* the Term time,   1 2 d.

And in the Vacation,   2 s.

For every Docquet for a pardon of *Pardon.* Alienation in Process of *Distringas,* or *Scire facias,*   2 s.

For every Writ of Entry of Lands *Entry of Lands* holden *in capite,* and entred in the same *holden.* Book,   6 d.

And in the Vacation,   1 2 d.

FOr indorsing every Writ of Entry, *Indorsing Bre.*
                6 d. *Writ B. e.*

For indorsing every Writ of Covenant in Term,   4 d.

In the Vacation,   6 d.

For entring unfiled Writs,   6 d.

For drawing the Discharges of Te- *Discharge of* nures in Parliament, and entring them, *Tenures.*
                3 s.

The

The *Under* Sheriff *of* Middlesex *taketh these* Fees *following in his* Majesties Court *of* Common Pleas.

Warrant.	FOr a Warrant upon a *Cap.* for every name, 4 d.
Return Venire facias.	For a return of a *Venire facias,* 2 s.
	For a Warrant upon a *Cap. utlegat.* 4 d.
Return Habeas Corpus.	For a return of a *Hbeas corpora Juratorum,* 4 s.
Sum. Jur.	For summoning the Jury, for every name, 4 d.
Cepi corpus.	For a *Cepi corpus,* for every name, 4 d.
Return exfa.	For return of an *Exigent,* for every name, 4 d.
Return Procl.	For return of a Proclamation, 12 d.
Scire facias.	For return of a *Scire facias,* 2 s.
	For return of a *Nihil habet* on a *Scire facias,* 12 d.

The

The Warden of the *Fleet* his Fees.

A Note *of the Fees due and belonging to to the Warden of the Fleet, and under-Officers, as appeareth by a Commission under the Great Seal of England, from the late Queen Elizabeth, in the third Year of her Reign, and confirmed in the seven and thirtieth Year of her Reign, what ever several Prisoner in their several degrees ought to pay.*

AN Arch-bishop, a Duke, a Dutchess, are to pay for their Commitment-fee to the said Warden and his Officers, having the first weeks diet with wine,   21 l. 10 s.

Also they are to pay for their ordinary weekly diet with wine, 3 l. 6 s. 8 d.

A Marquis, a Marquess, an Earl, a Countess, a Vice-countess, are to pay for their commitment-fee to the said Warden and his Officers, having the first weeks diet,   14 l. 11 s.

Also they are to pay for their ordinary weekly diet with wine,   2 l.

A Lord Spiritual, or Temporal, a Lady, the wife of a Baron, or Lord,

Commitments.

Commitments.

R 4   are

are to pay for the Commitment-fee as abovesaid, having the first weeks diet with Wine,   11 l. 4 s. 10 d..

Also they are to pay for their ordinary weekly commons, with Wine,   1 l. 6 s. 8 d.

A Knight, a Lady, the Wife of a Knight, a Doctor of Divinity, a Doctor of Law, or others of like calling, are to pay as aforesaid for their commitment-fee, having the first weeks diet with wine,   5 l.

Also they are to pay for their ordinary weekly commons, with wine,   18 s. 6 d.

Commitments. An Esquire, a Gentleman, a Gentlewoman that shall sit at the Parlour commons, or any person under that degree, that shall be at the same commons, are to pay for their commitment-fee as aforesaid, having the first weeks diet with wine,   3 l. 6 s. 8 d.

Also they are to pay for their ordinary weekly commons with wine, 10 s.

A yeoman, or any others that shalbe at the Hall commons, man or woman; are to pay for their commitment-fee having the first weeks diet,   33 s. 4 d.

Also they are to pay for their ordinary weekly commons.   5 s.

A poor man in the Ward, that hath part of the Box, is to pay for his commitment-fee, having no diet, 7 s. 4 d.

Al 3

Also there is due to the said Warden 20d per diem, for the whole day, and 10d. for every man, that he may lawfully licence to go abroad.

Licence to go abroad.

MOreover the said Warden hath for return of Writs, as Sheriffs and Bailiffs of Liberties have, by which he hath allowance for return of every *Habeas corpus* or Attachment,
2 s. 4 d.

Return of Writs.

Also for every *Habeas corpus cum causa*, there are Fees for returning the causes, *videlicet*,

For allowing the Writ,	2 s. 4 d.
For returning the first cause,	2 s.
For every Execution,	2 d.
For every Action,	12 d.

Which are due to the Wardens Clerks, and 5 s. to the Wardens Servants for bringing every Prisoner safe to the Bar,

Bringing a Prisoner to the Bar.

Also he hath for allowance of every *Superfedeas* and Discharge, 2 s. 4 d.

Allowance of Superfedeas.

Also when any man is committed by Order out of the Courts of Star-chamber, Chancery, Court of Wards and Liveries, Court of Exchequer, Court of Requests, and Court of Dutchy, the Wardens Servants (being sent to apprehend them, and bring them to the *Fleet*, according to the Tenour

Travelling charges for apprehending parties committed.

of

of their Commitment) have 4 d. the mile where they are apprehended, and 6 d. the mile back again, and the Clerk hath 2 s. for making the Writ.

A Table of the due Fees of the Prothonotaries Court in the Common Pleas.

These are the Fees due and belonging to the three Protho-notaries of the Court of Common Pleas at Westminster, for Entries of Declarations, Pleas and Judgments. And also for making and entring of Writs in their several Offices, and for other dues belonging to them, confirmed and allowed by the late King, by his Letters Patents under the Great Seal of England, dated at Cambury the 22. of July in the 12. year of his Reign, and are mentioned and expressed in a Schedule of Fees to the said Letters annexed, and recorded in his Majesties Court of Common Pleas at Westminster in the Term St: Michael next following, Rot quinto, sexto, septimo, octavo, nono.

Common Decl. and Pleas.

INprimis, for the entry of every common Declaration, common Plea in Bar, wherein no Free-hold is pleaded, common Replication, and Rejoinder in Actions personal, 12 d.

Special Narr: in Actions personal.

For the entry of every special Declaration, special Plea in Bar, or Abatement, Free-hold, Replication or Rejoinder, and Pleas subsequent, in sheets, every sheet containing 12. lines at the least, and every line containing ten words,   2 s.

And

And for every sheet exceeding, 8 d.

For every Declaration in Actions upon the case, *Ejectione firme*, accompt, annuity, conspiracy, covent, deceit, partition, *Plegits, acquiet,* and Debt upon Statutes, Plaint in Affize, and the like special Actions, and in real, mixt, and popular Actions, if the Declaration or Plaint exceed not three sheets, 2 s,

And for every sheet exceeding, 8 d.

For the entring of every Bar, Replication and Pleas, subsequent in every of the Actions last above recited, and in the like actions, not exceeding three sheets, 2 s.

And for every sheet so exceeding, 8 d.

For the Oyer of every Bill, Obligation, Indenture, Record, or Certificate, or the like, entred *in hæc verba*, not exceeding the length of three sheets, 2 s.

And for every sheet above that length, 8 d.

For recording of every appearance by the Court, 2 s. 4 d.

For the entry of every Recognizance without condition, challenge to the Sheriff, or Coroners, or to the Array, or other special Averments, 2 s.

And for the entring of every Recognizance with a condition, 4 s.

For every Judgment in Debt, Trespass, or Detinue, without a Tales for the Prothonotary, 2 s.

Special Nar. in special Actions.

Bar in special Actions.

Oyer de faits.

Appearances.

Recognizance.

Judgments.

And

Adjournments. And for entring every Adjournment, 4 d.

Judgments. For ever Judgment with a Tales, besides the Fee above recited, 2 s.

Remanets. For every *Remanet,* and Judgment or costs given to the Defendant by the Statute besides the Fee abovesaid, 2 s.

Judgments. For every Judgment in all other Actions, as well personal, as mixt, and real, and Prohibitions, and the like, 4 s.

Satisfaction. For every satisfaction, *Recordatur,*
Recordatur. Discontinuance, *Retraxit,* Relinquish-
Discont. Re- ment, *Nolle profequi,* or the like, in Acti-
traxit. ons personal, 4 s.
Nolle profequi. And in real Actions, 2 s.
Recoveries. For the entry of a single Recovery, 4 s. and the Writ of Seisin thereupon, 10 s. 6 d.

And for every Voucher more, 4 s.

For the entry of every *Mittimus &*
Dedimus poteftatem, for a common Recovery, 6 s.

For the entrance of a Summons *ad warr.* for a common Recovery, and the Writ of Summons *ad warr.* 4 s. 6 d.

For the entry of a *Certiorari* to certifie a Warrant of Attorney for the Tenant or Voucher, 4 s.

And if for both, 6 s.

Foreign Vou- For every foreign Voucher sent to
cher. the Common Pleas to summon the Vouchee, if the Record be not above three sheets, 2 s.

And for every sheet more, 8 d.

The like Fees are to be paid when the Record

Record is remitted back again, after the Voucher determined,   2 s. 8 d.

For the Entry of every special Verdict, whereupon a *Cur. advifar. vult.* is entred, being not above the length of three sheets, written as abovesaid, 2 s.   *Special Verdict.*

And for every sheet exceeding that length,   8 d.

For the entry of every general Verdict, with a *Cur. advifar. vult.* without a Tales,   2 s.   *General Verdict.*

And with a Tales,   4 d.

For the entry of every *Remittitur* of Debt or Damages,   12 d.   *Remittitur.*

For the entry of every Information upon any penal Law, and signing the *Subpœna* onely,   2 s. 8 d.   *Information.*

For the entring of every Surmise for a Prohibition to be granted, not exceeding the length of three sheets, as aforesaid,   2 s.   *Prohibition.*

And for every sheet above that length,   8 d.

For the entry of the Oath of every witness to prove the Surmise in a Prohibition, or *Audita querela* brought by an Infant, and the entry of the Proofs *de morte & vita virim,* Dower, and the like Actions and Suits,   2 s.   *Proof de fugg.*

For the releasing of any default in any real Action,   2 s.

And entring the recital of the grand Cape,   4 s.

And if under five Marks,   *Nihil.*

For

The Compleat Attorney.

Exam. Record.	For examining every Record of *Nisi prius,* 12 d.
Record in Coun. Palat.	For making the Record for trial of an Issue in any of the County Palatines, for the first three sheets, 2 s.
	And for every sheet more after, 4 d.
Exemplific.	For the exemplification of any Record, not exceeding six sheets, 5 s.
	And for every sheet exceeding that rate, 8 d.
Seizin in dower.	For the entring of Seisin in Dower, and dying seized, the Return of the Seisin, exceeding not above three sheets, 4 s.
	For every sheet exceeding, 8 d.
Non ponend. in assis. *Cog. de Pleas.*	For entring of Writs of Exemption de *non ponend. in jurat.* and Patents de *liberi. allocand.* and Protections, Cognizance of Pleas, and the like, according to the rates abovesaid, if they exceed not three sheets, 2 s.
	And for every sheet exceeding, 8 d.
Judgment per. default in wast. *Quare impedit.*	For the entring the default upon the Distress in Waste, *Quare impedit,* and the like, and Judgment thereupon, if the Title or Count do not exceed three sheets, 6 s. 4 d.
	And if it be more than as aforesaid, for every sheet, 8 d.
Quo warranto.	For entring of *Quo warranto,* if it exceed not three sheets, 2 s.
	For the entry of every Plea thereupon, according to the same rate before, 2 s. 8 d.

For

For the entry of a Plea of accompt pleaded before Auditors, if it be not above three sheets, written as abovesaid,

Account before Auditors.

2 s.

And if more, for every sheet exceeding, 8 d.

For the entry of every Summons, and Severance, and Aid Prayer, 2 s.

Severances. Aid Prayer.

For the admission of an infant to his *Prochein amie*, or Guardian 2 s.

And if it be by commission 4 s.

For entring of the Defendants discharge upon a *cap. pro fine*, or for a contempt, 2 s.

Cap. pro fine.

For the like upon Rescous, returned and admitted to his fine, 4 s.

For traversing of a Rescous, and Issue thereupon, 6 s.

For entring of the allowance of every general and special pardon of Outlary before Judgment, and after, 5 s. 4 d.

For entring of a *Dies dat*, in Debt, detinue and Trespass, 12 d.

And in all other Actions, 2 s.

For the entring of the Receit of a Feme covert, Tenant in tail, Lessee for years, or the like, 2 s.

And for the entry of the Plea, if it exceed not three sheets, 2 s.

And for every sheet exceeding, 8 d.

And if the Receit be by Writ, then more for entring of the Writ, 2 s.

For the entring of an Assize delivered in the Common Pleas by Justices

of Affize to be inrolled, for every fheet,
12 d.

And if the Affize come into the Common Pleas by *Certiorari*, then more for entring the *Certiorari*, 2 s.

Abridgment. For entring every Abridgment of the demand in Dower, Affize, or the like, 2 s.

Pone. For the entry of every *Pone* to remove a Plea by Writ out of the County Court there holden by Juftices, and for the return of the *Pone*, 4 s.

Mittimus. For the entring of any Record fent in the Common Pleas by *Mittimus*, or otherwife; and likewife for the entry **Rege inconful-** of every *Rege inconfulto*, or fuch like, if **to.** it exceed not three fheets, 2 s.

For every fheet fo exceeding, 8 d.

Certificate of For the entring of every Certificate **baftardy.** of baftardy certified by the Bifhop, and the awarding of the Writ and Judgment thereupon, 6 s.

Journeys ac- For the entry of the Licence of the **counts.** Court, to purchafe a new Writ by journeys accompts, 2 s.

Delivery of Re- For the entry of every Original writ **cord.** delivered of Record in real or mixt Actions, 8 d.

Challenge. For the entry of every fheet above three fheets of every challenge to the Sheriff or Coroners, or to the Array, or other fpecial Averments, or the like, 8 d.

Remanet. For the entry of every *Remanet* in real Actions, 4 s.

For the entry of every *Remittitur* in real

real and mixt Actions, 2 s.

For the entry of every sheet above *Aid prayer.* three sheets of every Aid-prayer, 8 d.

For the entry of an Admission of a *Admission to* Guardian, if it be by Commission, and *Guardians.* *Mitrimus,* 6 s.

For the entry of a Privy Seal, for *Privy Seal.* every sheet, 8 d.

For the entry of the Licence of the *Licence.* Court to compound upon penal Statutes, 2 s.

For entry of every Warrant of At- *Warrants of* torny made by the Tenants in common *Attorney.* Recoveries, or the like, after their Appearance at the Bar, 2 s.

For every Judgment by special con- *Quare impe-* fession of the Title in *Quare imp...*, *dit.* or the like, if it exceed not three sheets, 4 s.

And for every sheet after, 8 d.

For the entring of every special Im- *Special Impar-* parlance, 2 s. *lance.*

For the entring of every *Committi-* *Committitur.* *tur* of a Prisoner by the Roll, being brought to the Bar by Writ, and every tender of the body in discharge of the Bail, 4 s.

But if it be without Writ, then in either Case but 2 s.

For entring of every demand of a *Remand.* Prisoner to appear and remand the said Prisoner, 4 s.

For the entry of every Essoyn in *Essoyns.* the Plea-rolls, as upon Wagers of Law, 12 d.

For the entry of the Bail upon every

S Reversa

Reversal for insufficiency of *Exigent,*
or of the Return, 2 s. 4 d.

Narr.su'. de-mise. For the entry of every Declaration
in Debt upon Demise, or the like spe-
cial Declaration, if the Declaration
exceed not three sheets, 2 s.

And if such Declaration exceed the
number of three sheets, then for the
entry of every such sheet, containing
twelve lines, and every line ten words,
8 d.

Common Decl. For the entry of every several count
upon an Original in Debt, Detinue,
Trespass, and the like, 12 d.

Actions super casum. For the entry of every several count
in Actions upon the Case and Account,
Account. and the like upon several days, if the
count not exceed three sheets, 2 s.

And for every sheet so exceeding,
8 d.

Special condi-tion. For the entry of every special condition, or indorsment of any Obligation
entred *in hæc verba,* not exceeding the
length of three sheets, 2 s.

And for every sheet so exceeding, 8d.

Common condi-tion. But if the condition be in Debt for
payment of money, at one day, or un-
der the length of two sheets, then for
the entring thereof but 12 d.

Mittimus. For the entry of every *Mittimus* or
Certiorari. *Certiorari,* and the Return thereof, 4 s.

But if the Return thereof exceed
three sheets, then for every sheet so exceeding, 8 d.

Prohibition. For entring of the Count in a Prohibition, and pleadings thereupon
after

after an appearance of the Defendant, not exceeding the length of three sheets, 2 s.

And for every sheet above that length, 8 d.

For the entry of every Writ of Attaint, or false Judgment, 2 s. *Attaint, false Judgments.*

For the entry of the Return thereof and the Assignment of Errours or false Oaths, not exceeding three sheets, 2 s.

And for every sheet more, 8 d.

For the entry of every sheet above three sheets of the Oath of every Witness examined to prove the Surmise in a Prohibition, or *Audita querela* brought by an Infant, and the entry of the proofs *De morte & vita viri* in Dower, and the like Actions and Suits, 8 d. *Proof in a Prohibition. Audita querela and Dower.*

Fees due to the Prothonotaries for Writs, and the entries of them amongst other dues. *Fees for writs.*

FOr every Writ of Prohibition, or consultation, not exceeding four sheets, 2 s. *Prohibition.*

For every sheet so exceeding, 4 d.

For every Withernam return after appearance, second deliverance, Writ of Privilege, *Habeas corpus*, Proced. *Certiorari*, Summons and Resummons, *Petit. cape, ve. fac. sci. fa. Elegit, Extent. Supersed. Sub pæna*, Writ to the *Habend. Withe nam. Habeas corpus. Sum. & alikæc. Spenal.*

S 2 Bi-

Bishop, Attachment in *Aff. Diftring.*
Jur. Habeas corpu , and *Diftringas in*
Aff. & Attaint, and the like, *Habere fac.*
poffeffionem, Writs of View, *Mittimus,*
Indempnitat. nois, and every other fpeci-
al Writs,   2 s.

Entry of Writs.   For the entring of every fuch Writ,
which requireth an entry not exceeding
four fheets,   2 s.

        And if more, for every fheet as a-
bovefaid,   8 d.

Ca. fa. fi. fac.   For every *Ca. fa. & fi. fa.*   6 d.

Teftat: diftr.   For every *Teftat: fur. ca. fa. & fi. fa.*

Inquire in tref. *Dift-ing. ad deliberand.* and Writs to inquire of Damages in Trefpafs and Re-
plevin,   12 d.

Inquir. in cafu.   For Writs to inquire of Damages in
Cap. & Ex. pro Covenant, Ejectment, Actions upon the
fine.   Cafe, and the like,   2 s.

        For every *Capias pro fine,*   6 d.

        For the *Exigent* upon a *Capias pro fine,*
     10 d.

Intra.   For the entry of the Return of every
Return Bre. Writ in the Prothonotaries Roll other
than the *Ca. fa* returned *non eft invent.*
and the *fi. fa.* returned *nulla habet bona,*
whereupon further Procefs is awarded,
not exceeding four fheets,   2 s.

        And if more, then for every fheet, 8 d.

Bail fur. Priv.   For the entring of every Writ of
Habeas corpus. Privilege, or *Habeas corpus,* with the
Bail for one caufe,   6 s.

        And for every name more,   2 s.

Committitur.   For entry of every *Committitur* upon
a *Habeas corpus una cum die & caufa,*
     2 s.

        And

And for every other cause, 2 s.

For every Reversal upon an Outlary *Reversal.* for default of Proclamation with one name, and the Bail, or *nolle prosequi,* 4 s. 4 d.

For every name more, 2 s.

For every *Ca. fa. & fi. fa.* after a De- *Ca. fa. & fi. fa.* vastavit, 2 s. *pt. Devastavit.*

Whereof by allowance from the Prothonotaries the Clerk hath had, 8 d.

For every sheet exceeding four sheets *Inquir. in casu,* of Writs to inquire of Damages in *&c.* Covenant, Ejectments, Actions upon the Case, and the like Actions, 4 d.

For the Writ of *Liberat.* or the like *Liberat.* special Writs, 2 s.

Whereof by allowance from the Prothonotary, the Clerk hath had, 8 l.

For the entry of every such Writ, *Intra. Bre.* and the entry of every other special Writ which requireth an entry not exceeding four sheets, 2 s.

And for every sheet so exceeding, 8 d.

For every *Distringas* in Detinue, 12 d. *Distringas.* Whereof the Clerk by allowance from the Prothonotary hath had, 4 d.

For Writs to inquire of Damages in *Inquir. in case,* Covenant, Ejectment, Actions upon *&c.* the Case, and the like Actions, if they exceed not four sheets, 2 s.

Whereof by allowance from the Prothonotary the Clerk hath had, 4 d.

For the entry of every *Committitur,* *Committitur.* upon a *Habeas corpus una cum die & causa,* with one cause returned, besides the entry of the Writ, 2 s.

S 3 And

And for the entry of the Writ, 2 s.
And for every other caufe returned,
2 s.

Procefs. Su'. Information. For the figning of all Procefs upon information, excepting the firft *Sub pœ-na,* 1 s. 4 d.

The Prothonotaries Clerks Fees.

Copies. INprimis, for the copies of common Declarations and Pleas, for every fheet containing twelve lines, and every line ten words, 4 d.

For every fheet in real and mixt Actions, and Actions upon any Statute, and the like, 8 d.

Draughts. For drawing of every fpecial Declaration, and Plea for every fheet, 8 d.

Continuance. For every continuance every Term of every Iffue, Writ, *imparlance, demurrer* of fpecial Verdict, or adjournment, 4 d.

Exemplificat. For exemplifying every Recovery with a fingle Voucher, 4 s. 8 d.

For exemplifying of a double Voucher, 6 d.

And for every Voucher more, 12 d.

For exemplifying of any Record, not exceeding eight fheets, 5 s.

And for every fheet more, 6 d.

Drawing of Writs and Entries thereof. For drawing of every extraordinary long Writ after the rate of every fheet, 8 d.

And for the entry thereof (if it fo require) for every fheet, 4 d.

For

For a copy of Judgment for every *Copies of Judg-*
sheet, 8 d. *ments.*

For the entry of every Writ, and the *Entries in re-*
Return thereof into the Prothonota- *membr.*
ries Remembrance for drawing up of a
Judgment, if it exceed not three sheets,

6 d.

And for every sheet after, 4 d.

For entring of every common Rule *Rules.*
into the Bill of Pleas, or common Remembrance, 4 d.

For the entring and ingrossing eve- *Summons for*
ry Summons for a Recovery, and for *Recoveries.*
the making of the Writ of Summons,

2 s,

For the entry of every *Mittimus* and *Mittimus.*
Dedimus potestatem for a Recovery, 2s.6d

For the ingrossing of every *Nisi pri-* *Ingro. Nisi pri-*
us after the rate of every sheet, 4 d. *us.*

For entring of every *Testat. sur. ca* *Intrar. case te-*
sa & fi. fa. 4 d. *stat.*

For the search in every Term in the *Searches.*
Prothonotaries Office, in his Docquets,
or Remembrances, 4 d.

For the issuing out of the Court-mo- *Court-money.*
ney, of the party receiving it, 1d. in l.

For the making of every long Writ, *Making long*
as Prohibitions, and the like, for every *writs.*
sheet, 4 d.

For the prosecution and issuing out *Cap. pro fine.*
of Process for the King, to bring in the
party for to make fine for his contempt
untill the party render himself, or be
outlawed, besides the Fees of the
Court, 3 s. 4 d.

And if there be cause of prosecuti-

on after the *Exigent* returned , then
more.   3 s. 4 d.

Copy ſuggeſt. For the copies of ſuggeſtion to grant
a Prohibition, for every ſheet,   8 d.

**Traęt. Prohibit.
Special Ver-
dięt.** For drawing of every Surmiſe to
have a Prohibition, ſpecial verdięt, and
the like, for every ſheet,   8 d.

The Prothonotaries Clerks Fees for Informations onely.

Information. FOr ingroſſing of every Information,
                                          8 d.

For a copy of the ſaid Information,
if it amount to the number of five
ſheets of paper, or upwards,   3 s. 4 d.

If it be under the number of five
ſheets, then for every ſheet,   8 d.

For the making of every *Cap. pro fine*
upon an Information,   6 d.

For entring of the general Iſſue upon the Roll where the Information
was firſt entred in the Term it was firſt
exhibited,   8 d.

For the regiſtring of every Licence
to compound in the Office-book,   4 d.

An ancient Fee due to the ſecond Prothonotaries Clerk onely.

Fines. FOr recording of every Fine acknowledged at the Bar, by Writ, and mo-
ved by a Serjeant,   4 d.

Fees

Fees due to the Secondaries of the Pro- Secondaries
thonotaries in their several Offices. Fees.

FOr the copy of every common *Copies. of*
Rule, 4 d. *Rules.*
For taking a note of the Rule of the
Judges in Court upon a motion of a *Drawing and*
Serjeant, for drawing the same Rule in *entring of*
paper in *Latine* words, and entring it *Rules.*
into the Bill of Pleas, and the copy
thereof, the draught not exceeding six
lines in paper, 8 d.
If the Rule exceed 6. lines, then 12 d.
For every wager in Law, in Court, or *Wagers in*
Nonsuit of the Plaintiff, upon a wager *Law.*
of Law, 12 d.
For the entry of the *Committitur* of *Committitur.*
any Defendant to the *Fleet* in Executi-
on of any Judgment, or otherwise in
Court, and for making a copy thereof
for the Warden of the *Fleet,* containing the cause of the commitment, 12 d.
For the entring of every Commitment to the *Fleet,* of any person yield-
ing himself in discharge of his Bail,
and for the like copy, 12 d.
For attending the Judg from his
chamber to *Westminster,* to take a privy *Privy Verdict.*
Verdict tried at the Bar, 3s. 4d.
For reading the Record of a Demur- *Read. Record.*
rer in Court or Verdict, 12d. *Bails.*
For taking Bail in Court, 12d.

For

Admission to Guardians.

For entring of an admission of an Infant to his Prochin Amy, or Guardian in the Prothonotaries remembrance,
         1 d.

Copies of Issue and Jurors names.

For the Copy of the Issue and Jurors names to be delivered to the Jury upon any Trial at the Bar,   12 d.

Trials at Bar.

For reading of Evidences upon Trials at the Bar of each Party, Plaintiff, and Defendant,   3 s. 4 d.

Satisfact. Recordatur. Discontinuance. Satisfaction.

For entring of every satisfaction by special Warrant, *Rteo datur,* and discontinuance,   8 d.

For every satisfaction by general Warrant,   4 d.

For entry of every Will or Letters of Administration to enable an Executor or Administrator to acknowledg satisfaction, and the entry of the satisfaction,   12 d.

Interrogatories.

For every Copy of Interrogatories, Depositions of persons examined upon Interrogatories by Order of the Court for every sheet,   8 d.

Per Breve de Privato Sigillo,

Wolseley.

Fees

Fees of the Upper Bench.

A note of Fees due, and time out of minde used to be paid to the Prothonotaries, or chief Clerks of the Court of Upper Bench, and to their Clerks, as the same was presented upon Oath by virtue of Commission in Apr. 1630. by 29. Attornies of the same Court, and hitherto taken.

Writs.

FOr a *Latitat.*   5 s. 1 d.

Supersedeas.	*Prohibiton.*
Exigent in Appeal.	*Consultacon.*
Distring. in Attaint.	*Proprietate proban.*
Habeas corpus.	*Distring in Detinue.*
Certiorari.	*Inquir. de valore.*
Procedend.	*Resum.*
Elegit.	*Reattachmt.*
Sub pœna.	*Vesa. defend. in audita querela.*
Return bend.	
Withernam.	*Habere fac. sciam. & possession.*
Second deliverance	
Restitution.	*Respons. in Attaint.*
Scire facias.	*Rend. expon.*
Diminucon.	*Bre. expe.*
Libello bend.	*Mittimus.*

All these are accountable for to the Prothonotaries, *viz.* For every one 2 s. out of which they allow the Clerke for writing 4 d.

Venire facias.	*Sur. cepi corpus.*
Diftring. Jur.	*Averm. verf. vic.*
Ali. ~~Corpus cap.~~	*Fieri facias.*
Cafa.	*Teft. fi. fac. & cafa.*
Inquir. de Damnis.	*Diftr. nuper vic.*
Habeas Corpus.	*Non omittas.*

For every of thefe befides the Seal, 6 d. And for every *Deliver at de Recordo,* 4 d. And for the *Jura* of the *Diftr.* of *Ni. pri.* 4 d. But all thefe have been always to the Prothonotaries Clerks, and are not accounted for to the Prothonotaries.

In every Action wherein the *Pli.* recovereth damages to the value of 13 l. 6 s, 8 d. he payeth 12 d. in the pound for damage clear, when the Judgment is figned.

Upper Bench Fees for Entries.

For every Deed how fhort foever, 2s.
For every Action of Trefpafs, 1s.
For every not guilty, 1s.
For every Juftification in Trefpafs, 2s.
For every Replication, 2s. 8d.
For every Action of the Cafe not above three fheets, 2s.
For every general Iffue to it, 1s.
For every *Ejectione firme,* 2s.
For every Declaration in Appeal, 2s.
For every general Iffue therein, 2s.
For every Recogn. *Sur. He. corp.* for every Defendant feverally, 2s.
For every Depofition upon all Prohibitions, 2s.
For every Judgment by Circumft. 4s.

out

Out of which the Clerk is allowed, 8d

For every other Judgment, 2s

    whereof the Clerk is allowed, 4d

For every Difmiffion, 2s

For every Commitment in Execution, 2s

For every fatisfaction, 3s

For every Appearance recorded, 2s

For every *Non prof.* 2 s

For every Action of Debt, Detinue, or Trefpafs, 1s

For every general Iffue therein, 1s

For every condition performed, 2s

For every Replication to it, 1s

For a Writing denied, and keeping of the Writing, 2s

For every Juftification in Battery, 2s

For every *Aud. quer.* how fhort foever, 2s

For every fpecial Imparlance, 2s

For every general Imparlance upon the Plea-roll 12d

For every default upon Record, 2s

For fuch a fuggeftion upon a Prohibition how fhort foever, 2s

For every Recognizance to it, 2s

For every W. of Er. how fhort foever, 3s. 4d

For entring the Errours, 2s

For entring *in nullo eft Errat.* 2s

For every Diminution, 2s

For abatement of a Writ of Errour and licence to fue a new one, 2s

For entring of the fame, 2s

For every Recognizance fingle, or with condition, 2s

For every Inrolment whatfoever, longer than three fheets, 6s. 8d

After the rate for a Roll on both fides, 6s. 8d

The Compleat Attorney.

Venire facias.	*Sur. ceƒi corpus.*
Diſtring. Jur.	*Averm. verſ. vic.*
Ali. ~~*cay.*~~	*Fieri facias.*
Caſa.	*Teſt. fi. fac. & caſa.*
Inquir. de Damnis.	*Diſtr. nuper vic.*
Habeas Corpus.	*Non omittas.*

For every of theſe beſides the Seal, 6 d. And for every *Deliberat de Recordo*, 4 d. And for the *Jura* of the *Diſtr.* of *Ni. prł.* 4 d. But all theſe have been always to the Prothonotaries Clerks, and are not accounted for to the Prothonotaries.

In every Action wherein the *Plt.* recovereth damages to the value of 13 l. 6 s. 8 d. he payeth 12 d. in the pound for damage clear, when the Judgment is ſigned.

Upper Bench Fees for Entries.

For every Deed how ſhort ſoever,	2s.
For every Action of Treſpaſs,	1s.
For every not guilty,	1s.
For every Juſtification in Treſpaſs,	2s.
For every Replication,	2s. 8d.
For every Action of the Caſe not above three ſheets,	2s.
For every general Iſſue to it,	1s.
For every *Ejectione firme*,	2s.
For every Declaration in Appeal,	2s.
For every general Iſſue therein,	2s.
For every Recogn. *Sur. He. corp.* for every Defendant ſeverally,	2s.
For every Depoſition upon all Prohibitions,	2s.
For every Judgment by Circumſt.	4s.

out

Out of which the Clerk is allowed, 8d

For every other Judgment, 2s

    whereof the Clerk is allowed, 4d

For every Difmiffion, 2s

For every Commitment in Execution, 2s

For every fatisfaction, 3s

For every Appearance recorded, 2s

For every *Non prof.* 2 s

For every Action of Debt, Detinue, or

    Trefpafs, 1s

For every general Iffue therein, 1s

For every condition performed, 2s

For every Replication to it, 1s

For a Writing denied, and keeping of

    the Writing, 2s

For every Juftification in Battery, 2s

For every *And. quer.* how fhort foever, 2s

For every fpecial Imparlance, 2s

For every general Imparlance upon the

    Plea-roll 1 3d

For every default upon Record, 2s

For fuch a fuggeftion upon a Prohibiti-

    on how fhort foever, 2s

For every Recognizance to it, 2s

For every W. of Er. how fhortfoever, 3s. 4d

For entring the Errours, 2s

For entring *in nullo eft Errat.* 2s

For every Diminution, 2s

For abatement of a Writ of Errour and

    licence to fue a new one, 2s

For entring of the fame, 2s

For every Recognizance fingle, or with

    condition, 2s

For every Inrolment whatfoever, long-

    er than three fheets, 6s. 8d

After the rate for a Roll on both fides,

    6s. 8d

For half a Roll,   3 s. 4 d.

For every Bail by Recogn.   2 s. 6 d.

Upper Bench Fees of Clerks and Attornies.

FOr their Fee in every cause for every Term,   3 s. 4 d.

For their Fees at every *Ni. pri.* and inquiry of damages,   3 s. 4 d.

For their Fee in every Appeal, and Assize every Term,   6 s. 8 d.

For drawing every Declaration not exceeding a sheet,   1 s.

For every sheet above one,   8 d.

For drawing every Action on the case and covenant, how short soever, 3 s. 4 d.

For drawing every Ejectment,   2 s.

For every sheet ingrossed in Parchment,   4 s.

For drawing a Surmise upon a Prohibition, every sheet,   1 s.

For drawing special pleadings, every sheet,   8 d.

For copies of Declarations, Pleas or other things, every sheet,   4 d.

For continuing every cause every Term,   4 d.

For entring all things above three sheets, every sheet,   8 d.

For every Judgment by circumst. 5 s.

For making every Bail,   4 d.

For making every Bill of *Middlesex,* *Distring. super vic.* and *He. corp. per pre-ceptum* thereupon,   8 d.

For making every *He. corp. ad fac. Ht. corp. cum privileg. Certiorari, Procedend. elegit & habere fac. possessionem,* besides 4 d. allowed by the Prothonotary, 1 s. 8 d

For

For every sheet in a Writ of Inqui-ry, Prohibition, Consultation, &c. 4 d.

For entring every *Scire facias,*   1 s.

Fees received by the Secondary.

FOr taking the acknowledgment of a Deed in Court,   1 s.

For signing every Judgment by con-fession, *nihil dicit, verdict & damurrer.*

Also for acknowledgment of every Deed, for every Judgment pronounced in open Court, every Rule to alter a Visue, for every Rule, for a Prohibiti-on, Consultation, Attachment, &c. He receiveth for the Poors Box,   1 s.

For allowance of a Writ of Errour, *coram nobis residend.*   2 s.

Whereof to the Box,   1 s.

For an allowance of an *Audita que-rela,*   2 s.

Whereof to the Box,   1 s.

upper Bench Fees.

FOr every common Bail,   1 s. 2 d.

For a special Bail, upon a *Habeas cor-pus, Certiorari,* or Attachment, 4 s. 1 d.

Fees received by th Secondary for the Judges.

FOr every *Habeas corpus ad fac. & re-cipiend.*   4 s.

For every *Procedendo,*   4 s.

For every *Certiorari* to remove a fo-reign Attachment,   4 s.

For a *Procedendo* thereupon,   4 s.

For every *Habeas corpus cum privil.* 3s
Out of ever *Latitat* they have   8d

Fees received by the Judges Clerks.

FOr every Warrant for a *Hab. corp.* or any thing to which the Judg put-eth his hand in the Term time,   1s
And in the Vacation,   2s
For the acknowledgment of a Deed which he faith is for his Mafter, 6s. 8d
And for his own Fee,   2s
For taking the Depofition of Witneffes upon a Suggeftion for a Prohibition, for every Witnefs,   6s. 8d
And for his own Fee for every Witnefs,
                                       2s

Fees paid the Clerk for the Papers.

FOr copying every fpecial Plea, every fheet,   4d
For making the Paper-book either If-fue or Demurrer, every fheet,   8d
For entring into his Book every Record to be read in Court,   1s
For entring into his Book every caufe, to hear counfel on both fides,   1s
For entring every Trial at Bar,   1s

The Keeper of the Pofteas.

HAth for the receiving, marking, keeping, and delivery of every Po-ftea,   4d

                                   The

The Keeper of the files of Declarations.

HAth for the fyling, pying, and shewing the files of every Clark, for every Terme,   2 s.

Fees paid to the *Clerke of the Rules.*

FOR entring every Rule, except generall Rules for answer,   4 d

For a Copy of every Rule,   4 d

For every generall Rule for answer, being above three
                    2 s.

For every Rule given in Court, with a copy for a Prohibition, or consultation, he taketh 12 d. and the due is but 8 d. which hath been taken not above 25 yeeres.   8 d.

For every Rule with a copy given in Court the last day of a Terme he taketh 12 d. whereas the due is but 8 d. which hath been taken this two or three yeers,   8 d.

For evey copy of a Rule after the continuance day he taketh 8 d. whereas the due is but 4 d. which hath been taken this two or three yeeres,   4 d

All such Affidavits as are read in Court he claimeth this two yeers, or thereabouts to have the keeping of them, and taketh for copies both of Plaintiff and Defendant at his owne discretion, which formerly hath not been.

Doggetmaker.

THe Secondaries Clerk, for making and keeping the Remembrances of Entries, *&c.* hath of every Clerk, every Term,   8 d

Keepers of the Bailes.

FOR entring the common Bailes into Parchment Rolls every Terme, every Clerk of the Office giveth what he pleaseth.

                    T   *Keepers*

Keepers of the Rolls of writs.

FOR carrying the Rolls of the Writs to the Hall, and the Office, he hath of every Clerk every Term that he pleaseth.

Fees paid to the Custos Brevium *and his Clarks.*

FOr every record of *Nisi Prius* in a short Action of Trespasse,	4 s 6 d
For every other Record how short soever,	5 s
For every full Presse of *Nisi prius* or *Mittimus,*	6 s
For every *Nisi prius* out of the Crown side,	6 s 8 d
For every full presse there,	1 s 8 d
For every *Nisi prius* upon an Inditement of murther, for every name that pleadeth to Issue,	6 s 8 d
For every short Exemplification in Trespasse,	10 s
For every Exemplification containing a large skin 11 ·
For the like in the Crown side,	21
For every Exemplification in *Ejectione firme,* 13 s 4 d
For filing a Writ being a *Post diem* upon the *Angl.* 4 d.
For all pt. *Terminums* at any time after the first week ended in the second Term,	1 s 8 d
For every *Warrant* of Attorney in murther,	1 s
For every Sheriffs *Warrant,*	8 d
For every other *Warrant* of Attorney,	4 d
For every search for a Roll for ten years last past, 6 d
For every search above ten years last past,	3 s 4 d
For search for Rolls for the six last Terms	0 d
For search of every file of Declarations, Bails, Judicial, and other Writs after ten years	1 s 4 d
For the copy of every sheet between Party and Party,	4 d
For a copy of a Deed inrolled, for every sheet	8
For the File of an *Angl* for every Term after one,	4
For the copies of every *Writ* or *Appeale,* every sheete	8

Fee

Fees now paid to the Custos Brevium *his Clarks.*

FOR writing every *Nisi prius* or *Mittimus*, being but one presse,   1 s 6 d

For every presse more then one,   1 s

For writing every Exemplification in Trespasse or E-jectment,   3 s 4 d

For writing every large skin of Parchment Exemplified,   6 s 8 d

The Fees for writing every *Nisi prius* or *Mittimus*, were uncertaine untill about *Anno 2. Iac.* And then it was ordered by the Judges that the Clarks should have for writing of the first presse, 1 s 6 d. And if more, then every other presse, 12 d. And every full presse to containe 60 lines.

Fees claimed by the Cryer and Porter. As Cryer.

FOR calling a Jury.   2 s

For every Oath given in Covrt,   4 d

For taking a Privy Verdict,   4 s

For every argument in Law,   2 s

For every wager of Law   2 s

For every admission to a Gardian,   6 d

For a baile taken at the Bar,   2 s

For calling a Non-suit,   4 d

For calling the *Record*,   1 s

For calling a default,   1 s

When a Pardon is pleaded,   2 s

As Porter.

FOR every tryall at Bar   5 s

For every privy Verdict,   2 s

For summoning the Wager-men,   3 s

For a baile taken at Bar,   2 s

For a *Record* called,   6 d

For default called   6 d

For a Pardon pleaded,   2 s

For a discharge of a *Rescous*,   4 d

For a Baile taken in Court,   6 d

T ?   Of

Of all these Fees mentioned and claimed by the Cryer, and Porter, these following have been paid as due, during the time of our knowledge.

As *Cryer.*

FOR calling a Jury,	1 s
For swearing every witnesse,	4 d
For a wager of Law,	1 s
For a Non-suit,	1 s
For a default of a Record,	1 s
For a *defecit de lege,*	1 s

As *Porter.*

FOR summoning the Wager-men, 　　3 s
Also the *Porter* receiveth more for the Wager-men, where the Defendant wageth his law, or is ready to wage it, 　　1 s

Fees received by the Clark of the Errors immediatly after the Statute 27. Eliz.

FOR the Lord cheife Justices fee for the allowance,	17 s 4 d
For the Receipt,	5 s
For the Return,	2 s
For the Certificate of the first presse,	6 s
For writing the first presse,	2 s
For a *Super sedeas,*	2 s 7 d

These Fees amounting to 35 s. 3 d. were paid upon the allowance of the Writ, and for the Supersedeas.

FOR the certifying of the Record for every presse besides the first,	6
For writing of every presse after the first,	1
For the Roll,	1
For making *Non pros.* upon the Roll,	5

Al

*Also immediately after the making of the Statute of An.
Jac. the Fees taken for the Bail were as followeth,
upon a Writ of Errour.*

TO the Prothonotaries for the Recognizance, 2 s
To the Judges Clark,   2 s

Fees upon a Writ of Errour.

FOR making the Baile,   4 d
For drawing and entring the Recognisance,   4 s
Now, and for the space of thirty yeers last past, he
hath taken upon the Receit of every Writ of *Errour*
and *Supersedeas* in a gross sum   2 li. 6s. 8 d
Also for certifying every presse besides the last 6s. 8d
For writing every presse besides the first,   2 s
For every *Supersedeas* besides the first, with the Seale
     9 s. 3 d.

*These last mentioned were set down by Sir John Popham,
late Lord chief Justice, Ex relatione Edi. Page cler.
Error, but we do not certifie it upon our knowledge.*

ALso he taketh for every bail in gross sum, 19 s. 4 d.
For every Writ of Error, *Tam in redditione judicii,
quam in ajudicatione executiones,* he taketh double fees.

*The Marshals Fees as they were certified by Sir William
Knowls Knight, sometime Marshal of the Kings Bench.*

INprimis, for inlargement of every Prisoner which
is termed his admission fee   10 s.
Also he demandeth of every Prisoner upon his in-
largement, a Fine, for not wearing of Irons.
For execution in every pound   3 d.
For actions in every pound   1 d. ob.
    T 3   The

The Marshall taketh for every dismission more then the former fee of ten shillings 8 s. 8 d.

The Deputy Marshall, and Marshals men, take for every Prisoner that is committed in Court 5 s. 6 s.

And for every Prisoner committed from the Judges Chamber 2 s. 6 d.

The Deputy Marshall taketh for the allowance of every *Habeas corpus* 2 s 6 d.

The Clerk of the Fines.

THere was an Office invented and erected about 6. *Jacobi*, whereby is taken upon the filing of every Declaration in debt, where the debt is above 40 l. and not above 100. marks, 3 s. 4 d. And above a 100. marks, and not above a 100. l. 5 s. and after the same rate, and also in the every action on the case, and trespasse for goods, where the damages are land above 40 l. the like rates, so that the Plaintiff or Defendant be not a person priviledged, nor the Defendant in *Custodia Marr.* whereas before 6. Iac: in all our memories, no such monies were paid, or demanded.

Fees for trialls at Bar, taken by severall Officers.

THe Cryer for calling the Iury 2 s
For swearing every Witnesse 4 d
The Porter for keeping the doors 5 s
The Cryer for a Non-suit 2 s
The Deputy Marshall 2 s
The Tipstaves or Marshals men for a Verdict, *sedente curia* 8 s 6 d
If the Iury lye together all night 17 s 8 d

The

The Iudges Foot-cloathmeen, 12 d. a peece,   4 s
The Secondary receives for a Verdict in Court   2 s

And for a privy Verdict, 13 s. 4 d. which he faith is thus divided, *viz.* The Iudge that taketh the Verdict 6 s. 8 d. To the Secondary 2 s. and the reft being 4 s. 8 d. among the Officers that attend.

Of all the Fees mentioned, We prefent thefe following to be due.

TO the Cryer for calling the Iury   1 s
For fwearing every Witneffe   4 d
For calling a Non-fuit   1 s
To the Deputy Marfhall   2 s
To the Porter for keeping the doors   1 s
To the Secondary for taking a Verdict in Court 2 s
To him for a privy Verdict   13 s 4 d

And now they take no other Fees then thefe laft mentioned.

We pay into the Crown Office for eftreating every amercement.   1 s

Alfo there is paid to the Secondaries Clerk by every one of the Prothonotaries Clerks every Term that he faileth to bring in his Rolls within 24. daies next following, after Trinity, Michaelmas, and Hilary Terms refpectively, and within ten daies next after Eafter Term, 12 d. whereas formerly they had time untill the Effoin day of the next Term, to bring them in without paying any Fee.

Alfo there is paid to the Secondaries Clerk for the filing of every common Bail, after fix daies after every Term over and above the Fee.   4 d.

The Table of which feverall payments laft mentioned is remaining in the Kings Bench Office.

Fees due and received by Philizers.

FOr every *Cap. Alf. Plur. Exigit, Proclama. & Di-string.* in Trespasse   6 d

For every Exigent & Proclamation in Replevin, 6 d

For every *Pone cap.alf.plur.Testat. in Replevin*   6 d

For every *Supersed.* upon the mean processe afore-said   2 s

For every *Cap. Alf. Plur. Testat.* and *Exigit* in *Truf. sup. casum,* Action on a Statute, *Rap. custodie Truf. contra formam ordinationis,* Ejectments, and such spe-ciall Writts   1 s

For the Proclamation thereupon   1 s
For the *Distring.* thereupon   1 s
For every *Cap. Alf. & Plur.* in an appeal of *Mayhem*
                                                        1 s

For every *Cap. Alf. & Plur.* in an appeal of *Robbery*
                                                        2 s

For every name in every *Cap. Alf. & Plur.* in appeal of *Murther*   2 6

For every Proclamation in every appeal   2 s

For every general *Cap.utl.& delibatur de recordo* 10 d

For every speciall *Cap. utl. & delibatur de resordo*
                                                     2 s 4 d

For every Writ of *Withernam,* second deliverance, and return *habend.* before Avowry   2 s

For every *Venire facias*   6 d

For every *Distring. Iur. delibat. de recordo, & jur. Nisi prius*   1 8 2 d

For every *Subpœna* upon Issue by Originall   2 s

For entry of Declarations in trespasse by Originall
                                                        1 s

For entring not guilty thereunto   1 s

For entring every Ejectment and Action upon the case not above three sheets   2 s

If longer, then for every sheet   8 d

For every generall Imparlance   4 d
                                                        For

For every speciall Imparlance   2 s
Copies of Writs of Attaint, before judgment *per* sheet
                                               8 d

Fees due upon Tryals at Guild-hall, to the Officers
of the Court.

TO the Clerk that reads the Record and Evidence
                                               1 s

To the Associate   1 s
For every default   2 s 4 d
To the Cryer   1 s
For swearing every Witnesse   4 d
The Marshall   2 s
The Foot-cloath   1 s
The Green-cloath   1 s 6 d
The Doorkeeper   1 s
The Hall-keeper   1 s
The Jury men   8 s
Oyer-men, every one   4 d
For summoning and keeping the Jury   4 s 4 d
Lights   1 s
Bar-keeper   1 s
Return of the Postea   2 s

Also the Associate taketh in every cause where the
Plaintiffs Attorney is not present, and of every Defendant which appeareth, and hath not his Attorney
in Court, for a Warrant of Attorney   4 s

The Exchequer.

THis Court hath formerly been a Court of much
practise and in greate esteem ; but of late since the
Revenues of the Crown have been sold, there is but
little businesse to what formerly, and very likely to
be far lesse, when there will be little or nothing at all
left of what related to the Crown, save only the Customes, Impost, Tonnage, and Poundage.

But yet of late the Court hath had much increase
of businesse, by reason of many Suits which are
                                           brought

brought by Parſons and Vicars againſt their Pariſhi-oners for the detaining of their tythes, which courſe hath proved very ſucceſsfull to them in recovering and obtaining their juſt rights and dues.

The chief Iudges of this Court, are the Lord chief Baron, & three other Barons of the Coif, with whom alſo ſits one other who hath the name of a Baron, but hath no voice in Court as to any buſineſs, ſave the taking accounts of Sheriffs, Auditors, Bayliffs, Receivers, &c. The ſobordinate Officers are,

1. The Kings Remembrancer, now called the Lord Protectors Remembrancer, in whoſe Office are ſeverall Attornies.

2. The Lord Treaſurers Remembrancer, and in that Office likewiſe ſeverall Attornies.

3. The Clark of the Pipe.

The Controller of the Pipe, and ſeverall Clerks there.

4. The Clerk of the Office of Pleas in his Office; there are likewiſe ſeverall Attornies.

5. The Clerk of the Eſtreats.

6. The forraign Oppoſer.

7. The Auditors of the Court, which were anciently many.

8. Tellers, and one of them in chief, and under-Tellers their Subſtitutes.

9. The Clerk of the Tallies.

10. The Chamberlain of the Court.

The chief Uſher, and ſeverall other Uſhers.

The Uſher, and Porter of the Court, and Court-keeper.

The Keeper of the Records of the late Court of Augmentation.

This Court of Exchequer hath in it a divers way of proceeding.

As firſt, There is a courſe of proceeding ſuitable in
most

moſt things to the Common Law, proceedings in o-
ther Courts, and that is, of their (*Quo minus*) out
of the Office of Pleas, which Writ was anciently to
be granted to ſuch parly onely, who was either Tenant, or Debtor, or ſome waies accountant to the
King; and therefore the end of the Writ concludes,
that he is for default of the Defendant, giving him
ſatisfaction, leſſe able to ſatisfie the King; but at
this day the practiſe is grown generall in all caſes al-
moſt, but more eſpecially in *Wales*, where no Writ
out of the Upper-bench, and Common-bench lies,
ſave onely a *Capias ut legatum*, and this Writ which
ſo far relate together, as that they both pretend to be
by way of Prerogative for the King: The rules formerly given for proceedings at Common Law in
Upper-bench, *&c.* will ſerve you for this.

The Exchequer Chamber.

THis Court is as it were the Chancery of the Exchequer, in which ſits as the chief Iudge, or Iuſti-
cer, formerly the Lord Treaſurer, and Chancellor
of the Exchequer, being aſſiſted with the Lord chief
Baron, and the Barons of the Coif; and now that
there is no Treaſurer, nor Chancellor, the Lord chief
Baron, and the reſt of the Barons, and the proceedings had there before them, do much reſemble the
proceedings in the Chancery, and therefore I refer
you to what you will find following, of the proceedings in the Court of Chancery, which may be ſome
guide to you in this.

The whole practiſe and proceedings which are generally in uſe at the Exchequer Bar, do relate for
the moſt part to the two Remembrancers of the court,
which as I told you before, were the Kings, or States
Remembrancer, and the Lord Treaſurer, or Com-
mittee,

mittee, of the Revenue Remembrancer.

There hath been anciently very much businesse, and that very various in the Kings Remembrancers Office, relating to the Debters, Tenants, Farmers, Receivers, Accountants, Bayliffs, and Sheriffs, for debts or duties due to the King, &c.

In the Treasurers Remembrancer were wont to be all licences of Alienation pleaded, and all proces to issue out for the Fines not paid upon them, and also all proces for not payment of respite of homage, &c. And these severall Offices do in many things also follow the practise of the common Law.

The differences between this court, and the courts of Upper-bench, and common-bench, in point of appearance at the beginning of a Suit, take as follows.

In the Exchequer Chamber, the Process upon English Bill is subpœna, Attachment, Proclamation and Commission of Rebellion.

If the Defendant appeare, and no Bill be exhibited within foure dayes after the returne of the Proces the Defendant may be dismissed with Costs.

After the Bill is exhibited the Defendant hath eight dayes after his appearance to answer, if he answer not by that time a rule of foure dayes more is to be given, and if he doe not answer by that time, Proces of Attachment may be awarded against him for his contempt.

If the Defend. demurr or put in an insufficient Answer, the Plain. may put in his exceptions to the said Answer, and move to have the Bill, Answer, and exceptions or demurrer set down to be read in Court, and upon arguing thereof the Court give their opinions, whether such answer or demurrer be good or not, and award Costs accordingly, and if the Answer be adjudged insufficient or the demurrer be overruled, then the Court doth order that the Defendant shall put in a further Answer.   If

If a Bil be exhibited againſt a Peere of the Nation, there muſt be a Letter directed to him under the hands of two of the Barons, requiring his appearance, if he do not appeare, then Proceſs of *Subpæna* and after a *Diſtringas* or Attachment.

If the Bill be againſt a Corporation, Proceſſe of *Diſtringas* muſt be made againſt them, their Anſwer is without oath.

If a Bill or Petition be exhibited againſt the Lord-Protector, The Plaintiff muſt attend the Lord Protectors Atturney with a Copie of it, and procure him to anſwer it, which is without oath.

When the Defendant hath anſwered, the Plaintiff may goe to hearing upon Bill and Anſwer if he will, if he doe reply to the Anſwer, he muſt ſerve the Defendant with a *Subpæna* to rejoyne, upon Affidavit made thereof in the Terme time, if the Defendant do not rejoyne and joyne in Commiſſion for examination of witneſſes within foure dayes after the end of the Terme, the Plaintiff may have a Commiſſion *ex parte* to examine his witneſſes.

After Proceſſe ſerved to rejoyne and affidavit made as aforeſaid, both ſides may examine witneſſes in Court if they will, giving the names of their witneſſes each to other or to their Attorneys in Court, in convenient time before their examination.

Where the Plaintiff hath examined his Witneſſes he may move for Publication, and a rule is given ordinarily of a week in Terme, and if no cauſe be ſhewed according to the rule then Publication to paſſe and the cauſe to be ſet down for a hearing.

When the cauſe is ſet down to be heard the Plaintiff muſt ſerve the Defendant with Proceſſe of *Subpæna* to hear Judgement; And if at the day of hearing the Defendant do not appeare upon oath made of the ſervice of the ſaid *Subpæna*, the Court will cauſe the

Defendants

Defendants anfwer to be read, and fo proceed upon the Plaintiffs Proofes, but the Court doth ufually in fuch cafe give the Defendant a day to fhew caufe why a decree fhould not be made againft him.

If the Defendant attend the hearing, and the Plain. make default, the Defendant is difmiffed with Cofts. For breach of decrees and other great contempts, the Court doth award Attachments or a Meffenger or a Serjeant at Armes as the caufe requireth; And when the Defendant is brought in, he is committed to the Fleete or put in fecurity to attend until he be examined upon Interrogatories and licenfed by the Court to depart, and if he deny the contempt the Profecutor may examine Witneffes to prove it either in Court or by Commiffion: if by Commiffion the Defendant may joyne to fee an indifferent examination, but not to examine unleffe the Court order it, and if the contempt be proved the Court doth punifh it with Imprifonment, Fine, and cofts to the Profecutor; if it be not proved the Defendant is to be difmiffed with cofts. In cafe of Ordinary contempts for not appearing or not anfwering, the cofts are ordinary, *viz.* for every Attachment 10 s. for every Commiffion of Rebellion, 3 l. 6 s. 8 d. which is to be paid before the contempt be difcharged. In cafe where any Bill of cofts is to be taxed, the Attorney is to fee it before it be tendred to the Baron to be taxed.

The Fees in Court upon the Proceedings by English Bill together with fome other Fees.

FOr a *Subpœna*,	0 — 2 — 6
For an Attachment,	0 — 2 — 6
For a Proclamtion and Attachment,	0 — 2 — 6

For

For a Commission of Rebellion, to take an Anſwer, or to examine Witneſſes. } 0—18—8

For the appearance of every Perſon. } 0—0—4

Copies of Bils, Anſwer, *&c.* by the Leaſe. } 0—0—8

For Ingroſſments by the Leaſe,   0—0—8

The Attorneys Fee for every Terme,   0—3—4

For all Inrollments for every Roll   0—13—4

For every ſpeciall Writ, *Viz.* Writ of Priviledge, Injunction, *Supeſedeas,* Extent, *Scire Facias Fieri facias, Certiorari, &c.* } 0—7—10

For every Writ of *Venire facias* and Writ of Attendance. } 0—2—6

For every *Diſtringas Iuriſ.*   0—4—0

For every rule to plead or Anſwer. } 0—1—0

Filing each Bill.   0—2—0

For entring and inrolling a Recognizance. } 0—5—8

Drawing of Orders, Pleas, *&c.* by the Leaſe. } 0—1—0

To the Baron for allowing every Bill. } 0—2—0

To the Baron for ſigning every Common Order } 0—2—0

For ſigning a decree to each Baron. } 0—6—8

To each of their Clerks   0—2—0

For every Affidavit ſworne before him. } 0—1—0

For every Deed acknowledged before him. } 0—6—8

To his clerke   0—2—0
For every Bill of cofts taxed   0—2—0

Where an under-Sheriff is to paſſe his account in the Exchequer, the charge is as followes; ſome difference there may be, as the Account may lye, but not much.

                                  l. s. d

First for the Taley upon payment of proffers.   0 2-8
For the entry of the ſame Taley   0 1-4
Where the Sheriff is dead, for the *Diem clauſit extremum*, whereby upon account, execution is to be returned.   13 4
For the Warrant of Attorney   1-0
For the entry thereof   0-8
For the Uſhers Fees and the poore mans Box   13-4

To the Controller of the Pipe   16-8
To him more, in regard of, &c.   3-4
To the clerk to the Controller for ſummons in regard of, &c.   5-0
To the clerke of the Pipe in part of his fee   1-0 0

To the Lord Treaſurers Remembrancer   13-4
To the forreigne Oppoſer for charging of the greene Wax, and making the Scrowle thereof   1 6-8
To him for allowance of the wages of the Iuſtices of the Peace.   18 0

                                  To

To the Clerk of the Estreats for } As you can a-
the Portage of Books. } gree.

To the under Clerk of the Pipe } In like man-
for the like. } ner.

For the President of the Foreign } In like man-
Account. } ner.

The Fee in regard of the Justices of Assize for
their diet, 10 l.

To the Attorney for the entry thereof, and other
Petitions, 2 l.

To the said Attorney for his ordinary Fee, for the
whole year to receive the Writs and Precepts, &c.
1 l. 6 s. 8 d

To him in regard of, &c. for every Term during
the account till finished, 3 s. 4 d.

To his Clerk in regard of, &c. 10 s.

The copies of the Sheriffs, Seisures, according to
the number of them.

The old Seisures for each, 1 s.

The new Seisures for each, 1 s.

To the Clerk in regard of, &c. 3 s. 4 d.

To the Remembrancers Office for each thereof,
and for joining the tales of Professors, 3 s. 4 d.

On the Lord Treasurers Remembrancers side for
the like, 3 s. 4 d.

For allowance of the same tales of payments of
money in the Receit of the Exchequer, 1 s. 4 d.

For the joining of the same.

For allowance of the same, 1 s.

For every day that is given to the Sheriff, in respect of his Accounts, 6 s. 8 d.

For the entry thereof, 2 s.

To the Usher for Proclamation, when the Sheriff
is said to be cast out of the Court, 2 s. 6 d.

For the *Quietus est*, the making and allowing of
the same, 1 l.

V For

For the Baron, for his Fees, for taking and allowing of the foreign Accounts, 6 s. 8 d.

To the same Baron, for examining the Sheriffs Schedule, 6 s. 8 d.

The ordinary charge of passing another Account.

First, for the Delivery and Receit of three Certificates, 1 s.

For delivery of the Kings part of the Books of Extent to the Auditor, 6 d.

To the Auditors man for a Bag, 6 d.

For a Warrant of Attorney, 8 d.

To the Teller for receiving of the money, and making a Bill thereof, 4 d.

To the Auditors man for allowing the Certificate, 1 s. 6 d.

To the Auditors man for ingrossing the Accounts, 4 s.

To the Barons man for receiving and allowing the Warrants of Attorney, 2 s.

For entring the Accounts on the Kings Remembrancers side, 1 s.

For the like entry with M. 1 s.

For joining of their two Tales, 8 d.

For the *Quietus est,* 3 s. 4 d.

For entring of the *Quietus est,* 2 s.

For the Attorneys Fee, 3 s. 4 d.

Thus much shall suffice to have spoken of the Exchequer and of his Proceedings, and Fees relating to Sheriffs.

In the next place take the Fees of the Sheriffs them-
selves, as in the execution of their Office.

INprimis, for the return of a *Nichil*, or *Non eſt in-*
ventus,   4 d

But in *Scire facias* they take,   I s.

For making a Warrant upon ordinary Proceſs, if
it be directed to the ordinary Bailiffs, then for every
name,   4 d.

In many Counties they take far more, in ſome
16 d. in ſome more.

If the Warrant be directed to a ſpecial Bailiff or
Bailiffs, then for every name,   2 s.

For the Arreſt of every Defendant,   I s.

This ſhould be paid by the Plaintiff.

For making the Bond of Appearance,
wherein the Defendant with his Sureties is ⎫
bound to appear in Court, at the Day of ⎬ 4 d.
the Return of the Writ,   ⎭

They take 12 d. and more in ſome places.

For the return of a *Cepi corpus*,   4 d.
For the return of an *Exigent*,   I s.
For the return of a Proclamation,   I s.
For the return of a *Venire facias*,   I s.

They now take in moſt places,   2 s.

For the return of a *Habeas corpus*, or *Diſtringas*,
                                                                2 s. 4 d.

For a Replevin either in the County or otherwiſe,
                                                                      2 s.

For the return of a *Recordari*,   2 s.
For the return of an *Accedas ad curiam*,   2 s.
For the return of a *Diſtring. nuper Vicecomitem*, 2 s.
For the allowance of a *Superſedeas*, if it be after
the return of the *Exigent*,   I s.

They pay more now in many Counties.

V 2   For

For the executing of a Writ of Inquiry of Waste,

For the executing of a Writ of Inquiry of Damages in Trespass,

Trespass upon the Case, &c.

For the executing of a *Liberate* upon a Statute of Recognizance,

For the Execution of an *Habere facias possessionem*, or *seisinam* upon an *Ejectione firmæ*, a Writ of Right, of making Partition, &c. Dower, &c.

As you can make a-greement with the Sheriff.

For the executing of an *Elegit*, and for the Inquiry upon it.

For the executing of a Writ of Forcible Entry, or holding with force, whereupon the party moved, is to be restored by the Sheriff to his possession.

For the executing of a Writ of Inquiry upon Assault and Battery.

Upon a Rescous, and many other too long here to insert. The like as before.

For the returning of a *Mandavi Ballivo Libertatis, &c.*　　　　　　　　　4 d.

Upon the serving of an Execution for money, either Debt or Damages.

The Sheriff hath poundage allowed him, and is a general Rule allowed by the Statute in Q. *Eliz.* time. See the Statute what it is.

There are many other Fees incident to the Sheriffs in many Actions, and otherwise, which in respect the Actions themselves are most of them out of use, are not so well known; and indeed a man had need be well experienced in the Office of an Under-Sheriff, to know both what Fees he ought to receive, and what he ought in the Exchequer to pay.

The

Qeus. B. R.

The Compleat Attorney. 277

The Court of Upper Bench comes next to be treated of, wherein we shall be the breifer, in respect that many Actions treated of at large before, in the Court of common Bench, are here also brought and all that difference their proceedings, is for the most part matter of form.

THe Court of Upper Bench consists of a chief Justice, and three other Judges.

The subordinate Officers are as follow,

The chief Clerk of the Court, or Master of the Upper Bench Office, whose place is executed by his Secondary for the most part, or his Clerks under him, who write all Pleadings, and Declarations, and other proceedings upon Record, and are accountable to him for the same.

His Deputy also signs all *Latitats*, which is the first Writ whereby a Suit is commenced: and Writs of *Alias, Plures, Capias, Elegits, Habeas corpus, Protogendo, Habere facias possessionem, Certiorari, Distringas Ballivo, Distringas* against late Sheriffs, *Returno Habendo, Capias in Withernam,* second deliverance, and some others. He also keeps the Remembrances of all Records, whereby you may finde out any Record with little trouble, especially if you know the Term when it was entred, and the Attorneys name: and also all Writs returned, and *Posteas,* and Writs of Errour are kept and filed in his Office, and also common Bails, and especial Bails, after they are accepted of by the Plaintiff or his Attorney, are likewise filed and entred upon Record in his Office.

Secondly, the *Custos Brevium,* his Office is to file

V 3 all

all original Writs, and other Writs, wherein you proceed against any person you intend to outlaw. And also makes up all Records of *Nisi prius* for Trials at the Assizes in the several Countreys, and hath several Clerks under him, who write the same ; but many times the Plaintiffs Attorney, or the Defendants Attorney, if you go to trial by *Proviso*, write the same, that he may dispatch his Clients business the sooner, for which you pay for every press, which is to contain sixty lines, 6 s. 6 d.

The Secondary to the chief Clerk, he always attends the fitting of the Court, for to examine business, which is referred to him by the Judges ; and afterwards makes his report thereof, how the case stands. He also signs all Judgments, and taxes costs thereupon, and gives all Rules to answer and reply, and to go to trial by *Proviso*, and many other, and usually resolves all doubts and questions of the other Clerks. And if any difference arise between any of the Clerks, for matter of practice, it is usual with them that are fair Practizers, to refer the same to him for to determine, and not to trouble the Court with unnecessary motions, and expend their Clients money in vain, which may that way be saved.

The Clerk of the Papers, his Office is to make up all Special Pleadings and Demurrers, which the Plaintiffs Attorney most commonly speaks for, and afterwards by virtue of his Office, gives a Rule upon the side of the Paper-book, for the Defendants Attorney to bring the same to him again, to be entred within four days, or else judgment to go by default.

Keeper of the Files of Declarations, with whom after they are ingrossed in Parchment, and continued on the back, from the Term you declare, till it come to an Issue, are filed.

Keeper

Keeper of the Sign and Seal for the Bills of *Middlesex*, who keeps a Book, containing the Plaintiffs and Defendants names, and where you may search for any Appearance, or for any Writ that is taken forth.

The Clerk of the Rules, whose office is to attend the Court, and take short notes of all Rules and Orders that are made in Court (except those which belong to the Crown-office) and afterwards draws the same up, and enters them in a Book at large, for which you pay 8 d. and for the copy of every Rule 4d. if it be of the same Term, otherwise you pay 8d. He also files all *affidavits* that are used in Court, and hath the benefit of making copies of them, for which you pay for each sheet 4d. and with him you are to give all Rules of course, as Rules upon *Cepi corpus*, *H.b. as corpus*, for a *Procedendo*, *postcas*, Writs of Inquiry, and such like.

Phillizors, one for each County in *England*, who make out all Writs, wherein you intend to proceed by Original, and so to the Outlawry, except the Original it self, which you are to bespeak of the Cursitor of the County, where you intend to lay your Action, in such manner as you bespeak Originals, which are made in the Common Pleas. And they have the benefit of all Writs and Entries thereupon, and allow the chief Clerk nothing for the same.

The Marshal of the Upper Bench, who hath the custody of all Prisoners, who are sued in the Court, like to the Guardian or Warden of the *Fleet*, which a Prison properly belonging to the common Bench and Chancery; and every one that is sued and arrested in this Court of Upper Bench is supposed to be in custody: for you cannot declare against any man, who is arrested upon mean Process, in any county or City, and he remain in Prison there, for

want

want of Bail, untill he be removed by a *Habeas corpus*, and always either he himself, or his Deputy, or Servants, attend the Court for that purpose, to take Prisoners, who are committed to their custody.

Clerk of the Errours, he allows all Writs of Errour, and makes *Supersedeas* thereupon, into what County you please to have them.

Criers, who always attend upon the Court, either to call Non-suits, give Oaths to Witnesses, and Jury-men of Trials, or to any others whom the Judg shall direct, and at the end of every Term they do adjourn the Court.

Porter, who is to bring the Records out of the Office, when they are to be used in Court.

This Court of Upper Bench holds plea in all Actions of Debt, Detinue, Covenant, Account, and all Actions of the Case, either upon Promises, or for scandalous words, or for special nusance, *&c.* Trover and Conversion, and many other like, *&c.*

The course of proceeding there is by way of *Latitat*, as their first Process, if the Action to be brought, or the party to be arrested in any other County than *Middlesex.*

If in *Middlesex*, then you take out a Bill of *Middlesex*, with any Clerk of this Office, for which you pay 1 s. 6 d. and then you are to carry it to the under Sheriff of *Middlesex* his Office, who is to make out a Warrant upon it, for which he hath 4 d. and then you imploy what Bailiff you think fit, for the Arrest, except your Warrant be directed to the Bailiff of any particular Liberty, and then you are to imploy one of his Bailiffs.

If it be a *Latitat*, it supposeth a Bill of *Middlesex*, and that the party cannot be found in the County of *Middlesex*, as it appears by the later end of the Writ, where it is said, the Sheriff of *Middlesex* returns

that

that he is not found within his Bailiwick, but that he lies hidden in another County, and therefore command is given to the Sheriff of that other county, that he take him, *&c.*

This Writ or Bill of *Middlesex*, I conceive, is in the nature of the Original in the common Pleas, which warrants the *Capias,* and haply may have very anciently been in use for that purpose, for that otherwise 'twere vain to insert those words of the Sheriff of *Middlesex.*

The Form of a Latitat *is as followeth.*

Latitat.

THE Keepers of the Liberty of England, by Authority of Parliament, to the Sheriff of E. greeting Whereas we have lately commanded the Sheriff of the County of Middlesex, that he should take A.B. if he might be found in his Bailiwick, and him safely keep, so that he might have his Body before us, in the Upper Bench at Westminster, the Thursday next after fifteen days of Easter, to answer C.D. in a Plea of Trespass; And the said Sheriff of Middlesex, at that day returned unto us, that the said A.B. is not found in his Bailiwick; whereupon on the behalf of the aforesaid C.D. in the Court before us, it is sufficiently testified, that the said A.B. doth lurk and skulk in your County; therefore we command you, that you take him, if he shall be found within your Bailiwick, and him safely keep, so that you may have his Body before us in the Upper Bench at Westminster, on Wednesday next after three weeks of Easter, to answer the said C.D. in the Plea aforesaid, and that you have there then this Writ; Witness H. Rolle at Westminster, the seventeenth day of April, in the year of our Lord God 1651.

This

This Writ is ufually 4 s. 1 d. fome take 5 s. 1 d. And if you cannot arreft the party upon this, then you may have it renewed as followeth.

Alias Capias.

THe Keepers, &c. to the Sheriff of L. greeting. we command you, as formerly we commanded you, that you take A. B. if he shall be found within your Bailiwick, and him fafely keep, fo that you may have his Body before us in the Upper Bench at Westminster, on Saturday next after the Mor ow of the afcenfion of our Lord, to answer C. D. in a plea of trespass. And that you have there then this writ; Witness H. Rolle at Westminster, &c.   Wightwick.

This Writ 1 s. 1 d. but they ufually take 2 s. 1 d.

The Plures Capias.

THe Keepers, &c. To the Sheriff &c. we command you as many times we have commanded you, that you take A.B. &c. as in the Writ next before.

This Writ is likewife 1s. 1d. but they take 3s. 1d.

Bill of Midalefex.

MIddlefex ff. It is commanded to the Sheriff, that he take A. B. if, &c. and him fafely, &c. So that he have his Body before the Keepers of the Liberty of England, by authority of Parliament in the Upper Bench at westminster, on Wednefday next after the Moneth of Easter, to answer C D. of a Plea of Trespass, and that he have here then this Precept, &c.   by Bill   wightwick.

Thefe Writs you may have renewed every Term, untill

untill you get the party to be arrested. But if the *Latitat* remain unrenewed for five Terms, after you have taken it out, then you must have a *Latitat de novo*, for that you cannot renew the old.

Upon any of these Processes, if any of the Parties to be arrested, dwell within a Liberty, you must get the Sheriff to return a *Mandabo Ballivo* to your Process, and upon that the course is to have a *Non omittas, &c.* For which you pay 2 s. 4 d.

Where upon this, or any the other Writs, the party or parties be arrested, and have put in Bond for his appearance to the Sheriff, you must pay the Sheriff 4 d. and he will return you a *Cepi corpus*, upon which if the party do not appear at the return of the Writ, you may give the Sheriff a Rule to bring in his Body, on pain of 40 s. *&c.* which costs 4 d. and then if he do not come in and appear, you may have a *Habeas corpus* upon the *Cepi corpus*, which costs 2 s. 4 d. If the Sheriff will not return this Writ of *Habeas*, you may amerce him as before; if he doth return the Writ, and brings not in the Body, he can return nothing but a *Languidus in persona*, and upon that you may have a *Duces tecum licet languidus, &c.* upon the like price ; or else after the party is arrested, you may have a *Habeas corpus*.

At the Return of all or any of these you may amerce the Sheriff, and he shall pay it after those Rules given in the Upper Bench.

If you will extreat your Amerciaments into the Crown-office, the charge of every Rule extreated is 2 s. 4 d. unextreated 4 d. and in this course you may both amerce the Sheriff, and prosecute till such time as he doth appear, but if there be any great Amerciament, the Defendant will appear for fear the Sheriff sue his Bond : And after the Amerciaments are returned into the Crown-Office, if they

be

be not certified and returned into the Exchequer, which is once in every half year, where they are extreated before that time, if you be sued upon the Sheriffs Bond, you may upon motion of the Court, if the Plaintiffs Attorney (to whose Client the Sheriffs Bond is commonly assigned) will not consent otherwise, that you are content to appear, as of the same Term the first Writ was returnable; and to accept of a Declaration, and not to delay the Plaintiff in his Suit: the Court will usually order the Suit upon the Sheriffs Bond to stay, or if the Amerciaments be extreated, then upon the same offer, and also to take off those Amerciaments, the Court will order the like.

And when any one intends to appear, he must file a Bail with the Master of the Office, fairly written in Parchment, the form whereof is as follows.

If it be a common Bail thus,

A. B. *of* C. *in the County of* D. *Yeoman, delivered into Bail upon a* Cepi corpus.

To John Doe *of* London, *Yeoman, and* Richard Roe *of the same, Yeoman, at the Suit of* E. F.

If special Bail upon a *Habeas corpus,* then you must say (such a one) naming the Plaintiff, is delivered into Bail upon a *Habeas corpus,* to such persons naming his Bail, (instead of *John Doe,* and *Richard Roe*) at the Suit of the Plaintiff in the Plaint not naming the Defendant, as in the common Bail, which must also be filed with the Master of the Office.

In

In what cases you are to require, and may stand upon good Bail.

IF the Defendant do appear, and he stand indebted to your Client, either by Bond, Bill, or otherwise, to the value of 20 l. or 10 l. you may force him to put in good Bail, if you mistrust his sufficiency.

But if it be in any Action of the Case, for words, though the party be nothing worth, and you are likely to recover great Damages, yet can you very hardly hold him to good Bail: yet in some cases it hath been observed, that good Bail was required, as where one had made a Libell against another, who was a Magistrate.

In any Action of *Ejectione firme*, and in an Action of Trespass, good Bail is not insisted on, nor required, except in some special cases, then the Court will order that there be special Bail.

Nor is there good Bail required against Executors or Administrators, in any Action brought against them, unless in such case where you can directly prove they have wasted the Goods of the Testator.

If Bail be put in, either common or special, at another mans Suit, a stranger may upon this Bail put in a Declaration, but then he must declare of the same Term the Bail was put in, which is not used in the common Bench. But the party at whose Suit the Defendant was arrested, may declare the next Term after the Defendants appearance upon the Bail.

But if it be especial Bail that he put in, no stranger shall take the benefit of it, although he declare of the same Term.

If the Defendant appear in his proper person,
you

you muſt declare within three days, otherwiſe he will have coſts.

If you have declared, and do not call for anſwer, nor enter the Action within thꝛee Terms after the appearance of the Defendant, the Plaintiff ſhall be non-ſuited, and the Defendant ſhall have coſts.

And if you arreſt one in the County, upon mean Proceſs, and he is in the Sheriffs cuſtody there for want of Bail, for the ſpace of three Terms, and you do not remove him into the cuſtody of the Marſhal, where he muſt be, before you can declare againſt him, the party arreſted may have a *Superrſedeas*, and file common Bail.

The Declarations are uſually drawn by the Clerks of the Office, for they that are Clerks of the Office are to do the buſineſs of thoſe which are Attorneys at large, and their names are onely uſed as Attorneys, but thoſe Clerks are in right of their being Clerks of the Office, Attoneys of the Court.

Their manner of practice is ſomething different, in reſpect of the delivery of Declarations, from that in the common Bench.

In the common Bench, the Plaintiffs Attorney or Clerk, hath the benefit of both the Copies of the Declaration, both on the part of the Plaintiff and Defendant.

But in the Upper Bench, the Declaration being drawn by the Plaintiffs Clerk, the Defendants Clerk calleth for it, or elſe it is delivered unto him, and he maketh a Copy of it, and hath the benefit of it, and then the next Term after, or ſo ſoon as the Plaintiffs Clerk calleth for anſwer, is to plead or to confeſs the Action, or let it go by default, &c.

Their Declarations that are drawn, they ingroſs ſeverally in pieces of Parchment, and upon the back of them they enter their continuances, from the

Term

Term that is within written, unto the very Term that they either confefs the Action, or plead to Iffue, and that the Iffue be entred upon Record, and after Iffue is joined, many times they defer the entring of the fame, till the caufe be tried, which is otherwife in the common Bench, which is beneficial both to the Plaintiff and Defendant, being they may in the mean time agree the bufinefs, and fo fave that charge.

In their Declarations they begin with the name of the Plaintiff, and fay, that he complains of the Defendant, very feldom naming of what place, *&c.* unlefs upon a Bond where the *Alius dictus* muft be obferved, in the cuftody of the Marfhal, *&c.* for fo the Declaration fuppofeth every perfon they declare againft.

When they come to mention the Bond, Indenture, or Bill, if in an Action brought upon any Specialty, there they have (*Prof rt hic in Curia, &c.*) in the middle of their Declarations, whereas in the Common Pleas they conclude their Declarations with it; at the clofe of their Declarations they add underneath,

Pledges of profecuting { John Dove, Richard Roe.

Next that they add { J. B. *for the Plaintiff.* C. B. *for the Defendant.*

THe many and feveral Actions of the Cafe before mentioned in the practice of the Common Pleas, are much ufed likewife in the practice of this Court, and in thofe Actions they may proceed to Outlawry by Original, and fo through their Philli-

zers

zets Office, in which cafes, or in Trefpafs, or Trefpafs of Affault and Battery, if a man be outlawed in
that Court, he is half undone, if he be a poor man;
for befides that it cofts him 6 l. 13 s. 4 d. or upwards,
to reverfe the Outlawry, he muft although he live
200, or 150. miles diftant from *London*, come in perfon (if he be able) to reverfe it, and befides muft
procure good Bail; and in cafe he be impotent that
he cannot travel, then there muft be *Affu avit* made
thereof before a Judg, which done, he may reverfe it.

One may proceed to Outlawry in this Court, as
well as in the Common Pleas, in all cafes, except in
thefe four.

1. Debt. 2. Detinue. 3. Covenant. 4. Account;
but it is feldom made ufe of but upon good occafion,
that is to fay, when the Defendant hath a good
perfonal Eftate in Debts, Cattel, or Stock in his
Grounds, and is hard to be taken and arrefted; for
otherwife Outlawries are but meer Scare-crows, to
difable both the Plaintiff and Defendant, in put-
ing them to unneceffary charge, whereas upon a
Latitat you may procure a man to be arrefted prefently, and make him put in good Bail, which is all
you can do upon an Outlawry, after three Terms
fpace. And befide, upon a *Latitat* you may declare
againft the Defendant, in as many Actions as you
pleafe; whereas in the Common Pleas, you muft
have for every Action, one Original, and if it be a
Debt which exceeds 40 l. you muft pay as before is
told you, 6 s. 8 d. fine, and if 100 l. you pay 10 s.
fine, and fo proportionably; and as foon as you be-
fpeak your Original, before you have any benefit of
your Suit, whereas no fine at all is paid in the Upper Bench, and in the Upper Bench the Plaintiff
hath longer time to declare, than is allowed in the
                                                    com-

Common Pleas; (if the Defendant do not appear
in.perfon) and then you muft declare within three
days after.

When the Plaintiff and Defendant are at iffue,
the Defendants Clerk hath the benefit (as before of
making the Declaration) fo of making the Copy of
the Iffue for the Defendant, which is otherwife ufed
in the common Bench.

If there be efpecial Pleadings in any Action by
the Plaintiff or Defendant which either comes to
Iffue, or that there be a Demurrer, then they carry
the whole Book to the Clerk of the Papers, who giveth a Rule to the Defendant in the Margin of the
Book, to joyn in Iffue or in Demurrer, and he maketh up the Books, and is paid eight pence a fheet
for the fame, which is otherwife in the commonPleas
for there the Plaintiffs Attorney hath that benefit.

The Clerks of the Office are to account with the
Mafter of the Office, after the end of every Term,
for all Writs or Entries, &c. which they have had
of that Term fo proceeding.

After Verdicts, and that they have the *Pofteas* returned, and that the Mafter of the Office hath figned Cofts (which he doth as he doth all other bufinefs
by his Secondary) then they enter up their Judgments, every Clerk his own, and fo he maketh out
his Executions, either againft the Body, which is
commonly called a *Capias ad fatisfaciend.* or elfe a-
gainft the Goods, which is commonly called a *Fieri
facias,* or elfe againft the Lands and Goods, which is
called an *Elegit*; but if you once charge the Body
in Execution, you have no remedy againft the Goods
or Lands.

If it be an Iffue of any former Term, that is entred upon the Roll, or of the fame Term, then if
they will have a Record of *Nifi prius,* they muft have

X

it made by the *Cuſtos Brevium* of that Court, who keepeth particular Clerks for that purpoſe, for they are to pay him for them, although for expedition the Attorney or Clerk moſt uſually makes them himſelf, and then the *Cuſtos Brevium* ſeals them.

This Court of Upper Bench holdeth Pleas of the Crown, and to that purpoſe there is an Office called the Crown Office, and the Maſter of it called the Clerk of the Crown ; and here may be brought Inditements for all manner of Treaſons, Murder, Felony, Breaches of the Peace by Battery, &c Breach of the good Behaviour, for Perjury, all publick Nuſances, Appeals in caſe of Murder may come, and here likewiſe Informations upon penal Statutes are brought, and here iſſues out *Certioraries,* to remove Inditements from private Seſſions, and hither are all Convicts certified.

They have belonging to this Office a Secondary, who ſits in Court, and takes notice of what Rules are made on the Crown ſide. They have likewiſe ſeveral Attorneys of that Office who have the buſineſs of the Countrey, as to that Office divided amongſt them, who intermeddle not with any thing relating to the Court, other than in their own Office.

How to ſue upon a Statute Staple.

IF you would ſue forth Execution upon a Statute Staple go to the Clerk of the Statutes, and ſhew him your Statute, and he will make you thereupon a Certificate, which being made and ſealed by him, carry it to the Clerk of the Crown, (which is the Office whence all Patents ſpecial iſſue forth) and upon the delivery of the Certificate to him, he is to make you your Extent, which you muſt after deliver

unto

unto the Sheriff of the County where the Land lies, who will by virtue thereof impannel a Jury to inquire and extend Lands, Goods, and Chattels of the Cognizor, and may by virtue thereof apprehend the Body; if, &c. The Lands being thus extended into the Kings hands, the Sheriff may keep untill you bring your *Deliberate*, which you are to have (upon your Extent returned) from one of the Clerks of the Petty Bag; but it behoveth you to be very carefull how you sue forth of your *Liberate*, and that you do it not before you have fully informed your self what Lands or Goods there are in any other County, that you may extend, whereby fully to satisfie your Statute; for if you once execute your *Liberate* upon that which was first extended, you shall never have execution of more, although you make an after-discovery. And you are to deliver your Statute into the Petty Bag Office, before they will make you your *Liberate*.

How to sue upon a Recognizance acknowledged before one of the Masters of the Chancery.

WHere you will sue upon a Recognizance, you must bring it to one of the Clerks of the Petty Bag Office in Chancery, and he will make you out two *Scire facias*, directed to the Sheriff of *Middlesex.*

The first returnable of a Return past, and the other bearing *Teste* of the Return of the former; and returnable at a day to come, which you must get the Sheriff of *Middlesex* to return, & having them returned, you are to bring them back to the Clerk of the

X 2   Petty

Petty Bag Office, and then retain one of the Clerks for you, and give the Defendant day to appear.

At which day, if he appear, the Plaintiff is to declare, and the Defendant is to answer, and so proceed to Issue, and upon the Issue joyned, you may have the whole Proceedings ingrossed in Parchment, and by *Mittimus* sent into the Upper Bench or Common Pleas, or else the Lord Keeper, or Lords Commissioners for the Great Seal, for the time being, may deliver it so ingrossed into either Court without *Mittimus*, which is said to be delivered, *Propria sua manu*, where the Issue shall be tried, and Judgment given, for in the Chancery no Issue can be tried. But if the Defendant appear not, you shall have Execution by Default, which course is indeed most usual.

How to prove a Will, in Case the Party be present, the Inventory not exceeding fourty pounds.

First, you are to bring in your Will, under the hand of the Testator, and Witnesses names, and take Oath, that that is the last Will for ought you know; and in case the Party live in the Countrey, there must a Commission issue forth to that purpose, which being returned, you must retain a Proctor, and he will sue it out for you, the charge follows, but is alterable according to the length or shortness of the Will.

	l.	s.	d.
Inprimis, for registring of the Will,		1.	6.
For ingrossing the Will,		6.	0.
For the Register, for his hand to the same,		12.	0.

For

For the Seal and Probare of the Will,   6.8.

The Proctor's Fee and the ⎫
   Prox.   ⎬   4.8.

For proving the Will,   ⎭

For ingrofling the Inventory, ⎫ according as you
   and exhibiting the fame, ⎬ can agree.

Thefe Fees would be far lefs, could the Regifters Clerks be confined to walk by what the Statute directs, and in fome very fhort Wills they are lefs than what is above fet down.

The Dutchy Court.

THis Court before the Sale formerly made, and the large Grants of the Dutchy Lands, was much ufed in relation to Suits between the Tenants of thofe Lands, and alfo againft accountants and others for the Rents and Profits of the Lands, and is a Court of Record, wherein are Pleas both real, and perfonal, as alfo mixt pleadings, relating to the Dutchy Lands.

The Chancellour of the Dutchy is the chief Judg of this Court, and next to him the Attorney of the faid Court, who in all difficult cafes in point of Law, is ufually affifted by two Judges of the common Law out of one Court or other, to decide the matter or queftion in Law.

There is one chief Clerk or Regifter of the Court, to whofe Office it properly belongs to have the keeping of all the Rolls and Records of the Court, and alfo of the Proceedings therein.

There are divers Auditors of this Court, of which there are two more efpecial than the reft. The one whereof, his Office extends to all the Dutchy Lands on this fide *Trent;* and the other for the Lands beyond *Trent.* To thofe Auditours doth belong the keep-

X 3   ing

ing of the Kings Evidence; as Leafes and Grants of the Dutchy-land, as well of the Poffeffions and Copy-hold, as Fee-fimple and Fee-farm.

Although there be divers Surveyors for the Dutchy-land, for the furveying of it, yet do they not keep any Record to that purpose, unlefs fome fhort draughts of their own framing.

Thus much for Courts of Record at *Weftminfter*, which are for the common Law practice; come we now to the Court of Equity, which in many cafes abates of the rigour and feverity of the common Law, and is called,

The high Court of Chancery.

IN this Court the Lord Chancellour or Lord Keep-er of the Great Seal, were formerly, and now the Commiffioners of the Great Seal are the chief Judges; and in this Court, they, and in their ab-fence, the Mafter of the Rolls, do make Orders and Decrees.

The fubordinate Officers of this Court are many.

The twelve Mafters in ordinary, which are Af-fiftants to the Commiffioners, and fit with them, and to whom References are made, and before whom *Affidavits* are made, and Deeds acknowledg-ed, and Recognizances, &c.

The Regifter of the Court who hath divers un-der him, that fit in Court and take notice of all Or-ders, Decrees made in Court, and accordingly, after-wards draw up thefe Orders, and enter them and file them.

The fix Clerks, in whofe Office all proceedings up-on Bill, and anfwer unto the very Decree, and after Decre are acted, and from whom likewife iffue fome

Pa-

Patents as for pardon of men for chance-meddley, Patents for Embassadours, Commissions for Bank-rupts; and these by their Clerks, of which each six Clerk keeps a set number.

The Cursitors of the Court, who were incorpo-rated by Q. *Elizabeth*, by the name of the four and twenty Cursitors, amongst whom the business that lies in the several Shires, is severally distributed. These make all original Writs in the Chancery, which are returnable in the Common Pleas, and all Writs of Entry and Covenant.

The Register is a place of great note in this Court, and hath several Registers under him, who sit in Court by their turns, and take notice of all Orders and Decrees made in Court, and according-ly draw up the Orders, to which you must have a Re-gisters hand, and then you must enter it there, and in that Office likewise they file the Reports of the Masters. The Masters of the *Sub pœna* Office. The Clerk of the *Affidavits*, where you file such *Affidavits* as you use in Court.

The Clerks of the Petty Bag, who have many Clerks under them, and these Clerks have much va-riety of business that comes through their hands, and requires very much knowledg and experience for the managing of.

This Office hath the making out of all Writs of Summons to the Parliament.

To this Office are all Offices that are found *post mortem*, brought to be filed.

In this Office are all Pleadings of the Chancery concerning the validity of any Patent or other thing whatsoever, which passeth the Great Seal.

And these Pleadings were formerly in *Latine*, al-though most of the rest of their Proceedings were in *English*.

If

If any queſtion ariſe about the acknowledgment of any private Deed between Subjects, which is acknowledged in Chancery, before the Lord Keeper, the Maſter of the Rolls, or any of the Maſters in Chancery.

All Statutes and Recognizances taken before any Officers of this Court, to that purpoſe deputed, are here proſecuted and tranſmitted hither.

In theſe Offices are all Suits for or againſt any perſon privileged in the Court.

It is likewiſe a hand whereby to tranſmit divers things, from the riding Clerk ; and the Inrolment Office, to the Chapel of the Rolls.

The Examiners are Officers of this Court, who take the Depoſitions of Witneſſes, & are to examine them, and to make out Copies of the Depoſitions.

There are likewiſe Clerks of the Rolls, who ſit conſtantly in the Rolls to make Searches for Deeds, Offices, &c. and to make out Copies.

The Uſher of the Court, who hath the receiving and cuſtody of all Moneys, ordered to be depoſited in Court, and payeth it back again by Order.

The Serjeant at Arms who carrieth the Mace before the Commiſſioners, and to whom any Perſons ſtanding in contempt are brought up by his Subſtitutes as Priſoners.

The Warden of the *Fleet* attends likewiſe this Court, to receive ſuch Priſoners as ſtand committed by the Court.

This Court conſiſts of a double power, ordinary, as in the caſe of *Scire facias*, to repeal Patents in caſes of Traverſe, Endowment of a Woman, and the like, and herein the Court is limited, and confined to the Rules uſed in the Common Law.

The other is extraordinary, and unlimited, which is in caſes of equity, wherein relief is to be had by a

Suit

Suit here, by way of Bill and Anſwer.

By the power of this Court, are iſſued forth Commiſſions for charitable uſes, Bankrupts, and Sewers.

Here in this Court in ſome caſes, Commiſſions have been granted to examine Waſts, to ſet out meet ways for paſſages; to prove a Childe legitimate, to prove Cuſtomes, and to examine Witneſſes, *in perpetuam rei memoriam.*

It proceeds by way of Bill and Anſwer, in many caſes this Court will give relief againſt, beſides, and beyond the Rules of the common Law, ſome whereof follow. As where a charge lies upon one man alone, by the common Law, where in equity others ought to contribute a part to this charge, here in this caſe the Court will give relief.

So likewiſe will the Court relieve one againſt another who had falſified and broken his truſt with him.

It gives relief againſt the extremity of an Engagement, where either the Engagement is without any conſideration, unreaſonable, diſhoneſt, or diſcharged; or where there hath been either fraud, force, or the like, uſed to procure the thing to be done.

Where by a Law a man cannot be compelled to perform an agreement, this inforces it.

It inforces the Inrolment of a Deed, if need be.

This Court will reſtrain other Courts that take upon them a greater juriſdiction than properly they have, and removes the Suit into this Court, which is done by *Certiorari.*

This Court will reduce the general cuſtomes of a Mannour to a certainty between the Lord and Tenants, or the Tenants themſelves.

It ſerves to recover Land or Money given to charitable pious uſes, and miſimployed.

It inforces the Husband to give his Wife Alimony.

Where Creditors a e unreasonable, this Court inforceth them to take a reasonable composition of the Debtor, he being disabled.

Where Freehold or Copihold Land are confounded, it will distinguish it, or if it be lost, it will give a recompence for it.

This Court will ascertain the Fines of Copiholders.

This Court (where Executors or others have money in their hands there to ly long) inforces them to give security or interest for it.

This Court will inforce the recovery of a Legacy, or force the performance of a Will.

It serves for the recovery of ones Land, debt or duty, although he have lost the Conveyances or Writings, by which he should make his title to it, or otherwise be without remedy for it.

It inforces him that hath sold Land, and taken money for it, assured by defective conveyance, to make the same perfect and good.

It will inforce a Tenant to attorn, to perfect an Assurance.

In these and such like cases this Court of Chancery doth always, or for the most part, give relief, as you may see more at large in *Tothills* and *Caries* Reports.

In some other special cases likewise this Court doth exercise a power, as to prevent the desinheritance of an Heir, or restore it.

To avoid the extinguishment or suspension of rent or common.

To prevent an occupancy.

To avoid the bar of an Action, by the Statute of 21 *Jac.* of Limitations.

It

It will order the inclosure of Grounds or Lands that are common, give relief against the turning of a Water-course from a Mill, so as there be any special circumstance in the case, otherwise it is very shy and tender in making Orders in them.

But regularly this Court doth not give relief where the substance of the Suit by Bill and Answer tends to the overthrow of an Act of Parliament, made for publick peace and repose, or to the overthrowing any fundamental point of the common Law, or to overthrow and take from other Courts their peculiar jurisdiction, or the like.

In all such cases wherein the Plaintiff hath his remedy at common Law for the very same things, he shall not be relieved here.

Where a Promise is made to assure Land for a certain sum of money, in this case the Party may either sue at Law for Damages, or in Chancery for the Land it self.

The like case for a Nusance, where the Law gives me Damages, I may sue here to have the Nusance removed, or the thing it self restored : and yet there may be some special circumstances in the case, which may make the Court retain it ; as where a Suit is grounded upon a Will Nuncupative, Lease Parol, or long Lease, to avoid Wardship, or to establish Perpetuities, or to defeat Purchasors, or for Brokeage, or rewards to make marriages, or for bargains at play, or wagers, for bargains for Offices against the Statute of 2 *Edward* the sixth, or upon contracts for Usury or Simony, or if it be for Land not worth fourty shillings a year, or for any thing else under the value of ten pounds, those are regularly disallowed here : and sometimes upon notice taken hereof by the Court, upon motion or upon *Affidavit* onely, before the Cause comes to hearing, it is dimissed, but

if

if it ſtay longer till it comes to hearing, it is then diſmiſſed; yet there are ſome circumſtances that may make ſome of theſe retainable, as where the S it for ſo ſmall a matter be for the Poor of aPariſh, or the like.

In ſuch like caſes as theſe the matter being heard upon Bill and Anſwer, and the proofs of Witneſſes, the Court may (without any regard to form or miſpleading, ſo as the truth, *viis & modis,* may be diſcovered) proceed to ſentence it according to equity and good conſcience.

All perſons able in Law to ſue or be ſued, may in this Court ſue or be ſued.

Relief may be and is often given againſt or for an Infant in this Court, touching which matter theſe things are to be known;

As to Suits againſt an Infant.

Firſt, an Infant hath been compelled to anſwer a Bill in this Court, as in *Hares* caſe, *Hil.* 3 *Jac.* and *Mores* caſe, 11 *Car. Tothill* 108, 109. And being but twelve years old was bound by a Decree of this Court, 37 *Eliz. Wadhams* caſe, and upon a Review decreed again, *Crommells* caſe, *Mich.* 7 *Car.* and was committed to the *Fleet* for diſobeying a Decree, 12 *Eliz. Tothill* 108, 139.

Secondly, this Court may alſo if it pleaſeth appoint an Infant Defendant, a Guardian to defend his Suit, *Caries* Reports 38.

Thirdly, a Copihold was ſurrendred to the uſe of an Infant; for the Infant to pay an annuity to another at his full age, which he refuſed; it was decreed he ſhould pay it, and the arrears thereof, *Sawyers* caſe, 9 *Eliz. Tothill* 107.

Fourthly, *Young* purchaſed Lands in the name
of

of *Mason*, in truſt for himſelf and his Heirs, and dies not declaring any determination of his truſt, procures *Mason* to convey it to him being of kin, he conveys it to Infants, &c. ſues here as next Heir, the Court agrees, that if the benefit of the truſt did belong to **G.** that it ſhall be decreed to him, during the minority, and then that the Infants ſhall convey it. See *Caries* Reports 30.

Fifthly, a Mother conveyed her Leaſe to her Son in truſt, and after the Son conveyed it to his children Infants, and it was decreed againſt the Father and children, becauſe done without any conſideration, *Tothill* 98.

Sixthly, between the date and ſealing of the Conveyance of Land ſold, the Lord *Morley* paſſed it to an Infant, and it was decreed againſt the Infant and him both, 36 *Eliz.* Lady *Ruſſels* caſe.

Seventhly, the Father being Tenant in Tail, ſells his intailed Land, and leaves as much Free-land to deſcend to an Infant, the Court ordered when he comes of age to pay the money given for the Land according to his Fathers Will, or elſe that the Purchaſer ſhall have the Free-land, *Tothill* 184.

Eighthly, an Infant may by this Court be compelled to give a diſcharge of money due to, and received by him, as in *Rayners* caſe, 13 *Car.*

Ninthly, where one made an Infant Executor to prevent the payment of his Debts, and he was ordered by the Court to pay them notwithſtanding, *Mich.* 9 *Jac. Tothill* 108

Tenthly, an Infant may in ſome ſpecial caſes by this Court be concluded by his agreement.

But regularly if an Infant be twenty years of age, and make a contract never ſo much to his advantage, the Court will not conclude him, nor will the Court decree againſt him by his conſent or the conſent

sent of his Parents, but in some special cases upon the Merit of the cause, *Mich. 8 Car.* in Chancery.

A Father being about to convey some of his Land to his younger Son, and the eldest Son promised to give the younger Son a hundred pounds if the Father would forbear it; in this case the eldest Son being an Infant was ordered to stand to it. See *Stiles* his case, *2 Car. Tothill 95.*

Eleventhly, a Surrender was made of a Copihold by an Infant, to the use of *J. S.* for money paid, and no help could be had here, *Hughs* case, *Tothill 180.*

Twelfthly, if I take Bonds for my money in my childrens name that are Infants, I may release the Debts, and this Court will allow it, and forbid any Suit upon them.

As to Suits by or for an Infant.

First, he shall have the same relief upon a Breach of Trust, Fraud, or the like in this Court, as another man may have, notwithstanding his minority, *Tothill 108.*

Secondly, he may sue by himself or his Prochcin-amy or Guardian, as the Court will order.

Relief is often given by this Court, against, or for a woman under covert Baron, touching which, these things following are to be known.

As to Suits against her.

1. She shall be compelled to answer with, or without her Husband. See *Caries Reports*, 100, 101. *Tothill* 95, & 96. But more especially, if he be out

of

of the Land : and she shall be bound by the Decree of this Court, as in *westdeans* case *Totbill* 93. and she may be committed till she do obey it, as in *Sywards* case.

2. The Husband and Wife were ordered to levy a Fine, and perfect Assurances, *Totbill* 93.

3. The Husband was ordered to give security that the Wife should release her Right to Land. See *Totbill* 92.

4. An agreement in some cases will here be ordered, to conclude her where the merit of the cause requireth it. As if a man have two Tenements of his wifes Land, and they agree with the Tenant, that if he will surrender the one, he shall have three Lives in the other, and he doth so, and the Husband dy, the Wife was ordered to make it good. See *Irelands* case 37 *Eliz. Totbill* 91. but regularly it is otherwise ; and therefore where she hath Land with other Coheirs, and she with the consent of her Husband, agree to take a thousand pounds, to release her Right, the Judges did certifie she was not to be concluded, *Trin.* 7 *Jac. Dockwrays* case *Totbill* 98. yet in 10 *Jac. Randalls* case was, that a single woman did agree, and after her Marriage subscribed her name with her Husband to a later agreement, and was concluded by this later, by the Courts Order, *Totbill* 96.

But in *Slaters* case, 37 *Eliz. Totbill* 92. She and her Husband did article to forgo her Jointure, for other recompence, and a Decree was made thereupon (but without her consent) in her Husbands lifetime, and after his death the Court will not binde her to this agreement.

5. A Lease of Land was made to friends, to her use, to begin after her Husbands death, and they two levy a Fine of the Lands, this will not bar them

in

in equity, *Trin.* 15 *Car.* *Listers* cafe.

A. made over his Leafe for years, to the ufe of *C.* his Wife, after he and his Wife fold the Land, and levied a Fine of it to *D.* The Court ordered that the Purchafer fhould enjoy the Land againft the Wife, after the Husbands death, 2 *Car.*

One was feifed of Land to the ufe of a Feme fole, who after took a Husband, and the Husband fold the Land, the Wife had the Money, and fhe and her Husband defired the Feoffee in truft to convey it, and he doth fo, yet it feems the Court of Chancery will not bar her of the Land, after her Husbands death.

The Court ordered the Husband and Wife to levy a Fine of morgaged Lands, fetled in her; the Lady *Griffies* cafe, 4 *Car.*

One did convey Land to the Husband in truft, and he took the profit and left it with his Wife, and fhe married again; they two were fued in this Court, and yet neither as Executor nor Administrator to her firft Husband; as in *Acklands* cafe, *Tothill* 106.

As to Suits by and for her.

In fome cafes fhe may fue her Husband, as for Alimony or maintenance, where they be parted, but ordinarily fhe may not fue her Husband, nor her Husband fue her, *Sympfons* cafe, *Tothill* 94, 97.

Secondly, fhe hath been allowed to fue without her Husband, and without his privity, especially he being beyond the Sea, *Tothill* 95.

The Woman and her Husband agreeing to part up on difference, and he giving her a fum of Money for her livelihood, which was put into a friends hands for her, fhe was allowed to fue alone for this without her Husband. *Caries* Reports 87.

Thirdly, fhe was admitted to fue here for a duty releafed by her Husband, gone beyond Sea, as in

Farewels

Farewells case, 32. *Eliz. and Barkers case,* 5. *Caroli To-thill* 95. as for her Jewells, the Earle of *Darbies case, Tothill* 96. And yet shee having Goods, she pretended to be her *Paraphonalia,* the Husband devised them, and it was here allowed to be good, and she remedilesse, as in *Davenports case* 5. *Caroli.*

Fourthly, if a woman had goods at the Marriage, and the Husband doth use and dispose them al his life time, and then giveth them away, or maketh an Executor; this Court it seems will give her no releife, albeit the Husband leave never so great an Estate besides, unlesse they be goods set apart and preserved for her lively-hood, by some agreement or the like, *Tothill* 55.

5. A woman divorced from her Husband *Causa frigiditatis,* sued in this court for her portion, her Father being alive, and recovered it, *Burrows case.* *Tothill* 81.

6 The Wife being parted from her Husband, and having an Estate to her selfe, was allowed by the court to devise it by her will, *Mich.* 15. *Caroli Tothill* 97. *Georges case.*

7 If a feme sole being possessed of a Tearme, granteth it over, or a Tearm be granted by another to her own use, and then she taketh a Husband and dyeth, in this case the court ruled it to go to the Executor or Administrator of the wife, and not to the surviving Husband.

A. Being possessed of a Tearm, granted it upon a Marriage to be had between him and *R.S.* to *I.S.* her Brother to her use, and after marriage A. dyeth, and she marrieth again, and then she dyed. I.S. the Brother took out Administration of her Goods, and got the lease, and the second Husband sued him in this court for the Lease, but the court would not releive him *Pasch* 32. *Eliz: Withernams case* in chancery, *Cook upon Littleton* 350.   Y   8, A.

8. A. being possessed of a Lease for years, granted it to B. and C. to the use of A. and his Wife, and afterwards A. granted away all his Interest to a stranger, and the Court would not order it against the Wife, *Dyer, 369. Cromptons Jurisdictions 65.*

A. conveyed her Lease for yeares to Lessees in trust, to the use of her Daughters and Children : lyneally A. had a Daughter by one Husband, who had Issue, and it dyed, and the Husband also, then shee marries again, then the Lessees in trust convey the Lease to the Mother and her second Husband, and discharges the trust, she gives it to her Husband, and the Heir sued for it.

It was ordered that the Husband and not the Heir should have it : *Baskerviles case, Tothill 95.*

A Widow being about to marry, to prevent her Husbands disposall of the Land, conveys it to friends in trust, who with the Husband do sell it for valuable consideration, and shee sued in Chancery, and the Court decreed that the Purchasor should reconvey it to her, but should first deduct all his disbursements: *Fitziames his case, Tothill 43.*

A single woman Widow or Maid, may sue and be sued here as another Body, of which take some few cases.

1. A Widow of a Tenant in *Capite* sued here for her Dower, and had a commission to set it out; as in *Wilds case 25. Eliz.*

No woman shall recover Dower of a trust by this Court. *Mich, 2. Caroli. Kemps case.*

When the woman cannot tell who is Tenant to the Land, shee may sue, (albeit her writ of Dower here at Law) to discover the Tenant, to know against whom to bring her action, *Tothill: 99.*

A. conveys Land to B. and his Heirs, to the use of him and his Heirs, in trust for C. and his Heirs

(B having

(*B.* having then a Wife) B. dies, and his Wife fued for Dower of the Land, C. fued againft her for releif here, and it was denyed ; yet the Wife of C. should not have had Dower in this cafe, for a woman shall have no Dower of a Truft, *Hernes cafe Tothil.* 9.

So *A.* delivers B. 500 l. to put to ufe for him, and B. doth buy Land with it, and makes A. beleive it is for him and in his name, but it was in his own name : A. it feems fatisfied herewith, B. dyeth, and his wife fued to be indowed of the Land, and the Court would give A. no releife againft this Suit : *Trinity* 6. *Caroli.*

(A Copy-holder may not be fued for Land without the Lord, *Caries Reports* 57.)

An Heir alfo here in fome cafes shall fue and be fued, further then the Law bindeth him, as in the cafes enfuing.

An Heir of an Eftate in taile, having Lands in fee, difcended from the Anceftor, in lieu thereof is bound by decree to repay the purchafe money, or let the Purchafer have the free Land, *Peaces cafe* 8. *Jacobi Tothill* 184.

The Mother and Son bought tailed Land of her Anceftor, to the Plaintiff fome of the money due on a Bond which is loft, the Court thought fit to charge the Mother and the Son, becaufe of the Land in their poffeffion.

The Father fold his intailed Lands, but had little for them; it feems the Heir may compell the purchafer to give the worth, *Tothill* 182.

The Father articled for Land, the Son no party, but confented to it, and it was decreed againft him, *Pauls cafe Trin.* 4. *Jacobi. Tothill* 69.

A Deed not inrolled was decreed againft the Heir of the Land, *Tothill* 55.

The Father conceiving his Land to be Free-hold

gave

gave part of it to a younger Son, and it fell out that there was an old sleeping Deed of intaile, and yet it was ordered the younger Son should have it : *Pount-neys cafe, Tothil* 54.

Executors may charge or be charged in Equity, further then the Law doth charge, wherein as to fuits or Acts by them, take thefe infuing.

1. Here they may fue one the other, *Tothill* 8.

2. One of them may fue an Executor of an Executor, if he have gotten the Estate into his hands; *Briertons cafe* 6. *Iacobi, Tothill* 87.

3. Two Executors be, the one doth difagree, the Act of the other shall bind in Equity as it doth in Law.

As to fuits againft Executors, take thefe things.

First, one Executor alone without the reft may be fued here, but he shall be charged for no more then he hath, *Harbages cafe* 35. *Eliz. Tothill* 86.

Secondly, an Executor shall be bound by decree againft the Teftator, *Hil.* 5. *Caroli.*

Thirdly, He muft pay cofts adjudged here againft the Teftator, if he have affets.

Fourthly, he shall not be charged here for a Trefpaffe done by the Teftator, *Hollands cafe Tothill* 84.

Fifthly, nor may he be compelled here to give Bond to performe the will, without fpeciall caufe be shewed, as that he is decayed in Eftate, or hath broken the truft already in fome particulars, or the like, *Browns cafe* 32 *Eliz. Tothill.* 36.

Sixthly, He may here be ordered to pay a debt by word, before a debt due by fpecialty, *Tothill* 53.

One Ioynt-Tenant, or Tenant in common may here have releif againft another.

The Father may have releif againft his own Son in cafe of breaches of truft for a Leafe. *Pafch.* 1597. *Dormers cafe.*

Of

Of Trusts.

A Use of trust was, and still is either of Land or of Goods, and both these are either expressed or implied.

A use of trust of Land was a trust reposed in another, that he should suffer him that did trust, to take the profits of it, and he that was trusted, was to dispose the Land according to the direction of him that trusted him ; as when a Feoffment was made to *J. S.* and his heirs, to the use of *W. S.* and his Heirs: here *J. S.* had the Estate and property of the Land, but *W. S.* had or was to have the profits in honesty and equity. So if one had agreed with *W. S.* for a peice of Land for 20 l. paid, and had no assurance, yet the equity of the Land was in the contractor.

The use of Goods is when one man hath them in trust for another.

The use of Goods or Land expressed, is when the use or trust is expressed between the parties upon the making of the Estate, implied, when it is not declared upon the agreement, but left to the construction of Law, as if I bargain and sell my Land, levy a Fine, make a Feoffment, or suffer a Recovery of my Land without money, and no use expressed, this in Law is to my own use.

But if it be for money, it shall be to the use of the bargainee, conusee, Recoverer, or Feoffee.

If it be without consideration that I conveyed my Land by Feoffment to *J. S.* to have and to hold to him and his Heirs to the use of his Heirs, in this case *J. S.* and his Heirs have the use in Law.

To every of those uses, there are two inseperable incidents, confidence in the person, and privity in

the

the state expressed by the parties, or implied by the Law: And when either of those failed, the Use was either gone for ever, or suspended for a time at the least; and therefore if the Feoffee to Use upon good consideration, had infeoffed another of the land, that had notice of the Use, the Use had been gone for ever; because howsoever there was a privity of Estate yet there was no Confidence in the person; but if the feoffment had been without consideration, to such a one, in this case the use had remained still, because the Law did imply a notice: So also it seems the Law was, when it was made in consideration of Marriage only.

And if a Disseisor, Abator, or Intrudor, had come to the possession of the Land, whereof the use was, albeit he had notice of the use, yet the use was suspended during their possession, and they should not have been seised to the use as the Feoffee was, for they come not to the Land in the *Per*, but in the *post*.

If a Lord by Escheat, Lord of a Villaine, or one that had entered for *Mortmaine*, or that had recovered in a *Custodivit*, &c. had come to such Land, and had notice of the use, the use had been gone for ever, for those come to the Land in the *Post*, and above the use.

And the Tenant in Dower, and by Curtesie, should not be seised to uses in being, for all these wanted privity of Estate.

And if there had been tenant for life, the Remainder in fee in the use of another, and the Tenant for life had made feoffment in fee to one that had notice of the uses, this second feoffee should not have stood seised to the first uses.

So if the Husband had made a Feoffment in Fee of the Land of his wife, upon consideration, and without any use expressed, the wife should not have had a *Subpœna*, because the Feoffee was not in privity of the Estate of the wife.   And

And if *Cestui que use* for life, or in taile, the Remainder in taile with divers Remainders over in use, had made a Feoffment to one that had notice, hee should not have been seised to the first uses.

But now at this day, by the Statute 27 *Henry the eighth, chapter the tenth,* the use of trust and the possession of Lands are for the most part united, and in all such cases where they are united, and the use executed by the Statute, the Chancery doth not intermedle, but leave them to the Law. And such is this, where one seised of Land in fee, doth convey it to the use of one and his Heirs, or Heirs of his Body, or for life, or to the use of one of his Executors or Administrators for years.

But there are some uses and trusts still that are not Executed by the Statute, and those remaine as they were before, and are in the Conusance and order of the Chancery, as where Lands are conveyed without consideration in fee-simple after this manner, that the Feoffee and his Heirs shall take the profits, and deliver them to the Feoffor and his Heirs, or that the Feoffee shall account and give the profits to the Feoffor, or that the Feoffee shall convey the Land to the Feoffor, or to his Heirs, at his age of one and twenty years, or where it is conveyed to *J. S.* and his Heirs, in confidence that *J. S.* shall alien it to whom the Feoffor, or to whom *W. S.* shall appoint, or the like: Or where the Lands be conveyed to certaine uses expressed, and there no other secret uses be agreed upon between the parties.

So where Land is conveyed to one without consideration to one and his heirs, without expressing any use or intent, this is to the use of the Feoffor, who may dispose of it as he pleaseth; But if it be to any intent certaine, as to take back an Estate with remainders to others, &c. Here hee cannot change it.

Y 4

These

These and such like uses and trusts are not within, nor executed by the Statute, but they remaine as they were before the Statute, for all the state is in the party trusted, and the Grantor, or he to whose use the Grant is, hath nothing but a use, for which he hath his remedy only in Chancery, where matters of this nature are determinable, for it is a rule, that as the questions of uses and trusts that are within the Statute, are to be decided and ruled by the Judges of the Common-Law, so all other questions of uses and trusts that are out of the Statute are to be ruled and decided by the Iudges of the Chancery, *Cook* 1. 138. *Dyer* 369. 356. *Cromptons Jurisdiction* 65. 58. 59. And the Iudges in Chancery in ruling those cases, do proceed much after the rules they went by in the regulating of uses at the Common-Law, before the Statute.

Before the making of the Statute, these amongst other were the Lawes of the uses.

1. The Feoffor was to take the profits of the Land, and he might have disposed of it in his life time, or at his death to whomsoever he pleased; & his friends in trust were to settle it accordingly, or be inforced to it by *Subpæna* in this Court; and if hee did not dispose it, the use was to go to his Heirs, and if he had dyed without Heirs or disposition, it seems the Feoffees should have had the Land.

Secondly, If the first Feoffee had conveyed it to a second Feoffee to the same use, or to a second Feoffee that had notice of the uses, in these cases the second Feoffee had it to the same uses; but if the Feoffee had sold it *Bona fide*, or conveyed the Land to one that had no notice of the uses, in these cases the use had been gone, and hee, to whose use it was, remedilesse for the Land.

3. A bruit of a trust, or ones saying there was a
trust

trust to another, I being about to buy the Land; because he would not have me to buy it, it seemes is not sufficient, but a Suit about it, and proofe of it in Chancery, is sufficient notice to him that shall buy it.

4. If the *Cestuy que u'e* had appointed the Land to be sold by his Feoffees to pay his Debts, the Creditors might have compelled the Feoffee to sell it, if he in his life time, or by Will at his death had appointed them to convey it to *J. S. J S.* might have compelled them to it, and so their Heirs.

5. The Feoffees (if any occasion had been) were to bring or defend any Action for the Land, and to plead such Pleas as the Feoffers should appoint, or be inforced in Chancery to it.

6. If the Feoffor dye, and the Land descend to his Heire, the party to whose use, &c. as it seems had no remedy against him.

7. If the Feoffee or Donee to use, sell to one that knows of the use, the *Subpœna* shall go against them both, or otherwise against the party trusted only, who must make a recompence for the breach of trust, if the Land be gone.

These amongst other, were the rules by which uses at common-Law were guided, and much accordingly are uses now executed by the Statute, and trusts of Lands and Goods ordered and guided at this day, as in the cases following, of Inheritance and Freeholds, of chattells, of Goods.

Of Inheritance and Freeholds.

IF I without any consideration Enfeoff one and his Heire, of Land, to the intent he shall take the profits thereof, and deliver to me and my heires: Or

to

to the intent he shall account to me and my Heirs
for the profits thereof; or to the intent he shall reconvey it to me and my Heirs, or to my Heire at one
and twenty years old, or to the intent that he shall
alienate it to *L. M.* and his Heirs, or to whom I shall
appoint; or I convey it to certaine uses expressed,
but there are other secret uses agreed upon between
us, in all such like cases which are out of the Statute of uses, this Court of Chancery, if any complaint be, will order the parties trusted to performe
the trust.

If I without any consideration bargain and sell my
Land by Indenture, to one and his Heirs, to the use
of another and his Heirs (which is a use upon a use)
it seems the Court will order this: But if it were
in consideration of Money by him paid, here it seems
the expresse use is void both in Law and Equity.

And if a woman in consideration of four hundred
pounds paid her by her Son, bargaine and sell her
Land by Indenture to him and his heirs, to the use of
her selfe for life, and after of the heirs of her Son, in
which case by Law the Fee-wmple is to the Son presently, and the use for life to the Mother void; nor
is there as it seems any relief for her in this Court in
a way of Equity, because of the consideration paid,
but if there were no consideration, on the contrary,
Tothil. 188.

A voluntary conveyance was made to friends in
trust, to the use of the mans owne Children, with a
remainder over; the Feoffor being indebted much
Money, the Court inabled him to sell part of it to
pay his debts, *Grants case, Tothill* 42.

If one that hath Land in trust, convey it to one
that hath notice of it, and he convey it to one that
had no notice of it; in this case he that had no notice

tice is feifed to the firft ufes, *Pills Cafe*, *Tothill* 186.

If one convey his Land to friends in truft, and after fell the Inheritance, the truft in Equity goes to the Purchafer, *Decrees Tothill* 44.

Copy-hold was furrendred to the ufe of *J. S.* to the intent that he fhould pay an Annuity to a third perfon, the which he refufed, the Court ordered him to pay it with all the Arrears, *Tothill* 107.

Of Chattells real, and terme of years.

IF I be feifed of Land in Fee, and convey it to D. L. and his Heirs, to the ufe of W. S. his Executors and Adminiftrators for twenty years, or for any other number of years, in this cafe the ufe will be executed within the Statute : But in cafe where I be poffeffed of a tearm of years in being, and grant it to Friends to any ufes and purpofes in truft, this is out of the Statute of ufes, and orderable in Chancery onely, where if the truft be broken, I muft have remedy.

One poffeffed of a tearm in years, conveys it to Friends in truft, to the ufe of D. for life, and after of the Heirs Males of his body, in this cafe the Court refolved and ordered that D. fo long as he hath an Heire may difpofe it; and that an intail of, or out of a Chattell, is not good : but a Remainder in taile of a truft may be ordered in Equity, the Judges agreeing to it, *Tattons Cafe,* 2. *Jacobi. Tothill* 83.

The generall truft of an Executor is to pay debts and legacies, and for the furplufage to account to the Ordinary, *Ad pios ufus.*

Henry, Earle of Darby, conveyed certain leafed lands in truft to *Doughty* his feryant for payment of
his

his Debts, and upon a mediation of an end of contro-
verfies between the Daughter of *Fardinand*, Eldeſt
Son of *Henry Earle*, and *william* his younger Son now
Earle: It was ordered and agreed, that *william* the
now Earle ſhould pay all his Fathers Debts; whereupon *Doughty* conveyed all thoſe Leaſes to *william*,
and after the creditors ſued him in Chancery, but
had no releif, and were ordered to purſue their remedy againſt *Earle william, Hil, 1 Jacobi, Caries Reports*
25.

The Plaintiffs Wife conveyed away her Eſtate to
the Defendant her Son before marriage, and after
the Defendant conveyed it to his children: In this
caſe the court conceiving it to be done without any
conſideration, did decree it for the Plaintiff againſt
the Defendant and his children, *Poveys caſe, Totbil* 98.

Of Chattells perſonall, or Goods.

IF I deliver Money or Goods, or cauſe a Statute,
bond or other Eſpecialty to be made to another to
my uſe, or to any purpoſes or intents in truſt, and he
perform not the truſt, I may compell him to it, or
to give me recompence for the breach of the truſt
here, and therefore if he diſpoſe the money or goods
to his own or any other uſe, then I appointed it, or
will not diſpoſe it according to my mind, or releaſe
or diſcharge the duty, my remedy is by *Subpæna* in this
court, and if in theſe caſes the Goods or money be
taken from him, or he have any injury in them, he
muſt ſue for remedy, and I may compell him to it
here, *7. Ed 4. 14. 29. Cromptons Juriſdiction, 43. 62.*
65. Brook Feoffment 60.

If a Statute be made to *A.* and *B.* to the uſe of *A.*
alone

alone; and the Conufor get a releafe of it from B. a-
lone, in this cafe A. fhall have remedy here againft
them both, (as fome fay againft B. only; and not a-
gainft the Conufor.) See *Caries Reports* 14. *and* 15.

Of Bargaines, Agreements, or Promifes.

ARticles of Agreement were breifly drawne between two, and their hands to it; for the Sale
and affurance of lands for money; the Seller refufed,
and upon complaint here, was ordered to make the
affurance according to the agreement, the Manner
of the affurance referred to a Mafter of the Chancery,
*Chivers cafe,*Hil. 4. *Caroli.*

A Suit was brought here upon a paroll agreement
to execute an affurance of Land upon a Marriage a-
greement (the cafe thus.)

A. Suitor to B. the Brother of A. comes to B. and
tells her that if fhee will marry his Brother, he will
affure her of twenty pounds a year land for her Ioyn-
ture, and fhee did marry him, and after he refufed :
It was decreed in this Court, and the Court of Re-
quefts both, that he fhall be compelled to it; and
where it is faid, that heretofore the Chancery did
not ufe to decree paroll agreements for affurance of
Land, it is now otherwife; for where there is any Fx-
tcution of it by payment of all or any confiderable
part of the mony for the Land, there the Court doth
decree it.

In the Exchequer one fued by Englifh bill upon a
paroll agreement to have Land affured, and fhewed
that he had provided two thoufand pounds the purchafe

chafe money to his great loffe, *&c.* And the other refufed to affure the Land: in this cafe the Court would not decree the affurance of the Land, but decreed he fhould pay the Plaintiff damages for his loffe. So in the 13 *Caroli,* Olivers cafe.

The agreement was to convey the Land, as Counfell fhould advife, the Paper Book drawn, and agreed on to be ingroffed, and then the feller refufed to proceed, in this cafe the Court would not decree it to be done, becaufe no articles nor money paid, but a bare paroll agreement, and yet fome fpecial circumftance may make this binding, and therefore a verball agreement between Lord and Tenant, becaufe the Tenant was an ancient Tenant, and hath been at charge at building, was decreed, *Kings cafe,* and *Hunts cafe, Tothill* 65.66.

A. covenants with *B.* upon the marriage of his Daughter, to levy a Fine of the Land to *D.* And the Daughter being dead, and fome money unpaid, *A.* fold away the Land to others. In this cafe he was ordered for a hundred marks to make the Eftate good; *Mich.* 8 *Caroli,* Pages cafe, *Tothill* 47. and 48.

A Bill was preferred here, fuppofing ten fhillings paid; and two thoufand pounds to be paid for Land, to have the Land affured, and upon Demurrer it was over-ruled becaufe it may be to prepare for an Action of the cafe; but it feems in this cafe the Court would not decree the Affurance, *Trin.* 38. *Eliz,* villiams Cafe, *Tothill* 72.

The cuftomes of a Mannor were in queftion between Lord and Tenants, and Tenant and Tenant: And a generall agreement made by deed indented and inrolled here, and a Bill to eftablifh it, and nothing could be found but the Deed, and yet the court would not alter it, albeit it was objected that the Lord was at the time of the agreement Tenant in

Taill

Tail, and some of the Tenants infants and feme Coverts; *Caries Reports* 22.

If one enter into a Statute to *J. S.* who doth afterwards by Indenture of agreement promise and agree with the Conusee, that in case the Conusor did faile of payment, Execution should be done upon some certaine Land only: In this case, if after it he shall sue Execution upon any other Lands, the party grieved may have relief here, and compell him to perform his agreement, and have an injunction also if he desire it: *Pulvertofts case, Caries Reports* 37.

The Plaintiffs Bill was that he leased a house to the Defendant, and did covenant to repaire it, and then the Defendant did covenant to keep it so, and that the Defendant as well to make the Plaintiff break his covenant, as to free himselfe from his covenant, did interrupt and threaten the workmen, so that they durst not go on, and so the Houses are decayed, and the Plaintiff without remedy. The Defendant demurred, pretending the Plaintiff had remedy by Law, but it was over-ruled and put to answer; *Caries Reports* 59.

A Bill was brought to be relieved against the Defendant as Brother and Heir, for that the Plaintiff had paid to his deceased Brother, 34 l. for a Lease, and he died before it was made, and therefore desired his Lease or the money, and was relieved, *Caries Reports* 77.

One Joyn-Tenant promised the other, lying on his death bed, he would not take advantage of the survivorship, but suffer him to dispose of it by his will, by which he devised part of the payment of his debts, and the Survivor was ordered to make the Estate accordingly: *Caries Reports*, 81.

The Plaintiff bought of the Defendant the reversion of a copy-hold which he could not enjoy, as was

confessed

feffed by the Defendants anfwer, Ordered by the Court to fhew caufe why he fhould not repay the money back againe, which he had received on the Bargain: *Caries Reports 93.*

One brought his Bill to be releived here upon a promife made to him by the Defendant to furrender a Leafe upon the payment of a hundred Marks; and becaufe the matter was meet for the Common Law: *Caries Reports 95.97.*

The Bayliffs of a town promifed a leafe, the Court upon this would not give any releife againft any of their Succeffors, but againft the fame perfons, as common perfons upon the promife: *Caries Reports 103.*

What mifprifions in conveyances, or other Deeds are releivable here.

WHere there is any miftake in a Deed, fo that it is not made in purfuance of the intent and Agreement of the party, this Court gives Releife.

If the word Heirs being in fee fimple, or the like, be omitted; or that part of the land bought and fold be left out of the Deed, and that it do appeare that the conveyance was made upon good confideration, the Court in this cafe will rectifie: fee to this purpofe, *Caries Reports,* 16. and 17.

Dean and Chapter of *Briftoll* made a leafe, miftaking the name of the corporation, and the court held, that for leafes made for fome time of continuance, and upon good confideration, there fhould be releife given here, *Caries Reports 32.*

The leffee in the leafe was not named in the premifes of the leafe, but in the *Habendum* only, decreed

10

be good, and being referred to the two chief Juftices and the chief Baron, was by them certified to be good in Law, *Butlers* cafe, 22 *Eliz. Caries* Rep. 88. One brought his Bill here, to be relieved, for that he had conveyed by the Deed more Land than was intended and agreed; in this cafe becaufe it appeared that the Defendant was a Purchafer, upon a valuable confideration, the Court would not relieve the Plaintiff. *Cliffords* cafe, 4 *Jac.* in Chancery: and yet where more Lands paffed by a Fine than was intended, and the party relieved here by the Judges confent, *Caries* Reports 20.

Miftakes in making of a Bond in either of the parties names may be holpen here, *Colftons* cafe, *Tothill* 7.

If a power be referved to make Leafes by a Covenant without a tranfmutation of the Poffeffion, no help can be here, becaufe it is void in Law: and if it be upon a change of Poffeffion, and the power be not precifely followed, that is, doubtfull, and rather more ftrong againft help, for then the Eftate works and the power gone, and upon Wills no help. See *Caries* Reports.

If one be bound to me for money, and the fame day after the fealing of the Bond I give him a Releafe for other things, which by miftake is made too general, whereby this Bond is alfo releafed, in this cafe I may be relieved here, and fhall receive the Money notwithftanding, *Tops* cafe, *Tothill* 27.

Haddam the Husband was ordered to procure his Wife to levy a Fine, and to enter into a new Bond of five hundred pounds, becaufe the old Bond was worth nothing, by the miftake of the Writer, 1 *Jac. Tothill* 140.

where

*where an Assurance of Land is made defective, this
Court will inforce the perfecting of it.*

WHere a Conveyance is made for Lands or
Tenements, and it is found defective, and
the Estate not well executed to the Purchasor, according to the intent of the parties, for lack of words
sufficient in the Deed, or for lack of Livery of Seisin, Attornment, Inrolment, or the like : and there
was a good consideration given for the Land ; in
such like cases the Court in behalf of the Purchasor
will compell the party, in whose power it is, to perfect the Estate, *Tot: ill* 44.48,182,183,138.

Where a man for money, or other valuable consideration sells Land to one, and the word Heirs is left
out in the *Habendum*, in this case the party who sells
shall be compelled to amend it : And so when less is
granted than was intended, and so for any other
mistakes, *Caries* Reports 16,17.

A Messuage was demised (*cum pertinentiis* onely)
and because sundry Lands had been occupied formerly therewith for the same Rent, and by Lease of
the same words, the Lord Chancellour *Bromley*, and
the Judges ordered it shall all pass, though perhaps
in Law they will not pass by those words, but it
seems in such like cases it is very considerable in
equity, what the value of the Land is, and what money is given; for if the House with the appurtenances be sufficient for the money, unless the intent of
the parties were to grant the whole, it seems agree-
ale to equity that there should be no further extent
made of the words than what the Law makes.

The

The Anceſtour takes money for a Leaſe, and dies before it is made, the Heir muſt make it good, or re-pay the money, *Caries* Report 7.

Where a man for money, or other valuable conſi-deration, ſells Land by Deed, but Livery of Seiſin is omitted, I may compell him afterwards to do it, by this Court: So likewiſe, if upon the ſame conſidera-tion he ſell me Land in two Counties, and have gi-ven me Livery of Seiſin of the Land onely in one County, this Court will order him to make Livery in the Land in the other County, or pay back part of the money, *Caries* Reports 17.

Where a Conveyance is imperfect through the want of the Tenants Attornment; the Tenant in this caſe ſhall be compelled by this Court to attorn; and ſo it was decreed in *Hillary* Term, 3 *Car.*

A. was Leſſee for one and twenty years, and leaſ-ed to *B.* for ten years, rendring Rent; *A.* without the privity of *B.* did grant the Reverſion to *C.* and *B.* refuſed to attorn, and *C.* thereupon ſued *B.* in Chancery, to compell him to attorn; And in this caſe it was decreed by the Maſter of the Rolls with the aſſent of the Maſters of the Chancery, that he ſhould attorn and pay the Arrearages; But Juſtice *Whitlock* then Aſſiſtant was utterly againſt it, and of his opinion were the two chief Juſtices, chief Baron, and Juſtice *Dodridge*; but they all agreed the par-ties themſelves to the Aſſurance may be compelled to make Livery; and it hath been often denied here to compell him to attorn who is at liberty by Law, eſpecially where the party quarrelleth at the Tenants eſtate, or entreth into part of the Land, or hath covenanted for recompence in caſe of not At-tornment, *Caries* Reports 4.

where the Conveyance is made without good confide-
ration, this Court of Chancery will give no Re-
lief.

FOr instance, where there is a Rent granted, and
no Deed to warrant it, and nothing given for
it, or a Reversion is granted, and nothing is given for it, this Court will not inforce the Grantor to
perfect it.

Where Estate was made by Covenant, and not
good by Law, it was ordered by this Court to be
made good, *Princes* case, 40 *Eliz. Tothill* 85.

A Deed which was not inrolled was by this Court
decreed against the Heir of the Land, but agreed it
should not binde any other Estate challenged by
Survivourship, or otherwise, *Pauls* case, 14 *Car. Tothill* 54.

A Bill was here exhibited, to be relieved against
the Defendant, who would have avoyded an Estate
for lack of Livery of Seisin, and it appeared that
the Plaintiff had enjoyed it quietly five and twenty
years, in this case it was decreed he should continue
the quiet possession without Livery and Seisin, *Ri-
dens* case, 17 *Jac. Tothill* 54.

Upon Promises concerning Goods or Debts.

WHere there is a Contract made for Goods or
Chattels wherein the Contractor hath any
wrong

wrong done him, if he gives (*Quid pro quo*) that so it appears there is a good consideration in it: in this case the Contractor may be here relieved, but on the contrary, where there is no consideration, for there is *Nudum pactum.*

Where a man makes a promise without consideration, to build a man a house, make him such or such Goods, he shall not be here compelled to it, *Cromptons Jurisdiction* 49.

A spontaneous and general promise without any consideration was made by the Son to pay his Fathers Debts (no advancement coming to him by his Father) he being sued here, the cause was dismist, *Alexanders* case, 7 *Car.*

Where the Obligee agrees with the Obligor, to give him day for payment of the Debt, and he sueth him or his Surety before the day given, here this Court will relieve him.

What Relief shall be had where there is extremity used, upon a Statute Morgage, Bond, or other Ingagement.

WHere a man by way of Morgage conveys Land to another for security for money lent, in this case albeit the time of Redemption be past, yet upon the paying of the principal money, Interest and Damages, he may have the Land again by Decree of this Court; yet where the Morgage hath been of long continuance, as of twenty years or upwards, this Court will hardly give back the Land, unless in some cases extraordinary: and if the Morgager make a Feofment of it to a stranger, and so

Z 3 ex-

extinguiſh the Condition, unleſs it appear to be to the
end to pay the Debt, the Feoffee perhaps may not
have this advantage, *Caries* Reports 53. *Crowthers*
caſe, 39 *Eliz.* *Tothill* 79.

A Copiholder in Fee ſurrendred to the uſe of one
and his Heirs, upon condition of Redemption; after
this computing his Debts, and writing them down,
he doth will part of his Land ſhall be ſold to pay his
Debts; after his death one of the Creditors doth pay
the money at the day of the Mortgage, yet the Surrender was inrolled, and another Creditor ſued him
and the Heir here, and had a Decree that the Land
ſhould be ſold to pay the Debts, and if any remained
it ſhould go to the Heir, *Caries* Reports 7.

Where there was Leſſee for years rendring Rent,
and two men ſtriving for the Reverſion, he exhibibi-
ting his Bill againſt him, upon payment of his money into Court, according to his Leaſe, he had an
Injunction to forbid them both any further to trouble him, *Caries* Reports 46, & 47.

Where the Conuſee of a Statute extend the Lands
in the hands of one of the Purchaſers, and ſpare o-
ther Purchaſers: In this caſe he may be compelled
to extend upon the whole in all their hands, *Caries*
Reports 111, 112.

Where a man grants a Rent charge out of all his
Lands, and after ſells it by parcels to divers perſons,
and the Grantee force one onely to pay it, the party
ſo paying it may here be relieved, and force the reſt
to contribute, and the Grantee to take no more of
him than what is anſwerable to his proportion of
Land; but in ſuch caſe he muſt be ſure he make all
that have bought any of the Land, Defendants; that
ſo he may make them chargeable with the Rent,
and then they muſt ſhew cauſe why they ſhould not
contribute, *Caries* Reports 2, 23, 92.

When

When the Conusee in a Statute, or Plaintiff in a Judgment hath received satisfaction, the Plaintiff in Chancery, or Conusor, his Heirs, Executors or Administrators; or a Purchaser charged or chargeable by it, may force him, if he be living, or his Executors, or his Administrators, if he be dead, to acknowledg satisfaction upon the Judgment; or to deliver up the Statute: and if Statutes be very ancient, and nothing done upon them, this Court will inforce the Owners of them to deliver them up without satisfaction. In like case this Court will force the delivery up of old Bonds, *Tothill* 178,179. *Caries* Reports 145,146.

Where the Plaintiff had Judgment and Execution against the Defendant for three hundred pounds, he was by this Court here ordered to take it out for 100 l. onely, *Caries* Reports 51.

Where a man upon an Obligation, &c. either at, or after the day according to Law, hath paid any money, and hath no Acquittance for it, or have otherwise at, or after the day satisfied it, and hath no Acquittance for it, and it appears the Obligee hath accepted it, and is satisfied, and yet keeps the Bond, and refuseth to give the Party a Discharge; in these cases he or his Executors, &c. after his death may inforce him, his Executors, &c. after his death in this Court to discharge it, and to deliver up the Ingagement, *Caries* Reports 74. *Tothill* 26,27.

Where a man doth his utmost endeavour to pay money at the day, and to that purpose after he hath provided it, he is robbed, or let by some other chance, & afterwards makes tender of it in some short time. So where part of the money is paid, & yet the whole Ingagement lies, and the party that hath it doth refuse to deliver it up, or to receive the rest of his money, it being tendred shortly after the day, or acknow-

Z 4

ledg

ledg what is paid, &c. *Caries* Reports 1.

So where the Bond is to do any thing other than the payment of money, and the thing is done, and the condition performed, *Caries* Reports 45, 46.

Where a man takes a double security for one and the same Debt, as where he takes a Bond or a Bill and Goods in pawn, or any thing of the same nature, this Court will inforce him that hath taken this double security, to deliver up one of them, *Tothill* 26, & 27.

Where I appoint a Scrivener to put out and receive my money, and by my direction he doth receive the money due upon a Bond at the day, and the Bond remain in my hands, and I refuse to deliver it up, this Court will inforce the delivery of it up, *Hunts* case, 22 *Jac. Tothill* 175.

Where a man enters into a Bond or any other Ingagement, for money unlawfully gotten, as at Dice or Cards, or upon a cheating Contract, or the like, this Court will see him relieved against it, and have it took up or cancelled, *Tothill* 23, 24.

Where a man gives an Ingagement for that that is nothing worth, and which is neither gain to the Obligor nor loss to the Obligee, as for Debts, things in Action not recoverable, here this Court will give relief.

A. had a Son he intended to present to the Church of *Dale*, and he being sickly presented *C.* for the present, taking Bond of him of 600 l. to resign upon request, *C.* is instituted and inducted. After the Son of *A.* becomes healthy, and *C.* is required to resign, he refused, his Bond is sued, and he comes into this Court for relief, it was denied to him, and the Bond agreed to be good in Law and equity. *Trin.* 6 *Car. Wood* and *Berries* case in Chancery, *Tothill* 26, 27.

Where

Where a man makes a Bond not to marry without the consent of Friends, and the Bond becoming forfeit, is sued; it seems this Bond is not good, and this Court will give the Obligor relief, *Totbill* 26,27.

Where money is paid upon the Redemption of a Morgage by Indenture, without taking any Acquittance, this Court will inforce the Morgagee to bring in the Indenture to be cancelled here, *Carics* Reports 17.

The Son and the Father were bound to the Defendant in 500 l. to stand to the Award of the Lord chief Justice, who ordered that the Son who was Plaintiff, and had the Reversion in Fee, and the Father who had the Estate for Life, should make such Assurance as the Defendant should reasonably devise. The Defendant in pursuance thereof tendred an Assurance to the Father to be sealed, who being old and blinde, desired time to advise with his Friends, the Plaintiff the Son sealed, and the Father did afterwards offer to seal, and then the Defendant said, he did not care for his Seal, but he put the Bond in suit upon the Fathers refusal formerly, and it was staid by Order of this Court, *Caries* Reports 105

In any of the afore recited cases, if the party to whom such Ingagement is made, make use of it in any other Court by way of suit against him that entred into it, he may in this Court by Injunction stay the Suit, and shall have the matter ordered here as in equity is fit to be done, *To bill* 23,24. *Suckins* case, 11 *Car.*

This Court gives relief against the injuries of other Courts of Justice by their over-nice and strict observation of the Rules of the Law.

Where there is an extremity used against a man upon a Judgment had against him in any Court at Law, for money or Land, this Court although it will

not

not make void the Judgment, yet will it order the persons as it shall see cause in equity, and this was resolved upon a special debate by the Kings command in 14 *Jac.*

In all cases tending to overthrow of Judgments had in other Courts, this Court neither may nor will not examine or revoke them; for if so, it would render business endless. See *Caries* Reports 74, 75.

The Heir coming into his Fathers House, had of his Fathers Goods worth five shillings, and the Defendant sued a Bond of five hundred pounds against the Heir as Executour of his own wrong, and proving he sold or gave away the Goods, a Verdict passed for the whole five hundred pounds, which appearing by the Certificate of the Justices of Assize, an Injunction was granted to stay all Proceedings in this Action, and to forbid any new Action, till the Court have determined the matter, *Caries* Reports 49.

A Debt upon a single Bill satisfied, and the Bill not delivered, was sued, and Execution gotten, and the party was by this Court relieved, 22 *Eliz. Owens* case, *Caries* Reports 74.

If one man do unduly get a Judgment in any Court in the name of another, Relief may be had here, *Caries* Reports 76.

A drunken man being sued by another for words spoken in his drink, tending to Defamation, sought for Relief here, but could have none, *Qui peccat ebrius, luat sobrius, Caries* Reports 93.

One exhibited his Bill for Relief upon an Obligation of three hundred pounds, which he entred into, conditioned for the making a Jointure to his wife upon consideration of one hundred seventy four pounds promised to him by the Defendant in Marriage,

which

which was never paid to him ; he sued at common Law upon the Bond : In this cafe an Injunction was ordered to ftay proceedings, *Caries* Reports 112.

In what cafes the Tenant Copiholder fhall be relieved, againft the hard dealing of the Lord of the Mannour.

First, if the Lord will out his Tenant that pays his Rent or does his Services, or if the Tenant furrender in Court to the ufe of another, and the Lord refuse to admit him, to whofe ufe the Surrender was made, or will not keep Court for the benefit of his Copiholder, or exact uncertain Fees, they being certain ; this Court in thefe cafes will give relief.

Secondly, if he will not admit the Tenant copiholder upon a Defcent.

Thirdly, if the Tenant copiholder be outed of his Copihold, and the Lord will not hold a Court whereat he may fue for his Right.

Fourthly, if a falfe Judgment be had againft a Tenant copiholder, and he petition to the Lord to redrefs it, and he refufe.

Fifthly, if the Tenant copiholder petition the Lord to grant him a Licence to let, and he refufe it.

Sixthly, a woman Copiholder for Life, the Reverfion is granted two for their Lifes, *cum poft mortem, vel foris facturam* of a woman, it fhall happen, and fhe take a husband that doth furrender to the firft in Reverfion, who is admitted and dieth, and
after

after the next defireth admittance, and could not have it, but the Lord entreth as an Occupant, (as he might) and the Husband and Wife were willing to furrender to him in the Reverfion for Life, and the Lord refufing to keep a Court, or leave the poffeffion, was ordered to do both in this Court, *Totbill* 3, 44,45. *Caries* Reports 3. *Kitchin* 82,89.

A Copiholder granted by the Lord, at a Court held out of the Mannour, made good againft the Lord by Decree of this Court, *Marks* cafe, *Totbill* 45.

Where the Lord impofes an unreafonable Fine upon his Tenant upon a Surrender, &c. The reafonablenefs of the Fine fhall be here adjudged of, and this Court will give relief. A years value of the Land hath been here allowed good, *Caries* Reports 54

This Court gives relief to the Surety againft the principal Debtor or Creditor.

Where there is a Debtor with a Surety, and Creditor, and the principal Debtor, and Creditor, by compact, and agreement without the privity of him who is Surety, continues the Debt after the firft day of payment, when the Surety doth fuppofe it to be paid: in this cafe this Court will compell the Creditor to take his relief from the principal Debtor, and difcharge the Surety, his heirs, executors, &c. *Miles* cafe, 5 *Car. Bates* cafe, 10 *Jac. Saunders* cafe, 10 *Jac. Totbill* 181.

Where there is a Detainer of any Lands, Deeds or Goods, this Court will give relief towards the Difcovery and Recovery of them.

As where a man hath Title to Lands, and intends to bring his Action, but cannot difcover who is Tenant to the Land: in this cafe he may fue the Occupier in this Court, and he will be inforced to fhew what he, or any under whom he holds, claims to his knowledg, and then he may know whom to fue, and upon what grounds.   Where

Where the Defendant held beyond his term, this Court inforced him to shew what term his Lease was for, *Mich. 6 Car. Tothill* 183.

The Conusee of a Statute did by the power of this Court inforce a Lessee for years to declare all the particulars of his Lease, that so he might discover whether it were extendable or not, 11 *Car. Toth.* 183. *Creswells* case, *Tothill* 9. *Caries* Reports 16.

Where Writings are detained from a man, if the Court do see cause, it will inforce the Defendant to bring the Writings into Court by a *Duces tecum*, *Caries* Reports 43, 52, 53, 67.

This Court gives relief for the recovery of Land, Debt, or Duty, where the Law gives none.

Where a man hath a just Title to Land, but hath lost his Conveyances, this Court will give relief for the recovery of his Land, *Caries* R. 24. *Gossats* case.

Where a man hath a good Title to Rent, but no means to gain it, as if the Rent be seck, and he never had Seisin of it, or any other Rent wherein he hath had no Attornment of the Tenant, or supposing the Rent is by some accident (without any recompence for it) discharged: so if it hath been usually paid, but I can shew no Deed for it. In these and the like cases this Court will give relief for the recovery of it, *Tothill* 72, 172, 173.

Where a man hath a Debt due to him upon especialty, and hath lost his Writing, or cannot come at it: in this case if he have witness to prove it, he may be relieved here for the Recovery of it, *Caries* Reports 25.

Where an *Elegit* was returned and filed, and the time thereof elapsed, and yet the Plaintiff unsatisfied of his Debt, this Court will give him relief by reviving the *Elegit*, *Tothill* 179.

Where a man makes a Will with several devi-
ses

ſes, this Court will direct how they ſhall be taken and performed in equity.

The meaning of a Will is to be performed here, *Cobs* caſe, *Tothill* 141.

Where there was a Deviſe void in Law, by reaſon of a miſ-recital of a Grant, and lack of an Attornment, this Court did here decree it to be good, *Bacons* caſe, *Tothill* 79.

This Court doth give Relief againſt a fraudulent practice to avoid a Leaſe, *Caries Rep.* 18, & 22.

So likewiſe to avoid a Debt, *Caries Rep.* 18.

This Court will give relief in avoiding Conveyances fraudulently made, as where there is a Suit depending between two for Land, and the Defendant hanging the Suit, make ſecret Conveyances of the Land, this Court will order him to diſcharge the Land thereof, *Tothill* 108. *Harbynes* caſe, *Tothill* 9.

Thus much ſhall ſuffice to have ſpoken concerning the generality of the cauſes the Court of Chancery takes Conuſance of, in which for your further ſatisfaction, I refer to the Reports of Mr. Tothill and Sir George Carew.

It remains we ſhould now come to the particulick part of it, which directeth for the moſt part, their whole manner of Proceedings, wherein for methods ſake we will begin with their firſt Proceß, called a Sub pœna.

THis *Sub pœna* is the leading Proceſs of thisCourt, as to the procedure by Bill and Anſwer, and this doth require the Defendants appearance in this

Court

Court by a certain Day under a certain pain, to make Anſwer to the Complaint of the Plaintiff, which is indeed the Bill, which formerly was wont to be put in before the *Sub pœna* was ſued forth, but now otherwiſe uſed; this is called a *Sub pœna to anſwer*, and diſtinguiſhed by that name, in reſpect there are ſeveral other *Sub pœnas*, in order to further proceedings, as a *Sub pœna* for coſts, a *Sub pœna* to make a better Anſwer, a *Sub pœna* to rejoin, a *Sub pœna* to hear Judgment, a *Sub pœna* for Witneſſes to teſtifie, &c. a *Sub pœna Duces tecum*, &c. for Writings, Evidences, &c.

Touching the *Sub pœna* to anſwer, you muſt be very carefull there be no miſtake in the body of the Writ, for that may prejudice the Plaintiff, and the Defendant may take advantage if he finde any; but if there be a miſtake in the Labell onely of the Writ, no advantage is to be taken by it.

This Writ may be made returnable two ways, either upon the common Days of Return, as from the Day of *Eaſter* in fifteen Days, &c. or upon a Day certain, after any of the uſual Returns, or after any the great Feaſts, from whence the Returns take their names.

This word [Next] muſt be added where it is requiſite, as where the great Feaſts be either to come or paſt.

The Writ of *Sub pœna* is to be ſerved before the Return thereof be paſt, which they uſually do, either by the Delivery of the Writ it ſelf under Seal to the perſon of the Defendant, or by ſhewing the Writ under Seal unto him, delivering him a Note or Labell of the Day of his Appearance; and this is more uſual when there are more perſons than one in the *Sub pœna*, whereby the body of the Writ may be reſerved to be left with the laſt.

For

Or elfe the Writ may be left at the Defendants dwelling-houfe with one of his Family, or at his place of refidence. See Collection of Orders, &c.

It is conceived it may be a good fervice to leave the Writ hanging upon the Door of the houfe, or to put it into the houfe under the Door, or within the Window of the houfe where the party doth dwell or ufually refide at. But that is where it is perfumed it afterwards comes to his hands, or that he might be in the houfe at the time, or had notice of it.

Where a *Sub pœna* is ferved on the felf-fame day whereon it is returnable, it is a good fervice if it be before Noon, and the rifing of the Court in Chancery : and the Defendant fo ferved fhall be bound to an Appearance with all fpeed.

Where a *Sub pœna* is had againft a Husband and Wife, and the Husband alone is ferved, and hath notice that it is againft him and his Wife, this is a good fervice as to both, and for want of Appearance an Attachment may be had, either againft the Wife onely, or againft both. To which purpofe fee *Caries* Reports 89, 101, 103, 106, 109, 110.

The *Sub pœna* being ferved, the Bill muft be put in in due time, or elfe if the Defendant appear, and no Bill filed, they will get cofts. To prevent which, take notice what time is prefixed for exhibiting the Bill after the Day of the Return of the *Sub pœna*.

If the *Sub pœna* be returnable upon a general Return-day, as *Craftino, Octabis, Tres. Menfe, &c.* after fuch or fuch a Feaft, then hath the Plaintiff time to put in his Bill untill the fecond day before Noon next following, the fourth day following every of the faid Returns, and you muft account the Return-day, and the fourth day after it for two of the faid four days.

But

But where the *Subpæna* is returnable upon such or such a certaine day of the month, then the Bill must be filed the second day after it before Dinner.

Where the Bill is not filed, and the *Subpæna* returnable on a day certaine, as on any day of the Month, the Defendants appearance being entered, his Attorney may prefer costs the next day after: And if the Bill come not in the next day after costs so preferred before noon, or presently after Dinner, the Defendant is discharged with such costs as the Master of the Court taxes him.

Where the *Subpæna* is made returnable on a return day, in such case the next day after the fourth day is costs-day; and if the Bill come not in the next day at noon, or presently after dinner, (the *Defendant* having preferred his costs the day before) is discharged upon Atttendance with his costs.

Where the costs are not voluntarily paid for want of a Bill, either by the *Plaintiff* himself, or his Clark, to the *Defendant* or his Clerk, in such case the *Defendant* may have a *Subpæna* whereby to command the *Complainant* presently upon sight thereof to pay the *Defendant*, or the bringer thereof the said costs: And this *Subpæna* must be served on the *Plaintiff* personally, and upon such service, if the *Complainant* do refuse to pay the said costs accordingly, in such case the *Defendant* may (upon *Affidavit* made, that the *Subpæna* for costs was served) have an Attachment directed to the Sheriff of the County where the *Complainant* lives, to attach the *Complainant* for the said Costs.

And if the Sheriff of the County make return upon that Attachment, that the Complainant cannot be found, then an Attachment with Proclamation may be sued forth against him: And that Procla-

A a   mation

tion being likewise returned by the Sheriffs as aforesaid, then a Commission of Rebellion may be sued forth against the complainant.

On the other side, if the Plaintiff do in due time file his Bill, and the Defendant appeareth not the next day after costs day, then the complainant upon Oath made, that the Defendant was served with a *Subpæna*, may have an Attachment, and further processe, in case the Sheriff return, The party is not to be found, &c.

The *Affidavit* that must be made of the Service of the *Subpæna*, must be made according as the manner of the Service was: for if the *Affidavit* made do not prove a good service as before, no Attachment can be had upon it, and therefore he must swear as followeth.

That he delivered the *Subpæna* to the Defendant, or that he shewed the *Subpæna* to the Defendant, under the Seale of the Court, and delivered to him a Note of the day of his appearance, or a Labell of the *Subpæna*.

Or that he left the *Subpæna* at the Defendants dwelling house or lodging where the Defendant most abideth.

Or he may make *Affidavit*, that he heard the Defendant confess that he was served with a *Subpæna*.

If the party that makes *Affidavit* can sweare, that he saw another (naming him) so serve the Writ as before; this will be sufficient to maintain the Attachment.

There can be no Attachment regularly made out against the Defendant for not appearing, untill there be a certaine and positive Oath made of the Time, Place, and Manner of serving the *Subpæna*, inserting the return of the Writ.

And where any person served with a *Subpæna* do
injury,

injury, or wrong, either by word or deed to the party who acted in the Service of it, or doth set at naught, or contemn the Writ it selfe, or the Authority of the Court from whence it issues, upon Oath made thereof, and motion thereupon, such person will be committed to the Fleet, &c. *Caries Reports,* 19.92.110.

Where there is appearance made by the Defendant within the time limited, and by the Bill filed: In such case the Complainants Attorney may give unto the Defendants Attorney on the said day after the costs day, a Rule, that the Defendant do make answer to the complainants Bill by the same day seven-night then next to come: this rule and day must be entered into the Register; and in case the Defendant faile to make answer, by that prefixed day so entred, or if he do not otherwise satisfie the Court by shewing sufficient cause and occasion of such his delay, then the complainants Attorney may have an Attachment against the Defendant.

Now this writ of Attachment cannot be duly had, but where the *Subpæna* foregoing is duly obtained and served, for if the *Subpæna* be counterfeit, or if true, and not legally served, this Writ of Attachment in these cases is unduly obtained, and the Defendant arrested by it, upon disclosing the matter to the Court, will be discharged thereof.

An Attachment duly gotten for not appearing, may not bo discharged, till the Defendant have first paid twenty shillings costs, if the serving of the *Subpæna* were upon his person, otherwise it is ten shillings, and every succeeding process double so much: And upon payment hereof he is to be discharged of course: See *Caries Reports,* 32. 72. 79. 94. 105. *Tothill.* 15.

The Husband appeared, and the Wife not, an At-meat was granted against them both: *Abells* Cafe 39. *Eliz. Caries* Reports, 65.

So he alone appeared, and put in a Demurror, in both their names, without excufing her, Attachment was granted against both; *Spicers* Cafe, *Caries* Reports, 39.

The *Defendant* made Oath, he could not answer without fight of Evidences, & had time given him, and then afterwards put in a Demurrer: this Writ went out against him, *Pafch.* 21. *Eliz. Farmers* cafe.

Where the *Defendant* is ferved with a *Subpæna*, and afterwards for not appearing an Attachment iffues against him; if he do not appear upon the Attachment, and the Sheriff do thereupon return (as in the like cafes he doth) a *Non eft inventus*, then there will iffue forth against him a Proclamation of Rebellion, wherein obferve, that this proceffe of contempt, and all Attachments in proceffe are to be difcharged upon the *Defendants* payment, to tender to and refufall of it, by the *Plaintiffs* Clark of the ordinary cafes of Court, and filing of his Plea, anfwer, or Demurror, as the cafe is, without any motion in Court: And if the *Plaintiff* do profecute the contempt afterwards the *Defendant* will be difcharged with cofts.

Where an Attachment is had, if the Sheriff doe not make his Return, a day will be given, and if he do not by that time the Court will fet an Amerciament upon him: See *Caries Reports*, 44. 77. 78. *Collection of Orders, Totbill* 15.

Where any party is attached, and afterwards proclaimed, and he comes not in, but ftands further out in contempt, in fuch cafe a commiffion of Rebellion may be iffued forth against him for the apprehending of him and bringing him to the *Fleet* (the proper Prifon of this Court.)

This

This Commission of Rebellion is sometimes directed to the Sheriff, and sometimes to private persons, as in the case of *Cage* and *Efington*, *Trinity* 30. *Jacobi*, *Tothill* 37.

This course is likewise taken against those that make not obedience to Orders or Decrees, to pay costs or the like.

Where those private persons who are made Commissioners, having taken the person in contempt, suffer him to escape, they themselves will be committed till they bring him in; as in the case of *Sachaverell* against *Sacheverell*, *Hillary Term*, 18. *Jacobi Tothill* 38.

If any person rescue one taken upon a commission of Rebellion, the Rescuer is to be committed.

Where the Commissioners upon commission of Rebellion, let the party in contempt goe where he listed, whereby he made an escape, they were ordered to be committed to the Fleet till they pay the Debt: See *Nelsons* case against *Yelverton*, *in Trin.* 18. *Jacobi*, *Tothill* 39.

Where the party appears not, but stands further out in contempt, a Serjeant at Armes may be sent out to take him, and if he cannot take him, or that he resist, or having taken him, he make an escape, and so persist high in his contempt, in such cases a Sequestration may be had of his Land: And if the Suit be for Land, a Sequestration and Injunction for the profits of the Land, to be delivered to the Plaintiff by the Sheriff, or by other Commissioners for that purpose: as in the case of *Boles* against *Watley* and his Wife. *Caries* Reports, 38. 58. 105 106.

We proceed now to Bill and Answer.

THE Plaintiffs Bill is in effect the same that the Declaration after appearance had, is, either in the Upper-Bench or common Pleas, and laies down the cause of his complaint in Chancery, being such usually as is exempt from remedy at common Law, for that they insert commonly these words in the Bill, that the Plaintiff hath not remedy at Law.

This Bill by the practice of the present times may be put in after the *Subpœna* is both taken out and served, provided it comes in within the time before limited, to prevent costs.

Upon one and the same *Subpœna* served, two Bills may be put in, provided the matter contained in them appear not to be one and the same cause, for if it do so, one of them may be dismissed with costs and where two Bills are so put in containing severall matters, the Defendant must answer them both.

This Bill in Chancery, and all subsequent Pleadings and proceedings upon it, must be succinct and short, and not stuft with repetitions of Deeds, Writings, or Records, (*in hæc verba*) but the effects and substance of so much of them only as is pertinent & materiall to be set down, and that in briefe terms, without long and needlesse Traverses of such things not traversable, tautologies, or impertinences.

It must not likewise contain any matter criminall or scandalous against the Defendant, or any other and if it do, and concern the Defendant, he may refuse to answer it; and the Plaintiff and his Counsell whose hand is to the Bill, may be punished for it, and the party grieved may recover costs against such Counsell.

This Bill must be put in under counsels hand, who

s carefully to peruse it, if at least it be not drawn by himself, and so that it be such as is be re rejected, and likewise the Counsell must take care that it be such for the matter of it as the Court will allow, and take Cognizance of, and then he is to signe it.

Where any Bill containes matter not proper for this Court to give relief in, the Bill will be dismissed and so likewise will it be, if there want Counsels hand to the Bill, or if the Counsels hand be counterfeit or disallowed, See *Caries Reports* 89.

To this Bill in Chancery filed, the Defendant is to make answer, wherein many times he makes such delay, but in all cases of delay, he must upon Oath satisfie the Court of the cause of such his delay, which may be in severall respects; as.

First, where the matter contained in the Bill is such, as to which he cannot give answer, without conference had with some other persons named in the Bill, or to whom the Bill referes.

Secondly, where the Bill charges the Defendant with the having of Goods or Chattels of the Complainants, to make discovery what they are; in such case the Goods being in the Country, and he here, he may make Oath he cannot make perfect answer to the Plaintifs Bill without sight and perusal of the Goods: So likewise where he cannot make direct answer, without sight of some Evidences or Writings which he hath in the Country, he may make Oath thereof; but in such cases, that place in the Country where those parties live, Goods or Writings or Evidences lye, must be above twenty miles from *London*, for else he must answer within eight dayes after his appearance, unless further time be given him by order.

Upon Oath made as aforesaid, then his answer will

A a 4

will be spared till the first day of the next Term
following.

There may likewise Oath be made by another
person, either his Solliciter, Servant, or some
Neighbour to the *Defendant*, that he is sick, or disabled for travell without danger of life.

Upon such Oaths made as aforesaid, if the *Plaintiff* refuse to allow of a *Dedimus Potestatem* on the
behalfe of the *Defendant*, for the taking his answer
in the Country; This Court of Chancery upon
motion or petition will order it, and the order that
is so obtained must be carefully entred in the Registers Office, and the *Affidavit* upon which the Order is grounded must be filed in the *Affidavit*-Of-
ffice.

Where the *Defendant* doth not appear, or that after he hath made his appearance, he doth not answer within the time limitted him, nor by way of excuse sheweth any the reasons aforesaid, in such case
an Attachment as is aforesaid, is awarded against
him, which Attachment must be entred into the
House-Book of the six Clerks Office, and likewise in
the Registers Book, expressing the cause of the issuing of the said Attachment.

Where there is no day by rule given to the *Defendant* to answer, in such case the *Defendant* is at
liberty to answer at any time during the Term.

And wher the *Defendant* makes default within that
time to make answer, then an Attachment may be
sued forth against him of course. and the same with
the cause thereof (as before) must be entred with the
Register (*viz.*) That the *Defendant* appeared, and
went away without any answer.

Where the *Subpæna* is made returnable so neer
the end of the Terme, that there cannot be a day given to the *Defendant* to answer: in such case the
Defendant

Defendant must at his perill answer by the same day seven-night next following the day of his appearance, although it be out of Term, for the Court of Chancery is always said to be open.

Where the *Subpæna* is returnable on the last return day of the Tearm it selfe, then the *Defendant* is at liberty to appear the first return of the Tearm following.

But where the *Subpæna* is returnable upon a day certain, although the day be the last day of the Tearm, the *Defendant* is bound to appear and yet answer by that day seven-night next following the said appearance.

In all cases where the *Defendant* either makes Oath, that he cannot answer without Writings, Evidences, &c. or conference with some other person, or that he have a *Dedimus Potestatem*, and Commission to take his answer in the Country ; the *Defendant* must at his perill procure his answer to be put in before the day after the first costs day of the next Term following, unlesse it be in Trinity Term; then in such case it must be put in the second day after the second return, or otherwise the Complainants Attorney may upon such his default make an Attachment against the *Defendant* for not answering by the day prefixed.

VVhere the *Defendant* lives in the Country, and hath a *Dedimus potestatem* granted him for the taking of his answer to the *Plaintiffs* Bill, it hath been formerly the course, that in case the Counsell finde cause of Plea or Demurrer, that then the *Defendant* should move or petition to have a speciall *Dedimus potestatem* by order to answer, Plead, or Demur, for that the Commissioners upon an ordinary *Dedimus*, had not power to take any thing but an answer.

But

But by the late collection of Orders it is ordered, that where the Defendant is served with a *Subpæna ad respondendum,* and obtaineth a Commission to answer in the Countrey, he shall without more words have the same liberty thereby to answer, plead and demurr, as he had by the originall Process, if he could have appeared in person. See collect. of Orders, 29.

Where the Defendant doth demurr, or put in any just Plea which he hath, to the disability of the person of the Plaintiff or to the Jurisdiction of the court under the hand of learned Counsell, it will be received and filed, although the Defendant do not deliver the same in person, or by commission.

And if the Defendant do not put in his demurrer, or Plea into the Paper of Pleas and demurrers, in the Registers Office appointed for that purpose, within eight dayes after the same is put into the Court, that so the said Demurrer may be argued before the Lords Commissioners as it shal fall in course; and where this is omitted to be done, the Plea and demurter is over-ruled of course, and the Plaintiff may take forth a *Subpæna* against the Defendant, to inforce him to make a better answer, and in order for costs according to the late rules and collection of Orders.

Where a man exhibits his Bill in Chancery, and dies, the Suit depending, who ever have the Interest in the thing complained for, whether Heire, Executor, or Administrator, they may put in a Bill of Revivor against the Defendant; or in case the Defendant dye, the Plaintiff may exhibite his Bill of Revivor against the Heirs, Executors or Administrators of the Defendant.

Where there is a Bill of complaint exhibited against a man and his wife, and the matter contain-in the Bill wholly concerns the wife, and they both make answer unto this Bill, and after they have made answer the Husband dies; in this case a Bill of Revivor must be brought by the complainant against the woman, if he intend to proceed in that Suite; and the reason is, for that the woman shall not be constrained to abide by that answer, which shee together with her Husband, or solely as wife unto the man, had formerly made to the complainant, for that shee was at that time under coverture.

And in case shee survives her Husband, and continues possessed or seised of the thing in controversie, in *Statu quo,* she may as she shall think fit make a new answer, and shall not be bound up or concluded by that answer, which she made during coverture, or solely as Wife unto the man: and yet if she thinks fit, she may stand to that former answer of hers, and proceed accordingly in that Suit.

Where the Plaintiff exhibits his Bill in chancery against a feme sole, and she appearing, makes answer unto the Bill, and afterwards marrying, shee comes under coverture, the suit depending; In this case the Plaintiff may proceed against her and her Husband, and shall not need any Bill of Revivor: and her Husband shall be bound by that answer, which she made whilst a feme sole, for that she shall not advantage her selfe by her own act.

Where on the other side a feme sole Plaintiff exhibits her Bill, and the Defendant makes answer unto it, and afterwards she intermarryeth, here there can be no further proceeds by the Husband and Wife without a Bill of Revivor, because shee hath abated her suit by her own act of marriage, of which the Defendant may take his best advantage.

Where

VVhere the Man and the wife exhibit a Bill of Complaint, and to this the Defendant answereth, and the Man dyeth, the VVoman shall be at her choice whether shee will exhibit a new Bill, or proceed upon the Bill by her Husband and her selfe formerly exhibited.

VVhere there are two seized of joynt Estates, or where they are Executors of one VVill or Obligees, or Obligers; and they prefer a Bill in Chancery, to which the *Defendant* makes answer, and after one of them dye, here the Survivor may proceed in his suit against the *Defendant*, and shall need no Bill of Revivor.

Note, that the Bill of Revivor must pursue the first Bill exhibited; for where there is any variance between them, the *Defendant* may be discharged, and the Bill will be dissolved.

Where there are Administrators; *Durante minore ætate* of an Infant Executor, in the nature of a Guardian, and they sue on the Infants behalfe, and the Suit depending, the Infant comes to age, here it seems there needs no Bill of Revivor.

VVhere the complainant hath exhibited this Bill of Revivor, and hath procured thereupon a *Subpæna* to be served; he will be upon this in the same case as the Predecessor was, when the Bill first accrued, unlesse some good cause to the contrary (as that he is not Heire, Executor, nor hath the like interest, *&c.*) can by the Defendants answer bee shewed.

VVhere a man doth willfully refuse to answer, and stand out all the Processe of contempt, the Court will take the matter of the Bill *pro confesso*, and decree it, *Tothill* 69.

If the answer be good to common intent, the Plaintiff must reply and prove the matter if he can, and

no

not infist upon infufficiency of the anfwer.

No exception can be taken to an anfwer after a Replication put in, for it is then admitted to be good, but before Replication it may be excepted against.

But where it is excepted againft, the caufes muft be fhewn in writing, and delivered in to the *Plaintiffs* Attorney or Counfell, the fame Tearm the anfwer comes in, or within eight dayes after; and if he amend it in eight dayes, he is to pay no cofts.

VVhere an anfwer is excepted againft to be infufficient, it is ufually referred to a Mafter, to confider of the Exceptions, and he to certifie the court whether it be infufficient.

If the Mafter certifie it to be infufficient, then the *Plaintiff* may take out Proceffe for cofts, and the *Defendants* anfwer is not to be received, till he hath paid the cofts.

The firft anfwer being returned infufficient, the *Defendant* muft pay forty fhillings fingle cofts.

If it be an anfwer that came in by commiffion, and be infufficient, he muft pay fifty fhillings.

The fecond anfwer infufficient paies three pounds.

The third five pounds cofts, and you may have a *Subpœna* both for your cofts, and to make a better anfwer.

But in thefe cafes of exceptions, the infufficiencies appearing in the fame exceptions, are the point to be infifted on, and no new exceptions may be moved.

VVhere the Mafter upon reference to him finds the anfwer to be fufficient, and accordingly certifies, there the *Plaintiff* muft pay forty fhillings cofts.

If the Exceptions to an anfwer be put in after the Term, there fhall be time given to anfwer them untill the fourth day of the next Terme, unlefse the court haften it.

If the answer come in by commission, and be not good, no new commission will be admitted but upon Oath of the inability of the person, and his payment of fifty shillings costs as before.

Where a cause goes to hearing upon Bill and Answer, the same must be admitted to be true in all points, and no other Evidence is to be admitted, but what is matter of Record, to which the answer doth refer, and which is provable by Record if selfe: *Carles Reports* 78, 30.

Concerning Demurrers and Pleas, take these Rules following.

First, A Demurrer is alwayes where there is matter defective contained in the Bill, or where there is forrain matter.

The Plea of forrain matter may be of two sorts; Either where it is to the Jurisdiction of the court, or to the disability of the person, as where the *Plaintiff* is outlawed or excommunicate, or where there is in this or any other court, a Bill or suit depending for this very cause.

Or it may be that the cause hath been formerly dismissed this court, or the like.

Or if the matter of it appear upon Record, it may be put in without Oath, otherwise not.

In case it be a Demurrer, it must expresse the cause of the Demurrer, yet other causes may be insisted on at the time of the determination thereof by the court.

If the demurrer be over-ruled, the Defendant shall pay five marks costs, and where it is allowed, the Defendant shall have no costs.

If

If one plead a plea that is insufficient, and so over-ruled to be, as where it is an Outlawry pleaded, and it is not a good Plea, he must pay five Marks costs.

An Outlawry is not to be pleaded, unlesse you plead the Record, *sub pede sigilli*.

A plea of Outlawry, if it be in a Suit for the same thing for which a man sueth to be relieved in Chancery, is not to be allowed; but otherwise it is allowed, and will be in force to hinder all the Plaintiffs proceedings, till it be reversed.

But when it is reversed, the Plaintiff upon payment of twenty shillings costs, may upon a new *Subpæna* served, put the Defendant to answer the same bill.

Where the Plaintiff conceives the Plea for matter or manner naught, he may put it to the Judgment of the Court.

Where a man pleads a former suit, he need not set it down with the Register, but it shall be referred to a Master to certifie (which must be done within a moneth upon the Plaintifs procurement.) And if the Master do certefie against the Plaintif, he must pay five shillings costs: If there be no Report within a moneth of filing the Plea, the Bill will be dismissed of course, with seven Nobles coasts.

If the Demurror to any Bill be put in upon any slip or mistake in the Bill, the Plaintif of course laying down to the Attorny twenty shillings costs, may amend his Bill within eight dayes after the Demurror put in, but not after that time.

If the Demurror be admitted by the Plaintiff to be good within eight dayes after the filing of it and he doth pay the Defendant his Attorney, or Clark in court forty shillings costs, then the Defendant shall not need to attend his Demurror, but the Bill shall

stand

stand dismist of course without motion, unlesse both sides agree to the amendment of the same, but such dismission is to be no bar to a new Bill to be exhibited by the *Plaintiff*.

Where the *Plaintiff* finds sufficient cause for an Order in the answer, he may goe to hearing thereupon without further proofe, (of which he should be well advised) in which case he must procure his Attorny to present the same in course, to be set down to be heard upon Bill and answer: But in case the Court shall not find grounds to make a Decree or finall Order, the Bill shall be dismissed with costs, or the *Plaintiff* admitted to reply, if he desire it, first paying down five pound costs, within four dayes after such hearing, then the dismission to stand, and the conclusion of the order upon hearing is to be penned by the Register accordingly, and then such dismission shal be a good Plea in Bar of any new Bil for the same matter.

VVhere a *Plaintiff* proceeds so far as to proof, and upon the hearing it clearly appears the Plaintiff might have had full relief upon Bill and Answer, albeit he be releived in the cause, yet he shall pay costs. See more fully of these things in the collection of Orders 16. 18. *Caries* Reports, 39. 87.

Replication, Rejoynder, and Sur-re-joynder comes next to be handled.

THe Replication is the speech of the *Plaintiff*, in way of Reply to the *Defendants* answer.

The re-joynder is the *Defendants* answer, to the *Plaintiffs* Replication.

The Sur-re-joynder is a second defence to the Plaintiffs action, opposite to the *Defendants* Rejoynder.

First

First, the Replication must be short relating to the substance of the Bill, and it must avoid superfluous and criminous matter.

Secondly, the Replication must affirm and pursue the Bill, and confess, and avoid, traverse, or deny the Answer.

Thirdly, the Rejoinder, that must pursue and confirm the Answer, and must sufficiently confess or avoid, or traverse every material part of the Replication.

Fourthly, no new matter must be put into the Replication, and so much matter onely is necessary to be there, as will avoid the matter of the Answer.

Fifthly, if upon the Answer there be so much confessed, that the Plaintiff need not to draw into Pleading, and prove all the Points, he must see to it, and reply, and go to proof onely in those Particulars in question, and necessary to be proved.

Sixthly, when the Defendant doth demur or disclaim to any Bill exhibited against him, the Plaintiff cannot reply. And if the Defendant in those cases be served with a *Sub pœna ad rejungendum*, having before made no other Answer, but a Demurrer or Disclaimer, he shall have costs for unjust Vexation.

Where the case is such, that the parties cannot come to Issue, by reason of some new matter disclosed in the Defendants Rejoinder, that requires to be answered unto, the Plaintiff may sur-rejoyn to the Rejoynder, and the Defendant likewise to the Sur-rejoynder, if there be cause.

As for the time for the Replication to be put in after the Answer, you are to observe that the Plaintiff

B b   hath

hath time for all this Term, and all the next Term, and untill the begining of the second Term following, to put in his Replication.

The next Term after the Answer is put in, the Defendant may give the Plaintiff Rule to reply: and if such Rule be given, and the Plaintiff reply not, costs will be given against him.

And where he gives no Rule, and the Plaintiff doth not reply the second Term, after the Term, the Answer is put in, the Bill will be dismissed with the costs of course.

But in case the Plaintiff doth reply, and that the Replication be in Court, the Defendant can have no costs.

In case where the Complainant hath replied, the Defendant may if he will rejoyn *Gratis* to the Replication, and force the Complainant to joyn in Commission.

Where the Plaintiff intends to go to Commission, he must serve the Defendant with a *Sub pœna ad rejungendum*, before he can have Commission to examine Witnesses, and upon Return of the *Sub pœna ad rejungendum*, and Oath made of the serving of it, the Plaintiff may by entring Rules, force the Defendant to rejoyn and joyn in Commission, or go on to the examining of Witnesses without him; for having given him seven days to rejoyn, if within that time he refuse to do it, he cannot do it after.

In such case where the Defendant is served with a *Sub pœna ad rejungendum*, and does not upon the Plaintiffs Clerks Demand to the Defendants Clerk, deliver Commissioners names by the end of the

Term

Term, wherein this *Sub pœna* is returnable, there the Plaintiff may without Motion or Petition, give names, and take a Commission, *ex parte*. See *Caries* Reports 111. and Collection of Orders in Chancery.

The manner of joyning in Commission, and executing of it.

IN the joyning of this Commission to examine witnesses, the Complainant must first name one Commissioner, unto whom the Defendant may give general Exceptions.

The Defendant is to name the second.
The Complainant the third, and
The Defendant the fourth.

The Plaintiff is likewise to have, first the taking out, and carriage of the Commission, as oft as any is sued out, and he or his Commissioners must give either in person, or by a note left in writing, at the place of the usual abode of the other party, fourteen days notice to him, of the time and place of executing the Commission, and if there be default then made by the Plaintiff or his Commissioners, in the execution thereof, he must pay the Defendant such costs as he upon his Oath shall make appear he was put to in the intending of the Commission, and the Plaintiff must renew the Commission at his own charge, and the Defendant shall have the carriage of it. And so on the other side shall the Plaintiff have, if the Defendant have the carriage of the Commission, and it be lost by default of his side.

But

But where it becomes void by any Errour of the Clerk in making it, the costs shall be born by him, and that side for whom it was taken out.

Where the Defendant hath the carriage of the Commission, he must give notice to the Plaintiff, as is before directed; and if such notice be not given, either all the Examinations will be quashed, or otherwise the Court will grant to the other side a Commission *ex parte*.

Where there hath been Publication, there no Commission can be granted or renewed for examining Witnesses without special Order.

Where a Commission hath been to examine Witnesses, without Reference and Certificate upon it, it cannot be discharged upon a bare Petition.

Where a Commission is taken out by consent, and the one side at the speeding of the Commission do put in no Interrogatories, nor examine any Witnesses (unless upon a Motion, and by Order of the Court) he shall be never after admitted to have a new Commission.

•Where the Defendant had Witnesses to examine, and they being served did not appear, but make default, here a new Commission will be granted to the Defendant, *Curies* Reports 91. 43. *Totbill* 111. collection of Chancery Orders.

Touching the choice of Commissioners, or Examiners, and the Exceptions against them.

First, they must be men indifferent.

The Exceptions usually taken against the are, that he who is named Commissioner is of kin

die

dred, or allied to the party for whom he is named, and so may very well be deemed to side with that party.

Or that he is Master to the party for whom he is named, or that he is Land-lord to the party, or that he is of his Counsel, or Attorney for him, or one to whom he is indebted, or one that hath a Suit with the adverse party.

The Commission being to be set upon at the time and place appointed the Commissioners must call the Witnesses before them, where if they appear not, an Attachment issues against them, unless it be in such case where the Witnesses are impotent, and then a Commission shall be awarded, to examine them where they be, but usually they will have costs before they answer.

When the Witnesses appear to be examined, the Commissioners and Examiners must examine them themselves, and not leave so weighty a business, to the trust of their Clerks, or others to do it.

They are to hold the Witnesses to the point insisted on.

They should examine them but to one Interrogatory at a time, and see that answered first, and at one time.

They are to take what comes from them in answer to what they are examined, and not upon their sight of all the Interrogatories, to let them set it down themselves.

After they have been examined, upon better thoughts they may force them to attend their Examinations. They ought not either to ask them idle questions besides the matter of the Interrogatories, nor set down impertinent Answers.

They are to set down truly their sayings in Parchment, and that done, they are to set their hands to

every

every Schedule-examination, and send them up into the Court as they are taken, with a Certificate.

Where the Commissioners meet with any obstruction in the work, they must certifie that also.

After the Commission is duly executed, and that it be returned up, one of them must deliver it in Court, or they must send it by one that must make Oath, that he received it from one of their hands, and that it was not altered to his knowledg.

If any one of the Commissioners commit any misdemeanour about Examination, the party grieved, upon Oath of it, may have the Attachment against him, and cannot have a Commission to examine it upon the Certificate of the other Commissioners.

Where there is a disagreement of the Commissioners, or where there is any other special cause that obstructs the Commission, they may have an Examination sent down on purpose to do it. See *Caries* Reports 30,31,40,47,80,81. *Totbill* 189.

The interrogatories to examine Witnesses must be succise and apt.

When Witnesses are examined in Court upon a Schedule of Interrogatories, you cannot examine the same Witnesses upon putting in new Interrogatories.

Witnesses may be examined as well by Examiners in Court (in case they live in or near the Town) as by Commissioners in the countrey.

Either party, as well Plaintiff as Defendant, after answer put in, untill publication be past, may examine what Witnesses they please in Court, before one of the Examiners; but before Answer, and after publication no Examination will be allowed, but by special Order, some special cause being shewed.

Notice must be given both of the names and
dwelling

dwelling places of the perfons examined, in all cafes of Examination.

After an Order for Publication, and that deliver-ed to the Examiner, no Witnefs may be examined in Court, though he were fworn before, *Caries* Re-ports 27,58,93. *Tothill* 189,190,192.

Touching Depofition of witneffes.

NO abftract, or Copy of the Depofition of the Witnefles, is to be delivered till Publication be paft.

No Depofition of Witnefles may be fuppreffed up-on a bare Petition onely, without Reference and Cer-tificate upon it.

Where there are feveral Caufes which are meer-ly crofs Caufes between the fame parties, and touch-ing the fame matter, there the Depofition of Wit-nefles in the feveral Caufes may be ufed at the Hearing of both Caufes (being heard together) without any motion.

Where Depofitions are regularly taken, they may not be fuppreffed by motion; but the Depofiti-ons of Witnefles appearing to this Court to be got-ten by practice, may by Order of the Court be fup-preffed. Depofition of Witnefles taken in this Court, may by Order of the Court be made ufe of in any other Court, *Caries* Reports 35,56. Collecti-on of Chancery Orders.

He that will examine Witnefles (*in perpetuam rei memoriam*) to preferve a Teftimony, he muft firft ex-hibit his Bill, and fhew his Title to the thing, and that the Witnefles to prove it are old, and not like to live long, whereby he is in danger to lofe it, and then pray a Commiſſion to ſome Gentlemen of credit in the countrey to examine them, and a *Subpœna* to the parties intereſted, to ſhew cauſe if they can to the contrary.

If the party intereſted being duly ſerved within fourteen days ſhew cauſe, the Plaintiff muſt deſiſt; if he cannot, he may go on alone; if the other will not joyn with him, as he may if he will, and then fourteen days warning is to be given for Execution.

The Court in this caſe will appoint Commiſſioners, and give Articles to examine upon, or they may be examined in Court by an Examiner.

None but aged and impotent perſons may be examined upon this Commiſſion.

Where the Defendant takes Exceptions to the Proceedings in ſpeeding the Commiſſion, as whether he did appear or not, and whether Oath were made before them of notice given to him of the time and place of Execution thereof, in ſuch caſe the Commiſſioners muſt certifie up with the Commiſſion the Exceptions the Defendant ſo took.

This Teſtimony taken upon this Commiſſion, is not to be publiſhed while the Witneſſes live; but in ſome caſes, as either by conſent of the parties, or upon Oath made, that either the Plaintiff hath ſome Trial at Law, wherein he ſhall need it, and that the Witneſſes are not able to come to the place, or otherwiſe by Order of the Court, and then the Commiſſion is to be opened by a Maſter, and to be conſidered of, and afterwards it may, if the party will, be exemplified, and may by Order of this Court be given in Evidence in any other Court.

Theſe Depoſitions thus taken, ſhall not be made uſe of to be given in Evidence againſt any other, but the Defendant who was warned to defend it, his Heirs or Aſſigns, or ſome other claiming by, or under him,

by

by some interest which accrued unto him, after the Bill preferred, *Tothill* 189.190,191,192.

Where both Plaintiff and Defendant have examined what Witnesses they please, and are ready to go to Hearing, then either of them must first give the other a Rule for Publication; if it be the Plaintiff that gives the Rule, then thus (Day is given to the Defendant of Publication upon the Commission joyned) and if the Defendant give the Rule, then on the contrary thus (Day is given to the Plaintiff for Publication upon the Commission joyned.)

The Day so given is one Week, which being expired, and no cause shewn to the contrary, then Publication is granted.

After Publication so granted, neither party can examine Witnesses, unless it be by special Order of the Court, which is not granted without an Oath made, that the party which requireth the same, nor any of them hath seen, or been made privy to any Examinations of any the Witnesses formerly examined in this Court by either of the parties, and some good cause be shewn either by Oath or Certificate of Commissioners, why the party could not get his said Witnesses examined within the time limited for their Examination; in which case sometimes the Court giveth Order to examine Witnesses by a time prefixed, with this Proviso, that the party shall not in the mean time see the said former Examination.

Touching

Touching setting down the Cause for Hearing.

AFter Publication had, the Plaintiff, or in his neglect, the Defendant may procure a Day of Hearing of course, to be set down by his Clerk at the end of the Term, when the Lords Commissioners do set down Days for Hearing the next Term.

The Days must be set down according to their priority of Publication.

No Cause must be presented for Hearing, the same Term that Publication doth pass.

All Process to hear Judgments must be returnable six or seven days before the Day of Hearing, except it be in the begining of the Term, when the time will not bear it; and the Writ must have on the back of it the very Day of Hearing.

If the Plaintiff appear not, the Defendant is to be dismissed with costs, *Caries* Reports 45. collection of Orders in Chancery.

Touching Decrees take these ensuing Rules.

EVery Decree must be drawn up as short as with conveniency it may, and not recite the Pleadings largely, but the sum of it briefly.

If the Decree be made before the Master of the Rolls, or before any Judges, it being drawn, must be first signed by them, and a'ter by the Lords Commissioners, and then it must be inrolled.

The Decree must be signed and inrolled before the first day after the next *Michaelmas*, or *Easter* Term after the making of it.

Where

Where the Decree concerns Lands or Leases, it must be entred into the Registers Dockquet-book, within six moneths after the making of it, otherwise it shall not prejudice the Purchasers of the Land.

No Decree shall be binding to any but those who are served with Process, *Ad audiendum judicium,* or that did appear *Gratis .*

The Purchasor that comes in by conveyance, *Bona fide,* from the Defendant before the Bill exhibited, and that is no Party by Bill or Order, shall not be bound up by any Decree.

But where a man becomes a Purchaser (*pendente lite*) and without any colour of privity, or allowance by the Court, there it shall regularly binde him; yet in such case, if there have been any intermission of the Suit, or the Court be acquainted with the conveyance, the Court is to give order in it.

No Decree made by this Court can be crossed, altered, or explained upon a bare Petition onely, and yet hereby it may, for some special reasons, be staid for a while, till it can be moved in Court.

A Decree of this Court once inrolled cannot be reversed or altered but by a Bill of Review, unless it be in case of miscasting, where the case is demonstrative, and then it may be done by order.

A Decree will binde the persons, for where any do refuse to obey it, this Court will imprison him untill he do conform.

A Decree of this Court doth binde the right and title to Lands and Goods; for this Court by their Order of Sequestration and Injunction doth dispose of the Possession thereof for ever to him, the Court judgeth to have right thereunto in conscience.

Where a Decree is to be made upon a pretence
of

of Equity againſt the Judgment of another Court; this Judgment is firſt read, and then the Decree is not to vacuate the Judgment, but to order the unreaſonable party.

The courſe of the Court to inforce obedience to their Decrees, and to puniſh the breach of them.

Firſt, they are to ſerve the party with the Decree it ſelf, under the Seal of the Court; and if he yield not obedience unto, but ſtands obſtinate, they then proceed to take out of the Court all the Proceſſes of contempt againſt him, one after another, and the party being taken, is to be ſtraitly impriſoned, and not to be ſet at liberty till he yield obedience to it, (that is to ſay) That he perform that part of the Decree, which is preſently to be done, and give ſecurity to peform that part which is to be done for the future.

Alſo the Lords Commiſſioners for his contempt may fine him what they pleaſe, and afterwards extreat.

Where the Decree is for Land, and the party remain obſtinate and wilfull after his impriſonment, the Court doth uſe to grant an Injunction for the Poſſeſſion; and this being diſobeyed after it is ſerved. and Oath made thereof, the Court doth in that caſe grant a Commiſſion to ſome Juſtices, and if need be, a Writ of Aſſiſtance to the Sheriff, to put him in poſſeſſion. See *Caries* Reports 23,34,36 37. *Tothill* 56, & 57. collection of Orders in Chancery.

Where this Injunction is granted for poſſeſſion of the Land, and the party ſits out all the Proceſs

of

of contempt, and cannot be found by the Serjeant at Arms, or make a Refcue, a Sequeftration shall be granted of the Land, *Totbill* 107.

This Sequeftration is granted fometimes as well of the Goods, as of the Profits of a mans Land, and that for his wilfulnefs in ftanding out in contempt, and difobedience to the Court; as well where it is for difcharge and payment of Debts and Duties, as where the Decree is for the payment of a fum of money, *&c. Totbill* 175,176.

Concerning Contempts.

IN cafe of contempts upon force, or ill words ufed upon ferving of Procefs, or other words of fcandal to the Court, if they be proved by *Affidavit*, the party forthwith upon Motion will be committed, if the words fpoken deferve it.

For other contempts againft the Orders and Decrees of the Court, take as follows.

Firft, an Attachment goes forth upon *Affidavit* made of the contempt.

Then the party being taken is to be examined upon Interrogatories, which is ufually upon Motion referred to one of the Mafters in the Chancery.

The contemptor coming in *Gratis*, or upon Procefs, fhould give notice to the Clerk of the other fide of his Appearance; and if then there be not Interrogatories put in within eight days, or being examined, if no Reference be of the Examination, or Commiffion taken out by the other fide, nor Witneffes examined to prove the contempt in a Moneth; the contemptor fhall be difcharged, and fhall recover cofts, taxed by a Mafter without any Motion.

If

If after he hath appeared upon the Contempt, he depart, not examined, he muſt ſtand committed till he be examined and cleared, and if it be found, he muſt clear it, and pay coſts ere he be diſcharged.

Such as ſtand committed for Contempts upon Attachments, or Commiſſions of Rebellion, muſt enter into Bond to attend from day to day, not to depart without leave of the Court, *Caries* Reports 9, 44,70,71,82. Collection of Chancery Orders.

Impriſonment upon Contempts for matters paſt, may be diſcharged of Grace, after ſufficient Impriſonment, or it may be otherwiſe diſpenſed withall in ſuch caſe.

But where the Impriſonment is for non-performance of any Order of the Court in force, then the perſon ſo in contempt ought not tobe diſcharged, except the firſt obey, onely the Court may diſpenſe with the contempt for a time.

Concerning Bills of Review.

A Bill of Review ſhall not be admitted, except the Decree be firſt obeyed and performed.

No Bill of Review ſhall be put in, except the party that prefers it enter into a Recognizance with Sureties, for the ſatisfying of coſts and damages for the delay, if it be found againſt him.

Where a Cauſe is diſmiſſed upon full Hearing, and the diſmiſſion ſigned and inrolled, it cannot be retained again but by a Bill of Review, and that in ſome ſpecial caſes.

No Bill of Review is grantable but upon Errour in Law, appearing in the body of the Decree it ſelf, without Averment or further Examination of
any

any matter of Fact, which might have been had at the time of the Decree, unless he shew some new matter which hath risen in time after the Decree, whereof the Plaintiff could not have advantage of before: and then upon Oath made that there is a discovery of such new matter, this Bill (by leave of the Court) may be exhibited.

But he that so obtaineth this Bill must first give security by Recognizance to a Master, as is before directed.

Where the Decree is to yield the Possession of Land, deliver Writings, or to pay Money, he must first perform that before a Bill of Review: but if the Decree be to extinguish a Right, convey Land, release a Debt, acknowledg satisfaction, or to cancel Records or Evidences, or the like, it may be staid by the Order of the Court, till the Bill of Revivor be determined.

No Witnesses which either were, or might have been examined upon the former Bill, shall not upon this Bill of Revivor be examined to any matters: collection of Orders in Chancery, *Tothill* 273.

Having now gone through the general proceedings of Chancery upon Bill and Answer, there are some things which in some Cases are essential to those Proceeds, which take as follow; and first concerning Injunctions.

THis is looked upon according to the general acceptation, as that which makes stay of Proceedings at Common Law, although in many cases it is
like-

likewise to the end to gain the Poffeffion of Land in some cases it precedes, and in some cases it is subsequent to the Decree, and somtimes by writing, and other times by word of mouth, as when the party who is to be inhibited, is present in Court.

Where it ftays Proceedings at Law, in some cases it gives leave to go to Trial and Judgment, but ftays Execution.

Where the matter of Law is tried, it bars them from Judgment as the case may be.

Or where there is a Judgment, and that executed, it will ftay the money in the Sheriffs hands, after the party is arrefted at Law for the money.

This Injunction is commonly procured either upon some Writing, or matter of Record plainly appearing; or upon a very old Debt that hath flept long, Creditor and Debtor being both dead; or in such cases where the Defendant doth not appear, but fits an Attachment, or if he appears, either anfwers not the Bill, or confeffes fo much thereof as is fufficient.

Where either the Defendant is beyond the Seas, or being in the Kingdom, doth abfent himfelf, fo that he cannot be ferved, or where upon any pretence he hath gotten time to anfwer, the Court doth ufually in thofe cafes grant an Injunction to ftay Suit, till the Defendant doth appear.

Where there is a Commiffion granted to take an anfwer in the countrey, an Injunction will be granted to ftay the Defendants Suit at Law, (if any be) till the Anfwer come in, and of this the Defendant muft take notice without any ferving of it.

Where there is a Verdict at common Law in an Action of Debt, and a Bill be afterwards exhibited for relief, here the money muft be depofited in Court, before the Court will grant an Injunction, unlefs in

some

some cases where some speciall matter in Equity appears by the Defendants answer, or in some former Decree.

Where a person priviledged in this Court is sued elsewhere, he may stay that Suit by this injunction.

Where Timber is unjustly felled; Ancient Meadow ground plowed up, ancient pastures that have not been plowed up in twenty years before, or for the maintenance of inclosures kept in for 20 yeares before, there it is grantable according to the case.

Where an injunction is granted to quit a possession, it is granted of houses and Land onely, and not of Rent or such like thing, and it is not to be granted before the hearing of the cause, unlesse uppon oath, that the Plaintiff was in possession at the the time of the Bill put in, and then onely of that possession he had then, and three yeares before, and at the time of the motion, and not to be extended to the possession of those from whom he claimes: And this shall not hinder the Defendants Suit in Law, making of a Lease, taking of Distresse, &c. And this injunction where the Plaintiff delayes his Suit is to be dissolved again.

Where it is to stay or remove a Suit by *Certiorarie*, Bond must first be given that the Bill hath matter sufficient in it to beare it, and shall be proved true within fourteen dayes after he hath the Writ; and this if he doe not in this time, after a certificate of his neglect from the Examiners, it shall be dismissed with costs, and a *Procedendo* granted.

Where the injunction is to be obtained by motion for matter in the answer, there the Counsell must put the case in writing to the Court.

Where it is granted upon the merit of the cause, or upon speciall cause in Equity, it is to stand till the hearing, unlesse the Plaintiff delay his Suit.

This injunction must be served either on the

party himselfe, his Counsellor, Attorney, or Sollicitor, *&c.* as the case requires, and the manner of
the serving it is much like the serving of a *Subpœna.*

A bare petition only will not disolve this injunction, nor if it be had by motion is it to be dissolved
without motion of the adverse party.

Where an injunction is granted till the answer be
put in, and no order be made to continue it, within
fourteen dayes after the answer is come in ; in this
case it shall be disolved upon the Registers certificate thereof only, and if no motion be made that
Term, or at the next general seale after the Term; to
continue it for insufficiency of, or matter confessed in
the answer, it is disolved of course; so where it is to
stay a Suit at common Law, and the Plaintiff doth
not proceed for three yeares together.

Where the injunction is disobeyed (if you would
force obedience thereunto)upon Oath made thereof, all the Processes of contempt are to go out against
him, one after an other, and being taken, he is to
be imprisoned, till he doe yeild Obedience to it or
give security to doe it; nor is he to be heard in the
Principall case, till he yeild Obedience in every
thing in the Injunction, *Tothill* 107. *Caries Reports*
112. 113.

Touching dismission, take these things following.

THis is prayed by motion, and had upon Plea to
the Bill, or hearing of the cause, and not after
Examination of witnesses before hearing, but upon
a discontinuance of prosecution, by motion and order of the Court.

Wher

Where the Plaintiff discontinues his prosecution after all the Defendants have answered, above the space of one Terme, the cause is to be dismissed of course, but after a Replication put in, it cannot be dismissed without an Order upon motion.

Where a cause is dismissed upon a full hearing recorded and certified by the Lords Commissioners, it cannot be againe retained, or a new Bill admitted, but where there is new matter.

Where the Bill is duly dismist of course, or by order, no motion will be heard to retaine it, till the costs assessed upon the dismission be paid, and certified from the Attorney on the other side, that it is done.

No dismission, or Retainer upon a dismission will be granted upon bare petition only.

In cases of dismission not upon a full hearing, to a new Bill this may be pleaded.

But for the causes of dismission, the Court will retaine and dismisse as it doth see cause: See Collection of **Chancery Orders**, *Caries Reports* 34. 43. 74. 76. 110.

Touching References, and Reports, take as followes.

WHere there is a Demurrer to the Jurisdiction of the Court, there no Reference may be had to a Master upon it, but it must be heard before the Lords Commissioners themselves.

After Examination of Witnesses is past, there can bee no reference had to a Master to end and determine, unlesse it be in case of neere kinne, poverty or consent of parties.

Arese

A reference of the State of the case is sparingly granted, unlesse where there is consent of the parties.

The Examination of Court-Rolls is to be by reference, but there it must be to two Masters at the least.

No reference shall be made of the insufficiency of an Answer, without allegation of speciall causes: See the Collection of Chancery Orders.

The Reports of the Master upon the Reference must not exceed the warrant of Reference, which is the Order of Court by which it is referred to him.

After the Master hath seen the Order, he usually grants out a VVarrant, which is shewen unto the other side, whereby he gives notice of the time of his hearing the cause, where the other side with their Counsellor, or Sollicitor, may as they see cause attend.

The Report it selfe is usually briefe, and with some opinion, if the case be not very doubtfull, and if so, then it must be set forth the speciall case.

No order can be had to confirme the Report, till it be first filed with the Register, under the Masters hand, and a day given to the other side, for seven dayes at the least, to speake to it in Court; and yet where it is not to ground a Decree, and it be positive, it is to stand, and Processe may be taken out for the performance thereof, unlesse the adverse party upon notice thereof, do within eight dayes after (if it be in the Term time) or if the generall Seals for motions, or if after within four dayes of the beginning of the the next Term, get it controlled.

VVhere there is an appeale to the court from the Report of a Master, the party that doth so appeale, must deposite forty shillings with the Register, and a day will be set for the Judgment of the court, and

if

if the Court do adjudge it againſt the Appealor, the other ſhall have the forty ſhillings, and what more the Court ſhall judge fit; if otherwiſe, the money ſhall be reſtored. See collection of Chancery Orders.

The matters chiefly under reference are either inſufficient Anſwers, or matters of account.

Where the Maſter upon a reference to him reports the Anſwer to be inſufficient, the Complainant may take out two *Subpæna's* againſt the Defendant, the one for twenty ſhillings coſts, and the other to make a better Anſwer.

Touching Orders, and the Regiſter that draws them.

THe Regiſters being ſworn do ſit in Court, and take notice of all orders the Court doth make, and take ſhort Notes in their Book, by which to draw up ſome more full remembrance of that which paſſed in Court.

Where any order ſhall be made, and the Court not informed of the laſt materiall Order, formerly made, no benefit ſhall be taken by ſuch Order as being ſurreptitiouſly procured, and to that end the Regiſter doth mention the laſt former order in the preſent Order.

An Order made out of the generall rule, muſt ſet down the ſpeciall reaſons of it.

No order ſhall be explained by Petition, but by publick motion, both parties being heard.

No order but finall Orders and Decrees may be received to be entred after eight dayes after the pronouncing of it, that day being excluded.

The Regiſter is to keep copies of the Orders he

doth

doth deliver, and his hand is to be put to the Order before it be entred.

The Register after a hearing, and Reference to a Treaty, is to set down in the Order of Reference, what was the Opinion of the court, unlesse the court do direct it to be drawn otherwise.

All Orders drawn up by the Register are to be entred under the Registers hand in due time.

The Register is within ten dayes after the end of every Term to certifie the Commissioners, what References depend in the hand of any Master, and how long they have depended, that so if any of them have depended over-long, the court may require an account thereof from the Master, and quicken him to a speedy dispatch.

Touching *Suits in* Forma Pauperis.

THE counsell and Attorney assigned for *Paupers* may not refuse, but must attend their businesse, unlesse they shew cause to the court, why they cannot so do.

They must alwaies have their Order of admission with them, and first move that, before any other motion; and it hinders not, but that they may, if they have any other motion, make it afterward.

Where the Register finds that he is not a *Pauper*, he shall not draw up any Order upon the second motion; but the *Pauper* shall loose the Fruite of it.

No Counsellour, Attorney, or Officer of the court appointed to be for a *Pauper* by the court, is to take any thing of, or contract for any thing with him, and the *Pauper* that can be proved so to

hav e

have given or contracted, is to be dif-paupered for ever.

If a *Pauper* fell, or contract for his Suit, or any part of it, his Bill shall be difmiffed, and never after retained.

No proceffe of contempt shall go out for a *Pauper* untill it be figned by the fix Clark, who deale for him, and he muft fee there be caufe for it.

The courfe to obtaine the Admiffion is by way of Petition, either to the Commiffioners of the great Seal, or to the Mafter of the Rolls, who under-fcribe it, the Party having made Oath that he is not worth five Pounds, and affignes him counfell and Attorney.

His Admiffion muft be fhewen in the feverall Offices, where he hath occafion to paffe.

Touching petitions, for the avoiding of the multitude, of idle ones, drawn by perfons altogether ignorant of the practice and courfe of the court, or true ftate of the Petitioners bufineffe, it is directed, that Petitions before they be prefented to the commiffioners of the great Seale, or Mafter of the Rolls be fhewed to that fix clark, who is the Petitioners Attorney in court, or to his Deputy, and by him approved and fubfcribed; and for this no Fee is to be taken; but this not to be underftood of Petitions advifed, and figned by counfell. Nor of Petitions containing any matter of complaint against the Attorney, or his under clerke.

Touching Affidavits

Affidavits are moft generally made before Mafters of the chancery, but where it is for the ferving of a *Subpæna*, they are sometimes taken and certified by others.

An *Affidavit* may not be taken against an *Affidavit*, for if it be, the latter is not to be used.

An *Affidavit* ought not to be taken tending to the proofs or disproofe of the matter in question : Nor may any such matter be admitted, to be colourablely inserted into any Oath made of the serving of procelle : See more to this purpose, *Caries* Reports 63. 81. 82. 84. 85. 88. 98. 99. 103.

The way of Proceeding against a priviledged Person.

A Declaration against a priviledged man for Debt, or any thing whereof the Court holdeth Plea, is to be delivered to one of the six Clarks, whom the Plaintiff maketh his Attorney, and hee thereupon giveth a day (as it is commonly tearmed) which is a week, (*viz.* the whole next returne) to the Defendant to answer, which day is entred in the six Clarks costs Book in this manner, (*Roberts* against *Johnson*) A day is given from the day of Saint *Michael* in one Moneth, in a plea of priviledge.

Day being thus given, the Declaration under the Attorneys hand is sent over to the Petty-Bag, by one of the said Attorneys Clarks, which Declaration is briefly entred by one of the Clarks there, and likewise the day that is given to the Defendant to answer in a Roll there, which is called *Rotulum remembrance. Parvæ bagæ*; At which day by the course of the common Law, if the Defendant plead not, he is fore judged the court, but the course of the Chancery hath been of late to allow the Defendant a day of Imparlance, that is, day till the next return after the return given him to answer, which is in this manner.

The Defendant retaineth one or other of the six Clarks who imparleth for him, which is done in the six Clarks-costs Book in this manner, (*Roberts against Johnson*) Imparlance untill the Morrow of all-Soules, at which day it is sent over to the petty-bag, to be entred into the aforesaid Roll next under the said Declaration.

The said day of imparlance being past, another day, *Videlicet*, commonly five dayes in a week (which is commonly called a peremptory day) is given by the Plaintiffs Attorney and entred in the petty-bag as aforesaid, to the Defendant to plead, or else Iudgment is to be entred against the Defendant.

If the Defendant plead, his Plea is delivered by his Attorney to his Plaintiffs Attorney, and then if the Plaintiff will proceed to a Tryall, he is to joyne up the Issue (if he may, for in some cases he cannot) or else the Plaintiff is to reply, and to give the Defendant a day, *viz.* a whole Terme to joyne up issue which is given and entred as the day to answer: and if the *Defendant* by that day joyns not up the issue, Iudgment is entred up by *Nihill dicit*, and it is to be noted, that after a peremptory day given, the Defendant cannot pray *Oyer* of the Bond and condition, or such like, as of late is used for a meer delay: But if the Issue be joyned up, either by the Plaintiff or Defendant, then is the Record made up, and the same with a *Venire facias* is sent into the Kings Bench to be tryed, as an action there at Issue, and upon Iudgment there, Execution is thereupon there awarded.

But if the Defendant refuse or neglect to imparle at the day given him to answer or to plead, for hee

may.

may plead at that day if he will, then is Judgment entred against him, and Execution awarded.

Upon Judgment either by default, or *Nihil dicit,* some of these Writs of Execution are awarded; if for debt, the Plaintiff may have an *Elegit* by *westminst.*2. Chap. 18. or else *Levari facias,* or *Fieri facias* : and if the Plaintiff cannot levy his Debt and Damages, then he shall have a *Capias ad satisfaciendum,* either for all, or so much as resteth unsatisfied.

The Judgment being satisfied, the Plaintiff by himselfe or his Attorney (if the Defendant do desire it) doth acknowledge satisfaction upon the Judgment in the Petty-Bag Office.

It is to be noted, that whatsoever day is given by any of the six Clarks, and by them entred in their Booke, worketh nothing, if the same be not entred in the Petty-Bag.

The course used, where the priviledged person sues.

THE Defendant being arrested by an Attachment of Priviledge, at the Suit of a priviledged man, must retaine one of the six clarks to bee his Attorney and must put in Baile to the Plaintiffs Action, according to the course of the court, which is, to appear from day to day, untill the Plea be determined, to satisfie the Plaintiff all such summes of Money as the Plaintiff shall recover against him by reason of this Suit: Then the priviledged man putteth in his Declaration, and the proceedings thereupon are the same as before, against the priviledged man.

By the course of the court the Defendant is to put in foure Subsidy men, or sufficient Sureties (be
the

the action never so small) as appeares between *Archibald* and *Burall*, 23. *Eliz.* wherein the Defendant is bound in four hundred pounds, the sum of the action, and every Surety in a hundred pounds.

If Judgment be given for a priviledged man in this Court, he may if he will take out Execution against the Defendant as before; but it he will not then he may take out a *Scire facias* against the Defendant and his Manucaptors upon the Bail, whereupon if Judgment be had upon the *scire facias*, in the Chancery, Execution is awarded as in the former Actions: But if upon issue joyned, and sent into the Kings Bench, and upon a tryall there, Judgment be given, then is Execution there awarded; and upon satisfaction of the Debt and Damages, the Baile is to be discharged, upon the acknowledgment of satisfaction, as before.

If either the Plaintiff or Defendant upon a Declaration of Priviledge, or *Scire facias*, Demur in Chancery, the Demurrer being joyned, a day is set down by the Lords Commissioners for arguing thereof before them; and if upon the Argument it fall out to be a *Respondeas ouster*, then Judgment is entred thereupon, and if it be against the Defendant, then Execution is awarded, and if against the Plaintiff, then it is, that the Plaintiff shall take nothing by his Writ, or by the Declaration.

But if it be a *Respondeas ultra*, then is the Defendant to pay costs, and a day given for him peremptorily to plead, or Judgment to be entred, *Practice of the Chancery*, 93, 94, 95, 96.

A Table

A Table of Fees due unto the six Clarks and other the Officers of the Court.

FOR all first, second, or other Copies of all Bills, Answers, and other pleadings whatsoever, as also of all certificates and examinations made or taken, by vertue of any Commission but of this court, and of the Interrogatories therewith returned, and also of all Declarations or Proceedings by English Bill, or according to the course of the common Law, and for copies of records, Rolls, or Evidences, brought in to be copied, or remaining in the said court for every Leafe of Paper containing fifteen lines.

l	s	d
0	0	8

For the Inrolling of all Warrants whereby any Patents, commissions, Licenses, Pardons, Leases, or other Grants whatsoever, do passe by and under the great Seale, after the rate of every Skin so passing the great Seale.

l	s	d
0	2	0

For the inrolling of all Warrants for all commissioners for the Peace, for Goale-delivery, for a Liberty for *Oyer* and *Terminer*, for Piracies, for the preservation of the Game of the Swans, and for the commissions for Inquiry sued out for the benefit of any private person, for every of the said commissions   0 1 8

For

For the inrolling of all Warrants for all commissions of appeale, and for the admiralty, for every one of them,   0 4

For the Inrollment of every warrant for every ordinary licenfe, or pardon of Alienation,   3 4

But if it be of more then ordinary length, then according to the length after the rate of 20 s the skin and not above.

For the Inrolling of all warrants for all commissions in the nature of Writs, of *Diem clausit extremum, mandamus, Ideota probanda, Lunaticis inquirend. Melius inquirend.* for every of them,   3·4

For the inrolling of the warrants, for every patent or grant of the coftgdy of any Ward,   8-8

For the inrolling of the warrant for every prefentation, Donation, or Revocation, to any Rectory, Vicaridge, Deanry, Arch-deaconry, Chancellor-fhip Treafurer-fhip, or Dignity to any Metropoliticall, Cathedrall or collegiate Church, or for any Cannon fhip, or Prebend, in any of the faid Churches, or for the Maftership in any Hofpitall or other Eccclefiafticall living, or for the grant of any prefentation or prefentations, *pro unica vel pluribus vicibus* thereunto   3-4

For the inrolling of Warrants for every, *Mandamus ad inftalland.*   3-4

For the inrolling of all warrants, for all Licenfes for wines, for every life   3-4

Or fuch Fee not exceeding that proportion, as by the Commiffioners fhall be fet down, formerly they paid although granted for three lives   6-8

For the inrolling warrants for every pardon of Ontlawry   3 4

For inrolling of the warrants for every Denization, or commiffion of Bankrupts,   3-4

Eor the writing of every Exemplification, as well

of

of Records in the Tower, as of any Record whatsoever, being in their custody, after the rate for every Skin   1 6-8

Of every Client for every Term whilst his cause dependeth undetermined, by decree or by dismission the termly Fee of   0-3-4

If there were twenty Plaintiffs or more in one bill they all pay but one Fee for one Term   0 3-4

But for every three Defendants, accounting the Husband and the Wife but for one person, there is due for their first appearance   0-3-4

And upon the first appearance, if every Defendant appear severally by himselfe, he is to pay the Fee of three shillings four pence, but every Term afterwards during the continuance of the cause, there is only the Fee of three shillings four pence the Term to be paid for all the Defendants that appeared in any Term or vacation, in the same cause.

For a *Subpœna* Writ to answer   0-2 6

If there be three in the Writ, you pay more,   0-0 6

For the Attachment   0-2 10

For breaking it up with the Sheriff   0-2-0

For returne of the Attachment   0-0-4

For the proclamation upon the same   0-2-10

For the returne of the proclamation   0-0 4

For the Commission of rebellion   0-18-2

For the Inrollment of every *liberate* and *Allorate*   0-3-4

The rule which the Plaintiff gives the Defendant to make answer by a certaine day, in case where the Defendant appeares   0-0 4

For each rule of pulication, after Examination of Witnesses   4 d

For entring them with the Register, for each   0-0 4 d

The

The Defendants appearance   0-4-0

In which is included the Attornies Fee for the Term.

For the oath made that the answer is true,   0-0 4

The like for every Defendant   0 0 4

For the commission to take the answer in the Country, by *Dedimus potestatem*   0 7 10

Besides the ingrossing of the Bill, which is included in it, every sheet   0-0-6

For the *Subpæna* for costs where the Bill is not put in by the Complainant within the time limited   2 6

For a Bill of costs and the entry of it   2-4

A joynt commission to examine witnesses in the countrey.   7-10

So much the Plaintiff payes the Defendant   6-8

For the Examination of the first witnesse here before examiners,   0 2-6

For every witnesse afterwards   0-2 6

For the copies of the depositions of any witnesses returned by commission   0 0 8

For every sheet,

For copies of Depositions taken in the Examiners Office, for each Sheet   0-1-0

For the drawing of the Order upon motion, for every side,   0-1-6

For the entring of the Order, every side   0-0 6

The Fees of an injunction in all   1-2-6

For a *Subpæna* to rejoyn   0-2-6

For a *Subpæna* to hear Iudgment   0-2-6

For a *Subpæna super ordinem* to shew cause,   0-7-2

For a *Subpæna duces tecum*   0-7-2

For a *Subpæna de executione ordinis*   1-0-0

For the Rolls to publish witnesses, for each   0-0-4

For entring them with the Register, for each   4

For the copy of Replication, Rejoynder, Sur-rejoynder

re-joynder, Rebutter, and Sur-rebutter, as for Bill and anſwer.

Fees for a Decree for drawing up, as in caſe of an Order.

For every writ of Execution upon any order, 68

For drawing and inrolling every decree and diſmiſſion reſpectively   0 3 4

For every writ of Execution upon any decree after the rate for every skin   1 6 8

For the writing of every Sheriffs patent, writ of Aſſiſtance, writ of diſcharge, commiſſion to take the Sheriffs oathes, the warrant of Attorney, and the writing of the two oathes, and the Attorneys Fee;   1 2 8

For every *Superſedeas* for the diſcharge of any Commiſſion or other writ made in the ſix Clarks Office   0 6 8

For every *Superſedeas* of priviledge   0 6 8

For every ſpeciall *Certiorarie*, or *Procedendo Corpus Cum cauſa:* or *Habeas corpus*   0 6 8

For every bail upon every writ of *Corpus cum cauſa*, or nature of priviledge   0 2 9

For all manner of *Certioraries*, and *Procedendoes* of courſe.   0 2 0

For every recognizance or bond made to the Court.   0 2 0

FINIS.

An Abstract of the late Ordinance for the regulating of the Chancery, and the Fees now to be taken.

FOr the better regulating and limiting the jurisdiction of the high Court of Chancery, it is hereby ordained by his Highness the Lord Protector, by and with the consent of his Council.

1. That from and after the two and twentieth day of *October*, 1654. there shall be a certain number of Atturneys in Chancery, not exceeding 60. who shall be nominated by the Master of the Rolls, out of such of the present Clerks in the six Clerks Office of the Chancery, or othes, as shall be of ability and honesty, (and from time to time in case of death, or removal, to be supplied by his nomination) who being approved by the Lords Commissioners, shall be by them sworn Attorneys in the said Court, and shal receive thethree shillings four pence, termly Fee, which formerly the six Clerks received, and shall solicite and manage each Clients cause, without receiving any more for their pains of solicitation, than the said Fee of three shillings four pence.

2. That from and after the time aforesaid, instead of the six Clerks in Chancery, there shall be three chief Clerks, and no more. And that *Lawrence Maidwell*, *Matthew Pindar*, and *Robert Hales*, Esquires, shall be and are hereby made and constituted the first three chief Clerks; and that in case of death, or removal of any of them, the said chief Clerks shall be nominated from time to time by the Master of the Rolls, and approved by the Lord Chancellour, Lord Keeper, or Lords Commissioners for the time being; and that the persons before named to be the present chief Clerks, and such

as shall hereafter be named and approved as aforesaid being admitted in such manner as the six Clerks
formerly used to have been, shall do, execute and
perform all and every matter and thing which the
six Clerks heretofore might and ought to have done,
except intermeddling in any cause as Attorneys;
and that from and after the time aforesaid, no other
person or persons shall use or exercise the Office of
a six Clerk in Chancery; and that the Master of the
Rolls do take care, that all the Pleadings, Papers,
Books, Proceedings, and all other things belonging
to or filed in the several Offices of the six Clerks be
disposed of and filed in three Offices there, and that
the Attorneys aforesaid shall be distributed equally
into the said three Offices.

3. That all Bills, Answers, Pleadings, &c. shall
be filed with the chief Clerk in whose Office the
Attorney towards the cause for the Plaintiff is. And
that each of the chief Clerks shall have an inspecti-
on into the demeanour of the Attorneys in his Office, that they do their duties, both to the Court
and to the Client. And where they shall finde any
abuse, misdemeanour or unfaithfulness in any of
them, such chief Clerk shall acquaint the Court
therewith, who shall examine the same, and give reparation to the party wronged, and if they see cause
discharge such Attorney from his place.

4. That the first Process in Chancery be a *Sub
pœna*, which shall be open, and as many Defendants
as the Plaintiff shall desire be inserted into the same,
paying no more than one shilling and six pence for
every *Sub pœna* to be thus distributed, six pence for
the Seal and twelve pence to the Officer.

5. That no *Sub pœna*, shall be sued out, untill a
Bill be filed, and a Certificate thereof brought unto
the *Sub pœna* Office, under the hand of the chief
Clerk

Clerk or his Deputy, for which Certificate the said chief Clerk shall receive no Fee.

6. That in default of Appearance, upon Oath made of due service, or in default of an Answer within the due time (security being put in as is here-after provided) an Attachment with Proclamation shall issue to the Sheriff, who shall cause the same to be proclaimed at the Door of the Defendants dwelling House, Lodging, or last Abode, between the hours of ten in the forenoon, and two in the afternoon, by Bailiffs to be nominated by the Sheriff, or by special Bailiffs, (which shall not be denied, if required) and the said Bailiffs shall have power for the apprehension of the party (if need shall be) to break open any House or Door where the party is in the day time. Provided, that if the Warrant be to special Bailiffs, they shall not break open any House or Door, but in the presence of a Constable, who upon the shewing of such Warrant is hereby required to be assisting unto the said Bailiffs therein. And if the Defendant cannot be apprehended, nor shall appear by the Return of the Writ, the Plaintiff may renew the Attachment as often as there shall be cause, which Attachment shall be in lieu of a Commission of Rebellion, and Serjeant at Arms.

7. The Defendant shal not be compelled to answer untill the Plantiff, with one Surety at least, hath acknowledged a Recognizance before a Master of the Chancery in ordinary or extraordinary (the sum not to be under 20 Marks) conditioned to pay such costs to the Defendant in that suit, as the court of chancery shal award if they see cause to award any, for which Recognizance there shall be paid twelve pence only, and no more, and such Master of the Chancery shall forthwith certifie every such Recognizance into the Office of the Petty Bag in Chancery, to be there

filed,

filed, and the Officer there shall give a Certificate thereof to the Plaintiff, or his Attorney, upon request; and for the filing such Recognizance, making such certificate, and keeping an Alphabet thereof, he shall have and receive twelve pence, and no more; but where the Plaintiff shall he admitted *in forma pauperis*, no such security is to be required.

8. That where a Defendant might answer by Commission in the countrey, he shall not now be inforced to take a Commission, but without taking any Commission may answer upon Oath before a Master of the Chancery in the countrey in like manner, and by such time as if a Commission had issued. And that the Lords Commissioners for the great Seal do take care, that for that purpose, there be in every County a convenient number of such of the Justices of the Peace resident in that County, as they shall judg to be of the greatest ability and integrity, appointed to be Masters of the Chancery extraordinary; and that any such Master, or any Master in ordinary, after the Answer so sworn before him, shall sign the same, and give it into Court himself, or otherwise being sealed up, deliver it to some person to deliver the same into Court, and to make Oath that he did receive the same from the hand of such Master of the Chancery, and that since the receiving thereof the same hath not been opened or altered.

9. That upon delivering in the Answer, the Attorney for the Defendant do take care that he be provided with names of Persons for Commissioners, to be given by him upon a Rule given to rejoyn.

10. When an Answer is put in, the Plainti shal reply within eight days, if the answer come ini Term-time, otherwise within four days after the be
                                                  ginin

gining of the next Term, unlefs the Plaintiff fhall within eight days after the Anfwer come in, put in Exceptions thereunto, or procure the caufe to be fet down for Hearing on Bill and Anfwer, to be heard the next Term; otherwife the caufe to be difmiffed without motion, with cofts to be taxed by the chief Clerks.

11. That no copies fhall be given out of any Bill, Anfwer, or their Pleadings, untill the fame fhall be filed with the chief Clerks; and that each of the faid chief Clerk, where fuch Pleadings fhall be filed, fhall by himfelf, and fuch Clerk as he fhall appoint, for whom he is to anfwer, upon delivery out of fuch Pleading to be copied, take the name of the Atturney, to whom it is delivered, fubfcribed in a Book to be kept for that purpofe; and if any Atturney, to whom any Pleading is delivered to be filed, fhall neglect to file the fame, or after filing, if the Atturney to whom any Pleading is delivered to be copied, fhall neglect to bring back the fame in due time, if the fame be through negligence, and not voluntary, he fhall make fatisfaction to the party damnified thereby, as the chief Clerks for the time being, upon Examination thereof, fhall award; but if upon fuch Examination it shall be found that the fame was done voluntarily, he shall not onely make fatisfaction as aforefaid, but shall be expelled the Court.

12. That in cafe the Plaintiff think fit to except to the Anfwer for infufficiency, the Plaintiff shall deliver the Exceptions in writing to the Defendants Atturney within eight days after the Anfwer filed, and shall enter the caufe with the Regifter, and in the fame order as they are entred, the fame shall be heard by the Mafter of the Rolls, who shall appoint one or more days in every week for that purpofe,

an

and at every fitting shall appoint his next day of fitting, and how many of the said causes shall be then heard upon Exceptions, in the same order as they are entred, on which days the parties shall attend at their peril, and the Master of the Rolls upon hearing thereof shall give such costs as shall be fitting.

13. If a Defendant doth appear and answer insufficiently, and it be so ruled; or shall plead and demur, and the same be over-ruled, then if upon a Rule given he shall not answer within eight days, the Plaintiff may proceed in such sort as is before directed in case the Defendant had not appeared.

14. That after an Answer, if it shall appear at any time unto the Court, that no part of the matter of the Plaintiffs Bill is then proper for relief in that Court, the Court shall dismiss the Bill with full costs, upon a Bill to be allowed by the chief Clerks; but if some particular part of the Bill be thought fit by the Court to be proceeded in, the Court then shall direct the Examination and Proceedings upon that particular point, and the Defendant not be inforced to proceed to Examination upon any other matter.

15. The Plaintiff the next day after the Replication filed, or the same day if he will, shall cause a Rule to be entred for the Defendant to rejoyn and joyn in Commission; which if the Defendant shall not do within eight days, then the Plaintiff may take a Commission *ex parte*, and the Defendant shall have no new Commission in that cause.

16. That no Witness shall be examined in Court, but by one of the Examiners themselves, unless in case of sickness, and that one of the Examiners shall examine the Witnesses of the Plaintiffs part, and the other the Witnesses of the Defendants part,

part, if any be produced to be examined in Court, and that no Clerk in that Office shall be a Solicitor upon pain of losing his Place.

17. That all Commissions for Examination of Witnesses shall be open.

18. That a Commission to examine Witnesses may be issued out to be executed at any place, as well within ten miles of the City of *London*, as beyond it, if the party please.

19. That Commissioners for Examination of Witnesses shall take an Oath before execution of any Commission to execute the same faithfully, and impartially, which each Commissioner is impowred to administer to the other; and the Clerk or Clerks attending such Commissioners shall take an Oath, which is to be administred by the Commissioners, to write down the Depositions of the Witnesses truly and indifferently without partiality; and a clause shall be inserted into the Commission for that purpose.

20. That the Plaintiff having the carriage of the Commission, shall at his peril appoint a day and place for execution thereof at least eight days before the return of the Commission, and give due notice thereof, (unless in case where the day and place shall be agreed by the Attorneys on both sides, before the Commission go forth) and shall at the day and place appointed produce the Commission, and deliver the same to the Commissioners then present, to the end they may execute the same; or in default thereof the Plaintiff shall be absolutely concluded from having any other Commission, or examining any more Witnesses in that cause; but in such case the Defendant shall be at liberty to take out the then next Term, one Commission (or more) into several Counties (if he see cause) wherein the Plain-

tiff

tiff may joyn, but shall not examine. Nevertheless to prevent delay, the Defendant if he please may take out a Duplicate, when any Commission is sued out to examine any Witnesses; and the Plaintiff shall not give due notice to execute his Commission, eight days before the return of the Commission, the Defendant may execute his Duplicate at any time before the return, giving notice of the time and place where he intends to execute the same, one day at least before the execution thereof.

21. That there shall be no more than two Commissions at the most, for Examination of Witnesses in any one cause to be executed in *England* or *Wales*, unless where one shall be suppressed; and in case either party have any Witnesses in *Scotland*, or beyond the Seas to examine, setting down the names of such Witnesses, and delivering them to the Attorney of the other side, he may take out a Commission within the time before limited, wherein the adverse party may joyn, if he will, within four days after notice; otherwise the Commission shall issue *ex parte.* Provided, that the parties, or either of them, (if the Court see cause) may have several Commissions into several Counties of the same date.

22. That after the execution of one Commission, no second Commission shall be taken out, but by order of the Court, and upon *Affidavit* that some material Witnesses, whose names shall be therein expressed, have been discovered since the execution of the former Commission; or that some of the Witnesses intended to be examined at that Commission, and which are material, could not be found; or by reason of sickness, or like just cause, could not attend that Commission; in which case onely those Witnesses which shall be named, shall be examined by such second Commission; and the
same

same shall issue, and be executed at the charge of the party praying the same, unless the other side shall also desire to examine any Witnesses by any such second Commission; and then he shall likewise set down their names.

23. That after the return of a Commission executed, or Witnesses examined in Court, there shall be but one Rule for Publication; within which time, if the other side do not shew unto the Court good cause to the contrary, Publication shall pass accordingly.

24. That from and after the 22. day of *October*, 1654. no Order or Direction concerning any cause depending in Chancery be made or given, but upon motion in open Court; that then both parties concerned, or their Council, may be heard.

25. That the chief Clerks, and likewise the Atturneys, do diligently attend in Court, and do give an account touching any Proceedings in any cause depending in Court, as they shall be required.

26. That the chief Clerks shall have and receive one moyety of the Fees for copying, and for all other matters and things contained in the Table hereunto annexed, such and so much of the Fees therein set down, proportionably (with respect to the same, as they are by the said Table reduced) as the six Clerks formerly did and might receive.

27. That no Injunction be granted, but upon motion in open Court, satisfying the Court with such matter, which may induce the Court in Justice to grant the Injunction; but the Defendants taking Commission, or sitting an Attachment onely, shall not be a sufficient ground for an Injunction.

28. That no Injunction be granted before the hearing of the cause, to stay a Suit at Law, but upon matter confessed in the Defendants Answer, matter

ter of Record, or in writing under Hand and Seal
produced in Court.

29. That no Injunction granted after a Plea
pleaded at Law, or Rules given, shall stop a Trial at
Law, or any Pleadings or Proceedings preparatory
to a Trial.

30 That from and after the 22. of *October*,
1654. no Injunction be granted to stay the Morgagee from his Suit at Law, till the final hearing of
the cause; but an Injunction may be granted to
prevent the Morgagees pulling down Houses, cutting Trees, or making other waste and spoil upon the
morgaged Land.

31. That all differences touching irregularities
in Proceedings, or upon the Rules or course of the
Court, shall be determined by the chief Clerks, or
any two of them, whom the Attorneys on both sides
are to attend; and in case either side shall not rest
satisfied with their judgment therein, they may appeal to the Master of the Rolls, who upon hearing
the Attorneys on both sides (and the chief Clerks
who made the Certificate) if he see cause, shall settle the same, and give costs where he shall find the
fault.

32. All other References shall be determined
by the Masters of the Chancery, or Ordinary, which
shall be onely six in number, to be now, and from
time to time appointed by the Lord Protector for
the time being of which six, three shall fit daily at
some certain publick place, so long as any such References depend; and shall have a sworn Register
to attend them, who shall in presence of them and
the Council, reade the Notes taken in each cause
upon any Order made, or Report agreed; and the
same being so read, shall be subscribed by the Masters then present, or any two of them; and afterwards

wards the Report shall be drawn up by the said Register, and subscribed by the same Masters, and certified: And that from and after the two and twentieth day of *October*, one thousand six hundred fifty four, no other person or persons shall exercise the Office of a Master of the Chancery in ordinary.

33. That for every such Report, the party desiring the same, shall pay unto the said Register twelve pence for each side of the Report; and ten shillings upon every such Report to be distributed amongst the three Masters, before whom such cause was heard, for which the said Register is to account unto them.

34. For every Order which the said Masters shall make for new appointments or summons or of the like nature, the said Register shall have onely twelve pence and no more.

35. That all References made by the Court to the Masters, shall be set down by the Register, who draws such order in a Book, for publique view, and shall be heard in their order, as they are so referred and set down, without alteration; provided there shall onely eight be put in the paper to be heard at one time; and both parties are at their peril to attend the same at the time, or in default thereof, the cause to be proceeded in as if they were present.

36. If any Councell shall mis-inform the Court of any matter contained in the pleadings, proofs, or evidence, whereof he may have the perusall, or of any other matter whereof his Client did not inform him, and thereupon obtain an Order, which the Court shall afterwards see cause to discharge; the Counsell so mis-informing, shall be reprehended openly in Court; and before he shall be heard any more in Court, shall pay forty shillings to the party wronged by such mis-information, and twenty shillings to the use of the Lord Protector. But

37. But if such information be of matter of fact, whereof the Counsell cannot be otherwise certified, then by the information from his Client, Attorney, or Sollicitor, who gave such information, shall pay forty shillings unto the party wronged, and shall stand committed by order of the Court, till he pay the same.

38. That from and after the said two and twentieth day of *October*, one thousand six hundred fifty and four, every Attorney shall keep all and every *Affidavits*, whereupon he shall make forth any Writ or Process, in his own custody; and shall shew the same to the Attorney of the other side, and suffer him or any other person to take a copy thereof, if he shall require it: And that the Senior Register shall appoint a Clerk of honesty and integrity, to attend in Court, and at the Rolls, and at Seals, who shall take an Oath before the Lord Chancellor, Keeper, or Commissioners for the great Seal, to be faithfull in this imployment; and shall receive into his custody all and every *Affidavit* which shall be read in Court, or upon which any order shall be grounded, and shal duly file the same, and keep an Alphabet thereof. And in case the party, at whose instance such *Affidavit* was made, shall have cause to have a copy thereof, he shall pay unto the said Clerk for the same, four pence for the filing, and three pence for every side for a copy thereof; and the other side, or any other person desiring it, may also have a copy at the same rate; and the Register shall have for examining and signing such copy, six pence and no more.

39. That the former rules of the Court for admission of *Paupers*, be duly observed; and in such cases where by the Rules aforesaid, costs are to be paid, in case the party who ought to pay the same

be

be a *Pauper*, the Court shall give order, that unless the costs be paid, such person be whipped or sent to the house of Correction.

40. That all causes shall be set down for hearing, in order as they were published, without preferring one cause before another, and shall be so presented by the chief Clerks, without taking any Fee for the same; and the causes being so set down, shall be heard in the same order.

41. And that every cause shall be heard the same day on which it is set down for hearing; and for that purpose, the Lords Commissioners, if there be cause, shall sit for hearing such causes in the afternoon as well as the forenoon, except upon Saturdaies.

42. That from and after the five and twentieth day of *March* one thousand six hundred fifty and five all causes shall be heard the next Term after publication; or if they be more in number than may probably be heard that Term, they shall be set down on certaine dayes next after the Term, and attended and be heard upon those daies, as if they had been set down for that Term; and that *Subpœna's* to hear Judgment shall be made returnable upon such respective daies accordingly.

43. That no relief shall be given in Chancery against a Bond (which is only for payment of money) to be entred into from and after the five and twentieth day of *March*, one thousand six hundred fifty five.

44. That no trust or agreement made or declared after the five and twentieth day of *March* one thousand six hundred fifty and five, concerning Lands, or any other thing in the realty, shall be relieved in Chancery, unlesse it be contained in writing, and so averred in the Bill, save in such cases where the possession hath gone a long with the party claiming the trust. 45. That

45. That no Bill shall be admitted, nor any relief given in Chancery upon averment of any intention of the parties to a Deed to be made from and after the five and twentieth day of *March* one thousand six hundred fifty and five, other than what doth appear by the Deed it self.

46. That the Chancery shall not give relief in any case where the Plaintiff can have relief at Law, unless it be for the performance of the thing in kind where it cannot be had at Law.

47. That no Decree shall be made in Chancery, against an Act of Parliament.

48. That from and after the five and twentieth day of *March* one thousand six hundred fifty and five, Legacies shall be sued for at common Law, and not in Chancery.

49. That from and after the said five and twentieth day of *March* one thousand six hundred fifty and five, no relief shall be given in Chancery, on a Mortgage after three years forfeiture, or unlesse the suit be commenced within one year after the entry and possession of the Mortgagee continued, except upon some new agreement between the parties themselves in writing, and except in cases of Infancy, Coverture, *non sanæ memoriæ*, or beyond Seas. In which cases the persons concerned shall commence their suits within two years after the dis-ability removed, or in default thereof shall be debarred from any relief afterwards; and in case of such new agreement, the like rule to be observed after the time, by such new agreement limited, shall be expired.

50. That in case of Mortgages to be made from and after the five and twentieth day of *March* aforesaid, where the Mortgagee is in possession by recovery at Law, or otherwise, he shall not (except by speciall agreement in writing) be put to accompt for

the

the yearly profits accrued after such his entry before the suit for redemption be commenced, but the same shall belong to, and be retained by him without accompt, if by his answer, or at the hearing he shall elect to take the same in satisfaction of the Interest of his money, whiles he had the possession, except the Mortgagor shall rather elect to be concluded by the Mortgagees examinations upon Interrogatories concerning the profits by him received.

51. That such Mortgagee before the Mortgagor be admitted to redeem, shall be paid his whole principall money with damages, and his full costs incurred before his entry, and also after the suit commenced, to be taxed by the chief Clerks upon a Bill of costs, wherein and in all other cases of Mortgages to be made from and after the time aforesaid, the Mortgagee shall be charged (in case the Lands be letten to Tenants) with no more than what he did, or might fairely have received without fraud, or his own willfull default; And where the Lands are unletten, and kept in his own hands, with no more than four fift parts of the true yearly value. But if after such entry any casuall profits by fines upon copy-holds, wood-sales, or otherwise shall be received by the Mortgagee above the yearly revenue of the Lands Mortgaged, then the same shall go in abatement of Principall and Interest due before such entry. Provided that where in the cases aforesaid an account shall be, all lawfull Taxes and necessary disbursements and allowance shall be allowed to the Mortgagee.

52. That where upon a Bill exhibited by a Mortgagee, to inforce redemption or to have the Estate absolute, a Decree passeth, and is signed and enrolled, the time thereby limited for the payment of the Mortgage-money with damages, shall not be enlarged without consent of parties in writing.   That

53. That where Lands shall at any time from and after the five and twentieth day of *March* aforesaid, be extended upon any Statute, Recognizance, or Judgment, and an account sought to be had in Chancery; the Tenant by extent or elegit, shall not be put to account for more then the extended value, unless the Suit in Chancery be commenced within one year after such extent shall be executed, and possession delivered, and enjoyment thereupon accordingly; and that the same Suit be effectually prosecuted, except in case of Infancy, Coverture, *non sane memorie*, or being beyond the Seas: In which Cases, one year and no more shall be allowed to demand an account in Chancery, after such dis-ability removed.

54. That the Office of Register in Chancery shall not henceforth be executed by Deputies, but that there shall be four Registers of the said Court.

55. That the senior of them shall from time to time be Master of the said Office, and shall have the care, custody and government of the said Office, and of all the Books of Entries, Reports, Certificates, *Affidavits*, and other matters filed there, and also of the Clerks in the said Office; and shall take care that the businesse in that Office be done with faithfullnesse and diligence, and that no Fees be taken or required, other then what is contained in the Table hereunto annexed.

56. That in case of death, or removall of the said senior Register, the next in seniority shall succeed in his room; and as often as any Registers place shall be voyd, the senior Register for the time being, shall make choice of the most able & honest of the Clerks in that Office to that place, who being presented to the Lord Chancellor, Lord Keeper, or Lords Commissioners for the great Seal for the time being, and

by

by him or them approved, shall be sworn and admitted.

57. That each of the said Registers shall have and retaine to his own use, the Fees mentioned in the Table annexed, which shall be due for any the matters by him done, bearing his own charge, and his proportion of the Rent of the said Office.

58. That the Lord Chancellor, Lord Keeper, or Lords Commissioners for the great Seal, shall upon complaint to them made concerning any abuse, misdemenors, or unfaithfullness in any of the said Registers or their Clerks respectively, have power to hear and examine the same, and to order reparation to the party wronged, and also to discharge such Register or Clerk from his place if they find just cause.

59. That the Judgment pronounced upon every hearing, and the rule given on every motion, shall be truly taken, and fairly written by the Register and openly read before another cause or motion be begun ; to the end if the same be mistaken, it may be rectified by the Court, and that it be left to the Register afterwards onely to add the inducement, or reason of such Judgment or Order and other formalities requisite.

60. Where any Bill shall be dismissed by the rules of the Court, or order before hearing, the Defendant shall have his full costs, upon a Bill of costs to be allowed by the chief Clerks.

61. Every Plaintiff who shall not in all or some of the matters complained of, be relieved by the Court upon the hearing, shall pay the Defendant his full costs upon a Bill of costs to be allowed by the chief Clerks, or any two of them ; and in case the court upon the hearing shall find the suit to have been vexatious; the court shall give additional costs against the Plaintiff, to be pronounced by the court

E e   at

at the hearing, besides the said costs to be taxed upon the Bill.

62. Every Defendant against whom a Decree is made, shall pay the Plaintiff his full costs to be allowed as aforesaid, unless the court shall at the said hearing see cause to mitigate or discharge the same upon some speciall reason to be expressed in the order.

63. If any find him or themselves aggrieved by any Decree which shall be made in Chancery from and after the two and twentieth day of *October* one thousand six hundred fifty four, then the party or parties so aggrieved, first performing the Decree in all points (except in doing such Act which extinguisheth the parties right at the common Law, as making of an assurance, release, acknowledging satisfaction, cancelling bonds or evidences, or the like) and depositing the sum of fifty pounds in the hands of the senior Register for the time being, to answer full costs and charges in travell, attendance and otherwise, to the adverse party, in case such person be not relieved upon a petition to be exhibited in that behalf to the Lord Chancellor, Lord Keeper, or Lords Commissioners for the great Seal for the time being, within 3 moneths after the Decree made, having first performed so much of the Decree as within that time is to be performed, shall have the cause re-heard upon the proofs and evidence given at the former hearing, and no other; and that upon the preferring of such petition in open Court, the Lord Chancellor, Lord Keeper, or Lords Commissioners, being first satisfyed that the Decree is performed as aforesaid, and the fifty pounds deposited, shall the next day after, under their or two of their hands subscribed to the said petition; signifie their allowance of a re-hearing of such cause, and shall send notice thereof together

with

with the said petition to the Courts of the Upper Bench,
Common pleas and Court of Exchequer; whereupon the
said Courts shall appoint six of the Judges, that is to say,
two of each Court (of which six Judges the chief Justice of
one of the Benches, or chief Baron of the Court of Exchequer shall be one) and shall signifie the same to the Lord
Chancellour, Lord Keeper, or Lords Commissioners, who
together with the said Judges, shall appoint a day for
such re-hearing, at which time the said six Judges or the
major number of them shall be present. And the said
Lord Chancellor, Lord Keeper or Lords Commissioners,
together with the said Judges, or the major number of
them, shall re-hear the said cause upon the proofs and
evidence read and given at the said former hearing, and
no other, and shall have power to make void, alter or confirm the order or Decree made upon the former hearing,
as they or the major part of them shall think fit. And
such Order as shall be so by them made, shall be finall in
the said cause, and in case they shall not see cause to alter the order or decree made upon the former hearing,
then they shall order to the adverse party his full costs,
upon a bill thereof to be made and allowed by the chief
Clerks, together with such addition of costs for his caus-
less vexation, as they shall think fit. Provided, that if the
Decree be for payment of money, the payment of the
money into the Court, shall be accounted a performance
of the Decree, so far as to enable the party to have a re-
hearing as aforesaid.

64. That no Defendant who is prosecuted by an Officer, Clerk or Minister of the Court of Chancery, shall be
inforced either to appear in person in the petty-bag Office, or to put in any other Bayl then he should doe if he
were sued in another Court, at common Law, by a party
not Priviledged.

65. That the Master of the Rolls, and Masters of the
Chancery respectively shall not demand, take or receive

any other Fees than what are contained in the Table annexed, and that every offence in that behalf shall be and is hereby adjudged and declared to be extortion, and shall be punished as extortion.

66. That no Register, chief Clerk, Examiner, Attorney of the said Court, or Officer for making *Sub-pœna's*, shall either directly or indirectly demand, take or receive any other Fees, or sum of money, than what is contained in the Table annexed, for or in respect of any cause depending in the Court of Chancery, Writs, or Proceedings therein, Copies of Record or other thing there filed, registred or put to the Seal; and that every such offence shall be and is hereby ordained, adjudged and declared, and shall be reputed and taken to be extortion, and shall be punished as extortion; and that every person and persons so offending and thereof convicted, shall be and is, and are hereby disabled to bear any Office of trust or profit in the common-wealth.

67. That neither the Lord Chancellor, Lord Keeper, Lords Commissioners of the great Seal, Master of the Rolls, nor any Officer of the said Court shall either directly, or in-directly take or receive any sum or sums of money, gratuity or reward, for nominating or admitting of any person or persons to any Office or place within his or their disposition in the said Court, upon pain of losing his Office, and paying double the sum or value of the gratuity or reward so received; the one moyety thereof to the use of his Highnesse the Lord Protector, and the other moyety to the use of the party who shall sue for the same, by bill, plaint or information in any Court of Record.

And lastly, it is ordained by the Authority aforesaid that the Chancellour, Keeper or Commissioners of the great Seal for the time being, shall, according to the times, and in the manner by this Ordinance prescribed put in execution all the Rules, Lawes, Orders and Dirction rections before mentioned, and take care with all diligence and circumspection, that all the Officers, Ministers, Clerks and Servants belonging to the said Court, do honestly and faithfully perform the duty of their severall and respective places; and if they be found any wayes faulty, that they be publiquely rebuked, displaced, or otherwise punished according to their desert, that for the future there be no more cause of just complaints from the people.

Fees to the Master of the Rolls.

	l.	s.	d.
For every single perpetuity,	00	02	00
For every double perpetuity,	00	02	00
For every grant for life, except wine licenses	00	02	00
For every grant of any Office	00	02	00
For every license for selling wines	00	01	00
For every Sheriffs patent	00	02	00
For the Dedimus potestatem to take the Sheriffs Oath	00	06	08
For every Exemplifi.	00	06	08
For every cancellation	00	06	08
For every decree and Dismission	00	06	08
For the inrolling of every deed and recognizance	00	02	00
For every Venire fac. ad triand &c.	00	06	08
For every writ of Extent	00	06	08
For every Liberate upon an Extent	00	13	04

Fees to the Masters of the Chancery.

	l.	s.	d.
For allowance for robes out of the Hannaper	06	14	00
For Oathes upon Affidavits, Answers, and to witnesses to be examined in Court for every Oath	0	00	04
For acknowledgment of deeds and recognizance	00	02	00
For Oathes taken to articles for granting of Supplicavits	00	02	04

Ee 3

For

For examining all Records which are to be exemplified, for every skin of parchment ———————— 0 0 02 0

For every cause upon a Reference to the three Masters, who shall hear the same ——— 00 01 00

Subpæna Office.　　*l, s. d.*

FOr every Subpæna, of what nature soever and Labells thereof ———————— 00 10 00

For renewing the same ———————————— 00 00 06

For the Seal to each Subpæna ———————— 00 00 06

To every counsell under a degree of a Serjeant for a motion ———————————— 00 01 00

To every counsell on a hearing ———————— 01 00 00

To Counsell for the Lord Protector and Serjeants at Law, for a motion ——— 01 00 00

And for every hearing ———————————— 02 00 00

Cheif Clarks and Attorneys.　　*l. s. d.*

FOr every cause to the Attorney, the Termly Fee of ———————————— 00 03 04

For an Attachment besides six pence for the Seal ———————————— 00 01 02

For copying of all bills, pleadings, depositions, Records, Rolls, evidences, remaining in that Court, Certificates, &c.

For every Sheet containing fifteen lines, and every line ten words ——————— 00 00 04

For every Commission to examine witnesses — 00 00 04

For every joyning in such Commission ———— 00 03 04

For every injunction ———————————— 00 06 08

For signing by the Lords Commissioners ——— 00 02 00

For signing by the Master of the Rolls ———— 00 01 00

For a Distringas ———————————————— 00 03 04

For every speciall certiorari or Procedendo — 00 03 04

For every Habeas corpus ———————————— 00 03 04

For every Supersedeas ———————————— 00 03 04

For every speciall Commission ——————— 00 05 00

For

For every writ of execution of an order————00 03 54

For drawing and inrolling every decree or } 00 16 08
  difmiffion, if but one skin ————

If longer, then fix pence per she t afterwards·00 00 06

For every Writ of Execution upon a decree } 00 06 08
  directed to the Sheriff or Coroner ————

For every exemplification, every skin————00 13 04

The chaft wax ————————00 00 04

Signing the Dorquet————————00 01 00

For enrollment of all patents, Commiffions }
  Licenfes, Pardons, and other warrants
  whatfoever which pafs the great Seal, } 00 10 00
  after the rate of ten shillings for every (the skin
  skin ————————

For every Sheriffs Patent, writ of affiftance, }
  writ of difcharge, Dedimus poteft. and } 00 13 06
  the Attorneys Fee————

For every writ of Audita querela ————00 10 00

For every writ of Scire facias ————— 00 02 06

For a Superfedeas of priviledge————00 03 04

For every Mittimus that paffeth the feal—00 03 04

For the tranfcript after the rate of every skin 00 13 04

For every fearch ————————00 00 04

For every Writ of Baftardy ————— 00 03 04

For three Proclamations ———————00 02 06

For filing every Writ whereby one oath or ac- }
  knowledgment is received, of the tran- } 00 01 00
  fcript of any record thereby certified————

For every Dedimus poteftatem, to take an }
  acknowledgment or cancellation of any } 00 03 04
  patent, deed, Indenture or Recognizance

For writing of every Grant, Patent, &c. }
  belonging formerly to the fix Clarks— } 00 13 04

For every Liberate and every Allocate—00 04 00

For the enrollment thereof————— 00 01 08

For all writs of difcharge of tenths and fif- }
  teenths) for every of them ————— } 00 03 04

For every Writ of Superfedeas, for any }
    Parliament-man or his servant ——— } 00 03 04

For every writ of expence. Milit,& Burgenss—0 3 0 4

For every Certiorari of course ——— 00 01 00

For every Procedendo of course ——— 00 01 00

Registers Fees.

For the entring of an Attachment, ——— 00 00 02

For entring of a dismission upon the ge-}
    nerall order with costs ——— } 00 00 06

For entring of any other bill of costs taxed }
    by a Master ——— } 00 00 02

All ordinary rules to make answer, reply, rejoyn 0 00 02

For a rule for publication upon a joynt }
    Commission, or otherwise ——— } 00 00 02

For the entry of an appearance upon an At }
    tachment Bond or Commandment ——— } 00 00 02

For the Warden of the Fleet upon every }
    such appearance ——— } 00 01 03

The entry of every commission to examine }
    witnesses, ex parte ——— } 00 00 04

If it be a joynt ordinary commission ——— 00 00 08

The entry of every commission to hear and }
    determine ——— } 00 01 00

The copy of any of these if required ——— 00 00 02

The entring of a day given to the Sheriff }
    for returning an Attachment, or to bring } 00 00 06
    in the body upon a Cepi returned ——— }

The Copy of the Rule, if required ——— 0 00 02

For signing such copy of any Rule ——— 0 00 02

For a note of a day of hearing ——— 0 00 04

For the draught of every Order, decree }
    or dismission, not exceeding one side; } 00 01 06
    and for signing thereof ——— }

For entry of every such Order ——— 0 00 03

If such draught exceed one side, then accor- }
    ding to the proportion of 1 s 6 d per side } 0 01 06

And

And for entring, after the rate of three pence per side —————— 0 00 03

For any Order, decree or dismission not made upon motion or hearing, but by consent under the hands of the parties Counsell or Attorneys, and for the copies thereof signed by the Register, whereof either side hath one ; if it be but one side, the Plaintiff to pay one shilling six pence, and the Defendant to pay the like ; and if it exceed one side, then after the same proportion each of them —————— 0 01 06 per side

For the entring of such order, for every side — 0 00 03

For copying of any Order entred, Report, Petition, Certificate of Referrees account Cereificate of the chief Clerks being filed 0 00 03 per side

For signing such copy to the Senior Register — 0 00 06

For every search for Order, Reports or Petition for each yeare —————— 0 00 02

For a Certificate of no cause shewed, signed, to the Register that signeth the same ——— 0 00 06

For filing of every Report, Certificate, account or award ————— 0 00 02

For every Decree signed by the Lord Chancellor, Lord Keeper, or Lords commissioners, to whom the same is presented by the Register-- *l. s. d.* 0 02 06

For every dismission which he shall procure to be signed —————— 0 01 08

For entring of every cause, Demurrer, or other businesse in the paper of causes to be heard by speciall Order or Warrant to the Deputy Register ————— 0 00 06

For entry of any Decrees drawn up and enrolled, whereby any Lands or Lease is decreed or charged with any summe of money, annuity, &c. ————— 0 00 06

For

	l.	s.	d.
For a certificate thereof	0	00	06
To the Clerk that files an Affidavit, from party at whose instance it is made (if he come for a copy) for the accompt of the senior Register	0	00	04
For the copy of such Affidavit, for every side, to the same Clerk	0	00	03
For examining and signing such copy to the senior Register	0	00	06

Fees of the Examiners.

	l.	s.	d.
For the examination of every Deponent, Defendant or delinquent at	0	01	00
For the copies of all depositions and interrogatories, for every sheet containing fifteen lines unwastfully written	0	00	06
For all Certificates upon exhibits	0	00	06
For all other Certificates whereunto their hands are required	0	01	00
For the Exemplification of Depositions, for every skin	0	13	04
For the Examination of any copy of depositions, with the Record which is to be given in evidence in any other Court	0	03	04
For the examination of every deponent, unto whom the Examiner is required to travell out of his Office	0	03	04

THE TABLE.

B.

The Table.

chiefe

The Table.

The Table.

The Table.

The Table.

Exche-

The Table.

Ff *with*

The Table.

Fees

The Table.

Ff 2   Fees

The Table.

The Table.

L.

Latitat

The Table.

Outlawry

The Table.

Quaren-

The Table.

Q.

R.

The Table.

Teste

The Table.

T.

U.

Upper

The Table.

The Table.

FINIS.

Lightning Source UK Ltd.
Milton Keynes UK
UKOW04f1147050417
298393UK00001B/55/P